New Ideas on Development after the Financial Crisis

Forum on Constructive Capitalism
Francis Fukuyama, *Series Editor*

Publication of this volume is in collaboration with
the Bernard L. Schwartz Forum for Constructive Capitalism
and the Center for Global Development

New Ideas on Development after the Financial Crisis

Edited by

NANCY BIRDSALL

and

FRANCIS FUKUYAMA

The Johns Hopkins University Press
• BALTIMORE •

© 2011 The Johns Hopkins University Press
All rights reserved. Published 2011
Printed in the United States of America on acid-free paper
9 8 7 6 5 4 3 2 1

The Johns Hopkins University Press
2715 North Charles Street
Baltimore, Maryland 21218-4363
www.press.jhu.edu

Library of Congress Cataloging-in-Publication Data
New ideas on development after the financial crisis / edited by Nancy Birdsall and
    Francis Fukuyama.
        p. cm.
    "Based on presentations made at a conference that was held on April 22–23, 2009, in
Washington D.C."—
    Includes bibliographical references and index.
    ISBN-13: 978-0-8018-9975-1 (hardcover: alk. paper)
    ISBN-10: 0-8018-9975-3 (hardcover: alk. paper)
    ISBN-13: 978-0-8018-9976-8 (pbk.: alk. paper)
    ISBN-10: 0-8018-9976-1 (pbk.: alk. paper)
    1. Economic development. 2. Financial crises. 3. Global Financial Crisis, 2008–2009.
I. Birdsall, Nancy. II. Fukuyama, Francis.
HD82.N465 2011
338.9—dc22   2010028478

A catalog record for this book is available from the British Library.

*Special discounts are available for bulk purchases of this book. For more information, please
contact Special Sales at 410-516-6936 or specialsales@press.jhu.edu.*

The Johns Hopkins University Press uses environmentally friendly book materials,
including recycled text paper that is composed of at least 30 percent post-consumer
waste, whenever possible. All of our book papers are acid-free, and our jackets and covers
are printed on paper with recycled content.

Contents

Preface

THIS VOLUME is the product of collaboration between the Bernard Schwartz Forum on Constructive Capitalism at the Johns Hopkins School of Advanced International Studies (SAIS) and the Center for Global Development (CGD). The essays in it are based on presentations made at a conference that was held on April 22–23, 2009, in Washington, D.C.

The motive for bringing together noted analysts of development for this project was simple. In 2008–9, a financial crisis that began in the U.S. subprime mortgage market began to spread, eventually engulfing the largest financial firms on Wall Street, bringing about the most serious recession in the United States since the Great Depression, and then dragging the rest of the global economy down with it. Unlike earlier financial crises like the sterling crisis of 1991, the Asian financial crisis of 1997–98, or the crises in Brazil, Russia, and Argentina that occurred shortly thereafter, the 2008–9 crisis began in the heart of global capitalism, the United States, and occurred for reasons that seemed intrinsic to the U.S. model of relatively lightly regulated market-driven capitalism. Since the United States had been the main purveyor of ideas regarding economic policy and development strategies over the preceding generation, it seemed natural to wonder whether the crisis would call into question the U.S. model and lead to the rise of some alternatives. The Wall Street crash of 1929 and the ensuing Great Depression deeply discredited capitalism itself around the world and contributed heavily to the rise of antiliberal ideologies like fascism and communism. It is well worth contemplating whether changes in the dominant orthodoxy were going to be set in motion by contemporary events.

Background to the Crisis

The economic damage to the global economy from the 2008–9 financial crisis was huge and borne in large measure by poor countries that had no responsibility for bringing on the crisis in the first place. Global GDP growth dropped virtually everywhere in the world in the fourth quarter of 2008, and countries dependent on exports saw their export earnings shrink even faster (table P.1).

Due in part to lessons learned from that earlier crisis, central banks around the world engaged in heroic efforts to pump liquidity into the financial system and propped up huge failing financial institutions like Citigroup, AIG, and RBS. This, combined with fiscal stimulus from the United States, China, and other countries, appears at this juncture to have successfully prevented the severe recession from turning into a full-fledged depression. By the third quarter of 2009, many export-dependent countries saw a rapid rebound in their earnings and the early signs of recovery were evident in many parts of the world (see table P.2). It is, at this writing, still too early to know the long-term impact of the downturn. This is particularly true in United States and Britain, where a huge overhang of public and private debt threatens to delay any quick recovery. In order to stem the crisis and promote a return to growth, these highly indebted countries have weakened their long-term fiscal positions substantially. As Peter Heller indicates in chapter 12, these countries have made it even more difficult to address long-term problems of entitlement liabilities and have clouded the prospects for a return to sustained growth. Like Japan after the collapse of its

Table P.1. GDP growth (quarter to quarter % change)

Country	2008				2009			
	Q1	Q2	Q3	Q4	Q1	Q2	Q3	Q4
Brazil	6.3	6.5	7.0	.8	–2.1	–1.6	–1.2	4.3
China	10.6	10.1	9.0	6.8	6.2	7.9	9.1	10.7
India	8.5	7.6	7.5	6.2	5.8	6.1	7.9	6.0
Russia	8.7	7.5	6.0	1.2	–9.8	–10.9	–8.9	
Germany	2.9	2.0	0.8	–1.8	–6.7	–5.8	–4.8	–2.4
United States	2.0	1.6	0.0	–1.9	–3.3	–3.8	–2.6	0.1
United Kingdom	2.4	1.7	0.2	–2.1	–5.4	–5.9	–5.3	–3.3

Table P.2. Exports (billions U.S.$)

Country	Dec 08	Jan 09	Feb 09	Mar 09	Apr 09	May 09	Jun 09
Brazil	13.8	9.8	9.6	11.8	12.3	12.0	14.5
China	111.0	90.5	64.9	90.3	91.9	88.8	95.4
India	12.2	11.4	10.9	11.5	10.7	11.0	12.8
South Korea	27.1	21.1	25.3	27.8	30.3	27.9	32.5
Germany (EUR)	67.2	63.9	63.9.	69.4	63.1	60.1	67.3

	Jul 09	Aug 09	Sep 09	Oct 09	Nov 09	Dec 09	
Brazil	14.1	13.8	13.9	14.1	12.7	14.5	
China	105.0	103.0	116.0	111.0	114.0	131.0	
India	13.6	14.3	113.7	113.2	113.2	114.6	
South Korea	31.9	28.9	33.9	34.0	34.0	36.0	
Germany (EUR)	69.9	59.3	70.0	74.1	73.3	69.2	

bubble economy in the early 1990s, the United States may limp on for some time. Given the dollar's role as a global reserve currency, this is likely to portend serious long-term consequences that are not easy to foresee. There is by now already a massive literature on the causes of the financial crisis, and there will clearly be much more to come.[1] These causes can be divided into microeconomic and macroeconomic ones.

Microeconomic Causes

The financial crisis of 2008–9 started in the U.S. housing market, and particularly in the subprime mortgage sector, where financial institutions imprudently extended loans to large numbers of unqualified home buyers. There were a number of reasons for this. Quasi-public institutions like Fannie Mae and Freddie Mac were under congressional mandate to extend home loans to less well-to-do buyers for political reasons; implicit government backing permitted executives there to take risks that a purely private institution would not. But while those eager to exonerate free markets liked to point to this as "the" cause of the crisis, there were many other purely private lenders like Washington Mutual or Countrywide who similarly piled into the subprime mortgage market on their own. The fact that they were able to do so was vastly abetted by the repackaging of loans into complex securities (collateralized debt obligations, or CDOs) which could then be resold, reducing long-term risks to the loan originator. The complex mathematical models used by the financial industry to value CDOs provided a false sense of security to their purchasers, since they did not take into account rare events like a broad collapse of housing prices.[2] Many observers have noted large principal-agent problems in the finance industry, with traders and executives being rewarded for short-term gains that masked huge long-term risks. Principal-agent problems existed also among rating agencies, which had incentives to understate risks on the part of the firms that hired them.

Another large set of microeconomic causes, with large implications for future policy, concerned regulatory failures. A huge, unregulated shadow finance sector emerged in the period after 2002. Credit default swaps (CDSs) were used to insure CDOs and other complex instruments, thereby allowing financial firms to take them off their books and effectively increase leverage ratios. The market was misled to believe that such financial innovation dispersed risked when in reality it concentrated risk, often in unregulated institutions like the massive insurance company AIG, which collapsed in September 2008. In some instances, existing regulatory powers were not used (as when the U.S. Securities and Exchange Commission failed to detect and prosecute fraudster Bernard Madoff); in other cases, underfunding of enforcement capacity at agencies like the SEC prevented timely action; and in still other instances, Congress explicitly forbade the regulation of new instruments like derivatives (as in the Gramm-Leach-Bliley and Commodity Futures Modernization Acts of 1999–2000). The bigger problem was not statutory, however, but rather ideological. The apparently smartest economic minds in the country, from Robert Rubin to Larry Summers to Alan Greenspan, simply did not believe that regulation of this sector was necessary. As Greenspan was to admit in testimony in late 2008, "I made a mistake in presuming that the self-interest of organizations, specifically banks and others, were such as they were best capable of protecting their own shareholders and their equity in the firms."[3]

Macroeconomic Causes

In addition to these microeconomic causes, there were macroeconomic factors at play. As Martin Wolf has pointed out, many East Asian countries responded to the 1997–98 Asian financial crisis by restricting inflows of volatile foreign liquidity and by accumulating large reserves as a form of self-insurance.[4] The largest of these was China, which by late 2007 had amassed nearly $1.7 trillion in reserves. Since the dollar was the world's primary reserve currency, these excess savings flowed into U.S. capital markets at an astonishing pace, leading to the accumulation of over $5 trillion in dollar reserves on the eve of the crisis. The accumulation of these reserves was made possible by the export-led growth strategies followed by various countries in East Asia.

This huge movement of liquidity from emerging market countries into the world's richest country, the United States, was therefore the permissive condition for the overuse of leverage that took place not just in the U.S. mortgage market but also by private equity firms, commodity traders, and ordinary corporate finance officers in the period from 2002 to 2007. The transpacific flow of capital produced the apparent paradox of high global growth combined with historically low rates of inflation, or what U.S. Federal Reserve chairman Ben Bernanke was to label "the great moderation." The problem was that this moderation was the product of an unsustainable global growth model by which one part of the world produced and saved, while another part consumed and borrowed. Things that can't go on forever don't, but while this fact was broadly recognized during the 2000s, nobody acted in the short run as if it were really true. There are huge arguments as to the relative importance of macro- versus microeconomic factors, as well as many others not covered here in producing the crisis. As Wolf notes, the factor one picks as key is much like the fable of the blind men touching different parts of the elephant and deciding that their part represents the whole.[5] The multicausal nature of the crisis means, however, that there are a wide variety of implications and lessons that can be drawn from it for future development strategies.

Outline of the Book

In organizing the conference and this volume, we have asked the authors involved not to focus on short-term effects on trade, investment, and output but rather on long-term changes that may have been provoked in the way that people around the world think about development. As Zhou Enlai was once reported to have remarked about the consequences of the French Revolution, it is too early to say what these long-term effects will be. But as the contours of the crisis and its aftermath come into view, some preliminary assessments are already in order.

The introductory chapter by Nancy Birdsall and Part I of the book focus on the crisis itself and its background and the questions it raises for the future of development strategies. Many of the orthodoxies of an earlier era, such as the desirability of capital account liberalization and export-led growth, have been thrown into question, and the relative rankings of different developments models look much different now than they did in 2007. Part II encompasses perspectives from important emerging market countries in East Asia and Latin America. We have unfortunately not been able to include all parts of the developing world in this section, though the conference discussion did include a wider range of countries. Part III discusses international institutions and Part IV looks at new ideas in development thematically, including issues like reform of public sectors and migration as a potential route to development.

The conference and this volume would not have been possible but for the generosity of Bernard L. Schwartz, chairman and CEO of BLS Investments, LLC, and former chairman and CEO of Loral Space and Communications. Bernard Schwartz has been heavily engaged in promoting new ideas in public policy in recent years and contributed many of his own at the start of our conference. The Forum on Constructive Capitalism is structured as a high-level lecture and symposia series to take advantage of the substantial research and continued controversy over the consequences of globalization for social prosperity and harmony. By providing a forum for the discussion of whether and how increasing trade, financial and production interdependence affects the decisions of employers, labor organizations and government policymakers, it has sought to help formulate concrete policy proposals and recommendations.

The Center for Global Development is an independent, nonprofit policy research organization that is dedicated to reducing global poverty and inequality and to making globalization work for the poor. Through a combination of research and strategic outreach, the Center actively engages policymakers and the public to influence the policies of the United States, other rich countries, and such institutions as the World Bank, the International Monetary Fund, and the World Trade Organization to improve the economic and social development prospects in poor countries.

The editors of this volume would like to thank numerous individuals for their assistance in the production of both the conference and this volume. Dean Jessica Einhorn of SAIS lent her support early on to the whole project. Seth Colby, Executive Director of the Bernard Schwartz Forum on Constructive Capitalism, played an instrumental role in organizing the conference and provided editorial assistance for the present volume. Heather Dawson and Lawrence MacDonald of the Center for Global Development, and Robin Washington of SAIS, were invaluable for their work on the conference. We would also like to acknowledge the work of the late Henry Tom of the Johns Hopkins University Press. Henry, who unexpectedly passed away on the eve of the book's publication, made possible not just this book but also all of the other volumes in the Forum on Constructive Capitalism series.

Notes

1. Some recent books on the crisis include George Soros, *The New Paradigm for Financial Markets: The Credit Crisis of 2008 and What It Means* (New York: Public

Affairs, 2008); Paul Krugman, *The Return of Depression Economics and the Crisis of 2008* (New York: Norton, 2009); Andrew Felton and Carmen Reinhart (eds.), *The First Global Financial Crisis of the 21st Century* (London: Centre for Economic Policy Research, 2008).

2. See Nassam Nicholas Taleb, *The Black Swan: The Impact of the Highly Improbable* (New York: Random House, 2007).

3. Alan Greenspan, quote from testimony before Congressional Committee for Government and Reform, October 22, 2009.

4. Martin Wolf, *Fixing Global Finance* (Baltimore, MD: Johns Hopkins University Press, 2008).

5. Ibid.

New Ideas on Development
after the Financial Crisis

The Global Financial Crisis

The Beginning of the End of the "Development" Agenda?

Nancy Birdsall

BETWEEN THE COLLAPSE of Lehman Brothers in September 2008 and the September 2009 meeting of the G-20 heads of government in Pittsburgh, the global economic system could have been said to have gone through emotional and psychological states similar to those that follow a personal trauma: panic, denial, anger, and, at some point, adjustment to a new reality.

Three characteristics of the 2008–9 trauma make it memorable: it was truly global, bringing a decline in pre-crisis growth rates to virtually every country in the world; it began in and was blamed mostly on the United States, which for most of the previous 60 years was the acknowledged world economic champion on the grounds of its size, flexibility, and innovative and entrepreneurial strength. The United States and the mature democracies of Western Europe took a bigger and more long-lasting hit—both in relative and absolute terms—than did most of the world's middle-income emerging market and low-income economies.

Nor is it only the trauma itself that was special, but the rapid and largely coordinated international response was also largely unprecedented: the emergence of the G-20, a new global club at the head of government level eclipsing the G-7 and including the rising emerging market economies of the developing world; a globally coordinated stimulus package with the G-20 at the steering wheel; and a new impetus for making the International

Monetary Fund (IMF), the World Bank, and the newly formed Financial Stability Board more representative and legitimate in a global economy suddenly and stunningly more interconnected and vulnerable.

The nature of the crisis itself and the response to it already seemed remarkable in the early spring of 2009, when my co-editor Francis Fukuyama and I asked the contributors of this book to reflect on its implications for ideas about and models of the growth and development process. Would the prevailing model of successful development based on free and open markets espoused under the general rubric of what is known as the Washington consensus survive in Asia, Africa, and Latin America? What effect would the crisis have on the economic policies the international financial institutions—where for decades the American or Anglo-Saxon model of capitalism had dominated—would support in emerging markets and other developing countries?

In this introductory essay, reflecting on the contributions of the authors to this volume, I discuss two themes. The first is the pre-crisis subtle shift in the prevailing model of capitalism in developing countries—away from orthodoxy or so-called market fundamentalism—that the crisis is likely to reinforce. On the one hand, globalization—that is the global integration of nation-based domestic economies through trade, investment, and capital flows and the movement of people and ideas—will proceed apace. Despite the risks the crisis illustrated of an integrated and interdependent global market, globalization is here to stay. That is so completely taken for granted by the authors in this book that the point itself is rarely mentioned and certainly not contested; instead the contributors focus largely on changes in domestic policies in response to the risks the global market poses. Similarly, market-driven capitalism will remain the economic model of choice at the domestic level in many countries. Though the American or Anglo-Saxon version of capitalism has fallen from the pedestal it occupied for much of the latter half of the twentieth century, the contributions in this volume reflect the expectation that the market model will continue to dominate domestic policymaking in the developing world.

On the other hand, there will be a shift—in mind-set and in practical form—from what might be called the "mostly free" market (hereafter free market) to a "more managed" market (hereafter managed market) version of capitalism. The free market model is based on the notion that though market failures exist, government interventions to address them may well make the situation worse. Regulation of financial or labor markets is likely to introduce distortions more costly than the problems market failures pose in the first place (Friedman 1968) and may even put at risk liberty and freedom of individuals in the political sphere (Hayek 1941). In the managed market version of capitalism (Stiglitz 1989; and generalized in World Bank

1993), market failures justify specific interventions by the state, but, when there is no market failure, the market is left to fluctuate with little or no intervention.

In developing countries, the flexibility and efficiency associated with the American free market model is likely to be traded away in favor of domestic policies and interventions meant to ensure greater resilience in the face of competitive pressures in a global economy and of globally inflicted traumas. That implies more state involvement in financial and labor markets, more emphasis on the role of the state in catalyzing innovation in production, and a new round of attention to the domestic social contract, with higher public spending on social insurance programs and on universal health and education programs. In some countries, it is likely to mean a new round of twenty-first-century "new" industrial policy in the developing world.

Whether the outcome of a shift to a managed market model will be welfare enhancing is not clear. It may depend in the long run on what developing country leaders conclude about governance. In a crisis-prone global system, is there a trade-off between rapid and effective implementation of policy—the China model—and the messier but more accountable and responsive arrangements of mature Western democracies?

The second theme is better framed as a question than a prediction. It is a theme that is implicit in many of the chapters though like the reality of globalization rarely explicit: Will the financial crisis, which is likely to be remembered as marking the end of Western economic dominance, be a trigger for a new twenty-first-century approach to collective action on global problems? It is widely remarked that America's unipolar moment has passed; the global financial crisis verified for any doubters the rise of China and the reality of a "multipolar" world—with the United States still a leading power but no longer able to manage global affairs alone or even with a few close allies. A decade hence, will the financial crisis be viewed as a watershed in attitudes and practices with respect to global economic governance? Will it trigger a meaningful increase in the influence of China, India, and Brazil at the International Monetary Fund and the World Bank? Will it mark the beginning of the development of a more robust multipolar "polity" to cope with and better exploit the global market system? Or will efforts at global collective action falter in the absence of a single dominant player? What better presages the future: the successful coordination of a global stimulus at the London G-20 summit in March 2009 or the near-failure of a United Nations–led negotiation of a climate agreement, rescued at the last minute in the form of an "accord" agreed among a handful of countries in Copenhagen in December of the same year?

Whether and how global collective action proceeds on key challenges—

coordinated regulation of the financial services industry, climate change management, international migration, and correction of the global imbalance problem that helped precipitate the crisis in the first place—will matter tremendously for most of today's developing countries. The fact of uncertainty itself—whether the global economy can be managed in the absence of a global government—is already affecting approaches to development, as several of the chapters in this volume amply illustrate. A future in which global collective action is effective implies ultimately that the very idea of a "development" agenda (and the implied asymmetry of power and influence between developed and developing countries) will yield to the idea of a shared "global" agenda—across nation-states that cooperate in their own interests and in the interest of shared global stability and prosperity.

The Crisis and Domestic Policy in Developing Countries

At the World Economic Forum in Davos, Switzerland, in January 2009, at the near height of the panic among the global private and public leaders, it was Prime Minister Vladimir Putin of Russia and Premier Wen Jiabao of China who were most adamant about allegiance to the capitalist model. By the beginning of 2010 it was the United States, Europe, and other advanced industrial economies that were suffering a loss of faith in the benefits of a mostly free market—as they contemplated enormous public debt, populist fervor for punishing the bankers, and the long-run implications for the balance between market and state of having intervened heavily in their own markets. Indeed in 2010 at Davos French President Nicolas Sarkozy, while acknowledging the value of markets, studded his speech with multiple pained allusions to the risks and costs of market-led globalization.

Even in the throes of the global panic—before the March 2009 London G-20 Summit—Russia and China, the former communist states, had made clear to their domestic and foreign investors that they had no intention of abandoning the capitalist model. The BRICs—shorthand for Brazil, Russia, China, and India—and other emerging markets, and the developing world as a group, saw the United States as perpetrator and epicenter of the crisis; why would they alter an approach that for them was producing not only rapid growth but a visible increase in their geopolitical influence? These four countries, after all, had "emerged" not only as economic but also as geopolitical powers during the latest round of globalization—the two decades since the end of the Cold War.

In chapter 3, which was written early in the crisis in April 2009, Arvind Subramanian makes the point that globalization and market capitalism were working for emerging markets; they could afford to be smug about what were seen as financial excesses—not fundamental to the capitalist

Table I.1. Estimates of percentage growth in GDP, constant prices

| Country | Year | IMF 2009 estimates | |
		April 09	*October 09*
Brazil	2009	–1.301	–0.662
	2010	2.165	3.464
China	2009	6.52	8.504
	2010	7.51	9.028
Indonesia	2009	2.495	3.99
	2010	3.5	4.752
India	2009	4.523	5.355
	2010	5.607	6.421
Russia	2009	–5.977	–7.545
	2010	0.5	1.535
Thailand	2009	–2.969	–3.456
	2010	1.039	3.708

Source: International Monetary Fund 2009.

model—in the United States. Liliana Rojas-Suarez points out in chapter 7 that most emerging market economies in Latin America are and will remain firmly wedded to the capitalist model. Despite their greater vulnerability—given their far greater dependence on foreign capital inflows compared with Asia—Brazil, and Peru, among others, were reasonably well prepared to weather the initial round of financial contagion from the north. They had learned from the financial crises they endured in the late 1990s the logic, given their low domestic savings rates and resulting dependence on external capital, of shoring up reserves and maintaining flexible exchange rates.

The ensuing eight months (writing in January 2010) have apparently vindicated those reactions in Asia and Latin America. Except in Eastern Europe (with its heavy reliance on capital inflows from its Western European neighbors) and in Mexico (with its heavy reliance on the American market for its exports), the emerging markets were the first to recover and recovered not only sooner but also more robustly than expected. The IMF's upward revisions of its GDP growth estimates for 2009 and 2010 (made in early and late 2009) for many emerging economies are summarized in table I.1.

What are the implications for attitudes, ideas, and actual economic policy practices in developing countries? With the American version of capitalism in disrepute, both emerging market and low-income developing countries are likely to modify their approach to economic policy, and their modifications are likely to be tolerated and perhaps even applauded in the Washington institutions associated with the Washington consensus.

"Modification," not "reversal," is the appropriate word. The modifications will be neither dramatic nor universal across developing countries and will hardly represent a new capitalist "model." To some extent, modifications had already emerged as the norm prior to the crisis, as confidence grew within many developing countries benefiting from the pre-crisis boom that they could safely ignore "Washington" economic nostrums. Still in the next several years, modifications to the mainstream pre-crisis market model are likely to be more widely embraced and more deeply applied than they might have been without the crisis.

Modifications can be put into four categories:

1. The nail in the coffin of financial orthodoxy. The pre-crisis direction of avoiding premature opening of the capital account and of heavy reliance on regulatory and prudential "insurance" to gird economies against external financial shocks will be reinforced.
2. The vindication of progressive social and distributional policies as critical to reducing inequality and restoring social cohesion. A more European-style state approach to employment and social policy with greater attention to distributional measures.
3. New respect for "new" industrial policy. Greater admiration for and experiments with various forms of industrial policy—that is, engagement of the state as facilitator and coordinator, albeit in a twenty-first-century market-friendly manner, with an eye on the early success of the East Asian "tigers."
4. Increasing assertion, if not of the Chinese-style authoritarian state, then certainly of greater executive power and discretion in the implementation of economic policy, particularly in low-income countries, with an implicit nod to the impressive policy decision and implementation capability of China's top-down state system. For low-income countries, this should come at the risk of increasing tension with the traditional donors and the Washington institutions about any weakening of the rule of law and of the constraints on executive power associated with democracy and open political systems.

These four categories mirror to some extent the three capitalist models Mitchell Orenstein defines in chapter 1. However, they are also best seen in a particular light: the underlying rationale for them, post-crisis, is to increase the resilience of the economy and the protection of jobs and welfare in the face of external economic and other shocks. The global financial and economic crisis was a wake-up call—that periodic shocks and resulting uncertainty for individual countries are intrinsic to their integration into a globally integrated market. Vulnerability to poor policies and decisions elsewhere is a reality that emerging markets and low-income countries are now far more likely to take into account in their economic policies and implies a greater role for the state in managing the market and protecting people from its failings.

On the one hand, the benefits of integration into global markets and of embracing the free-market capitalist model are self-evident—higher growth. On the other hand, the crisis illuminated the logic and policies that factor in uncertainty and vulnerability.

The End of Orthodoxy

To the extent free market "orthodoxy" (or market fundamentalism or what is sometimes called neoliberalism, seen as the most disparaging label) includes an open capital account and a thoroughly liberalized domestic financial sector, most emerging market economies outside Eastern Europe even before the global crisis were hedging their bets. In Asia, India was moving slowly and cautiously if at all to liberalize domestic interest rates; in China, there is no sign the renminbi will become freely exchangeable on international capital markets anytime soon, despite the advantage having a reserve currency would provide in economic as well as geostrategic terms (as Minxin Pei notes in chapter 5). Latin America's liberalized economies (Brazil, Chile, Mexico, and Peru, but not Venezuela, Ecuador, or Bolivia, which by 2008–9 were revisiting state-led policies) had benefited from a dramatic increase in foreign capital inflows in the decade preceding the crisis. Self-insurance had taken the form of reserve accumulation, especially in Brazil, and of the begrudging acceptance of the costs to diversification of exports and export competitiveness overall of ongoing pressure on exchange rate appreciation—particularly given the offsetting advantages of flexible exchange rates and the inflation-dampening impact of strong currencies.

In the smaller low-income countries, open capital markets attracted relatively less capital and of incoming capital less in the form of footloose portfolio and other flows compared with investment. In most of sub-Saharan Africa, for example, financial and banking practices remained relatively conservative. In addition, public debt levels were relatively low when the crisis hit because sovereign governments had benefited from the debt relief movement of the previous 15 years, which saw major write-offs of external public debt by the IMF and the multilateral banks (the international financial institutions, or IFIs); internal debt was relatively low as local capital markets were small and governments had eschewed bad fiscal and quasi-fiscal policies as part of the IFI-led debt relief programs. As a result, these countries were less vulnerable to the financial contagion that hit the middle-income emerging markets in late 2008 and early 2009 (though within a few months they were of course hurt through trade and remittance losses).

Here it is important to distinguish between the free market fundamentalism including open capital markets that Stiglitz (2010) and others decry, and Williamson's original Washington consensus (Williamson 1990). Williamson's ten points included openness to foreign direct investment but no reference to the opening of capital markets. On liberalizing domestic financial arrangements, he was cautious, calling for abolition of preferential interest rates for privileged borrowers, for example, and only gradual introduction of modestly positive market-determined interest rates (Birdsall, de la Torre, and Valencia forthcoming). And it is true that the IMF (and the U.S. Treasury), which had pushed for opening of capital markets in developing countries in the 1990s, had already backed off from fundamentalism in this domain earlier in the 2000s, well prior to the crisis, as research at the IMF itself suggested there was no evidence that open capital markets were associated with faster growth and plenty of evidence that they are associated with high volatility, which, in turn, reduces steady state growth (e.g., Kose, Prasad, Rogoff, and Wei 2006; International Monetary Fund 2009).

Still it would be wrong to assume that throughout the mid-2000s IMF policy and practice was "heterodox" on financial market issues. It was accepted that developing countries would with good reason want to proceed with caution in liberalizing their financial markets and opening their capital markets; they should sequence reforms so that opening would come only after sound and stable regulatory and prudential arrangements and the macroeconomic policies associated with long-term price stability were firmly in place. However, to some extent the vision was still of a thoroughly integrated global financial system in which at some point developing countries would ideally open their capital markets completely. Indeed whether and to what extent operational guidance shifted toward helping countries manage moving slowly is not clear; Subramanian's plea that the IMF be more systematic on this issue suggests orthodoxy still dominated—at least until the crisis hit.

Post-crisis it seems far less likely that a temporary use of capital controls (as occurred in Malaysia during the late 1990s Asian financial crisis), or even a temporary closing of the capital market, will be so readily and completely condemned in Washington;[1] equally we will hear fewer squawks in the United States, at least in policy circles, if and when Chile or other Latin American countries reintroduce taxes on short-term capital outflows of the kind the United States tried to prohibit in the U.S.-Chile Free Trade agreement.

In a more concrete sign of growing tolerance of the managed market model, the World Bank and the other multilateral development banks are likely to become more supportive of domestic development banks, particularly following the success of BNDES (Brazilian National Development

Bank) in supporting initial stimulus in Brazil in 2009. That is likely to be the case even if development banks are used from time to time for political purposes, for example, to stimulate jobs or growth in election years. (After all, how different is that from interventions of the advanced countries to help their automobile and banking sectors at the height of the crisis?) Tanzanian Central Bank Governor Benno Ndulu argued strongly during the conference that development banks should be supported and strengthened and laid out the kinds of policy rules that would prevent the misdirected and regressive subsidies and abuses of quasi-fiscal powers of the past.

During the food price hike of 2008 that preceded the global financial crisis, some developing countries including India, Indonesia, China, Vietnam, Cambodia, and Egypt restricted food exports—a step broadly condemned in official circles. Lustig (2009) argues that such temporary heterodox quantity restraints can be justified as optimal, as they take into account the possibility that the hike is temporary and recognize the trade-off of costly adjustment to highly volatile prices as well as the economic logic of maintaining political stability. As with the financial and capital market issue, the challenge is developing resilience or robustness in the face of volatility that is often externally imposed.

It would be unreasonable for market-driven economies subject to external shocks that are out of their control and for which they are not the offending party to choose free market maximum "efficiency" over managed market policies that favor some measure of robustness. Surely that is the way in Eastern Europe countries, hit hard by the crisis because of the huge capital inflows they had welcomed, would see it. In fact, except in Eastern Europe, robustness was favored already by most developing countries before the global financial crisis; its origins and the resilience of many emerging markets to its effects suggests that managed market heterodox programs and policies—in the financial sector but also in other areas as the food and trade example suggests—will be more prevalent and in policy circles will be seen as increasingly sensible as well as legitimate (which will in turn make them more prevalent). Whether that will be a good thing overall in countries with weak governance will only become clear with time.

Vindication of Progressive Social and Distributional Policies

The second shift in domestic policy following the crisis is likely to come in the approach to employment and social policy. As with financial policy, a shift had already begun prior to the crisis but is likely to intensify post-crisis despite the fiscal challenges implied. Here the contrast between the American and European models of capitalism is relevant. For example Western Europe's success in quick and deep implementation of countercyclical policies—because of its preexisting automatic stabilizers in the form of guaranteed employment and other welfare programs—will not go unnoticed on the part of developing country policymakers, particularly those increasingly subject to the political pressures to attend to the needs of the middle-income majority that democracy entails. That is likely to be the case even in countries where tax revenues as a percent of GDP are lower than in Europe and even if the U.S. economy recovers more quickly than those in Europe, especially if it is a relatively jobless recovery.

In Latin America, a political move to the left was evident already early in the new century, as José Antonio Ocampo notes in chapter 6, when fatigue with the liberalizing reforms of the 1990s set in. Fatigue was not surprising, since the structural reforms had not produced high growth or reduced unyielding poverty and inequality (that the counterfactual might have been even less growth and greater increases in poverty was politically irrelevant). Populist governments in Bolivia, Venezuela, and Ecuador reasserted the primacy of the state in managing the economy directly for the benefit of the people, assuming control of their natural gas and oil resources. In Brazil, Chile, and Uruguay, center left governments put increasing emphasis on targeted redistributive cash transfer programs to reduce poverty and income inequality, while hewing to macroeconomic programs that assured external investors stable prices and predictable returns.

The financial crisis will reinforce the growing attention to social policy in Latin America, with more emphasis on social protection and fairness for the majority (compared with the traditional association of social policy with simply more public spending on health and education) in market-oriented democracies. Ocampo suggests it will be increasingly politically attractive to introduce more European-style universal social programs in Latin America, in contrast to highly targeted programs for the poor. The success of the automatic countercyclical stabilizers in minimizing social disruption and political instability in middle-class Europe as the global crisis unfolded may well influence policy views in Brazil, Mexico, India, and other developing countries, given the growth of the middle class in those countries (Birdsall 2010). That is likely to be the case despite the rigidities European social policies impose. Even in the United States, where unemployment rates are likely to remain high for several years after the financial shock, the European emphasis on social solidarity and the policy implication of more progressive revenue and expenditure policies is likely to be more politically salient.

Ideally the crisis will also help move the government in China toward an increase in social spending and greater emphasis on social insurance. For the global economy, such a shift would have the advantage of increasing domestic consumption relative to export-oriented investment in infrastructure; for the Chinese it might help minimize the risks of social unrest due to the growing gap between rural and urban incomes and within urban areas as well. In chapter 4, Yasheng Huang suggests rural incomes in China stagnated for more than a decade—contributing to the inequality gap—primarily due to a reversal of financial sector liberalizing reforms beginning in the mid-1990s, combined with increasing pressure on local authorities in rural areas to raise tax revenue. He argues that the global imbalance problem (Chinese do all the saving and lending, Americans and others do all the borrowing and spending) is in part due to stagnation of rural incomes and consumption power (as opposed to any increase in savings rates in the past decade or more). For the Chinese perhaps a trade-off will emerge between investments to keep the machine creating urban export-driven jobs greased and spending on more progressive social programs and distributional transfers.

As with financial sector policy, growing emphasis in some developing countries on the logic of the state leavening the injustices of the market did not arise out of nowhere in 2008–9. The development literature was extraordinarily thin on the inequality issue and its implications for sustainable growth for much of the post–World War II period. Only in the 1990s, after the fall of the Berlin Wall, did mainstream economists seriously revisit the distributional consequences of capitalism that Karl Marx had raised 150 years earlier. However the popular outcry in the United States and Europe over bankers' bonuses marks a kind of consolidation in the OECD countries of resentment of high levels of income inequality, which are viewed as grossly unfair because they are seen as not reflecting differences in skills or effort. The concern about inequality grew throughout the 1990s even in the United States, as the benefits of growth accrued to a tiny portion of the population while the median wage stagnated. This concern was also evident in the 2008 presidential election in which the Obama campaign in particular appealed to the beleaguered middle class as losers in a market-obsessed system in which the state had failed to provide such basic protections as access to universal health insurance.

Policy interest in reducing income and other inequalities may grow in developing countries (as in the United States—though so far more in talk than in reality) also as a result of the backlash everywhere against the bankers and other financiers. Whether justified by the evidence or not, the idea that income concentration on Wall Street contributed (along with cheap money, regulatory failures, and so on) to a sense of impunity and thus to excessive risk taking is likely to affect not only banking reform but also broader social policy change. In the emerging markets, including in China and Eastern Europe as well as in Latin America, perhaps there will be more interest post-crisis in the role of the state in ensuring minimal social protections for all—the universal programs Ocampo predicts. Where average income is still low—in South Asia and Africa—the crisis is likely to reinforce interest in replicating the success of Latin American countries with poverty mapping and direct cash transfers to poor households—if not universal programs. The crisis has already locked in what was growing policy and financial support for safety net programs of all kinds, including direct cash transfers to households, on the part of the international financial institutions.

On the one hand, markets will still reign across the developing world. On the other hand, at least for some years, politicians in the developing world will be less oblivious to the gap between the very rich minority and the large and increasingly politically salient poor and middle-income majority. In the rich world, we are seeing the end of smugness if not of big bonuses among free market fundamentalists. American pride in the United States's flexible and efficient labor market compared with that of Europe will diminish. In the developing world, it would not be surprising if future domestic policies and programs reflect, more than before the crisis, some experimentation with the European approach—both as morally responsible and in a volatile global economy as economically and politically smart.[2]

New Respect for "New" Industrial Policy

As with financial orthodoxy and inequality concerns, ideas about new, modernized, industrial policies were percolating in the late 1990s and the 2000s; the crisis could have the effect of increasing their currency. I referred above to development banks, written off as dangerous failures for subsidizing insiders at high fiscal cost in the 1980s but now back on the agenda. The ability of Brazil's development banks and those of other emerging markets to provide a quick and easy channel for quasi-fiscal stimulus in the first months of 2009 was noted by policymakers in low-income African countries. A government-sponsored development bank, as long as it avoids the sins of the past,[3] looks to be a market- and democracy-friendly vehicle for imitating China's remarkable ability, in a top-down policy system, to have so quickly and effectively implemented a major economic stimulus in late 2008 and 2009. More fundamentally, a modernized development bank is an institutional response to the interest of many developing country governments in jump-starting economic growth by underwriting or guaranteeing major private investments in high-risk sectors or regions. As Justin Lin outlines in chapter 2, that kind of public policy is a reasonable response to failures in the market—of coordination among private players where economies of scale cannot be achieved by single investors, of high costs to first movers and innovators in new sectors,[4] and of policy risks (creeping expropriation) that discourage investments in energy, water, and other areas in countries without a long track record of permitting adequate pricing of key public services and in general of honoring property rights.

The view of Lin and others marks a return to the early literature on development (Hirschman 1958; Leibenstein 1966; Rosenstein-Rodan 1943), now more explicitly grounded in the barriers market failures represent, that the state needs to play a facilitating role in fostering the growth process in low-income economies. For the three decades following the oil and debt crises of the late 1970s and early 1980s in the developing world, the prevailing orthodoxy (as reflected in the popular understanding of the Washington consensus[5]) was that the risk of government failure (incompetence, corruption) dominated any risks to growth of market failures. That was true not just in Washington but—as the reforms and adjustments of the 1990s took hold, and as the 2003–7 commodity boom raised exports and income—throughout the developing world. Except in China and a few countries such as Venezuela where governments took control of oil or other natural resource wealth, policymakers hesitated to increase the role of the state in production, and even in China the state dramatically loosened its hold on the market. The privatization movement slowed, but in part because it was so successful; only in a few countries are there today the large state enterprises that prevailed 30 years ago.

Ideas of a new generation of development economists about the benefits of the state doing more—guaranteeing, investing, coordinating, innovating—are likely to get far more traction in the real world of policy following the downfall from its pedestal of the American-style free market capitalist model. Whether a reentry of the state will be successful, particularly in low-income countries with weak rule of law where abuse of executive power is still a constant threat to responsible economic policy, is far from clear. What does seem clear is that there will be more sympathy for that idea and increased attention to the key rules that would keep state interventions of the managed market variety, meant to address market failures, off the slippery slope to government failure.

Increasing Assertion of Executive Discretion in Economic Policy, Especially in Low-Income Countries

China's remarkable bounce back from the immediate aftermath of the crisis illustrates the benefits of its tightly managed top-down policymaking machinery. As noted below, that its recovery relies on an undervalued exchange rate and its stimulus relied heavily on investment not on increasing domestic consumption can be faulted. But for many low-income countries, what is likely to be remembered is China's ability to go from policy decisions to effective implementation of those policies. The leadership of weak governments in Africa, for example, is bound to note that Chinese authoritarianism gets better results than Indian democracy with all its checks and balances. This is one way to interpret Lant Pritchett's chapter 9: that in the realm of development ideas, it is time to focus on the organizational capability of governments, especially in low-income countries, to implement policies—whatever those economic or other policies (industrial policy or back to the market) may be.

Pritchett associates organizational capability with a far more complex set of social dynamics, in which there are robust mechanisms that make the public sector accountable to its citizens, than is associated with the Chinese political system. But political leaders in low-income fragile democracies are likely to see a trade-off between the "capability" of a strong executive to get things done in an autocratic system and the accountability and responsiveness of electoral democracies. That was already the case before the crisis; China's effective crisis response is likely to make it more so. Larry Diamond in chapter 10 notes a kind of trend in low-income democracies to emphasize executive power to get things done over the freedoms associated with democratic systems. He suggests that though the financial crisis and ensuing economic hardship in developing countries had no marked effect on the state of democracy in the developing world, we should not be reassured that democratic gains are inevitable. He notes a pre-crisis trend of reduced "freedom" and accountability in low-income democracies in the last decade, even when economic growth was as high as 6 percent annually.

Orenstein emphasizes (and Pei and Lin seem to take almost as given) that the implementation capability of the state in China is associated with the lack of democratic accountability in a politically autocratic system. Huang provides an example; he links lack of private household savings in rural areas to local corruption, in turn associated with the lack of accountability of local officials to citizens. Perhaps this suggests that current policies cannot be sustained indefinitely in China without further political repression. Still, the lesson for ruling elites in many low-income countries is likely to be that executive discretion should not be too easily forsaken in the name of Western-style democratic accountability. What is likely to dominate as an idea in the developing world following the crisis is that China was succeeding before the crisis and succeeded in managing the pressures of the crisis very well indeed. Whether the right lesson or not, that will be associated with its ability to get things done without the perceived complications of more accountable political systems.

The Crisis and the Prospects for Global Collective Action

A key characteristic of the crisis is that it started in the United States and hurt the United States and the traditional Western European powers more—economically and psychologically—than most emerging market and developing economies. In fact, the crisis may be remembered more for marking the moment when the traditional transatlantic powers formally acknowledged the new reality: a multipolar global economy in which decisions and events in China, India, Brazil (of the BRICs), Nigeria (of OPEC), and Pakistan (of the nuclear club) among other "developing" countries (all except Brazil still low-income countries in per capita terms) have global, systemic implications. Will heightened awareness of systemic problems, including of many such problems that are fundamental to development, lead to new ideas and new approaches to global collective action? Will that matter for the way we think about development issues?

The possible implications of the crisis for global collective action, for development ideas, and for development prospects in developing countries, can be brought out in brief discussion of four topics:

1. The G-20 and governance reform of the IMF and the World Bank
2. Climate change and development
3. International migration and development
4. Changing views of traditional foreign aid

The G-20 and Governance Reform at the IFIs

Prior to the crisis, there were already clear signs that the post–World War II success of the Western allies in managing global challenges to peace and security and in building an open trade and investment system was under strain. The United Nations was from its beginnings weaker than it might have been because of its one-nation, one-vote governance structure, as Kemal Derviş points out in chapter 8, and because of fundamental differences in interests and ideology between the communist countries and the West. After the fall of the Berlin Wall, the UN's development contribution was blunted by the continuing tension on trade, human rights, and labor issues between the rich industrialized states led by the United States and the G-77 grouping of developing countries.

In contrast, the IMF and the World Bank (the original Bretton Woods institutions) had from their beginnings a more effective governance structure based on weighted votes; they also benefited for four decades from the ideological clarity associated with the absence of the Soviet Union and its satellites. By the end of the twentieth century, they were both well established as institutions in which the traditional Western powers used their financial clout to promote and support the market model in developing countries. It was the Western powers, grouped as the G-7 and after the Cold War with Russia as the G-8, that for all practical purposes constituted the informal steering committee for the two Bretton Woods institutions.

That situation began to change in the 1990s with the end of the Cold War. With the embrace of market reforms throughout the developing world and then the surge of growth with the 2003–7 boom, the Bretton Woods institutions came under increasing pressure to increase the voting power and other forms of influence of China and other emerging markets. But progress was minimal and painfully slow; when the crisis hit no meaningful changes in their governance had been made. The Europeans were unable to resolve among themselves how to share in a reasonable reduction in their voting power and seats given their reduced role in the global economy. The United States, during both the Bill Clinton and George W. Bush administrations, though generally supportive of greater voice and votes for developing countries, was not particularly eager to give up the prerogatives and power it had historically enjoyed, including its right to choose the president of the World Bank and to veto the Europeans' choice of the head of the IMF if it wanted.

The IMF and the World Bank suffered a loss not only of legitimacy (and that for many reasons, not just governance) but also of relevance, as rapid growth and their easy access to private capital reduced dramatically the borrowing of the big emerging markets and other developing countries, especially between 2002 and 2008. (To some extent, the success of major developing countries was, ironically, the outcome of their embrace of the macroeconomic and structural reforms the institutions had long advocated and supported.) By 2008, Turkey was the only major IMF borrower. The World Bank remained active in low-income countries but was becoming more of an aid agency, heavily reliant on contributions from the traditional Western donors for its activities in those countries, than the credit cooperative that John Maynard Keynes and its other founders envisioned. That in itself threatened its legitimacy with the new rising Asian and other emerging markets—since it continued to be dominated in its policies and governance by the advanced Western industrialized countries.

The crisis changed the situation dramatically, providing an opportunity for major strengthening of the system in two respects. First, it led to the elevation of the G-20 (first constituted in the late 1990s as a grouping of finance ministers with leadership from the U.S. Treasury) to its new status as a summit of heads of state. The first meeting of the G-20 group of countries at the head of state level in Washington, D.C., in November 2008 was a sudden and almost an ad hoc affair. But subsequent meetings in London in March 2009 and in Pittsburgh in September 2009 (after the conference on which this book is based) locked in the status of the G-20 as an obvious substitute for the G-8, at least on the global economy and financial system, and to some extent on global development challenges more broadly conceived as well.

Second, the crisis set the stage for a dramatic recovery in relevance of the IMF and the World Bank. This was especially true of the IMF, which, in retrospect, was rescued from what had looked like an inevitable slide into obscurity and irrelevance. In the first days after the collapse of Lehman Brothers, the IMF looked particularly irrelevant when the U.S. Federal Reserve Bank made quick and sizable lines of credit available to several large emerging markets. Within a few months, however, the IMF and the multilateral banks had a more representative new (if informal and unofficial) steering committee in the form of the G-20, which had endorsed for them a major role in ensuring adequate financial flows to developing countries to cope with the crisis. The replacement of the G-8 by the G-20 as the steering committee for the two institutions also helped somewhat to enhance their legitimacy in the developing world—though the modest pre-crisis adjustments in formal voting power and other governance changes were only slightly accelerated.

The switch of the G-20 from finance officials to heads of states, and the agreement at the London G-20 meeting in March 2009 on a coordinated stimulus, seemed at the time to be a breakthrough in the potential for global coordination. So did the commitment to ensure as much as $1 trillion of new resources would be available (primarily through the IMF and the multilateral banks) to help developing countries cope with the crisis. The same can be said of the resolutions at the G-20 summits, including in Pittsburgh in the fall of 2009, that all members would resist protectionist pressures at home.

However, within one year it was clear that global collective action in the interests of a larger global good had not suddenly become the norm. In retrospect, a coordinated global stimulus was relatively easy to agree to; it is not as politically difficult for governments to commit to spend more as it is to spend less. In the few countries that hesitated, such as Germany, the automatic stabilizers kicked in anyway. In addition the United States and Europe had considerable experience working together, including through multiple effective informal channels, and more easily so on issues like a global stimulus, where their immediate domestic interests and their customary role as chief stewards of the global system were well aligned. And of course an acute sense of urgency, including assurance that emerging market economies would continue to help fuel global demand, put the wind at their backs for the $1 trillion commitment.

As the urgency of the crisis diminished and the domestic political costs of any particular action rose, collective action faltered. As before the crisis, for example, the global collective was unable to address effectively the global imbalances that had contributed to the crisis in the first place, with the United States fueling imports and its consumption and housing boom with fiscal deficits and loose monetary policy and the Chinese fueling its investment and export booms with an increasingly undervalued renminbi and limited spending on social programs at home. A year after the Lehman collapse, the IMF still had no political ability to impose any kind of discipline on the major creditor, China, or the major debtor, the United States. Collective action of any kind at the global level was completely stalled. Decisions by the two big economies continued to be driven by domestic political and short-run economic concerns and not by even a small dose of concern about the risks of the imbalances to global stability and thus to their own long-term interests.

The stimulus China so effectively implemented with the emphasis on investment not consumption was driven by the same domestic imperatives to sustain job creation and experts as its pre-crisis stance; meanwhile it halted the minimal appreciation of its currency it allowed before the crisis hit. In the United States, the accumulation of public debt and effect of quantitative easing on global interest rates was also perverse from the point of view of a global adjustment (though few would argue there was any alternative as there was and continues to be in China); in particular there was the risk that U.S. policy was creating conditions for a dangerous bubble in emerging markets, as people and institutions holding capital sought higher returns in those markets than they could get in the United States.

Similarly, there was no real progress in coordinating new financial sector rules that would minimize the excesses that contributed to the crisis and ensure that the industry could not exploit differences in standards across major markets. The overall outcome a year after the crisis was that the risk of periodic financial collapse had not been reduced, and the policies in response to the crisis were adding to the risk of a long period of sluggish growth in the industrialized countries—with, as Peter Heller rightly emphasizes in chapter 12, attendant increased risks to the developing countries that depend on external demand for jobs and income gains.

In short, any benign effect of the crisis in inspiring global collective action on global economic challenges, including development, seemed limited and short-lived one year later. Better representation of some advanced developing countries in the global economy club—the G-20—did not provoke a sea change in global governance or the ability of nations to cooperate on fundamental economic problems that affect prospects for growth and development worldwide. Perhaps it is not surprising that the new ideas about development provoked by the crisis and set out in this book focus more on domestic policy within developing countries than on the inadequacies in what might be called a still-incipient or fragile global "polity." Though the increasingly integrated and thus increasingly risk-prone global economy lives on, more than two years after the Lehman Brothers collapse, it was hard to see much progress in creation of a global polity that would enhance its benefits and minimize its risks.

Climate Change and Development

In other areas where there are more obvious and immediate trade-offs between short-term domestic interests and the long-run benefits of a more stable and sustainable global economy, there is even less reason for optimism. Consider climate change. Throughout 2009, nations struggled to negotiate a global climate treaty. The traditional post-WWII powers had to engage with and accommodate the demands of rising Asia and other emerging market economies to an unprecedented extent. They also had to grapple with the question of their financial responsibilities, in their own interests and in the interests of global prosperity, to developing countries for mitigation at home and for financing mitigation and adaptation abroad—at a time when their own fiscal problems were daunting given their exploding debt levels due to the crisis.

As it turns out, progress toward a climate change agreement was painfully slow during 2009; the global financial crisis was a constraint and a distraction, not an opportunity. The December 2009 accord agreed at Copenhagen was better than nothing but at its heart amounted to little more than the summing up of what individual countries, especially China and the United States, could manage politically at home.

Whether there will be more progress in 2010 and beyond (not only on climate but on terrorism, drug trafficking, pandemics, and other risks that compound the development challenge) increasingly depends on the stance of China, India, Brazil and other members of a newly named group of "advanced developing countries." On climate, China's stance is especially crucial. Pei in his chapter argues that China's response to the crisis was to adhere to "realism" with only modest signs of any move toward "international liberalism"; China still feels strategically vulnerable—for example in terms of access to raw materials—and is unlikely to assume any role in global stewardship anytime soon. A good example of its approach was its willingness to contribute to the financing of IMF crisis programs—but at a modest level and not with permanent funding—and its taking the position that additional contribution would be contingent on faster and more meaningful gains in its formal influence at the IMF.

Would a continuing failure of collective action to address climate change matter for development prospects around the world? Yes. The potential for unabated climate change to damage growth and destroy livelihoods in developing countries is huge; countries closer to the equator and more dependent on agriculture are particularly vulnerable (Cline 2007), and in general poorer people are less able to cope with the adjustments climate change will bring (Dasgupta, Laplante, Murray, and Wheeler 2009).[6]

The realities of climate change—including China's and other advanced developing countries' own dramatically rising emissions due to their own rapid economic growth and population growth—and the mounting evidence of the high costs within China and other advanced developing countries—give them more incentives and more influence, as was evident in Copenhagen. These countries cannot afford to absent themselves from action, as their own contributions to greenhouse gas emissions assuming business-as-usual policy would alone be sufficient to put the planet at grave risk within a couple of decades (Wheeler and Ummel 2007). Nor can they insulate themselves from other global risks such as pandemics and nuclear proliferation. They are likely to insist in their own interests on more influence at major global institutions—and in the case of China, India, and Brazil, to see their own interests as increasingly aligned with sustaining stability and prosperity in the rest of the world.

Meanwhile, the United States and the Europeans may yet yield in their own interests to the pressure for more engagement of the advanced developing countries in the management of climate change initiatives, making climate the leading wedge of more fundamental institutional reforms. That is already the case with the shift from the G-8 to the G-20 as the key forum on global economic issues. At the institutional level, the new Climate Investment Funds are an example; these funds are housed at the World Bank and other multilateral banks and depend heavily still on contributions from the traditional donors. However their governance structure is already 50/50, in other words, 50 percent of votes are held by the developed and 50 percent by the developing world.

International Migration and Development

What does all this have to do with changes in ideas about development after the crisis? In a sense the crisis provided a wake-up call to the development community that the distinction between development issues and global issues is blurring. Already students of development were concerned with low-income fragile states because those states cannot be counted on to participate responsibly in dealing with cross-border problems. The crisis has driven home that the challenge to global collective action is bigger and more complicated. Emerging markets, especially China, may or may not take on global stewardship sooner or later. Even if they do, the traditional powers, especially the United States, may or may not be politically able to overcome their domestic problems sufficiently to cooperate even where their long-term prosperity depends on it.

The changing face of geopolitical power in the world, illustrated vividly by the crisis itself and its immediate aftermath, is bound to lead to a reframing of many development issues. Global problems and challenges will rise on the agenda, because they are more relevant than ever for developing countries' prospects for growth, and because some countries, while still poor, are economically big enough (and as Heller documents will be proportionally far bigger relative to industrialized countries by mid-century), are now systemically important; they are play makers not just takers in the global system.

Michael Clemens' chapter 11 provides a stunning example of a development issue already being framed differently than it was several decades ago because of the deep structural changes in both industrialized and developing countries. He and other development economists were calling attention to the logic of greater migration from poor to rich countries before the crisis. The crisis provided a reminder that though the United States, Europe, Japan, and a few other industrialized countries still dominate the global economy, their decisions alone no longer guide its fate. Among other changes, they are going to be dependent on immigration to maintain any reasonable measure of economic growth and vitality at home as their populations age (and this will be true of China in another couple of decades). Accepting greater immigration will also be sensible as a measure to increase social and political stability in the Middle East, Africa, and other settings where rapid increases in the number of young people will require stupendous efforts by relatively weak governments to create jobs and provide urban services—emigration can provide a safety valve where that process does not proceed smoothly and can contribute mightily through the return of human and social capital (what is sometimes called *circular migration*) and the spread of common norms and ideas, as well as obviously through remittances. The logic of increased migration as the last liberalizing force for a more prosperous and equitable global economy—after trade in goods and services and capital flows—is inescapable. Whether any collective global measures to minimize its social costs and maximize its benefits in both sending and receiving countries will follow is not clear.

Changing Attitudes about Aid and the Aid System

Ideas about development aid were not discussed at the conference where the chapters in this book were first presented. In retrospect that is surprising, since perhaps a decade hence looking back it will be remarked that the financial crisis undid forever the idea of aid as a vehicle for the rich, who know how to grow their economies and transform their societies, to the poor who apparently (or so it was assumed) did not.

As with other issues, prior to the crisis development practitioners had been advocating a set of reforms of the aid system for at least two decades, focused heavily on better aligning assistance to low-income countries with those countries' own priorities, rather than with the own political, diplomatic, or commercial interests of donor nations. That reform was often expressed as "putting the country in the driver's seat." But for the most part the domestic politics of aid and bureaucratic constraints had largely frustrated good intentions, and the prevailing if implicit view was that the donors knew more about the programs and policies that would bring transformation and modernization to low-income countries than the countries' own leadership and citizens. Aid-recipient countries may have been in the driver's seat but they often had donor passengers grabbing the steering wheel or shouting instructions from the back seat.[7]

The crisis illustrated that the traditional donors might not be good drivers of their own cars. By the time of the crisis, some low-income countries were increasingly taking charge of the wheel anyway. Also foreign aid had become no longer a solely Western activity. China, India, and Brazil had become donors too and saw aid as one part of a larger set of relations in their own interests, including growing investment and trade ties with low-income Africa and Asia. And Korea, the host of the November 2010 G-20 summit, began wresting from the G-8 the development issue, bringing an emphasis on growth, investment, trade, and financial stability to the agenda, not just or mostly aid.

The effect of the crisis was to reinforce this democratization of the aid system and to reinforce the view that the traditional Western powers did not have all the answers anyway on how to develop. Perhaps looking back ten years hence, the crisis will mark the moment when the conception of aid for the two post–Cold War decades began to change—from aid as primarily charity (with a heavy focus since 2000 on aid as a key input to help poor countries achieve the Millennium Development Goals) to aid as one aspect of global public policy central to a safer and more prosperous global system (Severino and Ray 2009).

Conclusion

The global financial crisis provided a dramatic illustration of the risks of the global market. For developing countries it underlined their vulnerability not only to natural disasters and terms of trade shocks but also to a sudden economic collapse of the advanced industrial economies. The crisis will not induce developing countries to give up the opportunities for growth the global market provides; after all globalization and market capitalism were working well for them before the crisis and they recovered more quickly from it than the rich countries did. Adherence to the market and to capitalism will endure. But there will be a subtle shift to an increased role for the state in managing markets, with greater recourse to policies and mechanisms to minimize vulnerability and ensure robustness, even at the cost of maximum efficiency and flexibility. That will be obvious in the case of slower opening of capital accounts, but it will also affect labor and social policies and it could inspire—despite the risks, especially where governance is weak—increased interest in Asian-style "new" (rule-based) industrial policy. Traditional Western ideas about good politics may also lose their grip. The crisis and its aftermath may be seen in the developing world as an illustration of the apparent benefits of resorting in the manner of China to executive discretion in the interests of an effective state that can act quickly and effectively—in contrast to the checks and balances that delay and complicate policy implementation in typical consolidated democracies. In that sense, the traditional Western idea about political progress (my co-editor's "end of history") will no longer go unquestioned in the developing world.

The crisis may also mark an important watershed in whether and how the international community manages global challenges to its common welfare. In the new multipolar world, there is less likelihood of the kind of change wrought after World War II, when, with the United States the unrivaled lead in the Western world, came the creation of the United Nations, the World Bank, the International Monetary Fund, and what became the World Trade Organization. The current crisis will be remembered as marking the end of Western economic dominance. With the creation of the G-20 replacing the G-8, China and other emerging markets now sit at the table of global collective action. Will that finally trigger meaningful reform at the IMF, and real engagement of China and other emerging markets in decision making there and at the World Bank? Will it confound or advance the negotiation of a climate change treaty and a more sensible approach to maximizing the benefits of international migration for all countries and peoples? Will it mark the end of the twentieth-century understanding of aid? Will the low-income countries get a seat at the table too, and if so when? With new issues arising on the global development agenda, do we have an international system of institutions, rules, and habits in place to address the resulting challenges? As we pick up the pieces after the global financial crisis, there are new issues—changing power shifts, demography, and continuing financial and other risks in a global system—and the answer is far from clear.

Will we look back on the crisis as the beginning of the end of "development" as an idea in itself—as the development agenda ultimately merges in this century into a global agenda for cooperation across nations in the interests of a more just, sustainable, and equally shared prosperity? Well, probably not. But I hope readers will read this book with that question in mind.

Notes

I thank Frank Fukuyama, Seth Colby, Lawrence MacDonald, Moises Naim, and the authors of the essays in this book, especially Michael Clemens, Peter Heller, and Mitchell Orenstein for their excellent comments on an earlier version of this introduction.

1. On February 19, 2010, the International Monetary Fund published a policy note on capital controls. Taxes and other restrictions on capital inflows, the IMF's economists wrote, can be helpful, and they constitute a "legitimate part" of policymakers' toolkit. Dani Rodrik wrote on his blog that this publication marked "the end of an era in finance." Available at http://rodrik.typepad.com/dani_rodriks_weblog/2010/03/the-end-of-an-era-in-finance.html

2. In his thoughtful comments on a draft of this chapter, Mitchell Orenstein suggested there is a change afoot about the objectives of development with the target of high growth rates no longer as widely shared. This was to some extent the case before the crisis, as the Millennium Development Goals agreed by more than 150 heads of state in 2000 would suggest, and see Sen (1999). However, I would say that developing country political leaders are still heavily focused on growth itself as the means to all the other good things that "development" implies.

3. At the conference, Tanzanian Central Bank Governor Benno Ndulu noted the potential benefits of development banks, and suggested the kinds of rules and constraints on their programs and policies, such as that would prevent the abuses that made them an economic liability in many developing countries in the 1970s and 1980s.

4. On the market failure due to risks that early adopters face, and the resulting logic of state interventions to encourage innovation, see Hausmann and Rodrik (2003).

5. On the popular understanding of the Washington consensus, and on the debate about its actual implementation, results and shortcomings, see Birdsall, de la Torre, and Valencia (forthcoming).

6. China's exchange rate policy is another example. A year after the financial crisis hit, in the absence of a rule-based arrangement on exchange rate management, or at least of prior agreed guidelines on good behavior as a basis for naming and shaming (in principle an IMF role; in fact a sign of the IMF's inability to discipline powerful members), protectionist pressures were rising in the United States, and wrangling between the two countries was creating a greater risk of disruptions to trade and investment flows around the world. To the extent the Chinese renminbi was undervalued in early 2010, it was undermining the competitiveness not only of the United States, but of many developing countries in Africa and Latin America whose rates were floating, as Subramanian (2010) among others argued.

7. For a discussion of the fundamental dilemma of making aid transfers from outside effective for development, and a summary of reform efforts and their limited traction, see Birdsall and Savedoff 2010.

References

Birdsall, N. forthcoming. "The (Indispensable) Middle Class in Developing Countries." In *Equity in a Globalizing World,* edited by R. Kanbur and M. Spence. Washington, DC: World Bank.

Birdsall, N., de la Torre, A., and Valencia, F. forthcoming. "The Rise and Fall of the Washington Consensus." In *The Oxford Handbook of Latin American Economics,* edited by J. A. Ocampo and J. Ros. Oxford: Oxford University Press.

Birdsall, N., and Savedoff, W. 2010. *Cash on Delivery: A New Approach to Foreign Aid.* Washington, DC: Center for Global Development.

Cline, W. 2007. *Global Warming and Agriculture: Impact Estimates by Country.* Washington, DC: Center for Global Development.

Dasgupta, S., Laplante, B., Murray, S., and Wheeler, D. 2009. "Climate Change and the Future Impacts of Storm-Surge Disasters in Developing Countries." *CGD Working Paper 182.* Washington, DC: Center for Global Development.

Friedman, M. 1968. "The Role of Monetary Policy." *The American Economic Review* 58(1): 1–17.

Hausmann, R., and Rodrik, D. 2003. "Economic Development as Self-Discovery." *Journal of Development Economics* 72(2): 603–33.

Hayek, F.A. 1941. *The Pure Theory of Capital.* Chicago: University of Chicago.

Hirschman, A.O. 1958. *The Strategy of Economic Development.* New Haven: Yale University Press.

International Monetary Fund. 2009. *World Economic Outlook, October 2009: Sustaining the Recovery.* Washington, DC: International Monetary Fund.

Kose, M.A., Prasad, E., Rogoff, K., and Wei, S. 2006. "Financial Globalization: A Reappraisal." *IMF Working Paper.* Washington, DC: International Monetary Fund.

Leibenstein, H. 1966. "Allocative Efficiency v. 'X-efficiency.'" *American Economic Review* 56: 392–415.

Lustig, N. 2009. "Coping with Rising Food Prices: Policy Dilemmas in the Developing World." *CGD Working Paper 164.* Washington, DC: Center for Global Development.

Rosenstein-Rodan, P. 1943. "Problems of Industrialization of Eastern and South-Eastern Europe." *Economic Journal* 53(210/211):202–11.

Sen, A. 1999. *Development as Freedom.* New York: Random House.

Severino, J.-M., and Ray, O. 2009. "The End of ODA: Death and Rebirth of a Global Public Policy." *CGD Working Paper 167.* Washington, DC: Center for Global Development.

Stiglitz, J.E. 1989. "The Economic Role of the State." In *The Economic Role of the State,* edited by A. Heertje. London: Basil Blackwell.

———. 2010. *Freefall: America, Free Markets, and the Sinking of the World Economy.* New York: W. W. Norton.

Subramanian, A. 2010. "It Is the Poor Who Pay for the Weak Renminbi." *Financial Times,* March 18, 2010.

Wheeler, D., and Ummel, K. 2007. "Another Inconvenient Truth: A Carbon-Intensive South Faces Environmental Disaster, No Matter What the North Does." *CGD Working Paper 134.* Washington, DC: Center for Global Development.

Williamson, John (ed.). 1990. *Latin American Adjustment: How Much Has Happened?* Washington, DC: Institute for International Economics, Conference Volume.

World Bank. 1993. *The East Asian Miracle: Economic Growth and Public Policy.* Washington, DC: World Bank.

Part I • Implication of the Crisis on Development Thinking

CHAPTER I

Three Models of Contemporary Capitalism

Mitchell A. Orenstein

FROM 1980 TO 2006, dozens of countries followed the lead of the United States and Great Britain in implementing free market economic policy ideas. Governments did so largely in the hope that this would lead to sustained high levels of economic growth. The financial shock of 2008–9 imperiled this trend. Emulation of the United States, a driving force of economic policy in both developed and developing countries in the recent past, seems unlikely to be so in the future. The days when economic policymakers worldwide eagerly sought advice from Washington and lionized the likes of Milton Friedman and Alan Greenspan are gone, possibly for good. The question is what comes next.

Where will countries turn now for new ideas about development and models for economic policy? In his book *The End of History and the Last Man*, Frank Fukuyama argued that capitalism and liberal democracy were the only viable systemic choices after the collapse of communism (Fukuyama 1992). Today, alternative models of capitalism are growing in importance. As the influence of free market ideas wanes, countries worldwide will explore other models of capitalist development that promise high growth without periodic collapse or implosion, an unfortunate hallmark of the free market model.

Looking at economic development policy as a search for models is relatively new in economic development theory. Standard analyses of policy choice assume that economic policymakers choose policy rationally, with full information, or that they try to and are prevented by politics. Yet decision makers often follow the herd, using bounded rationality, incomplete information, and emulation of neighboring and peer countries as guideposts of economic policy, or because they are forced, coerced, or encouraged to do so (Simmons, Dobbin, and Garrett 2008; Weyland 2005).

Sometimes emulation brings success, other times disappointment. Models may be (or appear to be) successful in one country or at one point in time, but unsuccessful in another. Since no one economic model has produced development consistently everywhere, most countries tend to try out one model, discover its strengths and weaknesses, and then search for new models of economic development over time as they continue their quest.

The effect is that at different points in time and under different circumstances, certain dominant economic models exert tremendous influence worldwide and then are surpassed by new models that offer seemingly greater promise. Fascism spread during the 1930s in Europe and Latin America, state planning was popular throughout the so-called third world during the 1940s and 1950s, and the 1990s were the heyday of free market capitalism. Today, we are again at a turning point. If emulation is an important part of economic policy choice, the future of economic policy will be determined largely by what models are perceived to be rising and waning in influence right now.

Three Models of Contemporary Capitalism

Since the collapse of communism in Europe and Eurasia, three main models of capitalist economic development have competed for influence as sources of economic policy ideas for development: free market liberalism, the European social model, and authoritarian state capitalism. These three models have been adopted by leading countries in the world economy and articulated in expert, academic, and policy discourse. They are models in both a descriptive and a normative sense. On the one hand, they more or less accurately describe the practice of the model leading countries. On the other, they claim superiority as templates in achieving desirable social, economic, and political outcomes.

Not all countries neatly fall into one model or another. While model leading countries tend to adhere most closely to the description, other countries adopt the model only in part. Significant deviations remain, particularly for countries that in a previous period adhered to a different model. Many developing countries are sui generis and tend to be model followers or partial adopters rather than model leading countries. One can no doubt identify additional variants or subvariants of capitalism. Despite these issues of categorization, it is useful to think about models of capitalism, because they are well-established and well-articulated sets of ideas about economic policy that influence policy in multiple countries.

In defining models of capitalism, which are normally distinguished according to the role of government in the economy, social policy, and the structure of labor markets and labor-management relations, I emphasize two additional elements here—the structure of enterprise ownership and the nature of the political regime—which are critical to a proper understanding of the different models of capitalism but are often left aside from standard definitions. In other respects, the definitions employed here follow standard approaches in international political economy (Hall and Soskice 2001; Katzenstein 1978; Schonfeld 1965), and in particular the typology proposed by Schmidt (2002, 107–18).

Free Market Capitalism

Free market capitalism is an economic model in which unencumbered markets are the core element. Free market capitalists claim that markets are superior to states as a mechanism of coordination and allocation of resources, except in cases of severe market failure and provision of certain public goods. Markets are thought to be self-correcting at most times and government regulation is thought to be best when it is minimal or even nonexistent. Advocates of free market capitalism suggest that removal of government regulation and interference in the economy is the best way to achieve growth, investment, and even public welfare. Limited regulation extends also to openness to the world economy, with an emphasis on free trade and capital flows. In free market economies, social policy is geared toward providing minimum guarantees or safety nets to protect people when—and only when—market provision fails. Labor markets typically are lightly regulated to enable flexibility in hiring and firing and wage setting by market forces, rather than rigid pay scales or union pattern bargaining.

A unique feature of free market economies is their widely dispersed share ownership through highly developed stock markets and minimal or nonexistent state ownership. In the United States and the United Kingdom (along with Australia, Hong Kong, Ireland, Japan, Korea, Mexico, and Switzerland), state ownership of the largest publicly traded enterprises in the country is effectively nil. In most other capitalist countries, the state owns a controlling share of between 10 and 50 percent of the 20 largest publicly traded enterprises (La Porta, Lopez-de-Silanes, and Shleifer 1999).

Most free market economies are liberal or electoral democracies. Economic and political liberalism both are rooted in a deeper tradition that extends also to the pursuit of science, technology, reason, individualism, and separation of church and state. "Free markets and free people" was one of the slogans of the free market revolution led by Ronald Reagan and Margaret Thatcher. And indeed most, though not all, countries that have achieved a high degree of free market liberalism also attained a high level of democracy during the period from 1980–2006, a period of rapid democratization worldwide.[1]

European Social Model

The European social model has often been defined in contrast to free market capitalism (Giddens 2005). While both rely on capitalist enterprise, free trade, and liberal economic policies to create growth and employment, the European social model leavens these policies with a substantial dose of state direction and regulation. It does so to achieve twin goals of economic and political stability by spreading the benefits of growth more widely and preventing economic crisis. In Europe, these are seen as crucial political imperatives because of its nineteenth- and twentieth-century history of unrest linked to economic uncertainty and struggle. Leading practitioners of the European social model are France, Germany, and Sweden, industrialized countries that have long been devoted to different variants of "coordinated market economies" (Hall and Soskice 2001; Pontusson 2005) with sectoral or national wage bargaining and different versions of state planning and economic intervention. Many analysts have pointed out that there are a variety of different European social models (Esping-Andersen 1990) and question whether there is a single one. While there is strong interregional differentiation, most European welfare states remain distinct from the rest of the world and constitute a separate, if very general, set of ideas and practices on economic policy.

According to Giddens (2005), the key elements of the European social model are a developed and interventionist state, high rates of taxation, an elaborate and well-funded welfare system to provide for the needs of not only the poor but also the middle and upper-middle classes, and an institutionalized role for trade unions and other social partners in economic decision making at all levels of policy. In some countries, such as Germany, this extends to enterprise decision making as well. Hall and Soskice (2001) note that coordinated market economies, firms tend to coordinate with one another through strategic interaction, rather than decentralized markets alone. The state plays a much more significant role in economic regulation than in free market economies, with a greater willingness to intervene.

In addition, state ownership and democratic governance are distinctive features of the European social model. In European countries, the median amount of state ownership is a controlling share in 20 percent of the largest companies. This is true of Denmark, Finland, France, Germany, Norway, and Sweden. Some of the more liberal European countries have less state ownership. Others have considerably more. In Austria, fully 83 percent of the leading firms are at least partly state-controlled. This state involvement in enterprise ownership marks a major distinction with free market capitalism, with its characteristic arms-length relations between state and market.

Democratic governance is a core element of the European social model. European social market economies are explicitly intended to protect and ensure the stability of democracy from social unrest that could undermine support for democratic rule, as occurred in the Weimar Republic. Democracy is a large part of their raison d'être. Conversely, democracy is widely seen as a causal factor in the development of the European welfare state, as citizens have demanded greater and greater social rights and protections over time, facilitated by proportional representation voting, coalition cabinets, and other consensus modes of decision making (Lijphart 1999). This emphasis on the democratic nature of the European social model helps us to understand its differences from authoritarian state capitalism.

Authoritarian State Capitalism

Authoritarian state capitalism was once thought in the West to be the most promising path to economic development for less developed countries. In the 1990s, it fell out of favor as scholars determined that democracies on average enjoyed similar growth rates to authoritarian regimes, despite the notable exception of China (Przeworski, Alvarez, Cheibub, and Limongi 2000; Rodrik 1998). However, the authoritarian state capitalist model of development has recently regained its potency in the international marketplace of ideas. It has been adopted by China, the major rising economy in the international system, and by Russia, which has sought to emulate China's development style after suffering a disastrous attempt to build democracy and free markets. Singapore and other East Asian and Southeast Asian countries have also developed under authoritarian state capitalism, as have Middle Eastern countries such as Saudi Arabia, the United Arab Emirates, and Kuwait. Authoritarian state capitalist economies differ in many ways, but they share a few key characteristics: an authoritarian political system, a state that owns, controls, and intervenes to a great extent in the economy, and relatively low welfare state effort, civil society mobilization, and trade union power.

It should be noted that many authoritarian state capitalist countries, including China and Russia, often have been portrayed as free market liberal economies because they have adopted elements of the free market model (Aslund 2007). This approach ignores major areas of departure from economic policies of free market capitalist countries. Authoritarian state capitalist countries can be distinguished from free market capitalist countries in important ways. While they have liberalized trade significantly and allowed some foreign direct investment, their economies are not fully liberalized. The state does not constrain itself to a regulatory role and behaves very differently. While in a free market capitalist country, the state provides a moderately extensive set of welfare guarantees and business regulations, authoritarian state capitalist countries typically provide minimal welfare coverage but are highly interventionist and regulate with a heavy hand, unconstrained by courts and law. Labor tends to be suppressed, while it is free to organize and often moderately powerful in free market economies.

Adding ownership and governance to the definition provides a sharper view of authoritarian state capitalism. Authoritarian state capitalist countries are unlike free market economies in both their degree of ownership concentration and state ownership. While exactly comparable statistics are not fully available, in China the five largest shareholders in the country held 58 percent of all shares in 1995. At that time, a typical publicly traded company was 30 percent owned by the state. The Chinese state continues to own controlling shares of the major banks (despite the much-publicized offering of some shares on the Hong Kong and Shanghai stock exchanges), including three of the largest banks in the world. Despite the large amount of private business in China, the state retains the "commanding heights" of the economy (Yergin and Stanislaw 2002) through ownership of banks and key enterprises. This ownership enables the state to control economic policy and facilitate development in ways that are impossible in free market economies. State ownership is also characteristic of countries such as Saudi Arabia (Aramco), Singapore (Temasek), and United Arab Emirates.

Finally, most state capitalist economies are also authoritarian. Authoritarian rule enables these countries to cut back on wages, welfare state

Table 1.1. Models of capitalism

Characteristic	Free market economies	European social market economies	Authoritarian state capitalist economies
Welfare state	Moderate	High	Low
Labor union power	Low/moderate	Moderate/high	Low
State regulation	Moderate	High	High
Political regime	Democratic	Democratic	Authoritarian
Ownership concentration	Low	Moderate/high	High
State ownership	Low	Moderate/high	High

spending, and private consumption in favor of investment and defense, to suppress labor organization, and to stop political shocks to the economic development model (Przeworski et al. 2000). Only through authoritarian governance can China, for instance, maintain a nearly 50 percent rate of investment. Authoritarian states do not depend on popular approval in the same ways or to the same extent. They can afford to ignore short-term discontent in the pursuit of long-term objectives. This provides a powerful set of tools for economic development, if used correctly. Authoritarian state capitalist countries differ from one another in important ways, but they share key features, outlined in table 1.1.

Emulation and Development

Having defined the three main models of capitalism, in the rest of this chapter I begin to develop a theory of the role of emulation in economic development and use the example of the spread of free market capitalism from 1980 to 2006 to frame some propositions about what might come next, after the shock of the 2008–9 world financial crisis.

Most theories of economic development focus on the domestic economic and political context to explain economic policy choices. Economic approaches often emphasize that political leaders do not choose optimal economic policies that can be discovered through the application of economic reasoning. Domestic interest group politics often trumps economic theory as a source of policy choice, except in unusual circumstances. This general approach overlaps in important ways with a dominant approach in political science, which emphasizes historical path dependencies that keep countries on the same developmental path and prevent them from fundamentally changing their model of development. Policies, as Pierson (1994) showed, create their own politics. Constituencies develop to support the benefits provided by existent policies and are often able to defend these policies against future changes. Institutions and politics thus tend to perpetuate existing policy regimes. For instance, Arvind Subramanian in his chapter in this volume entitled, "The Crisis and the Two Globalization Fetishes," notes that interest groups benefit disproportionately from capital account liberalization. It is this fact, rather than the economic merits of the liberalizing reforms, that explains why so many developing countries have liberalized their capital accounts.

While these interest-based theories explain a lot about economic policy choice, they do have shortcomings. One of the main ones is that these theories have an easier time explaining policy continuity than policy change. Since underlying power structures do not change easily, it is easier to use them to explain the way things are than why things change. To explain change, economic theorists often look to exogenous shocks, since these have the ability to shake up prevailing interest group structures. However, while crises create the environment for policy change, the content of change cannot necessarily be determined as interest group politics is reshaped in contingent ways under conditions of uncertainty.

Explaining why a certain policy is suddenly adopted in a crisis rather than another requires attention to the realm of ideas and the construction of interest. Theories, ideas, and models help to generate propositions about how the economy works, general frameworks for policy, and a set of practices for economic policy change that may be implemented at times of crisis. This is why the Chicago school with its emphasis on laissez-faire economic policies has been so important in the spread of free market capitalism worldwide. After the Second World War, U.S. universities became breeding grounds of a coherent ideology of economic development theory that gained influence in think tanks, governments, and international institutions worldwide, changing the way many countries approached economic development theory and practice.

To help understand the future of economic development theory, it is therefore helpful and interesting to look at the spread of free market capitalism worldwide from 1980 to 2006. Since we have little available data about previous episodes of economic policy emulation, the spread of free market capitalism offers a unique set of clues to understand the ways that emulation works as a source of economic development policy.

This section uses a global database on economic, as distinct from political, liberalization created by the Fraser Institute of Canada, a liberal think tank, to show how and how much policy emulation has affected countries around the world in the hope that observing these patterns can help to shed light on future directions.

The Fraser Institute Liberalization Index is based on 42 indicators divided into five areas of policy: (1) size of government; (2) legal structure and security of property rights; (3) access to sound money; (4) freedom to trade internationally; and (5) regulation of credit, labor, and business (Gwartney and Lawson 2008, xxi). These data are imperfect and may reflect subjective judgments, but in the absence of better data, we assume that they present a generally accurate picture of the spread of free market liberal economic policies worldwide, though results on individual countries may be suspect.

The first thing that jumps out of the Fraser Institute data is how widespread the trend toward free market liberalism has been. Out of 141 countries studied, 110 liberalized between 1980 and 2006, while only 12 went in the opposite direction (Gwartney and Lawson 2008). The others exhibited no distinct trend. Only a handful of countries like Myanmar (Burma), Venezuela, and Zimbabwe were seriously out of step with global trends during this period. The sheer enormity of the trend and the fact that most countries of the world could not or did not ignore it without risking international isolation suggest that emulation—voluntary or coerced—is a powerful force in economic policy choice.

While most countries adopted free market capitalist policies from 1980 to 2006, the extent of liberalization differed greatly. Exhibiting considerable path dependency based no doubt on domestic interest group politics and institutional rigidities, most countries liberalized only incrementally. However, there were some notable exceptions. Some countries liberalized by leaps and bounds, utterly transforming the nature of their economic system, somehow freeing themselves from interest groups and institutions that had dominated policy in the past.

Incremental Liberalization

Model leading countries—those that are strongly identified with a particular model of capitalism—tended to liberalize only incrementally from 1980 to 2006 both in terms of absolute changes in the index and relative to other reforming countries. This held true for the ten leading free market liberal economies in the world (Hong Kong, Singapore, New Zealand, Switzerland, the United Kingdom, Chile, Canada, the United States, Australia, and Ireland) that were already relatively liberal in 1980 and remained so in 2006. Few changes occurred in their global rankings during this period (see table 1.2 below). Only a few exceptional countries joined their ranks.[2]

Similarly, while the leading European social model countries liberalized significantly between 1980 and 2006, few liberalized enough to outpace the free market economies whose policies they emulated. Several, however, did exceed the degree of liberalism that free market economies attained in 1980. Calculating the rates of liberalization measured by the Fraser Institute, we find that France, Germany, Sweden, Denmark, Finland, the Netherlands, and Norway all liberalized at a rate that was within one standard deviation below the average rate of change for the entire sample (mainly because the size of government in these countries remained comparatively high). Path dependency matters and countries emulate policy from an existing baseline (Pierson 1994). Yet, the absolute level of liberalization did increase significantly in these countries, nonetheless.

The leading authoritarian state capitalist countries also liberalized incrementally. China, which is often portrayed as an example of radical liberalization, did not advance as quickly as one might expect in the Fraser

Table 1.2. Fraser Institute rankings of liberalism

1980 above 7.5	1990 above 7.5	2000 above 7.5	2006 above 7.5
Hong Kong	Hong Kong	Hong Kong	Hong Kong
Luxembourg	Singapore	United States	Singapore
Switzerland	United States	Singapore	New Zealand
United States	Switzerland	Switzerland	Switzerland
	Luxembourg	New Zealand	United Kingdom
		United Kingdom	Chile
		Canada	Canada
		Ireland	Australia
		Netherlands	United States
		Australia	Ireland
		Finland	Estonia
		Denmark	Iceland
		Austria	Denmark
		Luxembourg	Finland
		Iceland	Austria
		Belgium	Netherlands
			Germany
			Taiwan
			Kuwait
			Slovak Republic
			Costa Rica
			Luxembourg
			Norway
			Malta
			El Salvador

Source: Gwartney and Lawson 2008.

Institute ranking. While its overall score increased from 4.42 in 1980 to 6.17 in 2006, its world ranking actually decreased from 80 to 88 as other countries outpaced it in liberalization. China remains a heavily state-dominated economy, with a large state sector, government control of credit, and poor legal structure and property rights protections. Interestingly, both Iran and Russia liberalized more than China did. Iran's score increased from 3.82 in 1980 to 6.69 in 2006, 67th place in the world ranking, making it one of the world's most radical liberalizers. Russia increased from 4.09 to 5.91 between 1995 and 2006. Hong Kong did not increase its score at all during the period, but remained the most liberal economy in the world. Singapore increased modestly to the number two spot. Kuwait increased its score more dramatically, reaching number 20 in the global ranking by 2006. With the exception of Iran, none of the leading authoritarian state capitalist countries liberalized at a rate greater than one standard deviation above the norm for the rest of the world.

Radical Liberalization

Some countries liberalized so radically between 1980 and 2005 or 2006 that they effectively jumped categories, breaking free of their previous models of economic development and historical path dependencies. This list encompasses Ghana, Israel, Uganda, Jamaica, Peru, El Salvador, Hungary, Iran, Nicaragua, Tanzania, Iceland, Turkey, Chile, Bangladesh, and Mauritius. These countries liberalized more than one standard deviation beyond the average for countries in the Fraser Institute sample between 1980 and 2005.[3] Note that radical changes in most cases did not completely erase past legacies of state-directed economic policy. However, the change in these countries was simply greater than most. Add to this list several radical liberalizers among the post-communist countries that the Fraser Institute only began to track starting in 1990: Romania, Lithuania, Albania, Estonia, and Latvia. What do these radical liberalizing countries have in common? What factors account for their adoption of more radical policy change?

While there are undoubtedly multiple factors having to do with domestic politics and economics and external shocks (particularly in the case of the post-communist countries), one obvious commonality between this group is their level of development and their positioning vis-à-vis the core of the international system. For the most part, they are neither very rich nor very poor, but rather semi-peripheral countries in the world economic system—not at the core of the system but not entirely peripheral either.

The majority of radical liberalizers are classified by the World Bank as middle-income developing countries. Only four are low-income countries. The remaining ones are high-income countries like Estonia, Hungary, Iceland, and Israel—all relatively small, semi-peripheral European or European-style states. Notably, the high-growth East Asian miracle countries do not appear on the list of radical liberalizers. Another important fact: most of the radical liberalizing countries, with the exception of Iran, democratized during the same time period, ending in 2006 as electoral democracies.

Why are semi-peripheral countries (encompassing both middle-income and small, semi-peripheral high-income countries) seemingly more prone to emulate dominant economic policy trends? There are several reasons one could point to. First, semi-peripheral countries may have greater opportunity to reform. Because of their semi-peripheral status, domestic groups may be more likely to support risky policy changes that hold out the promise of joining the core of the international system. Compared with richer more centrally positioned countries, majorities may not view their country and its policies as already highly successful and be prepared to depart from the status quo. Second, as relatively wealthy states, they may have the slack resources and state capacity necessary to enact major changes that poor countries do not. Third, these countries may be better placed to benefit from radical change. With factor endowments and education levels that are more similar to their developed country rivals, they may benefit more than others from free trade and other forms of liberalization. In sum, middle-income, semi-peripheral countries may have greater chances to take advantage of the benefits of reform and the political and economic resources to deal with its costs. Compared with most wealthy incremental reformers, the political obstacles to emulation may be lower and prospective benefits higher in middle-income countries.

Other factors are no doubt at work. Neighboring countries tend to emulate one another to a greater extent, perhaps partly because of knowledge-sharing but also because of competition for comparative advantage. Thus radical liberalization tends to be concentrated in certain regions of the world where neighboring and peer countries compete to emulate one another. Radical liberalization is highly correlated with political democratization. Democratization may make countries more open to emulating foreign economic models through the opportunity structures created by a more open political system. Specific domestic political and economic factors may also explain a propensity to radical emulation and a lack of strong path dependency.

Deliberalization

If radical liberalizers tend to be semi-peripheral countries from regions with liberalizing and democratizing neighbors, what about those countries that have bucked the liberalization trend and opposed global influences?

Countries that truly have gone against the grain are very few in number. Of the 12 deliberalizing countries in the Fraser Institute sample, nine decreased only marginally in their liberalization scores. Interestingly, the United States (since 2000) falls into this group,[4] together with Belgium, Haiti, Luxembourg, Hong Kong, Malaysia, Nepal, Niger, and Bahrain.

The only countries to move more than marginally away from liberalism during the 1980–2006 time period were Venezuela, Zimbabwe, and Myanmar (Burma), three countries with strong dictatorships that have determined to resist influence from the international community. This suggests that bucking the trend toward economic liberalization has been politically difficult and incredibly costly. Domestic politics can trump international influences, but only if governments are willing and able to incur high costs for their citizens (Garrett and Lange 1996, 69).

Overall, the spread of free market capitalism shows that emulation is a powerful cause of economic policy change. When a particular model of capitalism is dominant, as the free market model was between 1980 and

2006, countries emulate its success. Most countries move incrementally toward the dominant policy regimes. Others undertake radical transformations. Only a relatively small proportion of countries buck the trend altogether. Path dependency is a powerful force in keeping countries within their traditional economic models, but policy emulation helps to explain why so many countries move within the constraints of the past toward the models of the future.

Financial Crisis and the Free Market Model

The 2008 world financial meltdown was more than a hard landing at the end of a business cycle: it precipitated a political and ideological crisis of free market capitalism. A few large banks were not the only things that died. Much of the justification for the idea of free market capitalism as a world-leading and world-beating economic model was also discredited. Former U.S. Federal Reserve Bank Chairman Alan Greenspan famously stated "I was wrong" about many of the fundamental assumptions of the free market approach. The crisis will have a global historic impact because it punctured the ideas that underpinned economic policy in much of the world.

There are four fundamental reasons for this collapse in confidence. First, the crisis had a traumatic effect on Western economies, destroying some of the leading institutions of contemporary capitalism. Banks such as Bear Sterns, Lehman Brothers, Bank of America, Citibank, and Merrill Lynch lost between 80 and 100 percent of their share value in 2008–9 and were swallowed up by their healthier competitors, forced into the arms of the state, or closed. Whereas in 2007, three of the top five banks in the world by market capitalization were American, in mid-2009, the top U.S. bank was ranked fifth.[5] In 2009, three Chinese state banks—ICBC, China Construction Bank, and Bank of China—stood astride the global top ten, moving ahead of many traditional Western banking giants from London and New York.[6] As a result, America lost stature in the eyes of the world.

Second, the 2008 crisis was so obviously self-inflicted. Most developing country economic crises are caused by external shocks beyond the control of the affected countries, but the 2008 crisis seemed to be caused by short-comings of free market capitalism itself. Failures of financial self-regulation, improper and irrational behavior of market actors, short-term incentives on the part of executives, and a lack of effective state oversight all seemed to indict the free market model. The 2008 crisis looked like something torn from the pages of Karl Marx's *Das Kapital*: unhinged speculation driven by capitalist greed ruining the employment prospects of the average worker.

Third, the U.S. response was so clearly hypocritical given its prior advice to the rest of the world. While U.S.-backed international financial institutions had advised countries to undertake austerity programs in the face of financial panics in the past, cutting budgets and increasing interest rates in an effort to stabilize economies at a considerable cost of unemployment, the United States turned its back on these policies when faced with a similar crisis. The country suddenly embraced Keynesian demand-management policies, expanding budget deficits to stimulate the economy, bailing out failing financial institutions and major firms and even nationalizing some industries, such as the once leading U.S. car maker General Motors. If the United States did not follow free market policies during its crisis, how could it continue to advocate them to the rest of the world?

Fourth, when the crisis hit, the free market model was already in decline worldwide. The collapse in New York was not the first straw, but the last one. A reaction against free market economic policies had already begun in the 2000s. Free market economic policies had failed to fulfill the promise of economic development in Latin America. After two decades of neoliberal reforms, Latin American countries experienced patchy growth and a sharp rise in income inequality, which seemed to be responsible for, not an antidote to, economic underdevelopment. Latin American countries began to turn, one by one, to leftist leaders (of different types) to adopt more growth-oriented economic policies.

The meaning of the 2008 global financial crisis has been the subject of much discussion. Interpretations are inherently controversial, since "what emerges as the dominating narrative of the crisis will have a profound impact" on the balance between state and market in economic policy.[7] Daniel Yergin, founder of a prominent Cambridge energy consultancy, noted 11 possible interpretations in an October 2009 article in the *Financial Times*. The top three explanations are (1) too much leverage in the financial system, (2) rapid innovation in financial instruments that created unforeseen systemic risk, and (3) failure of regulation to cover the "shadow banking" sector.

In fact, these three points are part of a single dominant narrative that has developed about the crisis: it was caused by an excess of financial risk and a dearth of prudential regulation. Financial companies had a growing amount of risky obligations on their books, overborrowed in general, and did not face adequate supervision. When the U.S. mortgage crisis began in 2007, panic soon spread into other financial markets and in 2008 the whole house of cards collapsed, leaving financial companies with trillions of dollars in toxic assets and bankrupting those institutions controlling the commanding heights of the economy. Tighter government regulation of banks and other financial companies could have averted the crisis. The solution to the crisis appears to most people not to be more of the same policies. Rather, leaders around the world will be forced to explore alternative models of economic policy.

Exploring Alternative Models

Based on the above analysis of the spread of free market capitalism worldwide and the devastating effects of the Great Recession of 2008–9, it is possible to generate several hypotheses about the directions of economic development policy in the years ahead.

First, we can expect less emulation of the free market capitalist model in coming years. Global emulation of the free market model was driven by perceived success of the U.S. and UK economies in beating average economic growth rates of other model leading countries. The crisis damaged perceptions of the relative success of the free market model. It is unlikely that countries will continue to emulate policies that are widely believed to have failed. Even countries like the United States and the United Kingdom appear to be moving away from their core policy approach and borrowing from other models, increasing the scope of the welfare state dramatically in the United States with health insurance reform and increasing state intervention and ownership of the economy.

Second, the leading free market capitalist countries have little ability to force their preferred policies on the rest of the world. The disrepute of the free market model is so great that it is difficult to imagine that countries would adopt many free market policies even if they faced significant coercion or incentives. Some of the leading institutions promoting free market capitalist worldwide, such as the International Monetary Fund, have a reduced ability and mandate to induce countries to adopt policies such as bank privatization or elimination of capital controls since requiring a new round of capital increases partly from the developing world.

Third, since countries always face incentives to emulate the policies of seemingly successful model countries, it is likely that in future years countries around the world will look toward the major alternative models: the European social model and authoritarian state capitalism. Because authoritarian state capitalist currently appears to be most successful, as China has pulled out of the crisis more quickly than other model leading countries, we should expect in particular a new era of influence for authoritarian state capitalism.

Fourth, the influence of both authoritarian state capitalism and the European social model will be incremental. Countries will not rush headlong toward the full adoption of these models, but starting from a particular baseline, will gradually, over time, choose to implement policies modeled on those of successful model leading countries. The result will be a gradual, but potentially long-term and significant trend toward both of the major alternatives to free market capitalism. This prediction is also underpinned by public opinion surveys, which show that most respondents in most countries wish to reform, but not to replace, the free market capitalist system.

Fifth, neither alternative model may be as dominant as free market liberalism was in its heyday. This is because both the European social model and the authoritarian state capitalist models have limits to their acceptability in some countries. The European social model may be increasingly relevant to wealthy and middle-income countries, while the authoritarian state capitalist model will have its greatest effect in poor and low-middle income countries that are already nondemocratic, hybrid, or poorly performing democratic regimes (see Larry Diamond's chapter in this volume for further evidence on this point).

The Pull of the European Social Model

Significant anecdotal evidence supports the view that wealthy and upper-middle-income countries already are emulating the European social model, in an incremental fashion, as a means of restraining the excesses of capitalism. U.S. economic policy after the crisis clearly has moved incrementally in the direction of social market capitalism, with significantly increased state control over leading enterprises, from AIG and Citibank to Bank of America to Chrysler and General Motors, where the government currently owns a 60 percent stake. Trade union ownership and involvement in corporate governance is also on the rise with the handover of 55 percent of Chrysler and 17.5 percent of GM shares to the United Auto Workers. Government regulation of the financial and other sectors has increased and will continue to do so, as has public employment as a percentage of overall employment. The government has sought to restrain income inequality by restricting executive pay. At the same time, it has sought to increase social guarantees by extending health insurance to all Americans. Some of these measures may be temporary, but together they mark a substantial shift toward the European social market model, with its emphasis on government ownership of leading enterprises and social equity.

Government spending and intervention also increased dramatically in Europe in the immediate aftermath of the crisis, as states bailed out failing banks and enterprises and the "automatic stabilizers" of the European social model came into effect: unemployment benefit spending and social supports of all kinds. Yet, this strong initial response caused a swift reaction from those advocating a new phase of austerity. European leaders imposed a severe austerity program on Greece after its 2010 debt crisis and the Tories under David Cameron have imposed deep cuts in government in the United Kingdom as well. The outcome of these countervailing trends is unclear. The result is most likely to be a continued commitment to social welfare, but within the bounds of fiscal sustainability. This compromise is evident, too, in Central and East European states that initially moved rapidly in the direction of free market capitalism. After gaining European Union membership, many have maintained the European social model's emphasis on welfare state spending and have acted to protect industries, regions, sectors, and groups affected by globalization and European Union accession. The extension of the European Union's Common Agricultural Policy (CAP) to Central and Eastern Europe played an important role in this, subsidizing agricultural incomes in Poland and Romania, where more than 20 percent of the population still works in agriculture. In many former communist countries, it has proven difficult to slash social spending. Most new member states have failed to fully transform themselves into free market capitalist countries, with the exception of Estonia. The European social model remains locked in a continuous process of transformation, attempting to balance goals of social protection and fiscal sustainability. European leaders want to maneuver between the Scylla of Greece, where social spending spiraled out of fiscal control, and the Charybdis of the United States, where homelessness, hunger, obesity, violence, and other social ills are tolerated as a matter of course. Europe's struggle will be mirrored by other developed and some middle-income developing countries where democratic pressures cause governments to rethink adherence to free market norms.

The Rise of Authoritarian State Capitalism

In developing countries, authoritarian state capitalism is making a comeback. These countries typically do not have access to the resources and governance capacity required by the European social model, and authoritarian state capitalism offers a more secure route to economic growth.

In large part, the appeal of authoritarian state capitalism is tied to the Chinese model and its status as one of the fastest growing economies in the world and one of the first to come out of the recent recession. China, in particular, has come out of the crisis relatively unscathed with its state-owned banks having taken a more conservative approach to risk than their Western counterparts. The same is true of Singapore, Hong Kong, and several other leading state capitalist economies. In real terms, China began to grow earlier, shaking off the recession more quickly than the liberal countries. As Chinese Chief Economist of the World Bank Justin Yifu Lin pointed out at the conference upon which this book is based, China has grown for 20 years—without a major economic crisis of the type the advanced Western countries are suffering. This achievement will count for much in the years ahead. The authoritarian state capitalist model also gains from the fact that the crisis of 2008–9 was not of its making and that significant state intervention in the economy appears to have dampened the effects of the crisis.

At the same time, the appeal of the authoritarian state capitalist model will primarily be felt in the developing world. This model will not be a relevant or important model in developed countries with well-established democracies. Instead, its relevance will be restricted primarily to poorer developing countries with weak, unconsolidated democracies. For democratic states, the model of an oppressive state mobilizing resources for economic development will remain unappealing. The end result of the crisis of free market liberalism may be greater differentiation in economic policy regimes between adherents of the different models, particularly over the issue of governance.

Conclusion

Emulation is a powerful force in economic development. Country leaders are often uncertain about how to pursue economic growth and development. Development paradigms change and countries have different experiences with similar policies. In conditions of uncertainty, policymakers tend to choose economic policies that appear to work in neighboring or model countries.

The financial crisis of 2008–9 marked the end of the intellectual dominance of the free market capitalist model worldwide. Signs of its waning were apparent before the crisis. Latin American countries that had been among the most vigorous adopters of free market policies soured on them in the early 2000s and began to pursue more social market oriented or authoritarian statist policies in countries from Chile to Venezuela. However, the severity of the current crisis, its obvious and embarrassing roots in the failure of regulation of the free market system, its destruction of some of the key institutions of free market capitalism, and the shocking scandals that went along with it, have drawn attention to the weaknesses of the free market model.

Economic policymakers in free market capitalist countries must find ways to address the legitimacy crisis that has shaken the free market model. This will be a difficult, but vital, project for those concerned with the future of liberalism. It will mean admitting the weaknesses of previous embodiment of the free market model. It will mean addressing the reasons why people believe that the free market model has failed, such as inequality, poor public infrastructure, weakening human capital development, environmental degradation, and fraying social bonds (Manzi 2010). It will mean finding solutions to these issues, without threatening the ability of the free market countries to generate growth.

Until the free market capitalist model receives an overhaul in ideology, perceptions, and practice, we can expect economic policy in developing and developed countries to be shaped by a process of lesson-drawing from the crisis and the rise of alternative models. To some extent, this will mean a strengthening of state regulation and welfare state institutions, consonant with the social market model in Europe. Meanwhile, developing countries will be drawn to authoritarian statism as a way of constraining the excesses of markets in countries without the state capacity to implement a European style of economic development. Political, as well as economic, freedom will continue to be threatened in countries around the world, particularly in those not structurally connected to Western alliances. None of this is particularly good news, but it will take many years for supporters of the free market model to rebuild confidence in this system, create new successes, and articulate them to the world.

Notes

1. The exceptions are Hong Kong, Singapore, and Kuwait, which I categorize as authoritarian state capitalist countries not only because they lack democratic rule but also because of the state's large ownership and regulatory role in the economy. Hong Kong had a strong democracy movement prior to its transfer to Chinese authority in 1997 and probably would have democratized under independent rule.
2. Estonia, ranked 11 in the Fraser Institute ranking, is one prominent case of radical liberalization.
3. This list was calculated from the Gwartney and Lawson (2008) data and includes those countries whose increase in liberalization scores between 1980 and 2005 were more than one standard deviation above the mean of all countries included in the study.
4. According to the Fraser Institute, liberalization increased in the United States under Presidents Reagan through Clinton and decreased under the second President Bush.
5. See Kirchfield 2008.
6. Thomson Reuters. Datastream. Figures from July 8, 2009. Available at www.the banker.com/cp/57/T1000_Top25.gif.
7. Yergin 2009.

References

Aslund, Anders. 2007. *Russia's Capitalist Revolution: Why Market Reform Succeeded and Democracy Failed.* Washington, DC: Peterson Institute for International Economics.

Campbell, John, and Ove Pedersen, eds. 2001. *The Rise of Neoliberalism and Institutional Analysis.* Princeton: Princeton University Press.

Esping-Andersen, Gosta. 1990. *Three Worlds of Welfare Capitalism.* Oxford: Polity Press.

Fukuyama, Francis. 1992. *The End of History and the Last Man.* New York: Free Press.

Garrett, Geoffrey, and Peter Lange. 1996. Internationalization, Institutions, and Political Change, in *Internationalization and Domestic Politics,* edited by Robert O. Keohane and Helen V. Milner. Cambridge: Cambridge University Press.

Giddens, Anthony. 2005. "The World Does Not Owe Us a Living! The Future of the European Social Model." Policy Network ESM Project.

Gwartney, James, and Robert Lawson. 2008. "Economic Freedom of the World: 2008 Annual Report." Fraser Institute/Economic Freedom Network.

Hall, Peter, and David Soskice, eds. 2001. *Varieties of Capitalism: The Institutional Foundations of Comparative Advantage.* Oxford: Oxford University Press.

Katzenstein, Peter, ed. 1978. *Between Power and Plenty: Foreign Policies of Advanced Industrialized States.* Madison: University of Wisconsin Press.

Kirchfeld, Aaron. 2008, February 4. "ICBC Deposes Citigroup as Chinese Banks Rule in New World Order," available at Bloomberg.com.

La Porta, Rafael, Florencio Lopez-de-Silanes, and Andrei Shleifer. 1999. Corporate Ownership Around the World. *Journal of Finance* 54(2): 471–517.

Lijphart, Arend. 1999. *Patterns of Democracy.* New Haven: Yale University Press.

Manzi, Jim. 2010. Keeping America's Edge. *National Affairs* 2 (Winter).

Pierson, Paul. 1994. *Dismantling the Welfare State? Reagan, Thatcher, and the Politics of Retrenchment.* Cambridge: Cambridge University Press.

Pontusson, Jonas. 2005. *Inequality and Prosperity: Social Europe versus Liberal America.* Ithaca, NY: Cornell University Press.

Przeworski, Adam, Michael E. Alvarez, Jose Antonio Cheibub, and Fernando Limongi. 2000. *Democracy and Development: Political Institutions and Well-Being in the World, 1950–1990.* Cambridge, UK: Cambridge University Press.

Rodrik, Dani. 1998. "Democracies Pay Higher Wages." NBER Working Paper 6364 (January). Cambridge, MA: National Bureau of Economic Research.

Schmidt, Vivien A. 2002. "Still Three Models of Capitalism? The Impact of Changing Policies and Growing Pressures on Economic Practices" In *The Futures of European Capitalism,* edited by Vivien A. Schmidt. Oxford: Oxford University Press.

Shonfield, Andrew. 1965. *Modern Capitalism: The Changing Balance of Public and Private Power.* Oxford: Oxford University Press.

Simmons, Beth, Frank Dobbin, and Geoffrey Garrett, eds. 2008. *The Global Diffusion of Markets and Democracy.* Cambridge, UK: Cambridge University Press. Weyland, Kurt. 2005. Theories of Policy Diffusion: Lessons from Latin American Pension Reform. *World Politics* 57, 262–295.

Yergin, Daniel. 2009. "A Crisis in Search of a Narrative," *Financial Times,* October 20, 2009.

Yergin, Daniel, and Joseph Stanislaw. 2002. *Commanding Heights: The Battle for the World Economy.* New York: The Free Press.

CHAPTER 2

Lessons from the Great Recession

Justin Yifu Lin

THE GLOBAL CRISIS, which erupted in developed countries and spread across the world in 2008 (the so-called Great Recession), has profoundly affected the economic outlook and economic thinking. Indeed, it has extended its impact to every corner of the globe. In advanced economies, the financial crisis and the global recession that followed have brought severe consequences in terms of employment and output. In developing countries, output contraction, growth slowdown, and rising unemployment came hand in hand with higher borrowing costs, sluggish export growth, and a reduction in international capital flows.

The efforts of governments and international financial institutions to buffer the impact of the crisis have been quick and aimed in the right direction. Bank recapitalization and countercyclical fiscal policy, accompanied by accommodative monetary policy, helped reduce the stress on the battered financial sectors and boost aggregate demand. As a result, recent trends are encouraging, showing indications that a slow recovery is taking place. The recovery has begun to take shape in several Asian countries (particularly in China). Most of these countries had little direct exposure to the financial roots of the crisis. They had the fiscal space necessary to apply strong policy stimulus programs. In advanced countries, growth remains modest with an important share still being attributed to the fiscal stimulus component. As households, financial and nonfinancial institutions, and governments make progress cleaning their balance sheets, it is expected that economic activity will pick up.

Trends in both the financial markets and the real global economy are indicating that the most critical phase of the crisis is over. Credit card and other interest rates have been returning to normal levels. Emerging and high-income countries' stock markets have gained ground generally since the spring of 2009. Trade and manufacturing production are on the rise. Interest rate premia in sovereign debt markets for developing countries have also fallen from a peak of more than 800 basis points in October 2008 to 350 basis points in September 2009.[1]

But it may be too soon to declare victory. Recovery is expected to remain weak, with significant excess capacity and high unemployment levels both in advanced economies and the developing world. The global financial crisis has left lasting effects on the structure of financial markets, international capital flows, and the cost of capital for developing countries. Many financial institutions have yet to clean their balance sheets.

Moreover, the implementation of exit strategies from the stimulus policies adopted to combat the crisis will be a major challenge: exiting too quickly may send the global economy on the path to a double-dip recession; exiting too late may carry the risk of high inflation, which would be damaging for macroeconomic stability, competitiveness, and poverty reduction strategies in developing countries. In light of growth rate projections, the World Bank is still estimating that the crisis added 50 million people to the count of the number of poor (living on under $1.25 a day) in 2009. It is now expected that a total of 64 million people will fall into poverty by 2010 (Chen and Ravallion 2009). These are people who live not just in the poorest countries in the world, but also in middle-income countries—now home to 70 percent of the world's poor.

Lessons from economic theory and history suggest that the poor and the underprivileged are the ones that suffer the most the effects of economic crises. Whereas the recession in most high-income countries is often temporary (as the unemployment rate will eventually fall as the economy recovers), in many developing economies, especially in Africa, consequences may be permanent. Child malnutrition can have consequences in future development and can even lead to death. Friedman and Schady (2009) estimated that 30,000 to 40,000 children may have died of malnutrition in 2009 in sub-Saharan Africa alone because of the crisis. In an increasingly globalized world—where fighting poverty is more than a moral responsibility but is also a strategy for confronting some of the major problems (diseases, migrations, violence) that ignore boundaries and contribute to global insecurity—thinking about new ways of generating and sustaining growth is a crucial task for economists. In this regard, the Great Recession provides a unique opportunity for researchers to rethink development strategies and to reflect on how to achieve sustained and inclusive growth, to reduce poverty, to increase resilience in a globalized economy, and to protect the poor from external shocks.

The remainder of this chapter is organized as follows: First, I provide a brief explanation of how the current global financial crisis originated and the underlying factors that turned a relatively small collapse in the U.S. subprime mortgage market into a global crisis. I also discuss the transmission mechanisms involved, which can help design the optimal response to the current situation and also prevent future crises or minimize their impact. Next, I offer a brief history of development thinking, its insights, gaps, and shortcomings. Then I discuss a development strategy based on comparative advantage, which can protect poor countries from homegrown crises, help them become more resilient to external shocks, and achieve sustainable and inclusive growth.

Understanding the Global Economic Crisis

One of the salient features of the recent financial crisis is the fact that it originated in advanced economies. Though some knew that the risks of a severe financial crisis were mounting, the necessary changes in policies and practices, both in mature economies' financial sectors as well as many new emerging markets (e.g., Eastern Europe) were stymied by procrastination during the 2003–7 boom. Few were willing to or capable of taking the punch bowl from the party[2] and the global institutional set-up did not have leverage to do so.

A combination of weak prudential and regulatory oversight, which began in the 1980s, and loose monetary policies, which dated from the dot-com burst in 2001, led to excessive leverage and risk-taking behavior by both businesses and households. To minimize the impact of the collapse of the Internet bubble, the U.S. Federal Reserve engaged in aggressive monetary policy, which showed in the drop of the Fed funds rate from 6.5 percent in January 2001 to 1 percent in June 2003. The excess liquidity in money markets—due to low interest rates and financial innovations that at the time were believed to be effective risk-reducing tools—soon translated into a boom in the housing market. Real estate and equity investment increased rapidly, and the housing boom turned into a bubble, with housing prices well beyond what they should based on economic fundamentals. Consumption expenditures rose, fueled by the wealth effects derived from these price increases in equity and real estate, and growth in the United States was strong.

At the same time, the rest of the world also experienced rapid growth during 2003–7, due to increasing capital flows searching for higher returns, and to the boom in oil and other commodity prices, combined with increased export demand from developed countries. As capital flows to developing countries soared in search of higher rate of returns, these funds were used to finance investment and build up capacity. Investment growth rose from 1.7 percent per year in the 1980s and 3.7 percent in the 1990s to 10.6 percent in 2003–7 in developing countries.[3] The investment boom in developing countries, in turn, further fueled the ongoing growth in developed economies.

However, lax prudential and regulatory oversight on the financial system was not free of consequences, as default started to mount in the markets for subprime mortgages in 2007. Losses associated with mortgage-backed securities left financial institutions on the verge of insolvency. With the fall of Lehman Brothers in September 2008, the subprime crisis developed into a full-fledged banking crisis and ultimately turned into a global financial crisis.

The main role of financial institutions is to channel funds from households and businesses to its most productive uses. When these institutions confront difficulties, this main role cannot be fulfilled, which has adverse consequences for the real sector. In the midst of the 2008 financial crisis, losses related to the subprime mortgage market and other risky investments led to a credit crunch. Financial intermediaries, worried about their capital base or facing difficulties raising fresh funds, cut back in commercial and consumption lending and tightened their lending standards. These decisions drastically reduced the credit available for consumption and investment in the real sector. As a consequence, both businesses and consumers had to cut back on spending, in some cases affecting working capital of firms, while leading overall to a fall in aggregate demand, mounting nonperforming loans, further credit tightening, and aggregate demand reductions.

The credit channel was only one of several mechanisms through which the financial crisis had effects on the real sector. Wealth effects derived from drops in housing and equity prices badly hit the pocketbooks of households, which responded with further cuts on expenditures. Finally, overall uncertainty about the magnitude and the duration of the crisis undermined consumer confidence and businesses investment decisions, on the one hand, and led to banks to hoard liquidity and reduce lending, on the other.

Eventually, crisis that originated in the U.S. subprime mortgage market spilled over across borders. The quickness of the contagion was facilitated by the fact that the credit boom in the years prior to the crisis was not limited to the United States but prevalent in other advanced and developing countries as well. Many of the preexisting conditions observed in the

United States were the same worldwide; credit risk and spreads were low and asset and housing prices in other advanced countries were too high. Many non-U.S. financial institutions also invested heavily in subprime backed securities and other complex derivatives. Because of the international linkages of financial systems, other advanced countries were not able to escape the financial turmoil when the housing bubble in the U.S. burst. Moreover, uncertainty over the exposure of other financial intermediaries further exacerbated the credit crunch in other advanced countries, with many banks and corporations hoarding excess liquidity.

Four main transmission mechanisms led to a contraction in the real economic activity of developing countries:

1. *International trade:* The international trade channel seems to have been a critical transmission mechanism. According to recent estimates by the World Bank, trade volumes had declined 18 percent in June 2009 from levels reported at the beginning of 2008.[4] The reduction in trade was due to three factors: a rundown of inventory in anticipation of a drop in consumption as a result of the bubble bursting in the United States and other advanced economies; the drop in household wealth, combined with increasing uncertainty about the future (job security), led to the postponing of purchase decisions on consumer durables; and the decline in investment as a result of excess capacity, due to the investment boom that preceded the crisis and the overall fall in aggregate demand after the crisis also contributed to the drop in trade flows.

2. *Financial integration:* Increased risk aversion and mounting uncertainty led financial institutions to pull out credit from risky assets in emerging economies, even though macroeconomic conditions in many of these economies did not show any signs of instability and their financial systems were relatively healthy. Moreover, bigger liquidity needs of many of these financial institutions due to the credit crunch in advanced economies also contributed to the reduction of capital flows (and hence the availability of private financial flows) and an increase in the cost of capital.

3. *Remittances and tourism:* Developing countries were also affected by the drop in remittances from relatives living in the United States and other countries affected firsthand by the crisis, which represent in some cases an important source of income for households. African countries were particularly hit by the decline in remittances, which were estimated to have fallen by about 8 percent in 2009, compared with an annual increase by about 13 percent over the past few years. Another important transmission channel is the fall in tourism revenues. Tourist arrivals in Gambia for instance fell by an astonishing 32 percent in one year. Tanzania, Mauritius, Kenya, and Senegal also experienced significant drops in tourist arrivals.

4. *Commodity prices:* The drop in consumption and investment globally was accompanied by drop in prices of commodities, hurting the resources exporting countries' revenues. The drop in commodity prices, especially oil, has particularly affected African countries, such as Angola, Gabon, Nigeria, and Sudan.

The longer-term implications of the global financial crisis for developing countries are more difficult to discern. What is more certain is the long-term growth challenges facing developing countries and the rethinking of economic growth strategies that will be required. This is because poverty reduction is still the most challenging development issue in our time. There were 1.4 billion people living on under $1.25 a day international poverty line before the crisis. Sixty-four million more people may be trapped in poverty because of the crisis. A sustainable and inclusive growth is essential for poverty reduction.

It is therefore essential to revisit the frameworks that have dominated development thinking.

A Brief History of Development Thinking

From Adam Smith in the late eighteenth century to Milton Friedman in the mid-twentieth century, most economists believed that laissez-faire was the best vehicle for achieving sustainable growth. It was assumed that in striving economies, all decisions about resource allocation are made by economic agents interacting in markets free of government intervention. The price system determines not only what is produced and how but also for whom. Households and firms pursuing their own interests would be led, as Smith famously said "by an invisible hand" to do things that are in the interests of others and of society as a whole. This approach to economic development assumed that productivity increases in the agriculture and manufacturing sectors are due mainly to incremental refinement of old, traditional technologies for the purposes of exploiting widened markets and specialization. It basically ignored the possibility of successive introduction of big innovations that could create new industries or radically alter methods of production.

While this view was challenged by Marxist economists, it was the dominant intellectual framework for the study of growth in all countries for a long time. It took Rosenstein-Rodan's well-known paper to bring development economics to the agenda of the discipline of economics (1943). In this paper, Rosenstein-Rodan suggested that the virtuous circle of development depended essentially on the interaction between economies of scale at the level of individual firms and the size of the market. Specifically, he assumed that modern methods of production can be made more productive than traditional ones only if the market is large enough for their productivity edge to compensate for the necessity of paying higher wages. However, the size of the market itself depends on the extent to which these modern techniques are adopted. Therefore, if the modernization process can be started on a very large scale, then the process of economic development will be self-reinforcing and self-sustaining. If not, countries will be indefinitely trapped into poverty.

Rosenstein-Rodan's framework sparked a wave of similar ideas from Arthur Lewis, Gunnar Myrdal, Albert Hirschman, and others, which came to be known as the structuralist approach to economic development. In Latin America, for instance, political leaders and social elites were influenced strongly by the steady deterioration in the terms of trade, the economic difficulty encountered during the Great Depression in the 1930s, and the thesis developed by Raul Prebisch (1950). Rosenstein-Rodan and his followers believed that the decline in the terms of trade against the export of primary commodities was a long-standing trend, which resulted in the transfer of income from resource-intensive developing countries to capital-intensive developed countries. They argued that the way for a developing country to achieve high growth rates was to develop domestic manufacturing industries through a process known as import substitution.

Yet, the results were disappointing. Instead of converging to the developed countries' income levels, the income levels in developing countries stagnated or even deteriorated and the income gap with developed countries widened. This was the case across Latin American, African, and South Asian countries in the 1960s and 1970s, when import substitution policies that were intended to promote industrialization by protecting domestic producers from the competition of imports became the source of high tariffs, quotas, or restrictions on foreign trade and of distortions, rent seeking, and economic inefficiencies.

As government-led economic development strategies based on structuralist teachings failed in many countries, the market-led growth model appeared to triumph and to influence development thinking. This trend was reinforced by a new revolution in macroeconomics. The prevailing Keynesian macroeconomics was challenged by the emergence of stagflation in the 1970s, the Latin America debt crisis, and the collapse of socialist planning system in the 1980s. Multilateral lending institutions and bilateral lenders—especially the United States—soon called for a comprehensive set of reforms of Latin American economies and advocated a set of policies, which follow the canons of rational expectation macroeconomics, later expounded on by John Williamson and known as the Washington consensus.

Finally, the collapse of socialist economies in the 1980s, which prompted Francis Fukuyama (1992) to proclaim "the end of history," seemed to mark the complete victory of free market economics over proponents of structuralist state interventions and centrally planned economic systems. Most mainstream economists explained at the time that government intervention in the economy was bound to fail because of the inevitable distortion of the allocation of resources, supply, and prices and the absence of a viable incentive system for economic agents. They interpreted the economic collapse in Eastern and Central Europe and the former Soviet Union and the stagnation and frequent crises in Latin America and other developing countries as evidence that the state should refrain from playing a leading role in initiating industrialization. These views fueled the sense of triumph of capitalism and centered development thinking on the neoliberal, Washington consensus policies. They promoted economic liberalization, privatization, and the implementation of rigorous stabilization programs. Unfortunately, the results of these policies were at best controversial.

The story of economic development in the past half-century has often been one of disappointments. But there are also a few success stories. The contrast in economic strategies and performance among developing countries has been intriguing to economists. On the one hand, many countries that followed dominant economic theories of the time in formulating their policies often failed to change their economic structures and narrow the gap with industrialized countries. On the other hand, some other countries such as Japan and the four dragons (Korea, Singapore, Taiwan, Hong Kong), started from a low agrarian foundation and were able to quickly climb the industrial ladders and to achieve convergence to the structure and income level of advanced industrialized countries by the 1980s. Likewise, China, Vietnam, and Mauritius achieved rapid and sustained growth by following a gradual transition approach to a market economy in the 1990s, instead of the "shock therapy" prescribed by the Washington consensus. In fact, it appears that, for economies that were centrally planned, the resilience to the 2008–9 crisis has been inversely correlated to the speed of transition.[5]

In all the successful cases, the market was the fundamental mechanism for resource allocation as predicted by rational expectation macroeconomic theory and the Washington consensus. However, the state also played an active role in the development and transition process as the Keynesian theories and structuralism envisioned. Still, economists do not seem to have derived the same lessons from these experiences. It is therefore useful to take a closer look at the fundamental reasons of success in economic development.

The Structural Dynamics of Economic Development

What policies and factors make it possible for some countries to be successful in processes that generate sustained and inclusive growth, while others languish? To answer this question, which is at the heart of development economics, it is useful to start from the observation that, throughout history modern economies have moved successively from subsistence agriculture to light industry, then to heavy industry, high-tech industry, and eventually to the postindustrialization phase. This evolution provides the basis for an understanding of economic development as (1) a process of continuous technical innovation leading to improved quality of the same goods or lower production costs for the same goods and (2) a dynamic process of industrial upgrading and structural change with new and different goods and services produced continuously.

The modern economic literature has devoted a lot of attention to the analysis of technological innovation but not enough to the equally important issue of industrial upgrading and its corollary, which is structural change. While no economist believes that all rich countries are alike and all poor countries are alike, growth models feature only minimal differences between countries. Some of them have only one sector and completely overlook the industrial differences between developed and developing countries. Even the well-known Kuznets three-sector model of savings, consumption, and investment assumes that all countries produce the same goods, with only differences in their relative weight. Clearly it is a modeling choice to introduce a suitable level of abstraction. Nevertheless, it can have misleading implications for growth analysis.

One consequence of such modeling choices is the neglect paid by economic analysis to structures, which should be the starting point for the inquiry of economic development. It is crucial to consider the fact that countries at different stages of development tend to have different economic structures due to differences in their endowments. When the endowment structure is upgraded, the country's industrial structure must also be upgraded. And, these changes in industrial structure necessitate changes in the social and economic structure so as to reduce transaction costs (such as transportation or financial costs) for production and exchanges. Industrial structure in an economy is endogenous to its endowment structure. For the developing countries to upgrade their industrial structure, they must first upgrade their endowment structures (Ju, Lin, and Wang 2009) from labor intensive to capital intensive. Developing countries can upgrade their endowment structure by increasing their relative share of capital. The best way to do this is to develop industries and adopt technology that is consistent with their comparative advantage as it stands, given their level of economic development. This is because when firms choose their industries and technologies according to the comparative advantages determined by the country's factor endowments, the economy is most competitive.[6] As competitive industries and firms grow, they claim a larger market share and create the greatest possible economic surplus, in the form of profits and salaries. Furthermore, reinvested surpluses earn the highest return possible, because the industrial structure is optimally organized given the endowment structure. Over time, this strategy allows the economy to accumulate physical and human capital and enables upgrading the factor endowment structure in the fastest way. As capital becomes more abundant and hence relatively cheaper, their production shifts to more capital-intensive goods and labor-intensive goods are gradually displaced. This process generates an endless V-shaped industrial dynamics—the so-called flying geese pattern of economic development.[7]

In order for a country to exploit its comparative advantage in the process of economic development, it must have an open economy and participate in the global economy. The adverse impact of global crisis on developing countries has caused some concerns about globalization. However, China, India, and certain other emerging economies that have coped well with the crisis all had strong external balance sheets and ample room for fiscal maneuvering, which allowed them to apply countercyclical policies to combat external shocks. They have also nurtured industries in line with their comparative advantage, which has helped them weather the storm. China, for example (which has been able to meet its 8 percent growth target in 2009 in the middle of the global recession), became an economic power-house only after turning from an inward-oriented to an outward-oriented economy in the 1980s. Indeed, all 13 economies with an average annual growth rate of 7 percent or more for 25 years or longer and identified in the Growth Commission Report led by Nobel laureate Michael Spence adopted an open economic system to fully exploit the potential of globalization. Their experience confirms that comparative advantage—determined by the relative abundance of labor, natural resources, and capital endowments—is the foundation for competitiveness, which in turn underpins dynamic growth and strong fiscal and external positions.

By contrast, if a country attempts to defy its comparative advantage and adopts an import-substitution strategy to pursue the development of capital-intensive or high-tech industries in a capital-scarce economy, the government will have to resort to distortive subsidies and protections. Such measures will be eventually detrimental to the country's economic performance. They will weaken both the government's fiscal position and the economy's external account. Without the ability to implement timely countercyclical measures, such countries fare poorly when confronted with crises. There again, for any given country, following its comparative advantage is the best long-term development strategy, as it also ensures that the economy is more resilience to external shocks.

When a country follows its comparative advantage in choosing new industries, it accumulates capital in the process of economic development. Its endowment structure is then upgraded, and the country climbs up the industrial and technological ladder. Many other changes must take place as well. First, the type of technology needed by firms becomes more sophisticated and riskier, as they move closer to the global frontier. Second, capital requirements become more important, just like the scale of production and the size of markets. Third, market exchanges among domestic and foreign agents increasingly become more complex and often require taking into account time and distance.

A flexible and smooth process of industrial and technological upgrading also requires simultaneous improvements in education, financial, and legal institutions, as well as other infrastructures. Yet, individual firms cannot internalize all these changes cost-effectively, and coordination among many firms to achieve these changes will often be impossible. At that point, the only entity that can coordinate the desirable investment or change is the state, which has to play a facilitating role in dealing with market externalities.

The important question at that stage is to delineate the respective responsibilities of the market and the state in sustaining the dynamics of structural change. The market's role is clear and often easily understood: firms aim to make profits, which are determined by the prices of inputs and outputs used in their production. But for firms to enter the right industries and choose the appropriate technology according to the comparative advantage consistent with the country's endowment structure, the economy must exhibit prices that reflect the relative scarcity of factors. This only happens in an economy with competitive markets.[8] Therefore, a competitive market should be the economy's fundamental mechanism for resource allocations.

The state's role seems less clear and remains subject to controversy. Yet, it becomes more apparent when one focuses on the need to sustain the dynamics of infrastructure development. With the upgrade in factor endowment and industrial structure, infrastructures and other social and economic institutions need corresponding improvement in order for the economy to achieve cost-efficiency. Firms that were once viable[9]—under the previous endowment structure—become nonviable. To become viable again, firms need to upgrade to industries with higher capital intensities. And, as mentioned above, this upgrading process is an innovative and unavoidably risky venture. Successful upgrading requires that firms overcome issues of limited information regarding which industries are viable. It also requires coordinated investments—including by other firms. In addition, issues of information externalities may arise from the success or failure of pioneering firms because many are reluctant to be the first mover.

Development thinking has not focused on such issues. Despite their insights on issues of market failures, old structuralist economists treated industrial structure as exogenous and recommended that the state in developing countries change its industrial structure through direct intervention and other administrative measures. Attempting to change the industrial structure in this way caused all kinds of distortions. The neoclassical critics of structural economists rightly highlighted the importance of government failures. However, by treating the distortions introduced previously under the structuralist policies to protect nonviable firms in designated priority sectors as exogenous, their critics recommended an approach to eliminate those distortions without sufficient consideration of the endogeneity of those distortions. They also ignored the structural differences between the developed and developing countries and missed the specific responsibilities of a facilitating state in the process of industrial upgrading and structural changes.

It is now time to revisit both frameworks and to extract the good insights each can provide to further our quest for sustainable and inclusive growth. The analysis of growth dynamics should begin with an economy's endowments and the way they evolve over time. Following the tradition of classical economics, economists tend to think of a country's endowments as consisting only of its land (or natural resources), labor, and capital (both physical and human). These are simply *factor* endowments, which firms can use for production. Conceptually, it is useful to add infrastructure as one more component in an economy's endowments.[10] Infrastructure can be hard (tangible) or soft (intangible). Examples of hard infrastructure are highways, port facilities, airports, telecommunication systems, electricity grids and other public utilities. Soft infrastructure consists of institutions, regulations, social capital, value systems, and other social and economic arrangements. Both of these types of infrastructures are critical to the viability of domestic firms: they affect individual firm's transaction costs and the marginal rate of return on investments. Most hard infrastructures and almost all soft infrastructures are exogenously provided to individual firms and cannot be internalized in their production decision.

Both hard and soft infrastructures are needed in high-income countries and are likely to be quite different from those optimal in low-income countries. For countries at the early stages of development, factor endowments are typically characterized by a relative scarcity in capital and a relative abundance in labor or resources. Their industries that will have comparative advantage in open, competitive markets tend to be labor-intensive or resource-intensive (mostly in agriculture and the mining sector) and usually rely on conventional, mature technologies, and produce "mature," well-established products. Except for mining and plantations, production in the earlier stages of development tends to have limited scope for economies of scale. Their firm sizes are usually relatively small, with market transactions often limited to personalized local markets. The types of hard and soft infrastructure required for facilitating this type of production and market transactions are limited, relatively simple, and rudimentary.

At the other extreme of the development spectrum, high-income countries display a completely different endowment structure. Their relatively abundant factor is typically capital, not natural resource or labor. Therefore, these countries tend to have comparative advantage in capital-intensive industries with large-scale production. Because they are situated on the global technology frontier, their economies rely on the invention of new technologies and products for sustained growth. Their firms must engage in risky R&D activities. In that context, the appropriate financial arrangements are big banks and sophisticated equity markets that can mobilize large amount of capital and are capable of diversifying risks. The types of hard infrastructure such as roads and port facilities and soft infrastructures such as regulatory and legal frameworks must comply with the necessities of national and global markets where business transactions are long distance, large in quantity and value, and based on rigorously designed and implemented contracts.

By moving up the industrial ladder in the process of economic development, developing countries increase their scale of production. Larger firms proliferate and the need for a bigger market becomes evident. In such situations, infrastructures are often the bottlenecks to economic development. The growth process tends to render existing institutional arrangements obsolete, as it induces shifts in the demand for institutional services, which have the nature of public good. Changes in institutions require collective action and often fail because of free-riders' problems.[11] For this reason, governments need to play a proactive role in facilitating timely improvements of hard and soft infrastructures and the changing needs arising from industrial upgrading.

In developed countries where industries are already on the global frontier, there is always uncertainty on what the next frontier will be. Therefore government's policies to sustain industrial upgrading, or "vertical innovation,"[12] are typically in the forms of support to research in universities, which has externalities to R&D in private firms, patents, preferential taxes for capital investments, defense contracts, and access to procurement opportunities.[13] In developing countries, their industrial upgrading moves within the global frontier. At each stage of their development, firms in developing countries can acquire the technologies and enter into those industries appropriate for their endowment structure, rather than having to reinvent the wheel by themselves. When the capital accumulation necessitates the upgrading of their industrial structure, the state could potentially play a proactive role to facilitate the process by providing information about the likely new industries of comparative advantage; coordinating investments in related industries and providing the required improvements in soft and hard infrastructure; subsidizing activities with externalities; and catalyzing the development of new industries by incubation or attracting foreign direct investment.[14]

To sum up, the proposed new structural economics approach is organized around the three main ideas:

1. *The economy's structure of factor endowments (defined as the relative abundance of natural resources, labor, and human and physical capital) is given at each stage of development and differs from one stage to another.* Therefore, the optimal industrial structure of the economy will be different at various stages of development. Industrial structures can have differences in capital intensity of industries, optimal firm size, scale of production, market range, transaction complexity, and nature of risks. As a result, each industrial structure requires corresponding soft and hard infrastructures to facilitate its operations and transactions.

2. *Each stage of economic development is a point in a wide spectrum from a low-income, subsistence agrarian economy to a high-income industrialized economy, not a dichotomy of two economic development stages ("poor" versus "rich" or "developing countries" versus "industrialized countries").* Due to the endogeneity of industrial structure at each stage of development, the targets of industrial upgrading and infrastructure improvement in a developing country should not necessarily refer to the industries and infrastructures that are in place in high-income countries.

3. *At each given stage of development, the market is the fundamental mechanism for effective resource allocation.* In addition, economic development as the dynamic process of moving from one stage to the next requires industrial upgrading and corresponding improvements in hard and soft infrastructures. Industrial upgrading is an innovation process. Pioneering firms in the upgrading process generate non-rival, non-excludable public knowledge to other firms in the economy, that is, consumption of the new knowledge by one firm does not reduce availability of that knowledge for others and no one can be effectively excluded from using it. In most cases, improvements in infrastructures cannot be internalized in an individual firm's investment decision. Yet, these improvements have large externalities to other firms'

transaction costs. Thus, in addition to an effective market mechanism, the government should play an active, facilitating role in the industrial upgrading process and in the improvement of infrastructures.

Conclusion

We now have a reasonable understanding of the origins of the global financial crisis: excessively lax macroeconomic policies, in a context of weak prudential and regulatory oversight, led to excessive leverage, mispricing of risk, and the build-up of global systemic risk. The Great Recession has exposed a number of previously known, documented, but unresolved fragilities within the increasingly integrated financial system. It has also offered the opportunity to identify new areas of research on how to help developed and developing countries cope with the challenges of shocks and how to bring sustainable, inclusive growth. Long-term sustainable growth is indeed the key for narrowing the gap between developed and developing countries and an important element of world stability. Yet, with the exception of a few successful economies,[15] there was little economic convergence between rich and poor countries before the current global crisis in spite of the richness of development thinking, and the many efforts that made by developing countries and multilateral development agencies since the end of World War II.

This chapter has suggested a framework based on comparative advantage that enables developing countries to be more resilient to internal and external shocks, achieve sustainable growth, eliminate poverty, and narrow the income gaps with the developed countries. The proposed approach, called a neoclassical approach to structures and change in the process of economic development, or new structural economics, builds on some of the insights from the old structural economics. It emphasizes the idea that the structural features of developing economies need to be taken into account in analyzing the process of economic development and the role of state in facilitating a developing country to change its backward structure to a modern one. However, this new approach considers structural differences between developed and developing countries to be endogenous to their endowment structures and determined by market forces, rather than resulting from the distribution of power or other exogenously determined rigidities as assumed by the old structural approach. The implications of this framework for research are challenging but exciting, as we need to better understand the roles of the market and the state and how they interact in the process of economic development.

Notes

1. J. P. Morgan Emerging Market Bond Index Global, 2009.
2. Perhaps the gradual tightening by the U.S. Federal Reserve beginning June 2004 represented the first calculated bet to try to smooth the cycle.
3. Source: World Development Indicators 2009, World Bank. Investment growth is the annual growth of gross fixed capital formation. The average growth rate reported is the simple average of the growth rate over the indicated time period. Developing countries are defined as those countries in the low- and middle-income group (2008 GNI per capita of $11,905 or less).
4. Source: DEC Prospects Group, World Bank.
5. This point was made by P. Murrell at the panel "The Great Transformation after Twenty Years: What Is Left to Be Done?" American Economic Association Meetings in Atlanta, GA, January 3–5, 2010, and in his forthcoming paper "Is the Transition Over?"
6. M. E. Porter made the notion of "competitive advantage" popular in his book *The Competitive Advantage of Nations.* According to him, a nation will have competitive advantage in the global economy if industries in the nation fulfill the following four conditions: (1) they intensively use the nation's abundant and relatively inexpensive factors of production, (2) their products have large domestic markets, (3) each industry forms domestic clusters, and (4) markets are competitive. The first condition reflects the fact that the industries are consistent with the economy's comparative advantage, which is determined by the nations' endowments. The third and the fourth conditions hold only if the industries are consistent with the nation's competitive advantage. Therefore, the four conditions can be reduced to the following two independent conditions: comparative advantage and domestic market size. Among these two independent conditions, comparative advantage is the more important because if an industry is the nation's comparative advantage, the industry's product will have a global market. This is the reason why many of the richest countries in the world are very small. See Lin and Ren 2007.
7. This pattern was documented in the literature by Akamatsu 1962 and Chenery 1960 and formalized in Ju, Lin, and Wang 2009.
8. See Lin 2009 and Lin and Chang 2009.
9. A firm is viable if with a normal management it can survive in a competitive market without external subsidies. Lin (2003, 2009) shows that a firm will be viable if it is operated in the optimal industry determined by the economy's endowment structure.
10. The difference between factors of production and infrastructures is that in a market economy the former are supplied mostly by individual households, whereas the latter are supplied by the community or the state.
11. See Lin 1989.

12. See Acemoglu, Aghion, Griffith, and Zilibotti 2009.
13. Because of budget constraints, governments need to prioritize their support to basic research. This explains why supports to basic research, such as preferential taxes, defense and procurement contracts, and mandates, are often industry specific. Among the measures used by the advanced countries to support structural change only the patent system is industry neutral. All others actually correspond to in fact to "picking winners."
14. An important caveat here is the need to recognize the downside risks associated with serious governance problems and political capture by certain corrupt elements and powerful groups in many developing countries. However, if the industrial upgrading facilitated by the state follows its comparative advantage, the government only needs to compensate the externalities generated by the pioneer firms in the upgrading. The required compensation should be very small. The political capture in developing countries is more likely to occur when the industries promoted by the government's industrial policy go against the country's comparative advantage. As such, firms in the government's priority industries are not viable in open, competitive market. The government needs to introduce various distortions to protect and subsidize the nonviable firms and is thus subject to political capture (see Lin and Li 2009 and Lin and Tan 1999). The effectiveness of the facilitating role also relies on the government capacity. If the industries promoted by the state's industrial policy are consistent with the country's comparative advantage, it will be more likely to be successful and the requirement for the state's capacity will be smaller. Moreover, the success may increase the government's confidence and enhance its capacity.
15. See, for example, those 13 economies studied in the Growth Report (Growth Commission 2008).

References

Acemoglu, D., P. Aghion, R. Griffith, and F. Zilibotti. 2010. "Vertical Integration and Technology: Theory and Evidence," *Journal of the European Economic Association* 8, no. 5, 989–1033.

Akamatsu, K. 1962. "A Historical Pattern of Economic Growth in Developing Countries," *The Development Economies* (Tokyo) 1: 3–25.

Chen, S., and M. Ravallion. 2009. "The Impact of the Global Financial Crisis on the World's Poorest." VOXeu papers. www.voxeu.org/index.php?q=node/3520.

Chenery, H. B. 1960. "Patterns of Industrial Growth," *American Economic Review* 50(September): 624–54.

Friedman, J., and N. Schady. 2009. "How Many More Infants Are Likely to Die in Africa as a Result of the Global Financial Crisis?" Policy Research Working Paper Series 5023. Washington, DC: World Bank.

Fukuyama, Francis. 1992. *The End of History and the Last Man.* New York: Free Press.

Growth Commission. 2008. *The Growth Report: Strategies for Sustained Growth and Inclusive Development,"* Washington DC: Growth Commission.

Ju, J., J. Y. Lin, and Y. Wang. 2009. "Endowment Structures, Industrial Dynamics, and Economic Growth," World Bank Policy Research Working Paper 5055. Washington, DC: World Bank.

Lin, J. Y. 1989. "An Economic Theory of Institutional Change: Induced and Imposed Change," *Cato Journal* 9(1, Spring/Summer): 1–32.

———. *Economic Development and Transition: Thought, Strategy, and Viability,* Cambridge: Cambridge University Press.

Lin, J. Y., and H. Chang, 2009. "DPR Debate: Should Industrial Policy in Developing Countries Conform to Comparative Advantage or Defy It?" *Development Policy Review* 27(5): 483–502.

Lin, J. Y., and F. Li. 2009. "Development Strategy, Viability and Economic Distortions in Developing Countries," World Bank Policy Research Working Paper 4906.

Lin, J. Y., and R.N. Ren. 2007. "East Asian Miracle Revisited" (in Chinese) *Jingji Yanjiu (Economic Research Journal)* 42(8): 4–12.

Lin, J. Y., and G. Tan. 1999. "Policy Burdens, Accountability, and the Soft Budget Constraint," *American Economic Review: Papers and Proceedings* 89(2): 426–31.

Murrell, P. 2010. "The Great Transformation after Twenty Years: What Is Left to be Done?" American Economic Association Meetings in Atlanta, GA, January 3–5.

———. forthcoming. "Is the Transition Over?" University of Maryland University College.

Prebisch, R. 1950. *The Economic Development of Latin America and Its Principal Problems.* New York, United Nations. Reprinted in *Economic Bulletin for Latin America* 7(February 1962): 1–22.

Rosenstein-Rodan, P. 1943. "Problems of Industrialization of Eastern and Southeastern Europe," *Economic Journal* 111(June–September): 202–11.

CHAPTER 3

The Crisis and the Two Globalization Fetishes

Arvind Subramanian

IN THE INDUSTRIALIZED COUNTRIES, and in the United States in particular, the 2008–9 financial crisis has raised fundamental questions about capitalism and the so-called Anglo-Saxon version of it that had elevated the status and role of finance.[1] The crisis may well do to finance what the government's response to John D. Rockefeller's activities did to oil: pruning the sector back to size through stronger and more intrusive regulation (Yergin 2008).

Surprisingly, across the emerging market world, there has been no such existential angst about capitalism, no serious questioning of the role of the market. It is not that these countries have not been affected by the crisis. Indeed, all countries—rich and poor—have found themselves in the same financial maelstrom, if not in the same boat, and the effects have been substantial.[2] There has also been serious discussion and action on the appropriate short-term responses to the crisis. But, there have been no serious calls or indeed actions to roll back capitalism, to erect protectionist barriers, or to renationalize the economy. Most surprising, there has not even been a pitch to restrict inflows of fickle foreign capital that were arguably at the center of this crisis for many emerging markets. The crisis may have exposed the claim of a decoupled world economy, but it seems to have emphasized the decoupling in policy debate and long-term policy choices.

Coupled Economies, Decoupled Debates

What explains this decoupling? First, the crisis originated in the United States and to a lesser extent in Europe. The rest of the world has been affected, and in some cases, seriously. But the original sin was committed in the "core" not in the periphery, which has therefore had less reason therefore to turn inward. And many emerging market countries, especially in Asia and parts of Latin America (Brazil and Chile, for example), as a consequence of prudent economic management, have been less affected by the crisis and managed to mitigate its worst impacts. So, what should we be introspecting about, they are entitled to ask?

Second, another big question thrown up by the crisis in the core countries: the role of the state and the appropriate demarcation between state and markets, especially in the financial sector. In the emerging markets, particularly in the more successful ones such as China and India, this is simply not an issue. The line still favors state over markets and in the financial sector heavily so: in both these countries, most of the banking system assets and liabilities are still controlled by the government. The issue is not how to claw back the role of the state so much as how to continue reducing its role in the gradual and pragmatic manner that these countries have been doing over the past two decades.[3]

Perhaps the most important reason for the decoupled debate phenomenon is that the big development question in the emerging markets is not the state-market boundary but the more difficult question of how to improve the state, its basic capacity to deliver law and order, security, and other essential services.[4] My colleagues Lant Pritchett and Larry Diamond make similar points in their chapters included in this volume.

Even if capitalism is not up for debate in the developing world, globalization strategies of developing nations will be because financial and trade integration has been the transmission mechanism for the impact of the crisis. Emerging market governments are not going to revert to socialism and dirigisme but they are likely to ask what lessons the crisis offers for the globalization strategies and in particular whether to embrace or persevere with one of the extreme models of globalization.

The Two Fetishes: Extreme Models of Globalization

The crisis has served as a very useful natural experiment to test two extreme models of globalization that countries had adopted going into the crisis. These models of globalization, reflected choices about openness to foreign capital and to exports. The first can be described as the "foreign finance fetish" model and relied on importing a lot of foreign capital, especially financial capital. The second can be described as the "export fetish," or the mercantilist, model, which entailed a reliance on exports as development strategy assisted by government intervention, for example through an undervalued exchange rate, and combined with a curtailment of some forms of foreign financial capital.

These two models are sharply drawn, but in practice, they represent the two ends of a continuum along which emerging markets situated themselves in the lead-up to the crisis. Of course, there is another extreme model of globalization, or rather the lack thereof, exemplified by North Korea and Myanmar (Burma), which have shut themselves off from world trade and capital markets. But that model is too discredited to risk emulation.

The foreign finance fetish can be measured in different ways. It can be measured in terms of a country's policy stance toward financial globalization (sometimes referred to as "de jure" financial globalization); or the actual flows of foreign capital to a country (referred to as "de facto" financial globalization). In turn, flows can be measured in net terms (which is broadly the current account deficit in the country's balance of payments) or gross terms.[5]

Viewed in terms of actual net flows, countries in Eastern Europe were the best exponents of the foreign finance fetish model. As part of their regional integration, many of them sucked in large amounts of foreign capital—not just foreign direct investment but also hot flows of portfolio capital and debt—from countries of the European Union. The most dramatic cases were Latvia and Bulgaria: their current account deficits exceeded 20 percent of GDP in the run-up to the crisis in 2008. But other countries including Estonia, Hungary, Lithuania, and Romania ran current account deficits that exceeded 3 percent of GDP, a threshold that if exceeded is generally considered to warrant concern.[6] Foreigners—banks in Austria and Italy— were willing to lend to these countries because they seemed to be growing rapidly as part of converging to the standards of living of their western neighbors.

Consider next the export fetish model. The export fetish model—of which China has been the great recent exemplar—must be distinguished from export-led development strategies such as those pursued by Korea in the 1970s and 1980s. The distinction is captured in the idea of the fetish or the overreliance on exports often achieved through government intervention and manifested in substantial levels of exports but especially in substantial excesses of exports over imports (i.e., in current account surpluses).

The distinction is not that China has intervened and that Korea did not. Korea did provide cheap credit and other incentives for exports. But in the case of China, there was a conscious policy of maintaining a substantially undervalued currency, which was achieved through a combination of restricting inflows of foreign financial capital although not foreign direct investment) and intervening heavily in foreign exchange markets to prevent the currency from rising in response to the excess supply of foreign exchange that was building up in the economy. China's policy consistently thwarted the pressure on the currency to appreciate and find its equilibrium level. Goldstein and Lardy (2009) have estimated, for example, that the Chinese currency has been undervalued relative to some norm by about 20–30 percent during the period 2003–8. Thus, the difference between Korea and China, or the difference between reliance on exports and export fetishism, is related both to instruments and to the magnitude of the government intervention.

As a result of this policy, China's ratio of exports to GDP has risen significantly to over 50 percent today. These levels may, at first blush, not seem very striking when compared with other countries such as Singapore or Korea or even countries within Europe. In fact, though, China's export integration is phenomenal. It is a well-accepted dictum that large countries tend to trade significantly less than smaller countries. China's export fetish is revealed in a comparison of its export-to-GDP ratio of 50 percent with that of other big countries such as the United States, India, and Brazil for which exports account for about 20 percent of their GDP. Its export integration is more than twice as large as comparator countries.[7]

Of course, the more glaring indicator of the consequences of export fetishism achieved through a policy of undervalued exchange rates has been China's current account surplus, which reached about 11 percent of GDP in 2007. Korea too had current account surpluses but these were brief (between 1986 and 1988) and not of the same magnitude (average of about 7 percent of GDP).

One can situate other emerging market countries between these two extremes. Brazil and India, with their surprisingly low share of exports and nonnegligible amounts of foreign capital, are in the middle of this continuum as are the Philippines and Indonesia. Mexico and Turkey, being close to big neighbors, resemble the foreign finance fetish model of the Eastern European countries, as does Korea. Malaysia and Thailand, like China, have been relatively impervious to foreign capital market but remain highly export-oriented economies.

The Better Fetish

The global financial crisis affected emerging market economies through two main channels: financial and real. The first phase of the crisis was marked by deleveraging as firms and households in the United States and other industrializedcountries scrambled to acquire liquidity. They pulled back all the investments that they had made in the emerging market countries. The effects took the form of sharp declines in their currencies and in other asset values such as stock prices and land values.

In its second phase, the global financial crisis became a global growth crisis. As growth and demand collapsed in the major economies, the impact was transmitted to the emerging markets via trade. Exports in all the emerging market countries have spiraled downward (Eichengreen and O'Rourke 2009).

Which of the two extreme models did better? It is clear that the finance fetish model did not emerge well from this crisis in two respects: severity of impact and effectiveness of response. The greater the foreign capital that flowed into an emerging market country, the more it was affected. Countries in Eastern Europe saw their currencies plummet, their financial systems plunge into bankruptcy, and many of them (Latvia, Hungary, and Belarus) have been forced to go to the IMF for emergency financial assistance. In contrast, other countries such as China, Malaysia, and Thailand, as well as countries with moderate exposure to foreign capital saw smaller declines in their currency values. China was one of the few emerging market countries that saw its currency strengthen.

Even more important, the ability of countries to offset the financial and real impact of the crisis has been significantly weaker and more constrained in countries adopting the foreign finance fetish model. This is most sharply illustrated in comparing the experience of the Asian and Latin American countries in this crisis with their own experience in the financial crisis of the 1990s.

Then, the crisis-ridden countries faced an acute dilemma on how to respond. Should they raise interest rates to retain confidence in their currencies or should they lower interest rates to provide a boost to investment and growth and to help the financial situation of the banking system? Debate raged and the IMF was accused of favoring the former course over the latter. In this crisis, that debate was notable for its absence, it was the dog that did not bark. Almost without exception and anxiety, policymakers in Asia slashed interest rates without having to worry about retaining investor confidence.

Why were they able to do so? Above all, unlike in the earlier emerging market crises, this time most investors, especially residents, believed that the reasons for declining currency values and asset prices had little to do with the domestic economy and almost entirely to do with external factors.

As important was the fact that these countries followed sound policies and importantly had insured themselves by accumulating sizable foreign exchange reserves and by not allowing too much financial capital to come in. Some countries such as China and Malaysia had not just saved for a rainy day; they had built their Noah's Ark (Summers 2006). Holdings of reserves, which central banks deployed to defend the currency, helped reassure residents and dissuaded them from rushing to exit. This strategy worked and, after an initial period of disturbance, relative calm returned to many currency markets in the developing world.

In contrast, countries in Eastern Europe in this crisis faced the same dilemmas and were more constrained in their policy responses as the Asian countries had been a decade ago. Overall, countries that embraced foreign finance wholeheartedly were battered more than those who were cautious about foreign finance.

Of course, in some ways, the country that was the most foreign finance fetishist of all was the United States. There will be endless debate on whether the crisis in the United States was due to its dependence on foreign finance or due to the failure its own regulatory and monetary policies. Most agree that the easy access to foreign finance (facilitated by the export fetishism of China discussed below) was the rope that the United States chose to hang itself with. Without the rope, there would not have been the same excess of liquidity that facilitated the build-up of the debt-financed asset price bubble. To that extent, the experience of the United States, the epicenter of the crisis, perhaps is the best case for the prosecution against foreign finance fetishism.

How did the export fetish model of China fare? It is not that countries such as China were spared the effects of the crisis. Global trade has plummeted in this crisis, in fact by a greater extent than even during the Great Depression of the 1930s. Across the emerging market world, exports have declined, taking the real economy down with it. The greater the exposure to exports, the great the growth impact that a country suffered. There are likely to be two narratives about how China fared during the crisis. The first upbeat narrative will go something like this. China's export fetish model performed remarkably well. By being cautious about hot flows of capital, it avoided the worst of the financial impact. By maintaining an undervalued exchange rate, it boosted exports and its long-run growth substantially. And, although export fetishism led to a dangerous vulnerability to foreign demand and prosperity overseas, China mitigated the costs of this exposure by superb "boom-time" management of its economy.

In particular, the low levels of public debt (less than 20 percent of its GDP) and a very strong public balance sheet built up during the boom years, helped China to counteract the recessionary impact of the crisis. Even though exports collapsed, it was able to embark on a countercyclical fiscal strategy, which has been among the most ambitious anywhere in the world, matching the fiscal efforts of the United States and surpassing those of several European countries. And this strategy may have even been more effective than that of the United States because it started off from much stronger initial conditions. The strong recovery of the Chinese economy in the second half of 2009, reflecting the sizable fiscal stimulus, would provide ammunition to this upbeat narrative.

But there is an alternative narrative that might emerge especially from within China itself. It is true that China has been able to offset the crisis through effective countercyclical action. It may also well be the case that its development strategy of large levels of reserves helped China in this regard. Equally, though, China had a close shave with social unrest. Its high export exposure increased considerably the social and political risks associated with the economic dislocations. Manufacturing was particularly badly hit, excess capacity increased; nearly 20 million people had to be physically relocated. China may have pulled it off this time but it could easily have gone the other way.

Persisting Fetishes

The continuing appeal and embrace of these two models may, however, depend on factors other than the experience of this crisis. First, let's consider foreign finance fetishism.

Insofar as the foreign finance fetish model has been further battered, countries should be more cautious about being open to foreign capital going forward. As a result, we should expect some financial deglobalization that would be the international counterpart of the pruning back of finance that is expected to happen domestically. But will this financial deglobalization actually occur?

That a wholehearted embrace of foreign capital can be costly is not a new lesson.[8] If anything what is surprising, given the regularity of crises associated with foreign capital in the developing world—think of the Latin American debt crisis of the 1970s and 1980s and the financial crisis of the late 1990s—is that countries have not been more cautious about foreign capital. Indeed, the period after the Asian financial crisis of the late 1990s has seen the most rapid pace of financial globalization around the world.[9] On foreign finance, the disconnect between past experience and future practice is the real puzzle.

Part of the explanation must lie in the political economy of opening up to foreign capital, in the combination of interests and ideology that, as much as experience, appears to have shaped countries' attitude to foreign capital. Jagdish Bhagwati (1998) famously noted that a Wall Street/U.S. Treasury complex drove financial globalization in Asia in the 1990s. But this has turned out to be only a partial explanation. It explains the push factor, namely, why foreign financial firms push for opening abroad. It does not explain why foreign governments have voluntarily and enthusiastically embraced foreign finance even when they are not forced to under World Bank/International Monetary Fund tutelage. The interesting question therefore is: why do emerging market countries chose to open up to foreign capital?

The bias toward opening to foreign capital is not just the result of the U.S. financial sector pushing its interests in foreign markets. It seems that, increasingly, the political economy within developing countries is also biased toward opening up to foreign capital. The parallel with trade protection is instructive. Societies are predisposed toward protectionism because of the imbalance in its impact. The costs of import restrictions—higher prices—are diffused over many consumers while their benefits are concentrated in the hands of a few producers. Concentrated interests have more at stake and are therefore able to mobilize easily whereas collective action is more difficult for the consumers.

Something similar applies to foreign capital. The benefits of foreign capital often accrue to firms and producers in the form of lower borrowing costs. And where domestic financial systems are inefficient, as they often are in many emerging markets, access to foreign capital is particularly valuable. So, the benefits are concentrated. More importantly, these benefits are frontloaded: firms see immediately the lowering of the costs of borrowing. The costs, in contrast, happen in some distant future because financial crises—one of the major costs of foreign borrowing—occur only after a certain period of overreliance on foreign capital.

The other cost of foreign borrowing is its tendency to drive up the exchange rate and make a country's exports less competitive. In principle, therefore, if exporting interests are strong and a country follows a flexible exchange rate, this political economy imbalance in favor of opening up to foreign capital can be rectified. Flexibility leads foreign capital flows to put upward pressure on the currency, jeopardizing the profit margins of exporters, who can mobilize to complain about the outcome.

In practice, few countries follow such a pure float: central banks often try and dampen upward pressures on the currency, which actually makes it even more attractive to embrace foreign capital. But this cannot go on and at some stage, a combination of asset price bubbles and overheating leads to the inevitable financial crisis, but that of course happens well after foreign capital has flooded in and well after the pressure from domestic firms has favored such capital coming in.

In addition to interests, ideology has also played a prominent role in capital account opening. A belief system was created around the elevated status of finance domestically and internationally.[10] In the case of opening up to foreign capital, the belief system operated subtly, and the International Monetary Fund played an important role.

Leading up to the Asian financial crisis, there was a strong push for opening to foreign capital. After the crisis, the IMF appeared to change tack. It did a partial and strategic mea culpa. Yes, it was a mistake to push capital account opening, admitted the IMF. But it never went on to argue that countries should be cautious toward foreign capital. Rather the line was that foreign capital remained fundamentally beneficial and that reaping the benefits required a series of complementary reforms such as macroeconomic stability and a sound and well-regulated financial system.[11]

This view precluded the IMF from providing guidance to emerging markets on the serious practical question: if these complementary reforms could not be undertaken should countries regulate the inflow of foreign capital and if so, how? Setting itself to answer this question would have legitimized the view that foreign capital could be potentially harmful, which would have run counter to the ideology that supported the foreign finance fetish. Interests and ideology may once again triumph over experience, so that financial globalization will continue going forward more rapidly than might be desirable.

What about prospects for the export fetish model? If the China model is seen as having succeeded, the systemic implications are grim. Many emerging markets and even some richer countries may also draw an ominous lesson from the crisis for their longer run policies: that they need to export to grow and that they need to accumulate even larger war chests of foreign exchange to defend themselves against similar shocks in coming years. More countries will increase their savings in order to accumulate foreign exchange reserves. If countries believe that they must export and that they must accumulate a war chest of foreign reserves to combat future crises, we are in for the proliferation of a "new mercantilism" across the emerging market world.

This new mercantilism will create serious systemic tensions because in the aftermath of the crisis, external conditions are likely to be much less favorable for trade and global imbalances. On the trade side, if countries start to use government policy to gain export advantage, there will be a backlash from importing countries, which will complain about unfair trade practices abroad and start contemplating unilateral trade action. The world got a preview of this in the exchanges between the United States and China over China's exchange rate policy. If more countries embark on mercantilism, these frictions will escalate.

Moreover, for mercantilism by the many to be feasible, there will have to be a consumer of last resort. For every surplus there must be a counterpart deficit. Over the past decade, the United States has been such a net consumer, willing to suck in cheap goods from abroad. Going forward, though, it may be unwilling to do so for both trade reasons but also for foreign policy reasons. On the trade side, the Obama administration is more receptive to the interests of labor groups than the previous administration. Mercantilist practices abroad have a greater impact on labor than on corporations, which are more mobile and can shift their operations overseas, including to the countries engaging in mercantilism. Calls for trade actions from labor are more likely and are more likely to receive a sympathetic hearing under the current administration.

The crisis has also underlined the tension between superpower status and international indebtedness. The United States knows that further sizable increases in its net foreign debt, already exceeding $3 trillion, would jeopardize its economy and undermine its international influence. The United States has experienced the vulnerability of being a debtor. Early on in the financial crisis, many cash-strapped financial icons went pleading to sovereign wealth funds in the Middle East for cash and equity infusions, leading to the fear that Wall Street might become the property of foreign governments. And more broadly, the United States is in perennial fear of a sudden withdrawal of foreign financing from U.S. bond markets. These financial vulnerabilities constrain the exercise of U.S. power internationally.

Moving to the Middle: Changing Ideology, Reforming Institutions

The best outcome, therefore, for the international financial and trading system would be a repudiation of both these extreme models of globalization and a move toward the middle. Caution about (not a repudiation of) foreign finance can help minimize the risks of future crises. Shifting from export fetishism toward more balanced growth would minimize trade frictions and the risk of imbalances reemerging. How can the international community fashion its responses to facilitate such a move toward the middle? Responses must be both at the level of ideology and institutions.

The IMF must lead the intellectual charge in combating foreign finance fetishism. Without a shift in ideology, it will be difficult to overcome the strength of interests that systematically tilt the outcome in favor of more rather than less foreign capital. One concrete way to achieve this would actually be to give the IMF jurisdiction over capital account issues on the clear understanding that it will be more open toward analyzing and giving advice on managing the capital account. For example, it could be given the concrete task of preparing a best practices manual for countries on when and how best to throw, in James Tobin's famous phrase, "sand in the wheels" of international capital flows.

This manual would attempt to find answers to a number of important but unexplored questions: For example, should controls on capital flows be price-based or quantity-based? What kinds of flows are best addressed, debt or portfolio? Over what duration are limits most effective? When should they be withdrawn? In addition to demonstrating its usefulness to countries, such an exercise can allow the IMF to shed its image as doctrinaire and ideologically biased and address the perception that it has acted as an instrument of rich countries and their financial companies. An IMF that produces such a manual could do as much to endear itself to the developing world as it is trying to do now by reducing the conditions it is attaching to its loans.

What about addressing export fetishism? Even if China's experience during the crisis is seen as favorable, other countries could spurn the export fetish model. Small countries could realize that are so overexposed to exports that no amount of fiscal action can realistically offset the effect of external shocks. Others might come to realize that they can neither emulate China's boom-time management nor acquire its state capacity to spend well and effectively during a crisis. In other words, countries might conclude that the export fetish model may have worked for China but less likely to do so for others.

But even absent such a voluntary distancing from export fetishism, a series of institutional changes can steer countries away from it. Clear multilateral rules against government activism to support exports would help. What would these look like and what is the appropriate forum for discussing them?

The International Monetary Fund is, of course, the natural forum for addressing exchange rate issues. But the IMF suffers from problems of inadequate leverage and eroding legitimacy. The IMF has successfully changed the policies of countries that have borrowed from it. However, it has rarely, if ever, effectively influenced the policies of large creditor countries even where such policies have had significant negative effects on others. Moreover, emerging market countries chafe at its governance structure, which reflects the receded realities of an Atlantic-centered 1945 rather than those of an ascendant Asia of the twenty-first century.

As argued in Mattoo and Subramanian (2009), the World Trade Organization (WTO) is one alternative to the IMF, since undervalued exchange rates have large and direct trade consequences. What is needed is a rule in the WTO proscribing undervalued exchange rates that are clearly attributable to government action. An undervalued exchange rate is in effect a combination of export subsidies and import tariffs, each of which is currently disciplined by the WTO. The IMF would continue to be the sole forum for broad exchange rate surveillance. But in those rare instances of undervaluation, we envisage a more effective delineation of responsibility, with the IMF continuing to play a technical role in assessing when a country's exchange rate was undervalued, and the WTO assuming the enforcement role.

This change would be consistent with the WTO's better record on enforcement. Its dispute settlement system, although not perfect, has been reasonably effective in allowing members to initiate and settle disputes. Effectiveness, and indeed legitimacy, are related to the WTO being perceived as less asymmetric in the distribution of power between the industrialized-countries and emerging markets. Power and influence evolve organically in the WTO because they flow from market size rather than being historically determined as in the IMF. One sign of effectiveness and legitimacy is the fact that developing countries, even the smaller ones, have been as active in bringing disputes to the WTO for settlement as they have been at the receiving end.

How would this new rule against undervalued exchange rates be incorporated in the WTO? Through negotiation. Clearly, Chinese concerns have to be addressed for any new rules to be crafted and commonly agreed. The United States and European Union have been the principal demandeurs for action by China in the past. But it is important to remember that until very recently, a number of developing countries—Brazil, Mexico, Korea, Turkey, and South Africa—were affected by the competitive pressure from the undervalued renminbi. Indeed, the Indian prime minister has also urged China to follow a more market-based exchange rate policy. For obvious reasons, more emerging market countries have not voiced their concerns, but it is possible that a coalition of affected countries could unite on this issue.

It is possible that China has attained a degree of power and status that has put it beyond outside influence, especially on such a key issue as the exchange rate. Chimerica (to use Niall Ferguson's phrase) may just be an identification of two countries that are not just intertwined but beyond each other's influence.

But insofar as China can be persuaded to agree to multilateral rules to tame mercantilism and export fetishism, there are two possible carrots. First, China's major trading partners could pledge granting China the status of a "market economy" in the WTO contingent on its eliminating currency undervaluation and moving to a market-based system. This status would have significant value for China by shielding it against unilateral trade actions such as anti-dumping and countervailing duties by trading partners. Second, as part of radical governance reform of the IMF, which is desirable in itself, China should be offered a substantially larger voting share in the IMF commensurate with its economic status.

For other countries, contemplating export fetishism and building their own Noah's Ark of foreign exchange reserves, their incentives to go down this path can be diluted if there is a credible guarantee that liquidity will be quickly, cheaply, and unconditionally available from the IMF. Credible multilateral insurance for self-insurance is the bargain to be struck here (Goldstein 2009). The IMF has made a good start in this direction but reforms need to be more ambitious to ensure that the IMF has the resources, incentives, and legitimacy to be a provider of multilateral insurance. Of course, all these changes at the IMF will only be acceptable to many emerging market countries if they can feel that the IMF is their institution and not just that of the richer countries. Thus, governance reform at the IMF will be crucial if this bargain has any hopes of being realized (Truman 2006).

In short, the world needs a stronger WTO as well as a new IMF—ideologically less doctrinaire, financially better equipped, perceived to be more legitimate, and endowed with greater regulatory authority—to nudge countries away from the twin fetishes of foreign finance and exports. In the aftermath of the crisis, sustaining successful globalization may require repudiating some of its excesses.

Notes
1. The London-based *Financial Times* ran a series on the future of capitalism over several months, and many of the world's leading economists and other intellectuals weighed in on this topic.
2. For the estimated effects of the crisis on a selected group of important countries, see Subramanian and Klasnja (2009).
3. In India, for example, the only bank threatened by the crisis was a private one that chose to deal in the toxic assets that wreaked havoc in western financial markets, resulting in a flight of deposits to the safety of public sector banks. Yet, it is remarkable that the debate on finance in India has not lurched in the direction of triumphalism about the public sector model of finance and the need to ensure its permanence.
4. On the importance of the state or the quality of public institutions, see Acemoglu, Johnson, and Robinson (2001); Rodrik, Subramanian, and Trebbi (2004); and Fukuyama (2004).
5. See Kose, Prasad, Rogoff, and Wei (2009) for different definitions of financial globalization.
6. By way of comparison, in the run-up to the Asian financial crisis of the late 1990s, Korea's current account deficit peaked at 4 percent of GDP, and Thailand's and Malaysia's at 8 percent and 10 percent, respectively.
7. So-called gravity models of trade relate a country's trade to standard determinants such as income, size, and distance from trading partners. These models

show that all these factors cannot account for a lot of China's trade. One such calculation for how much China overtrades and India does not can be found in Rodrik and Subramanian (2005).

8. Skepticism about foreign finance has an impressive intellectual pedigree going back to Bhagwati (1998) and Calvo and Reinhart (2000).

9. See Kose et. al. (2009) for trends in financial globalization over the past three decades.

10. See Johnson and Kwak (2009) on this belief system and how it came to grip the United States and Fukuyama and Colby (2009) for a discussion of the role of economists in falling prey to the finance fetish.

11. This view is expressed well in Mishkin (2006).

References

Acemoglu, Daron, Simon Johnson, and James A. Robinson. 2001. "The Colonial Origins of Comparative Development: An Empirical Investigation." *American Economic Review* 91(December): 1369–1401.

Bhagwati, Jagdish. 1998. "The Capital Myth: The Difference between Trade in Widgets and Dollars." *Foreign Affairs* May/June.

Calvo, Guillermo, and Carmen Reinhart. 2000. "When Capital Flows Come to a Sudden Stop: Consequences and Policy." In *Reforming the International Monetary and Financial System,* edited by Peter B. Kenen and Alexander K. Swoboda. Washington, DC: International Monetary Fund.

Eichengreen, Barry, and Kevin O'Rourke. 2009. A Tale of Two Depressions. Available at www.voxeu.org/index.php?q=node/3421.

Fukuyama, Francis. 2004. *State-Building: Governance and World Order in the 21st Century.* Ithaca, NY: Cornell University Press.

Fukuyama, Francis, and Seth Colby. 2009. "What Were They Thinking? The Role of Economists in the Financial Debacle." *The American Interest* 5(1).

Goldstein, Morris. 2009. "A Grand Bargain for the London G-20 Summit: Insurance and Obeying the Rules." Available at www.voxeu.org/index.php?q=node/3100.

Goldstein, Morris, and Nicholas Lardy. 2009. "The Future of China's Exchange Rate Policy." Policy Analyses in International Economics, no. 87. Washington, DC: Peterson Institute for International Economics.

Kose, M. Ayhan, Eswar Prasad, Kenneth Rogoff, and Shang-Jin Wei. 2009. "Financial Globalization: A Reappraisal." *IMF Staff Papers* 56(1): 8–62.

Johnson, Simon, and James Kwak. 2009. "The Quiet Coup." *The Atlantic.* Available at www.theatlantic.com/doc/200905/imf-advice.

Mattoo, Aaditya, and Arvind Subramanian. 2009. "Currency Undervaluation and Sovereign Wealth Funds: A New Role for the World Trade Organization." *World Economy* 32(8): 1135–64.

Mishkin, Frederic S. 2006. *The Next Great Globalization: How Disadvantaged Nations Can Harness Their Financial Systems to Get Rich.* Princeton: Princeton University Press.

Rodrik, Dani, and Arvind Subramanian. 2005. "From 'Hindu Growth' to Productivity Surge: The Mystery of the Indian Growth Transition." *IMF Staff Papers* 52(2): 193–228.

Rodrik, Dani, Arvind Subramanian, and Francesco Trebbi. 2004. "Institutions Rule: The Primacy of Institutions over Geography and Integration in Economic Development." *Journal of Economic Growth* 9(2): 131–65, 206.

Subramanian, Arvind, and Marko Klasnja. 2009. *The Global Economy Takes a Grimmer Turn Especially for Europe and Japan.* Washington, DC: Peterson Institute for International Economics. Available at www.petersoninstitute.org/realtime/?p=633.

Summers, Lawrence. 2006. "Reflections on Global Account Imbalances and Emerging Markets Reserve Accumulation," L.K. Jha Memorial Lecture, Reserve Bank of India, Mumbai.

Truman, Edwin. 2006. "Reforming the IMF for the 21st Century," Peterson Institute for International Economics, Washington DC.

Yergin, Daniel. 2008. *The Prize: The Epic Quest for Oil, Money, and Power.* New York: Free Press.

Part II • Emerging Market Perspectives

CHAPTER 4

China

Getting the Rural Issues Right

Yasheng Huang

TO OFFER SOME NEW PERSPECTIVES on the current global financial and economic crisis, one has to start with a "standard" perspective as the baseline. A prevailing perspective interprets the current global financial crisis as rooted in "macro" and "cross-country" dynamics. The idea is that some countries—principally developed countries, such as the United States—save too little while other countries—principally developing countries, such as China—save too much. The global imbalances are the structural cause behind the current economic and financial difficulties.

Much of the responsibility has been assigned to two principal players in the current financial crisis—the United States and China (and rightly so). Policy analysts and economists argue that the huge bilateral trade imbalances—accumulated over many years—between the United States and China reflect the different consumption propensities of the two countries. But this perspective is derived from the arithmetic of international flows of goods, services, and capital rather than from a deep insight into the workings of the economies of the United States and China. It begs the deeper question why such glaring imbalances have arisen in the first place and why they have persisted—or are being allowed to persist—for such a long period of time. There is also a framing issue. If the excessive exports from China are identified as a problem, then the logic is to recommend a policy course that tackles such imbalances head-on. This policy course could encompass, among others, a further revaluation of renminbi and curtailing explicit and implicit export subsidies.

In this chapter I argue that the origins of the macroeconomic disequilibrium lie in the micro development of rural China. Though on the surface the connections between the Chinese peasantry and the free-spending American consumers seems to be tenuous, some data digging and hard thinking reveal that they are deeply enmeshed in myriad ways. First, the underconsumption by China's huge rural population—estimated to be between 700 million and 900 million as of 2008—has significantly contributed to the slowdown of the aggregate consumption of the Chinese population. Secondly, the rural population has contributed to the massive supply increase of China's manufactures. So both the demand and supply sides make the rural economy an important topic in our research into the deeper causes behind the global imbalances.

Just as in the United States where the lax financial regulations of the 1990s fostered and encouraged reckless risk taking on the part of households and financial firms alike, the decade of the 1990s sowed many of the seeds that have engulfed China deeply in the current global imbalances. It was not so long ago when many foreign economists celebrated China's integration into the global economy. Globalization—taking the specific forms of foreign direct investment (FDI) and export manufacturing—is believed by many to be the most effective platform to reduce poverty and lift income (and, implicitly, raise consumption). GDP data are often cited to support this reasoning as are the poverty numbers. During the 1980s and 1990s, more than 200 million Chinese were lifted above the absolute poverty level (Dollar 2005).

I do not repeat these well-known success indicators. Rather, this is a focused treatment of those topics that have received less attention in the academic literature.[1] This chapter focuses not on national accounting data but on household income and consumption dynamics (obtained through surveys). It turns out that the household surveys reveal some substantial heterogeneous performances during the 1979–2008 period in a way that is not discernible through the GDP data. To some extent, offering new perspectives on financial crisis hinges on offering some new facts.

One curious fact is that China's domestic consumption declined sharply right in the wake of a signature event heralding China's entry into the global economic order—its joining of the World Trade Organization (WTO) in 2000. On the eve of its WTO entry household consumption stood at 45 percent of GDP. By 2007, the ratio shrank to 33 percent. The much-cited poverty findings in fact do not support at all the view that globalization single-handedly drove down poverty. An impressive portion of China's poverty reduction took place in the 1980s, not in the 1990s. By various estimates, about 80 percent of the 200 million people who grew out of poverty did so in the 1980s and a huge portion of this 80 percent did so in the first five years of the 1980s.[2] There was virtually no FDI in the first half of the 1980s and China's exports, while growing, were only a small fraction of Chinese economy. Taken as a whole, China's record in poverty reduction is impressive but not all of this can be traced to FDI or to foreign trade. Something else was afoot driving down China's poverty level.

The analytical bias by the economics profession toward attributing economic growth to globalization is, to some extent, based on weighting heavily those observable factors in constructing explanations of China's economic success. GDP, FDI, export production, tariff reductions are observable to outside analysts and these data series appear to correlate with each other closely. The conventional view on China is that the country has continuously reformed its economic system and that its economic performance has been consistently robust.

The idea of this chapter is to demonstrate some substantial discontinuities in Chinese reforms. One such a discontinuity has to do with rural finance. In this chapter, I show that beginning in the early 1990s (although it is hard to pin down the exact timeline) many of the innovative and liberal reforms in rural finance implemented in the 1980s were reversed. Increasingly, in the 1990s and continuing to this day (although with some easing), it became more difficult for rural households to access China's vast pool of savings and that China's financial system became less supportive of small-scale entrepreneurship in rural areas. Another development is that China began to curtail, restrict, and then ban altogether the operations of informal finance in rural areas. Informal finance, itself a form of private entrepreneurship, had played an instrumental role in supporting private entrepreneurship in the 1980s.

But what does this development have to do with the central theme of this volume—the unfolding financial crisis and the global imbalances? The connection lies in China's consumption. As I have shown, China today has probably the lowest consumption-to-GDP ratio of major economies in the world. The idea of this chapter is that to understand this low consumption-to-GDP ratio we have to understand what has happened to the income development of the nearly one billion Chinese rural residents. Low income growth—rather than high domestic savings rate—is probably the reason why consumption growth has been slow, despite rapid GDP growth.

The empirics of this chapter are organized to offer this revisionist perspective on how China became so deeply enmeshed in the story of global imbalances. The standard perspective is right in that one precipitating and contributing factor is the underconsumption by the Chinese. Nothing in this chapter contradicts this perspective but hopefully the gain of the exercise is to provide more details on the dynamics behind China's under-consumption. These historical details are important because they help us identify a productive solution to get China out of the current binds of production-consumption dilemma. The right policy lesson for China, contrary to the new orthodoxy of stressing the failings of capitalism, is that the country can use more capitalism, especially in its financial sector.

In the first part of this chapter, I try to get history right about China. In the second part, I go into more historical details and present data on rural household income and consumption since the early 1980s. I show that both income and consumption growth in the 1980s were robust but that this was followed by a drastic slowdown in the 1990s. As a simple descriptive piece of evidence, the income and consumption developments were bunched closely together, that is, consumption grew when income grew and vice versa. This is a prima facie contradiction of a prominent view that the sluggish consumption growth was due to a precautionary savings dynamic in which income grew fast but households saved away the ever-larger increment of income rather than spending it. There is no substantial evidence in support of this hypothesis. It should be noted that since 2003, there has been some recovery in the rate of consumption growth.

In the third section of the chapter, I identify financial policy reversals in rural China in the 1990s. In the 1980s, credit flows were made available to rural households but in the 1990s credit flows were reduced. Is there a connection between the consumption boom and bust and this financial development? This chapter does not explore the actual linkages between them but suggests that this is a reasonable hypothesis that warrants a further exploration.

Getting the History Right

The policy reversals in the area of rural finance are virtually unknown outside of China and to those academics studying Chinese economy.[3] Rural finance has not received nearly the same level of analytical attention as the state-owned banking system and capital market developments. For example, *China's Unfinished Revolution,* Nicholas Lardy's excellent book on Chinese banking system, devoted about six pages to rural credit cooperatives, an important rural financial institution.

Because China has produced consistently strong GDP growth performance, it is only natural that analysts have not contemplated the possibility that there might have been policy reversals. I show that these policy reversals mattered substantially by presenting the data on rural household income growth and that the rural household income growth in the 1990s slowed down substantially compared with the decade of the 1980s. I further show that since 2003, the year when the current leadership of Hu Jintao and Wen Jiabao came into power, the rural household income growth has recovered somewhat from its anemic growth in the 1990s.

Why do we need to pay attention this period of Chinese economic history in a volume on the unfolding economic and financial crisis in 2009? There are three reasons. One is the sheer size of the rural population. Domestic consumption on the part of both urban and rural residents is important in understanding China's role in the current global imbalances, but in this chapter I focus on the consumption dimension of China's rural residents—officially 727 million strong and 55 percent of the Chinese population—even after 30 years of rapid economic growth. In fact, the true size of rural population is larger. The 727 million figure does not include 230 million rural migrant workers who reside in cities but lack the status of being full legal urban residents. Rural economy matters for the demand side of the analysis simply because of the sheer size of the rural population. The rural sector also matters on the supply side. Rural residents have played a vital role in the success of China's export industries, especially those located in the coastal regions of the country, and in boosting China's manufacturing productivity. There is a related supply-side issue. In the 1980s and the early part of the 1990s, the rural entrepreneurs created the miracle growth of what came to be known as TVEs (township and village enterprises). TVEs, unlike the coastal export industries that have taken off since the mid-1990s, were mainly domestically oriented. And herein lies the connections between financial reversals and the current global imbalances: China's TVEs began to atrophy in the mid-1990s due, among other reasons, to the increasing financing constraints (Woo 2005). It is plausible that the rural financial policy reversals played a role, if not a central role, in the increasing financing constraints facing the TVEs in the 1990s. Shifting the economic gravity from the TVEs to the export-oriented industries in the coastal regions of the country may have contributed to a production shift from domestic to a foreign orientation of the Chinese economy.

My purpose in this chapter is to settle historical debate. The main motivation behind writing this chapter was to come up with the right diagnosis and to identify right policy prescriptions. But here there are some strong headwinds. One of the likely legacies of the financial crisis originating from Wall Street is ideological in nature. The view that the lax financial supervisions of Wall Street lay at the heart of the financial exigencies of 2008 has reinforced the considerable political and intellectual priors toward statism in China. Because of China's massive stimulus program, the bank lending to the state sector has completely eclipsed that to the private sector. In 2009, there have been numerous instances of "reverse takeovers"—the state-sector companies, armed with massive liquidity—have acquired controls of private-sector firms in many industries and have branched out into new product and business territories.

If history is any guide, these developments are likely to exacerbate China's underconsumption woes. One of the main ideas of this chapter is that stronger financial controls on the part of the state, at least in the Chinese context, are actually associated with a depression of domestic consumption. I demonstrate this point not by theoretical speculations but by taking advantage of the considerable heterogeneity in China's reform experiences. Because China experienced both periods of financial liberalization and of financial reversals, we can then examine and contrast income and consumption developments during these different policy periods.

The third reason is that getting history right also helps us settle a theoretical debate on why consumption has declined relative to China's GDP. There are two schools of thought on the causes behind China's consumption decline. One emphasizes the role of rising savings rate in explaining China's declining consumption; the other stresses the importance of income growth (or lack thereof). (I will come back to these two hypotheses in greater details in the next section.) We can again go to history to see which theory is correct.

China's dramatic consumption decline—relative to GDP—coincided very closely in timing with the period of financial policy reversals. This consumption-finance nexus—in the context of China—was first identified by a pair of IMF economists. In their paper entitled, "Explaining China's Low Consumption," Jahingir Aziz and Li Cui showed that the often alleged role of rising private savings rate actually played a relatively minor role in explaining China's declining consumption. It was the low income growth, induced by financial repression, that led to the declining consumption (Aziz and Cui 2007). This chapter further explores this hypothesis but does so by presenting a counterfactual: What would happen to China's consumption if the financial repression were absent?

As it turns out, one does not have to resort to a counterfactual analysis to get at this question. One little-noted fact about Chinese economy is that the country experienced a massive consumption boom but it did so only in the 1980s. (This is true of China's overall consumption but especially true for rural consumption.) This consumption boom in the 1980s also coincided with a substantial extent of financial liberalization in the countryside.

Low income growth—induced by financial policy reversals—can lead to low consumption growth. The other channel is more direct. As will be shown below, during those periods when rural consumption grew rigorously, the rural consumption outpaced rural household income growth by a wide margin. This suggests, prima facie, that Chinese financial system was pro-consumption, if only episodically so. The view that Chinese financial system privileges production over consumption should not be generalized across all periods of economic reforms in China.

In order to fully understand the twists and turns in China's rural economy, it is important first to go over some high politics during this period. From the outset, we should note that we know far more about the "personnel" changes in the high politics of China than we do about why these "personnel" changes have contributed to economic policy changes. The policy deliberations are not observable while the personnel changes are. All I can do here is to offer some conjectures as to why these political twists and turns may have contributed to the policy changes. They are conjectures and should be interpreted as such. They are not hard and fast facts.

The starting point in our analysis is that Chinese economic reforms have been a highly heterogeneous process, that is, the reforms were, at one point in history, pro-income and pro-consumption rather than being single-mindedly pro-export and pro-production. The pro-income and pro-consumption phase of Chinese reforms tends to coincide with financial and broader liberalization episodes. This perspective has some policy relevance. If a part of solution to the unsustainable global imbalances is to create a policy environment to nurture a domestic consumption base, the best bet is to study how the country has successfully managed the balance between internal and external consumptions in its own history and what China needs to do to re-create those conditions.

If the household income and consumption growth is used as a metric (rather than GDP growth alone), the decade of the 1980s is the golden era of Chinese growth. It had all the telltale characteristics of a balanced and welfare-enhancing growth. GDP growth was rigorous but so was household income growth. Export was developing rapidly but so was domestic consumption. Far less known is the fact that the country implemented substantial financial liberalization—in the rural economy where the income and consumption growth was the most impressive.

Deng Xiaoping was at the helm of the political leadership but the daily management of the economy was in the hands of two individuals who were probably the most liberal—in both politics and economics—among all the Chinese leaders: Hu Yaobao and Zhao Ziyang. This era ended abruptly in 1989, the year when the Tiananmen crackdown ushered in a new group of leaders—Jiang Zemin as the party secretary and Zhu Rongji as the steward of economy. (Zhu became the executive deputy premier in 1991, governor of China's central bank in 1993, and then premier in 1998.) This is the period in which China was propelled to the forefront of the global economy. FDI increased sharply beginning in 1993, from less than 4 percent of China's fixed asset investments to a level approaching 15 to 20 percent. China entered into many bilateral trade and investment treaties and then culmi-nated its economic opening by making the most sweeping—and almost completely one-sided—concessions to the United States in its bid to join WTO. This was the golden era of globalization for China.

Much of the rural financial policy reversals documented later in this chapter occurred during this period. Rural income and consumption slowed down substantially in the 1990s. The rural household income grew at one-third the level of the 1980s; rural household consumption contracted even more, to about one-fifth the level. In fact, by one measure at least, rural household consumption contracted not just relatively but absolutely—in 1990, 1993, and 1998. It is also the period in which the divergence between external and internal liberalization was at its sharpest. Rural finance col-lapsed while the country lavished tax concessions and exemptions on for-eign investors. To understand the current underconsumption problem in China, it is critical to understand the policy orientation of the group of leaders who ruled China between 1989 and 2002.

This group of leaders—who can be best described as globalizers or the Chinese equivalents of technopols in Latin America—stepped down from power at the end of 2002. Since 2003, the new policy era—known as that of Hu Jintao and Wen Jiabao—represents a mix between reversing some of the rural policy legacies of the 1990s and exacerbating the state controls of investment and financing instruments (such as strengthening the state monopolies). For the rural sector as a whole, the leadership of Hu and Wen is a much welcomed relief. There were efforts to restart rural finance and to reduce rural taxation and service surcharges. As a whole, rural household income and consumption have recovered from the lackluster performances in the 1990s, although still far from the level prevailing during the decade of the 1980s.

What was the political economy background behind these three policy periods? Here we can offer some conjectures only. One observable effect of the Tiananmen event in 1989 is that the backgrounds and outlooks of Chi-nese leaders before and after Tiananmen were very different. Many of the reformist leaders before Tiananmen—symbolized by Zhao Ziyang in par-ticular—had first gained national prominence as a result of their economic stewardship of the poor rural provinces. More than any other politicians, Zhao and Wan Li had launched China's transformative rural reforms, in Sichuan and Anhui provinces, respectively. The leaders of the 1980s rep-resented the rural and, by implication, the more market-driven part of China.

The leaders of the 1990s came from entirely different backgrounds. The two top leaders, Jiang Zemin and Zhu Rongji, had built their political cre-dentials in the most state-controlled and least-reformed urban bastion of

China—Shanghai. This portrayal of Shanghai will be unfamiliar to many analysts of China. Contrary to the popular image, Shanghai for many years repressed private sector development to support large-scale state-owned enterprises. Using statistical analysis and a large-scale dataset, my colleague Yi Qian and I showed that Shanghai underperformed the rest of the country significantly in terms of private sector and entrepreneurial development (Huang and Qian 2010). The political ascendancy of urban bureaucrats to national positions ushered in a policy shift from rural bias of the 1980s to the urban bias of the 1990s.

Rural issues are once again the priority of the policy agenda of the current leadership. In a sign that signals a return to the policy model of the 1980s, since 2004 the leadership of Hu Jintao and Wen Jiabao has issued consecutive No. 1 documents focusing on rural issues. The Chinese government has also begun to acknowledge the dire situation of rural finance. Some efforts have been made to revive the deeply troubled rural credit cooperatives and to permit more competition in financial services. During his five years of leadership, Hu has also begun to address many of the social imbalances. The government has completely abolished agricultural taxes, started to reduce or waive educational charges in the rural areas, and experimented with a basic health insurance program that will cover the entire rural population by 2010.

There is emerging evidence that the rural situation has begun to turn around. The bad news is that the long neglect of the rural issues between 1989 and 2002 has created a "small base problem," that is, the faster rural household income growth was on the basis of a very small household income base. The rural per capita net household income in 2003 was only $327 (on the basis of official exchange rate conversion) compared with the per capita GDP of the country as a whole of $1,317. The gap is huge and by 2008, because of an acceleration of GDP growth—powered mainly by investments—the gap only became larger. The ratio of per capita net rural household income was 0.24 in 2003 but only 0.2 in 2008. The momentum of the urban bias that was firmly established and entrenched in the 1990s cannot be fully offset by a moderate change in the policy direction.

Debating China's Consumption Decline

A few stylized facts about China have captured the attention and imagination of the academic, policy, and corporate worlds. One is its rapid and consistent GDP growth. Since the early 1980s, China has led the world in the growth league, averaging a GDP growth annually around 10 percent for 30 years. The other fact is the rise of China as a global economic player. Its $2 trillion of foreign exchange reserves, its massive export machinery, and the ubiquitous presence of "Made in China" labels are all testimonies to the rise of China.

In this chapter, I also analyze two areas that are usually neglected in favor of China's GDP performance and its rise in the status of export producer. They are the virtual collapse of both rural household income growth and rural household consumption growth—all relative to GDP growth—during the same period when China established its substantial footprints in the world economy.

While much of the policy discussion on Chinese contributions to solving global imbalances has centered on its China's export prowess, it is not clear that this is the most productive way to frame the central issue. The right way to frame the issue is not why China exports so much but why it consumes so little. Framing the issue this way is important because it is not axiomatically obvious why China should be so dependent on exports. After all, China is or can be a relatively self-contained continental economy. It has a massive domestic market that has attracted attention of corporations all over the world and therefore should, in principle, attract the attention of its own corporations.

Probably the most important development—second only to the rise of the Chinese economy itself—is the dramatic decline of consumption within China, by some 20 percentage points since the late 1980s. A parallel development is the rising share of investment in Chinese GDP. That ratio has now well exceeded 50 percent, the highest ever in the history of the People's Republic of China and possibly in the world during the peace time.

Figure 4.1 presents data from World Bank's World Development Indicators database on household consumption as a ratio to GDP in China and in the United States. It shows a remarkable difference between the two countries that lie at the heart of the global imbalances: China's ratio, especially since 2000, declined substantially from 47 to 30 percent, whereas that of the United States rose. This is, in a nutshell, the genesis of the global imbalances.

The magnitude of China's consumption decline cannot be overstated. In 2000, the household consumption stood at 47 percent of the GDP; by 2007 it stood at 33 percent. China is not just underconsuming compared with the United States. No other major economies come remotely close to this low level of consumption. India's consumption is 20 percentage points higher; Brazil's, 25 percentage points higher. And there is nothing East Asian about China's low consumption level. Korea and Japan, two other quintessentially East Asian countries, consume more than 55 percent of their GDP.

The right set of questions to explore is about those factors that have shaped and oriented its domestic consumption pattern. On this issue, there

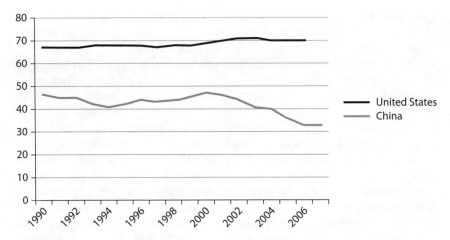

Figure 4.1 Household consumption/GDP ratios in China and the United States, 1990–2007. Source: Based on World Development Indicators database of the World Bank.

are two competing hypotheses. The first hypothesis—accepted by many economic, business, and policy analysts—states that Chinese low consumption is due to the high and rising savings rate. The second hypothesis—the one that this chapter will illustrate—states that the low consumption growth is due to low household income growth. And the low household income growth is in turn due to China's financial repression.

The established view among economists and Chinese policymakers is that China's consumption decline is a result of voluntary decisions on the part of the Chinese households to forgo current consumption in order to smooth out consumption pattern for the future (Chamon and Eswar 2008). The idea that Chinese households save a large portion of their income for precautionary purposes has also influenced the policy actions of the Chinese government. One part of the current stimulus package is devoted to rebuilding China's social protection. The rationale is to reduce the precautionary savings and to increase household consumption. This is considered as a vital part of the strategy to move China away from export-dependent model of economic development.

One implication of the precautionary-savings hypothesis is that savings rate has risen. Even on this seemingly factual point, the conclusion is not straightforward. In July 2009, Zhou Xiaochuan, the governor of the People's Bank of China—China's central bank—observed at a conference that "Chinese household savings rate, although high, has remained highly stable" and therefore household savings rate cannot explain China's consumption decline. According to the data he provided, between 1992 and 2007, China's household savings rate fluctuated closely around 20 percent of GDP. There was no substantial increase. But during the same period, corporate savings rate doubled from 11.3 percent of GDP to 22.9 percent and the government savings rate doubled from 4.4 to 8.1 percent.[4] There is no rudimentary support for the most basic point of the precautionary savings hypothesis.

Another implication of the precautionary-savings hypothesis is that income growth has to exceed consumption growth, but this is simply not what we observed in the data. Take the Chinese rural households as an example. A comparison of rural household income data with rural household consumption data shows that in most of the years between 1981 and 2005, consumption growth actually outpaced income growth rather than the other way around, which directly contradicts the precautionary savings hypothesis. The consumption growth in the 1981–88 period exceeded income growth by some 5 percentage points and by 3.3 percentage points between 2003 and 2005. Only during the 1989–2002 period did consumption lag income growth, but only by 1.5 percentage points. The whole idea that Chinese households are holding back their purchases despite sitting on a substantial pool of savings has very little empirical support, at least as far as the rural population is concerned.

There is, however, an entirely different hypothesis explaining why Chinese households are not consuming. This hypothesis assigns the main blame not to high savings rate but to low income growth. Indeed, there is descriptive evidence that this is the case. During the 1980s when the rural consumption grew at the fastest rate, rural income also grew at the fastest rate. In the 1990s, rural household income growth lagged GDP growth by more than 50 percent and the population-weighted rural and urban household income growth also lagged GDP growth (Huang 2008). Aziz and Cui (2007) first pointed out that the alleged rise of Chinese savings rate only explains about 1 out of 8 percent consumption decline in the 1990s and the 2000s. The two IMF economists speculated that it was the low household income growth—induced by financial repression—that caused the Chinese to underconsume.

In this section of the chapter, I first present data on rural household income development during the three decades of Chinese economic reforms. The main finding is that during these 30 years the Chinese rural household income performance has been highly heterogeneous, in sharp contrast to its consistently high GDP growth. The second section presents data on rural household consumption that reveals exactly the same pattern. At least descriptively, the Chinese rural household consumption patterns closely match the rural household income patterns. When income

grew rigorously, so did consumption. When income growth modera
consumption growth moderated as well.

Rural Household Income: A Story of Three Decades

As is well known, the Chinese GDP growth has been rapid and con
tent—in the range of 9 to 11 percent per annum for the last 30 years. Ma
analysts assumed, often implicitly, that the personal income—incoi
available to households to finance their consumption and savings—h
also grown at a comparable rate as GDP during the same period. (In fa
the terms, "GDP" and "income" are often used interchangeably in muc
of the discourse on Chinese economy, further reinforcing the view that th
two go together.)

This chapter presents data that calls into question this assumption.
show that in sharp contrast to the consistency of the GDP growth, house
hold income, especially on the part of rural households, has grown at a sub
stantially lower rate compared with GDP. My analysis and the policy impli
cations I draw explicitly treat household income growth as a more mean
ingful measure of economic performance. The household income measures
personal income or take-home pay. It refers to money that actually flows to
the household sector in the form of wage, benefits, transfer payments, property income (rental income, interest payments on bank deposits, or stock
dividends), and profits from operating small businesses. In other words,
unlike GDP, which is an abstract and mathematical construct, household
or personal income is closer to the concept of welfare than GDP.

Figure 4.2 presents Chinese economic performance broken down along
two dimensions. One is the familiar GDP dimension and in this case it is
the period average of the real GDP growth rates. The other is the relatively
less familiar dimension of the Chinese performance—the growth of the
household or personal income. Both types of growth statistics are in per
capita in terms calculated on the basis of their values expressed in the 1978
prices.

The graph breaks down the Chinese reform era by the three policy periods that were described at the beginning of this chapter: (1) 1979 to 1988,
the liberal period of Hu Yaobao and Zhao Ziyang; (2) 1989 to 2002, the
period of heavy-handed industrial policy approach that characterized the
rule of Jiang Zemin and Zhu Rongji; and (3) 2003 to 2008, when the leadership of Hu Jintao and Wen Jiabao, with a heavier focus on social issues,
came into power.

Let's first look at the GDP series. During the 1979–1988 period, Chinese
GDP per capita grew at an annual average rate of 8.5 percent, compared
with 8.1 percent during the 1989–2002. This is a small difference, and since

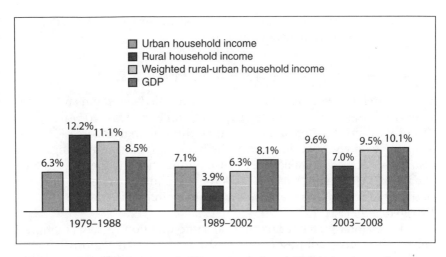

Figure 4.2 Rural and urban household income growth and GDP during three policy periods. Source: Rural and urban household surveys by NBS, various years.

the Chinese data are prone to substantial fluctuations, one can dismiss this difference of 0.4 percent as inconsequential and random. On the basis of GDP data alone, one would naturally draw the conclusion that the Chinese economic performance has been consistently robust.

In sharp contrast to the consistency of the high GDP growth, household income performance exhibits a highly varied pattern. In the 1980s, the per capita household income growth exceeded GDP per capita growth by 2.6 percent (11.1 percent minus 8.5 percent). In the 1990s, the pattern reversed itself. Then GDP growth kept up its fast pace from the previous decade, averaging at 8.1 percent annually between 1989 and 2002. But per capita household income growth slowed down sharply, from 11.1 percent in the previous decade to only 6.3 percent. The gap between household income growth and GDP growth is now negative: –1.8 percent (6.3 percent minus 8.1 percent). Between 2003 and 2008, the situation improved substantially. There was still a gap but the gap was narrowed to –0.6 percent. The biggest change between the 1980s and the 1990s has to do with the growth rates of rural household income. Rural household income in the 1980s grew at an extraordinarily robust rate. The average growth for the 1979–88 period was 12.2 percent (after inflation is excluded). In the 1990s, the growth slowed down to 3.9 percent. This was a momentous change between the two decades and it was the single most important factor contributing to the gap between GDP performance and the household income performance.

Consumption Boom and Bust

Now we turn to the consumption side of the equation. Figure 4.3 presents the real growth rates of per capita rural household consumption between 1981 and 2002. The deflators used in the calculation are the rural income deflators with 1978 as the base year—in order to make the comparison with the income side easier. Using other deflators, such as the rural retail price indexes, produces qualitatively similar results.

Several interesting patterns are easily discernible in the graph. First, there is a high degree of variance in the data. In the early 1980s, the rural household consumption grew extremely fast, 28 percent in 1981 and then 15 percent and 16 percent in 1982 and 1983. But there are also years in which rural consumption declined absolutely. For example, in 1990, the growth rate was –11.7 percent and then in 1993 it was –0.28 percent. (Another measure, detailed later, would show even steeper declines.) In sharp contrast, China's GDP per capita grew at 2.3 percent in 1990 and 12.7 percent in 1993. The divergence between rural household consumption and GDP growth is huge.

There are three general patterns in the data—boom, bust and recovery. The consumption boom in rural China happened in the 1980s. On aver-

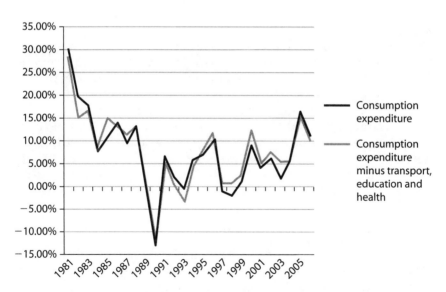

Figure 4.3 Real annual growth of per capita rural consumption (%), 1981–2002.
Source: Based on rural household surveys by NBS.

age, between 1981 and 1988, the rural consumption averaged 15 percent per year. This rapid consumption boom was followed by a bust that was extraordinarily long in duration—13 years between 1989 and 2002. During that period, the annual growth rates averaged only at 3.8 percent. Since 2002, the growth rate recovered. On average, the growth was 9.7 percent.

This is not a random periodization. These three different phases of rural consumption coincided closely with Chinese political cycles, as previously explained. What is significant here is that the consumption dynamics, just as income dynamics, closely follow the Chinese political cycles in ways that GDP does not. The third pattern in the data is that different measures of rural "consumption" produced slightly different results. This chapter uses two measures of consumption. One is the consumption expenditure on both goods and services. This is the most comprehensive measure of consumption. One problem with this measure is that it incorporates those expenditures on service items that are provided by the state monopolies. The prime examples of these service items are education, medical care, and telecommunication services. In the 1990s, the prices of these state-controlled monopoly services rose substantially, forcing the Chinese households to expend an increasingly larger share of their income on these items. This would make the consumption growth appear faster than the actual increase of rural welfare. So I have devised an alternative measure that nets out these monopoly service items. This is our narrow measure of consumption and is shown in by the line that netted out transportation, education, and medical services.

The two broad and narrow measures of consumption dovetail with each other in many years but in general the broad measure of consumption outpaced the narrow measure of consumption. This is especially the case in the 1990s. During the 1981–1988 period, the narrow consumption measure grew at an average annual rate of 15.4 percent, virtually identical to the broad measure growth (at 15.3 percent). However, between 1989 and 2002, the narrow consumption only grew at 2.4 percent, a sharp decline from the 3.9 percent in terms of the broad consumption measure. Since 2002, the two measures began to converge again: 8.8 percent in narrow measure vis-à-vis 9.7 percent in broad measure.

Rural Financial Development: Liberalization or Closure?

According to a famous formulation in the economics literature, the Chinese reform has been Pareto-optimal, in that it has created winners without creating losers (Lau, Qian, and Roland 2000). It is time to reassess this claim about the Chinese reforms.[5] The fact that the Chinese rural population has reaped decreasing returns from China's "miracle growth" is at direct odds with the view that the Chinese reforms have been Pareto-optimal.

Why did rural consumption in China fail to take off in the subsequent decades after an auspicious start in the 1980s? An accurate diagnosis of the causes of rural consumption stagnation is important for two reasons. First, it shows that a solution of the global imbalances is fundamentally domestic in nature rather than external. Thus the prevailing policy discussion fixated with exchange rate policies and bilateral trade imbalances is secondary to the issue at hand. Second, the prognosis being offered here—that it was China's dysfunctional financial system that played a role in curtailing China's domestic consumption—is particularly poignant today. In the United States, much of the policy and intellectual diagnosis of the financial crisis has heavily focused on the role of reckless financial innovations and a financial regulatory system in disarray. This makes eminent sense in the context of the United States, but for other developing countries, which start overwhelmingly from an initial position of heavy statist controls, the policy implications from the perspective of Wall Street are far from straightforward. The biggest concern is that China, and other developing countries, may draw precisely the wrong policy lessons from the financial crisis. Instead of further deregulations and liberalization, the Chinese policymakers may now feel intellectually empowered to strengthen the state controls of finance. This is why a case for financial reforms should not be made on the basis of theory or logic alone; it should be based squarely on China's own record of successes and failings. This is what I will do next.

It is well established that the Chinese financial system allocates credits poorly. In 1998, Nicholas Lardy argued that the Chinese reforms were unfinished because the financial system was unreformed (Lardy 1998). Some scholars, although acknowledging credit constraints in general, believe that the credit constraints varied considerably across different regions in China (Brandt and Li 2002). A number of researchers have noted the lack of progress in financial reforms. For example, Park and Shen (2001) note that authority to issue new loans became highly centralized during the course of the 1990s and a study by the International Finance Corporation, based on a survey in the late 1990s, shows that newer private firms faced greater financing constraints than older firms (Gregory, Tenev, and Wagle 2000). Other studies have reported on the deteriorating rural finance in the 1990s (International Fund for Agricultural Development 2002; Nyberg and Rozelle 1999).

What is less well known, however, is that China substantially liberalized its financial system in the 1980s. Elsewhere I have provided a detailed account of this development, using data as well as bank documents that went back as far as the early 1980s to reconstruct the history of this important period (Huang 2008). The inefficiency of the Chinese financial system is not simply a function of the historical legacies of central planning. Very early in the 1980s, as a part of the rural reforms, China moved quite far in financial liberalization in the countryside. Banks were instructed to support start-up businesses and to experiment with interest-rate liberalization. Widespread practices of informal finance were tolerated. In the 1980s, the vast majority of the start-up entrepreneurs were rural residents, and a sizeable fraction of them, ranging between 30 percent and 50 percent, reported being able to obtain loans from the banking system.

The new freedoms and a moderate amount of financial resources enabled these rural entrepreneurs to build thriving businesses, and some grew quite big in a matter of just a few years. The land leases were granted and then progressively lengthened. In some regions of the country, markets for land exchanges spontaneously sprang up. With more income and with a sense of security about their future, peasants began to spend on housing, clothing, home appliances, and other expenditures. These new expenditures, on top of a genuine sense of optimism about the future, contributed to the huge consumption growth documented in the previous section.

Microfinance flourished in China long before the term became popular in the economic lexicon. Early research by the World Bank reports very high levels of credit availability to the private sector in the 1980s. Lin (1990, fn. 3, 188) reports on a survey of 56 private firms in Tianjin in 1985. Of those firms with a total investment of less than 50,000 yuan, bank loans accounted for 38.8 percent of their funds; of those with an investment between 50,000 and 100,000 yuan, bank loans accounted for 43.6 percent; and of those firms with investments more than 100,000, bank loans accounted for 69.9 percent. One of the World Bank researchers, William Byrd (1990, 209), thus observes, "Banking institutions already see well-established private enterprises as solid borrowers." Byrd also reports that local banks that lent heavily to private-sector firms had lower nonperforming loan ratios.

In the 1990s, many of these productive policies were reversed. The authorities began to recentralize controls over financial resources, mainly to launch huge infrastructural projects in the urban areas. The milestone event was the 1994 tax reforms, which reassigned tax revenues massively in favor of the central government. Local governments, starved of resources but not reduced in size or political power, began to tax the peasants aggressively. In the wake of the Asian financial crisis, in the name of effecting financial stability, many of the small-scale financial institutions that supported rural entrepreneurs in the 1980s were closed down. This was a curious move as the state-owned banks instructed to take them over were in fact far less healthy and saddled with nonperforming loans. The state also forcefully imposed itself on land transactions. Conversions from agricultural to nonagricultural uses of land required not just approval from the state but also the state assumption of the land title itself.

It is important to stress why characterizing what happened to rural China as a reversal rather than simply as a steady-state financial repression is analytically important. Recall the earlier finding that China did experience a massive consumption boom but it was in the 1980s. The consumption constriction, however, occurred in the 1990s. The financial reversal story fits with this pattern of consumption data, that is, when China's financial system was relatively liberal, rural household consumption grew rapidly. When the financial system was more controlled, rural household consumption slowed down.

The modest recovery of rural consumption since 2002 also fits with our story. It is widely known that the leadership of Hu Jintao and Wen Jiabao—who came to power in 2003—began to address the rural problems in a proactive manner, by increasing investments in the rural sector, by reducing taxes and service charges, and by some modest financial liberalization. One can debate whether their measures are adequate to the monumental task—many of these measures were designed to reduce the rural tax rates rather than to augment income growth, but there is no doubt that Hu and Wen take rural issues more seriously than did the leadership of Jiang Zemin and Zhu Rongji (1989–2002).

Are there more systematic data illustrating this financial reversal? Our empirical investigation is based on "fixed-site rural household surveys" (FSRHS) conducted by the Chinese ministry of agriculture. One huge advantage of FSRHS is its longtime series that goes back to the mid-1980s. FSRHS is, to my knowledge, one of the most detailed datasets on Chinese rural households. Because of its longtime series, we are able to document the policy changes during the 1990s. In this chapter, I use a subset of FSRHS covering six provinces, Liaoning, Shandong, Hubei, Guangdong, Yunnan, and Gansu. My data set includes two well-known reformist provinces (Shandong and Guangdong) and it is not prima facie plausible to argue that financial policies retreated in these provinces but otherwise became more liberal in other provinces not covered by my dataset.

Let's take a look at the trends of loan access between the two waves of the FSRHS. Figure 4.4 shows the percentage shares of rural households reporting receiving either formal or informal loans in the survey. The blue bar represents the 1986–1991 wave of FSRHS and the red bar represents the 1995–2002 wave of FSRHS. The pattern is very clear: Far fewer rural households in the 1995–2002 wave reported receiving loans compared with the 1986–1991 wave. For example, the share of rural households reporting receiving formal loans declined from 37 percent to 13 percent. As pointed out before, rural China experienced a consumption boom in the 1980s and

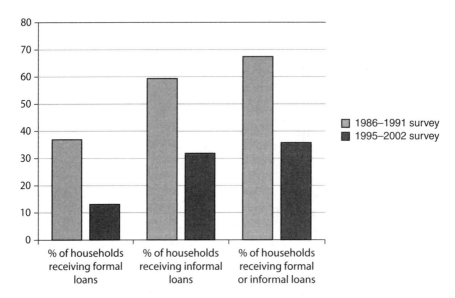

Figure 4.4 Percent of households receiving formal or informal loans. Source: Based on six-province sample of fixed household surveys by Chinese ministry of agriculture.

a consumption bust in the 1990s. At least descriptively, the consumption and financial developments correlate with each other closely.

Before I conclude that the financial access to rural households was reversed, it is necessary to also look at what happened to informal finance. One may argue that formal and informal loans are substitutes, that is, the decline of formal loans in the 1990s might have been partially or fully compensated for by the rise of informal loans. Since informal loans are less directly controlled by the state, the rising informal loans can be said to be a sign of financial liberalization (Allen, Qian, and Qian 2005). The evidence in my dataset does not support this assertion. The graph shows that formal and informal loans are not substitutes; they are actually complements, in other words, when formal loan access decreased, so did informal loan access. Access to informal loans declined from close 60 percent of the rural households in the 1980s to 30 percent in the 1990s. The graph also shows that loan access—whether formal or informal—was substantial in the 1980s. The last two bars denote access to either formal or informal loans. More than 67 percent of rural households reported receiving either formal or informal loans in the 1980s. This compares with 35 percent in the 1990s. The magnitude of financial reversal is extraordinary.

Conclusion

It should be noted explicitly that this chapter has not demonstrated the actual mechanisms that link the financial reversals in the 1990s with the changes in the rural income or consumption pattern in the 1980s and the 1990s. This fact-finding chapter identifies three significant developments in China that are not sufficiently highlighted in the literature as compared with its GDP growth and export performance. First, the rural household income and consumption grew in China but at a rate that lagged GDP growth rate by a wide margin. Second, there was an income and consumption boom in China but this boom occurred in the 1980s and that the boom was followed by an income and consumption bust in the 1990s. Third, this income and consumption boom and bust followed closely in timing with the cycles of financial liberalization and reversals in the 1980s and 1990s. In this chapter, I have established a coincidence in timing between these two developments. A future research agenda is to uncover and unpack the actual linkages between this financial development and the patterns of rural income and consumption developments.

The empirics of this chapter provide a basis for pondering the larger implications of the particular path whereby China has "risen." It is a rise that depends much more on domestic supply rather than domestic demand. One can debate whether this is the right strategy to steer a country the size of the Chinese economy but its global imprint is now very noticeable.

Below I offer some broad conjectures on the effects of this nature of the Chinese rise as well as some additional ideas explaining the income and consumption dynamics in rural China. China's rural economy holds the solution to China's macro imbalances. This is the first and the most important insight from my analysis. Understanding this basic fact—that a majority of the Chinese population experienced significant income and consumption slowdowns—points to the reason why the decoupling failed to work and why the Chinese growth is so appended to the growth in the United States. Not so long ago, Western analysts were peddling the idea that China had become a powerful economic center of its own, able not only to drive its own growth independent of the United States but also to power the global economy forward. The decoupling idea failed because its proponents have failed to understand that different components of the Chinese economy have churned out very different performances during this period of rapid GDP growth. The component of the Chinese economy that is most needed to "decouple" Chinese economy from the United States—its consumption base and its final demand—has grown much more slowly than China's GDP. That China grew matters for global imbalances but how it grows matters even more.

It should be noted that the massive liquidity-driven investment program China launched in 2009, while being effective in decoupling China from the recession in the United States, is almost certain going to exacerbate the imbalances in the Chinese economy and its effect is unlikely to be long-lasting.

There is also an issue whether the Chinese growth can be sustainable with a large portion of its population reaping a relatively small share of the growth dividends. This is where the standard analysis of the Chinese economy has faltered. In their enthusiastic pronouncements about the GDP numbers, few Western analysts have noticed that the household income actually grew very slowly, especially so in rural China, as demonstrated in the chapter. The slow household income growth, combined with rapid GDP growth, means that China has created a huge production capacity but it has done so at the expense of its own consumption potentials.

A deeper question is why Chinese growth has not unleashed China's domestic consumption potentials as rapidly as its rapid GDP growth would have implied. To answer this question, one needs to examine how the rapid GDP growth happened in China in the first place. Part of that growth is a result of economic liberalization but the market-driven part has fluctuated over time in its contribution to growth. Much of the GDP growth since the mid-1990s has been a result of government-organized massive investment drives in infrastructures, urban construction, and urbanization. The government- and investment-heavy growth strategy has not brought about a broad distribution of the benefits of growth. One little-known fact about China's consumption decline, as shown in figure 4.1, is that the consumption decline not only coincided in timing with China's entry into WTO but also with the acceleration of the pace of urbanization in China. The size of urban areas of China expanded dramatically since 2000. Urbanization would have normally raised income through productivity improvement and asset appreciations, so the question is why income growth has been slow during this period of rapid urbanization?

I started with an observation by Governor Zhou Xiaochuan about the stable household savings rate and rising government and corporate savings rate. Let's go back to his speech in which he made an observation about Chinese urbanization. Governor Zhou specifically singled out the role of urbanization in explaining why corporate savings rate has risen so fast. He argued that during the urbanization process personal income rose slowly relative to corporate profits. "The vast majority of Chinese laborers," he observed, "failed to share the rising profits with the corporate sector." In particular, he advocated increasing household asset income—income from stock ownership and land transactions—as a way to reduce the aggregate savings rate.[6]

My ongoing research on the linkages between some of the salient features of the Chinese growth strategy and its final demand formation has looked into this issue of urbanization and income nexus. So far, my research has not uncovered any statistically significant linkages between urbanization and household income growth (Huang 2009). One conjecture is the state ownership of land assets. China's rural-urban income inequality is already among the highest in the world and on top of this income inequality, another development closely associated with Chinese urbanization—the land grabs by local governments—is particularly worrisome from the point of view of preserving and growing wealth on the part of Chinese households. A huge portion of net worth on the part of the rural residents—more than 60 percent of the book value according to one estimate—was tied up in the housing structures on the land. One effect of the land grabs is to have enriched the coffers of the local governments rather than allowing the value of the appreciating land assets to accrue to the incumbency right holders.

Ultimately the question how to understand and resolve the Chinese portion of the global imbalances comes down to the nature of the Chinese economic growth. The basic point here is that the state-driven component of the Chinese growth—such as financial closures in the 1990s and state ownership of land assets—may be efficient mechanisms on the supply side but is not as efficient to create income growth and wealth on the part of households. This internal demand-supply imbalance lies at the heart of the external imbalances between China and the United States.

How to move China away from this set of economic imbalances? During the current economic downturn, a lot of policy and analytical attention has been focused on one particular form of economic imbalances—China's massive current account positive balances. The analytical framework behind this emphasis is that, for China to play a meaningful role in righting the current global imbalances, it needs to reduce its current surpluses and one of the policy instruments to do so is through current revaluation.

This chapter argues focusing so exclusively on China's "export fetishism" is the wrong framing of the entire issue. The right question to ask is not why the country exports so much but why the country consumes so little.

To get China out of its unsustainable dependency on external markets is not a narrow, technical export policy issue. Increasing the massive income and consumption potentials of China's population requires more and not less financial reform. Taking a page from China's own development in the 1980s and 1990s is highly instructive and points to a direction of bold institutional reforms rather than financial retrenchment. These reforms should encompass financial support for the small and medium businesses, legalizing informal finance, abolishing the *hukou* regulations (a system that restricted rural migrants from accessing urban public services and from acquiring full urban residency), granting full trading rights of land to rural residents, and above all improving village governance by strengthening village elections—another product of the 1980s.

Unfortunately, if the recent policy measures—such as the massive stimulus program that has strengthened China's state sector—are any indication, China is moving in the opposite direction (despite some positive developments in the rural economy). The current policy emphasis in China is on state controls rather than on liberalization. The lessons of history from China itself seem to be too easily ignored in favor of the lessons of recent history of the United States. If a new perspective on financial crisis is needed, it is one that argues that the right policy prescriptions should be firmly rooted in an accurate understanding of the reality on the ground in China itself rather than from lessons and experiences from a socioeconomic context that lacks any immediate empirical relevancy for China. This by no means is a new perspective and it is the type of thinking that has been traditionally used to resist the idea that countries should listen to Washington and to liberalize their economic and financial system. The supreme irony is that China is more willing to listen to Washington now when the policy message is more state controls of the financial sector. The fact that the Wall Street should be better and more stringently regulated should not imply that the Chinese rural residents should be denied financing and that Chinese private entrepreneurs should be banned from engaging in informal finance. China's own experience suggests precisely the opposite—that the right policy course is to undertake more financial liberalization.

Notes
1. For a comprehensive account of the Chinese economy, see Naughton (2007).
2. See the various estimates by Ravallion and Chen (2007).
3. In contrast, the fiscal centralization of 1993 is relatively better known to outside analysts although that development is often heralded as a positive development. It is beside the scope of this chapter, but I would argue that the fiscal recentralization of the early 1990s directionally affected rural income growth in the same way as the financial policy reversals described here.
4. This was widely reported in China. See http://news.stockstar.com/info/darticle.aspx?id=JL,20090704,00000676&columnid=1581
5. One issue that clouds an assessment of Chinese performance is whether the Chinese growth rate is as truly impressive as the official figures suggest. Young (2000) and Rawski (2001) raise questions about the veracity of the Chinese data. This is a complicated issue that I will not deal with here, except to note that bet-

ter research is needed to reconcile the well-documented microeconomic inefficiencies in the Chinese economy with the apparent macroeconomic success.
6. See http://news.stockstar.com/info/darticle.aspx?id=JL,20090704,00000676& columnid=1581.

References

Allen, Franklin, Jun Qian, and Meijun Qian. 2005. "Law, Finance and Economic Growth in China." *Journal of Financial Economics* 77(1): 57–116.

Aziz, Jahangir, and Li Cui. 2007. "Explaining China's Low Consumption: The Neglected Role of Household Income." Washington DC: International Monetary Fund.

Brandt, Loren, and Hongbin Li. 2002. "Bank Discrimination in Transition Economies: Ideology, Information or Incentives?" Ann Arbor: William Davidson Institute Working Paper No. 517.

Byrd, William A. 1990. "Entrepreneurship, Capital, and Ownership." In *China's Rural Industry,* edited by W. A. Byrd and Q. Lin. Oxford: Oxford University Press.

Chamon, Marcos, and Prasad Eswar. 2008. "Why Are Savings Rates of Urban Households in China Rising?" Washington DC: International Monetary Fund.

Dollar, David. 2005. "Globalization, Poverty, and Inequality since 1980." *World Bank Research Observer* 20 (2): 145–75.

Gregory, Neil F., Stoyan Tenev, and Dileep Wagle. 2000. *China's Emerging Private Enterprises: Prospects for the New Century.* Washington, DC: International Finance Corporation.

Huang, Yasheng. 2008. *Capitalism with Chinese Characteristics: Entrepreneurship and State during the Reform Era.* Cambridge, UK: Cambridge University Press.

———. 2009. "Urbanization, Hukou System and Government Land Ownership: Effects on Rural Migrant Workers and on Rural and Urban Hukou Residents." In *Paper Prepared for the OECD Conference on "Global Development Outlook."* Paris: OECD.

Huang, Yasheng, and Yi Qian, eds. 2010. In *Is Entrepreneurship Missing in Shanghai?* edited by J. Lerner and A. Shoar. Chicago: University of Chicago Press.

International Fund for Agricultural Development. 2002. *Rural Financial Services in China.* Rome: International Fund for Agricultural Development.

Lardy, Nicholas R. 1998. *China's Unfinished Economic Revolution.* Washington, DC: Brookings Institution.

Lau, Lawrence J., Yingyi Qian, and Gérard Roland. 2000. "Reform without Losers: An Interpretation of China's Dual-Track Approach to Transition." *Journal of Political Economy* 108(1): 120–43.

Lin, Qingsong 1990 "Private Enterprises: Their Emergence, Rapid Growth, and Problems In *China's Rural Industry: Structure, Development, and Reform,* edited by W. A. L. Byrd and Lin Qingsong. Washington, DC: World Bank.

Naughton, Barry. 2007. *The Chinese Economy: Transitions and Growth.* Cambridge, MA: The MIT Press.

Nyberg, Albert, and Scott Rozelle. 1999. *Accelerating China's Rural Transformation.* Washington, DC: World Bank.

Park, Albert, and Minggao Shen. 2001. "Decentralization in Financial Institutions: Theory and Evidence from China." Ann Arbor: Department of Economics, University of Michigan.

Ravallion, Martin, and Shaohua Chen. 2007. "China's (Uneven) Progress against Poverty." *Journal of Development Economics* 82 (1):1–42.

Rawski, Thomas G. 2001. "What Is Happening to China's GDP Statistics?" *China Economic Review* 12 (4): 347–54.

Riskin, Carl. 1987. *China's Political Economy.* Oxford: Oxford University Press.

Woo, Wing Thye. 2005. "China's Rural Enterprises in Crisis: The Role of Inadequate Financial Intermediation." In *Financial Sector Reform in China,* edited by Y. Huang, T. Saich and E. S. Steinfeld. Cambridge, MA: Harvard University Asia Center.

Young, Alwyn. 2000. "The Razor's Edge: Distortions and Incremental Reform in the People's Republic of China." *Quarterly Journal of Economics* 115 (4): 1091–1135.

CHAPTER 5

China's Response to the Global Economic Crisis

Minxin Pei

GLOBAL CRISES, whether wars among great powers or depressions, present serious challenges and create rare opportunities for countries to expand their power and influence—as long as they follow the dictates of realism and have the capacity to capitalize on the momentary weaknesses of their neighbors or chief competitors. In history, world order was profoundly reshaped each time such a crisis took place. For the international community today, one of the most important questions is whether the ongoing global economic crisis will produce a new world order. Will the crisis precipitate, if not accelerate, the decline of the West, particularly the United States? Will rising powers, especially China, take advantage of their relative short-term economic strengths and press for long-term geostrategic gains? Where will the new leadership for a post-crisis world order come from? Will rising powers like China and India, instead of competing for power, answer the call for global leadership and cooperation? Will the global economic crisis undermine China's economic growth model, which is heavily dependent on exports and an open world trading system?

Answers to these questions are important not only because they are on the minds of the leaders and policymakers around the world, but also because they can shed some light on the world order that is emerging from the wreckages of the worst economic crisis since the end of World War II. In this chapter, I attempt to use China as a test case to illustrate the competing forces and the complex dynamics that are pulling China's economic policy and the country's relationship with its most important trading partners—industrialized countries in the West—in different directions. I start with a general discussion of the conflict between China's dominant foreign policy philosophy, realism, and an ascending intellectual force, international liberalism. I then briefly analyze four examples that are representative of China's policy response to the global economic crisis. I finally assess the findings from these four examples and address the issue of whether China is integrating into the global economic order along the traditional realist route or the international liberal route.

Realism, Liberalism, and China's Role in the World

Specialists on Chinese foreign policy have long noted the dominant role played by realism in Chinese foreign policy (Christensen 1996). Realism has powerfully informed the perspectives of China's current leadership on international affairs for several reasons. First, the post-Mao leadership has apparently learned an important lesson from the dismal failures of Mao's radical foreign policy, which recklessly sought confrontation with the world's superpowers, almost simultaneously, frightened neighbors, plunged China into self-imposed isolation, and gravely undermined China's core national interests. As a result, Chinese foreign policy in the post-Mao era has been consistently based on China's national interests and not on leftist ideological values. Second, given the overriding priority accorded to domestic economic development by the ruling Chinese Communist Party, Beijing understandably views foreign policy as an instrument to advance its domestic objectives. A foreign policy based on realism apparently suits this requirement because such a mind-set combines cool-headed strategic calculation with clearly identified core foreign policy goals of the state (in the Chinese case, the pursuit of power through economic development).

Third, even though deep and extensive economic integration between China and the West has made China more vulnerable to the shocks to the global security order and economic system, China has not demonstrated a willingness to transform itself from an underpaying consumer of global public goods, such as access to markets, secure sea lanes, and East Asian regional stability, to a provider of global public goods. Free-riding on the status quo, which is underwritten in large part by American hegemony, China has become adept in extracting various types of benefits from the status quo without having to pay for its (costly) maintenance. In other words, adherence to the principles of liberal internationalism would have dictated that China contribute more to the maintenance of a global order it deems as beneficial. Fourth, and most importantly, realism has retained its grip on

China's strategic thinking because its ruling elites, despite their enormous success in delivering sustained rapid economic growth and raising China's international status since 1979, remain deeply skeptical about the West's true intention toward China. They constantly worry about the West's plot to subvert the Communist Party's rule through engagement and political infiltration (even though Beijing simultaneously welcomes such engagement because it provides huge economic benefits). America's apparently insuperable advantage in military capabilities adds additional anxiety to China's strategic planners because of its inability to protect its own vast trading routes. The rise of China as a trading nation that has become reliant on imported raw materials and energy further increases Beijing's sense of strategic vulnerability.

The policy response flowing from such a deeply engrained realist perspective is predictable: China will be pragmatic, calculating, and tactically flexible in the pursuit of its national interests. As a rising power haunted by the prospect of a hegemonic confrontation with the United States, China has managed to curb its ambitions and imposed strict self-restraints on challenging American hegemony. Yet, at the same time, it has implemented consistent policies that seek to protect China's core national interests through the means and instruments dictated by realism. The most illuminating example is China's military modernization. Acutely aware of its weaknesses in military capabilities, Chinese leaders have steadfastly implemented a program of military modernization designed to reduce China's vulnerabilities and develop critical capabilities that can deter the United States from taking actions harmful to core Chinese national interests (such as Taiwan).[1]

In the realm of international economics, however, realism offers limited useful policy guidance because of the interdependent nature of global commerce. While Chinese policymakers more or less are able to identify their core national interests and the means of protecting such interests in the realm of national security, they face greater difficulties when their core national *economic* interests are intertwined with countries that are and will likely be strategic competitors, such as the United States, Japan, or India. Under such circumstances, realism may not provide the most effective or productive guidance for policy. But will the alternative, international liberalism, offer a better solution?

Some leading scholars of Chinese foreign policy argue that, since the late 1970s, the Chinese government has gradually "socialized" itself into the international order (both the international security system and the global trading system). Beijing has adapted not only to the behavioral norms imposed by these systems but also accepted them as legitimate and binding (Johnston 2008). The idea of institutionalized integration into the international system—or *jiegui,* in Chinese—has become part of the official lexicon (Wang 2007). Rosemary Foot, an authority on Chinese foreign policy, carefully traced China's evolutionary cooperative behavior in world affairs and attributed such change to the ascendance of the "idea of a responsible state" among Chinese policymakers (Foot 2001). China's much-praised cooperative behavior during the East Asian Financial Crisis of 1997–98 was also cited as evidence of Beijing's shift toward international liberalism (at least in the area of global finance; Sohn 2008). A leading Chinese international relations expert bluntly asserted that even Chinese nationalism, a driving force of Chinese foreign policy, has acquired a more positive tendency toward international cooperation (Zimin 2005). However, some skeptics are not persuaded that Beijing's rhetoric on its international responsibility and recent examples of Chinese cooperative endeavors suggest a fundamental shift in Beijing's foreign policy philosophy (Lynch 2009).

Scholarly debate aside, conclusive evidence of a shift away from its realpolitik approach to international affairs to a new foreign policy paradigm remains elusive. A reasonable thing to say about Beijing's evolving thinking on its role in the world would be that while realism continues to serve as the principal guide for policy, Chinese leaders are open to ideas of multilateralism and other aspects of international liberalism and have taken tentative steps to incorporate these ideas in its foreign policy. The mixing of realpolitik thinking and liberalism unavoidably sends out mixed signals about China's intent. Chinese actions often confound foreign governments (even the Chinese themselves). Beijing can simultaneously appear a Machiavellian master of great power politics solely preoccupied with its narrow national interests and a responsible and cooperative player eager to fulfill its international obligations.

Nowhere is this contradiction more evident in how China behaved during the current global economic crisis. On the one hand, considerations of domestic political legitimacy and geopolitical interests dictate a realpolitik approach to the crisis. In terms of domestic political concerns, the essence of realism is subordinating foreign policy objectives to the internal political and economic constraints of maintaining elite unity, generating employment and demonstrating governmental effectiveness in face of an unprecedented economic shock. Another dimension in domestic politics is the power of various major domestic interest groups—the exporting sector, the bureaucracy, the financial industry, state-owned enterprises, and local governments. Even though China is ostensibly ruled by a one-party regime, it has a relatively weak central leadership that must make decisions through consensus and bargaining. As a result, powerful interest groups can influence key macroeconomic policy decisions. For instance, Beijing faced

If anything, the international community's expectations turned out to be too low. In less than a year after the announcement of its large stimulus package, China reported economic results that greatly exceeded these expectations. The earlier suspicion that the Chinese government double-counted some expenditures to boost the total amount of fiscal stimulus became a moot point because the fiscal stimulus appeared to have played a much less important role than the massive increases in new bank lending (roughly $1.2 trillion in new lending in the first six months of 2009) in bringing about a rapid rebound in the Chinese economy. In the second quarter of 2009, economic growth reached an astonishing annual rate of 15 percent.[10] The Asian Development Bank estimated in September 2009 that China's growth rate for the year would be 8.2 percent, slightly above the 8 percent target set by the Chinese government.[11] Although China's recovery appeared impressive, it did not get as an enthusiastic a reception as the stimulus package itself originally received. The international community was worried that China's huge increase in new bank loans could lead to lower credit quality and a large build-up of non-performing loans in the banking system in the future, thus brewing another banking crisis. More importantly, China achieved such a strong recovery mainly by repeating its tried-and-true growth strategy: investing in infrastructure and capital-intensive projects. While delivering a powerful boost to the growth rate in the short run, such a strategy further exacerbated China's structural imbalances (such as low consumption and overcapacity in the manufacturing sector). Most worrisome, government spending and bank lending (which favored state-controlled firms) crowded out private sector activities, creating new structural distortions in the economy.[12]

It is obviously too early to tell whether China will pay a high price for the stimulus package in the future. But one thing is sure: by managing to reignite its economic growth so quickly, China has demonstrated to the rest of the world the efficacy of its decision-making and policy-implementing apparatus.[13] More important, the Chinese government also showed that it would play by its own rules. Despite international criticisms of its unbalanced growth and mercantilist trade policy, Beijing appeared to believe that the most effective response to such criticisms is not accommodation, but perseverance and self-help. The top leadership of the Chinese Communist Party must be deeply aware that failure to achieve a quick economic recovery could be far more costly than the failure to accommodate the demands of its main trading partners that China rebalance its economy and adjust its currency policy. Should economic growth remain stagnant as a result of the global recession, China risked heightened domestic social tensions, erosion of the legitimacy of the ruling Communist Party, and elite disunity (since economic setbacks tend to set off power struggle within the authoritarian regime). In comparison, failure to rebalance its economy and reduce its huge current account surpluses might get Beijing bad press and, in the worst-case scenario, fuel protectionism abroad. Such consequences were by no means costless, but they were definitely bearable relative to the prospects of domestic social unrest and political instability.

The case of China's stimulus package offers a valuable lesson in understanding Chinese behavior as a great power. Its actions were centered on the principle of self-help: China deployed its vast financial resources to confront a dire crisis, without counting on its trading partners to come to its rescue. In designing and implementing its package, China apparently did not consider whether its proposed actions would further exacerbate the structural distortions in its economy that had substantially contributed to the global imbalances and the credit bubble in the West. All it cared was how to raise domestic growth rates. To be fair, China was not acting alone. Other major economies took similar actions to stave off an economic collapse. Nevertheless, it can be argued that China missed an opportunity to try out the liberal alternative. It could have redesigned its stimulus package so that its component policies would lift household consumption, boost the private sector, revalue its currency to reduce trade surpluses, and reorient its economy toward domestic consumption growth instead of exports. The fact that China did not do so with its stimulus package must have disappointed those who had initially expected Beijing to adopt a more liberal policy. Perhaps such expectations were naïve in the first. They were based neither on the realist principle in Chinese foreign policy nor on the complex domestic political realities in China that dictated a growth-at-all-cost policy response to the crisis.

Dethrone the Dollar?

As the epicenter of the global financial crisis, the United States has suffered significant losses both in terms of economic strengths and of political prestige. Although it is hard to determine whether the economic fallout from this crisis will irreversibly damage America's global hegemony, the U.S. dollar's position as the global reserve currency became a subject of debate and speculation. With ballooning budget deficits estimated to cause the net national debt to exceed the U.S. GDP within the next decade, foreign investors holding dollar-denominated assets understandably have grown concerned about the safety of their investments in American assets.

For China, which has become the largest holder of dollar-denominated assets (based on official U.S. Treasury data as of July 2009, China held $800 billion in U.S. Treasurys),[14] the dollar question has both economic and geopolitical implications. As an economic issue, China is legitimately worried about the safety of its dollar-denominated assets. America's long-term fiscal health and monetary policies, if generating inflationary pressures, are sure to lead to the devaluation of the dollar and result in massive losses for China. As a geopolitical issue, the dollar question poses a more tricky challenge for Beijing. Without doubt, the United States' ability to borrow in its own currency confers enormous strategic advantage to Washington because such ability allows Washington to tap global savings to fund its needs (whether excess private consumption or government borrowing). More important, Washington also has the capacity to reduce its foreign debt in real terms through inflation, at the expense of its foreign creditors. For China, America's enjoyment of this seigneurage right provokes both resentment and relief. On the one hand, China's ruling elites clearly understand how such seigneurage can further cement America's hegemony and make it even more difficult for China to challenge the United States' global dominance. On the other hand, such seigneurage allows the Americans to overconsume and run large current account deficits, thus creating the excess demand for Chinese exports and directly contributing to China's growth, which underwrites the political legitimacy of the Chinese Communist Party.[15]

Prior to the crisis, Beijing maintained a studious silence on the future of the dollar even though China's central bank had already accumulated massive dollar-denominated holdings. But during the crisis, particularly after the Federal Reserve began to pump liquidity into the U.S. financial system through the purchase of Treasurys and mortgage-backed securities, the perception that Washington was deliberately inflating away its foreign debt started to take hold in China.) "These purchases would expand the central bank's balance sheet, probably via printing money and would therefore be dollar-negative," according to a well-known Chinese economist (Huang 2009). Heated discussions on the intent of Washington's actions filled China's business press and Internet, gradually generating rising pressure on the Chinese government to defend its policy of investing in the U.S. Treasurys and mortgage-backed securities. In response, Chinese premier Wen Jiabao publicly raised worries about "safety" of China's investments in American assets in a press conference on March 12, 2009. "We have lent a huge amount of money to the U.S., so of course we are concerned about the safety of our assets. Frankly speaking, I do have some worries," Wen said (Baston 2009). But the most powerful, if not the most controversial, statement on the status of the dollar was made by Zhou Xiaochuan, the governor of the People's Bank of China, which is the country's central bank, on March 23, 2009. In three published essays, Zhou elaborated China's official position on the international monetary system. In one essay, "Thoughts on the Reform of the International Currency System," he called for a new "super-sovereign" reserve currency decoupled from sovereign nations, thus explicitly needs to be created. Specifically, Zhou's idea of a "super-sovereign" reserve currency is based on the expansion of the "special drawing rights" (SDRs) issued by the IMF. Technically, SDRs are a basket of four hard currencies (the U.S. dollar, the euro, the Japanese yen, and the British pound). The replacement of the dollar by SDRs, should it happen, would significantly weaken the position of the dollar.

Senior American officials reacted negatively to Zhou's proposal. President Barack Obama, Treasury Secretary Timothy Geithner, and Federal Reserve Chairman Ben S. Bernanke dismissed such a move publicly (Yanping 2009). However, Zhou's idea elicited sympathetic response from other countries, particularly Russia, India, and Brazil. The IMF's Dominique Strauss-Kahn also voiced his tentative support by saying that a "conversation over a new type of international reserve currency would be completely reasonable."[16] Interestingly, while Zhou's proposal subsequently became the official policy of the People's Bank of China, which in June 2009 reiterated that China would push reform of the international currency system to make it more diversified and reasonable,[17] none of China's top leaders, such as President Hu Jintao, Premier Wen, or Vice Premier Wang Qishan (who was in charge of China's strategic economic dialogue with the United States) officially endorsed Zhou's proposal.

Beijing's subtle position on the dollar contrasted sharply with Moscow's. During the crisis, top Russian leaders seldom missed an opportunity to call for the replacement of the dollar as *the* international reserve currency. For example, on January 28, 2009, Russian premier Vladimir Putin, in keynote speech to the World Economic Forum in Davos, Switzerland, warned that "excessive dependence on what is basically the only reserve currency is dangerous for the world economy."[18]

So the question remains whether China was genuinely seeking to dethrone the U.S. dollar as the international reserve currency, both to reduce its financial exposure and to undercut the U.S. geopolitical influence derived from the dollar's role as the international reserve currency. Some American observers saw a dark plot. The *Wall Street Journal* considered Zhou's move to be "part of China's increasingly assertive approach to shaping the global response to the financial crisis" (Batson 2009). However, as this brief discussion shows, the evidence is mixed. The motivations for Beijing to publicly cast doubts on the future of the dollar were complex. Chinese leaders voiced worries about the dollar and called for a new international reserve currency in part, at least, to respond to rising domestic criticisms of their decision to purchase massive quantities of U.S. Treasurys. Even though China remains a one-party dictatorship, public opinion, especially that nationalistic variety, has begun to constrain its leaders' foreign policy choices,[19] Moreover, Beijing's interests in protecting the value of its dollar assets are legitimate and genuine. Even though they are reluctant to admit it openly, Chinese leaders also realize that their policy of using undervalued Chinese currency, the RMB, to gain export price competitiveness was responsible for the soaring trade surpluses and the rapid increase in their foreign currency reserves. As a result, China finds itself trapped in a love-hate relationship with the dollar. As Nobel laureate Paul Krugman (2009) observed, China "can neither get itself out (of the dollar trap) nor change the policies that put it in that trap in the first place." Another dimension of China's dollar trap is that, as the largest holder of dollar assets, China has the capacity to inflict enormous financial damage to itself if it keeps up heated rhetoric on the undesirability of holding dollar assets. Its prognosis about the future weakness of the dollar can become self-fulfilling. Such economic interdependence has greatly constrained Chinese leaders' realist instincts to seek geopolitical advantages when the United States is weak. They fully understand that China cannot credibly undermine the status and the future of the dollar, hence America's geopolitical influence, without also suffering huge financial losses themselves. As a result, Chinese leaders resorted to a third way: using a well-respected technocrat to call for a new international reserve currency on purely economic grounds to ward off domestic political pressure, but refraining from expending real political capital to push for this move.

Acquisition of Natural Resources

As a trading nation dependent heavily on the import of commodities, China has long acutely felt its strategic vulnerability to the lack of secure access to natural resources, particularly oil and critical minerals. As a result, the central government in Beijing has encouraged Chinese firms to "go out"—extending their reach beyond Chinese borders. Even though the "going-out" strategy encompasses many economic sectors, ranging from telecom services, manufacturing, and natural resources, it is China's focus on acquisition of natural resources assets (such as equity stakes) that has received most attention in the international community and sounded alarm to Western governments and firms.[20] Indeed, the 2009 U.S. National Intelligence Strategy explicitly identifies China's "natural resources diplomacy" as a challenge to American national interest.[21] In addition to reducing its vulnerability to insecure access to natural resources, significant acquisition of natural resources has another valuable function of diversifying China's foreign investments. As a result of its huge trade surpluses, China has amassed more than $2 trillion foreign exchange reserves, nearly two-thirds of which are invested in dollar assets. As the value of the dollar is likely to fall due to America's deteriorating fiscal conditions, a defensive diversification strategy would call for acquiring real assets, such as natural resources. However, since purchasing current stocks of commodities is not a feasible solution due to the costs of storage and the upward pressures on their prices caused by Chinese purchases, the most sensible approach would be equity stakes in natural resources producers which could yield managerial control and financial returns.

Unfortunately, prior to the onset of the global financial crisis, China's strategy to acquire natural resources assets has encountered strong resistance abroad and yielded mixed results.[22] Its most high-profile failure was undoubtedly the abortive attempt by the China National Offshore Oil Corporation (CNOOC) to buy the American oil and gas company Unocal in 2005 when the U.S. Congress effectively scuttled the deal by raising the national security concerns about the proposed Chinese acquisition. But China's efforts in other regions produced better results. For example, before the outbreak of the global economic crisis in September 2008, China had invested $7 billion and, in returned, obtained around 400,000 barrels a day of oil from new and relatively small producers in Africa and Latin America, high-risk regions that had deterred Western companies from entry (Hulbert 2009).

How has the global financial crisis affected China's ability to carry out its natural resources strategy? On the surface, with the world plunged into a deep recession and commodities prices collapsing, China should be in a much stronger position during the global economic crisis to advance its strategic objectives in this area. Compared with liquidity-constrained foreign companies and financial institutions, Chinese firms have ample liquidity, healthy corporate balance sheet, and strong government support. The crisis, as the saying goes in Chinese, is an opportunity too good to miss.

Published reports seem to confirm that Chinese companies, nearly all of them state-controlled entities, indeed significantly intensified their efforts to acquire natural resources assets during the current economic crisis. According to *Caijing* magazine, in January and February 2009, Chinese companies initiated 22 overseas acquisitions worth $16.3 billion in total. If the pace continues, the total value of acquisitions would be nearly double 2008's of $52.1 billion. Almost all the major acquisitions in 2009 were in the natural resources sector. Such a percentage is a noticeable change from 2008 when 60 percent of China's outbound investment was in the natural resource sector (Zhen 2009). Particularly noteworthy were energy deals struck by China with Russia and Iran, two major oil producers whose interests are often at odds with the West.

In the case of Russia, China agreed to provide a $25 billion loan secured by Russia's oil exports. The huge loan would help Rosneft Oil Company and Transneft Pipeline Company, both Russian state-run entities, supply

300,000 barrels a day of oil to China over the next 20 years (the agreement will take effect in 2011 once the East-Siberia Pacific Ocean pipeline is completed; Hulbert 2009). As the largest trade financing agreement between Russia and China, the loan-for-oil deal apparently has strengthened both countries' economic ties and improved China's energy security.

In January 2009, China also signed a $1.7 billion oil contract with Iran to develop a portion of the North Azadegan oil field between the National Iranian Oil Company (NIOC) and China National Petroleum Corporation (CNPC) that will produce 75,000 barrels a day over a four-year period (Hulbert 2009). In August 2009, PetroChina, Asia's largest oil company, agreed to purchase $41 billion worth of Australian natural gas from a field off Australia's northwestern coast. The biggest energy prize won by China during the crisis was the Canada-based energy firm, Addax Petroleum. In October 2009, Chinese oil company Sinopec successfully closed a $7.22 billion takeover deal for the multinational oil and gas exploration company Addax Petroleum, which has stakes in oil fields in West Africa and Iraq. Another major state-controlled natural resources firm, China's Minmetals, paid $1.4 billion for an Australian miner, OZ Minerals. Although Australian officials were uncomfortable with its natural resources in foreign hands, it was unwilling to turn away the opportunity to help its oil industry.[23] Other countries with which China seeks oil from include Venezuela, Brazil, Angola, and Sudan (Cook and Lam 2009).

With respect to China's mining ventures abroad, private enterprises have signed important deals with Australian and Zambian mining groups. February saw the Shenzhen Zhongjin Lingnan Nonfemet Company Limited, China's third-largest zinc producer, buy a majority stake in Perilya, a medium-sized zinc and lead producer, for about $29 billion.[24] In addition, Hunan Valin Iron and Steel obtained a 16.5 percent stake in Fortescue Metals Group Limited, Australia's third-largest iron ore producer, for $771 million. As the largest acquisition by a Chinese company in the Australian mining sector, the purchase of OZ Minerals gave the Chinese access to an immense range of mining assets, such as the Sepon copper and gold mine in Laos and the Century and Rosebery zinc mines in Australia.[25] In Zambia, the Chinese firm NFC African Mining PLC has taken over and promising to inject $400 million in Zambia's top cobalt producer, Luanshya Copper Mines (Cook and Lam 2009). By maintaining a financial stake in various mining companies, China can ensure a steady supply of long-term materials to support domestic infrastructure development. However, China's most important attempt to strengthen its natural resources security during this crisis—a planned $18 billion deal to acquire nearly 20 percent of Rio Tinto, the world's second largest mining giant—came to nothing after opposition from shareholders and Australian politicians forced Rio Tinto's management to abandon the proposed acquisition by Chinalco, China's state-owned aluminum producer, dealing Beijing a severe blow reminiscent of the infamous CNOOC's failed attempt to buy Unocal.

All in all, China's intensified attempts to acquire natural resources assets are perfectly understandable from a realist perspective. Beijing has no faith in the current system that allocates natural resources. Unlike markets for manufactured goods, the global markets for natural resources are severely distorted due to the concentration of control by either a small number of Western giants (such as energy and minerals) or sovereign nations that view natural resources as their instruments of power (such as Russia and OPEC member states). China has little confidence in those players' reliability as suppliers of its imported natural resources. Although the "go-out" strategy to acquire assets in the natural resources sector is fraught with political and economic risks, Beijing sees no alternative but to continue its efforts. In the crisis, Beijing apparently achieved greater success, as market conditions gave Chinese cash-rich firms greater bargaining power. But the failure to clinch the Rio Tinto deal shows that the goal of achieving secure access to natural resources remains elusive for China.

Summit Politics

Summit meetings of the leaders of the world's most powerful countries are important symbolic affairs even though expectations of substantive achievements of these summits are generally low. Nevertheless, the gathering of G-20, which consisted of the world's 20 largest economies, in London in April 2009 was an important milestone for China. The second G-20 summit was given greater importance largely because the first G-20 summit in Washington in November 2008 was a desultory affair, with hasty preparations, little leadership, and no actionable agenda. For China, the London summit should have been an opportunity to demonstrate leadership and commitment to international cooperation. Compared with other participating nations at the London summit, China was in a much stronger position. With the implementation of its large stimulus package under way, the Chinese economy appeared to have bottomed out in the first quarter of 2009. The call for a new international reserve currency by China's central bank governor, Zhou Xiaochuan, in late March had seized headlines around the world. With its $2 trillion foreign exchange reserves, China was counted on by the international community to play a key role in supplying the fresh funds to recapitalize the International Monetary Fund. Some Western leaders, such as then British Prime Minister Gordon Brown, even suggested that China contribute a substantial sum to supporting poor countries hit by the economic crisis. Perception of China's economic strengths and diplomatic clout was such that prominent opinion makers had started proposing the establishment of a "G-2"—the United States and China—as a partnership for resolving global economic crisis. Fred Bergsten, an influential international economist and director of Washington-based think tank the Peterson Institute for International Economics explicitly called for "a partnership of equals" between the United States and China in an essay in *Foreign Affairs* (Bergsten 2008).

Did China Deliver?

In rhetoric, China certainly did not disappoint. Its president, Hu Jintao, emphasized the right themes in his public pronouncements. He called for international cooperation in achieving a speedy recovery of the world economy; he urged improving regulation of the financial sector and giving developing countries a bigger say in global economic decisions. In addition, he challenged developed nations to provide additional support to developing countries in order for them to weather the crisis. To further put the West on the defensive, Hu warned that trade protectionism would violate the consensus reached at the Washington summit in November 2008 in which protectionism was rejected.[26]

Rhetoric aside, China's actions at the London summit sent a mixed signal. Resoundingly rejecting the suggestion that China contribute more to a new IMF new lending program on the ground that it would not pay additional capital in excess of four percent of the total new recapitalization program (because China has only 4 percent of the voting rights at the IMF), Beijing nevertheless agreed to purchase $50 billion in IMF bonds (a promise China carried out in September 2009), in an apparent gesture to demonstrate that it was both principled and flexible. Except for this important concession, China worked hard to defend its core national interests. When French president Nicolas Sarkozy proposed an initiative on off-shore banking that would put Hong Kong and Macau on an OECD list as "tax havens," Hu strenuously opposed such a move and managed to keep these two Chinese cities off the list, in a relatively rare case of asserting China's influence openly. Hu's action was particularly noteworthy because China is not a member of the OECD.

Notably, despite international perception of its strengths and expectations of its ambitions and assertiveness, China kept a low profile during the London summit, as it did during the Washington summit. It did not advance new proposals for reforming the world's financial markets or regulatory framework, nor did it make any promises of development aid or trade liberalization measures. China's cautious behavior at the London summit was perfectly understandable. Its realist instincts constrained China from making commitments or participating in international cooperative schemes that could result in significant outlays of its precious economic resources for practically no real gains in national interests. Of course, China would be praised as a responsible "stakeholder," but this would have been very expensive public relations. China was loath to create a precedent, such as contributing to the IMF's recapitalization program beyond Beijing's legal obligations. As a power that cherished its freedom of action but also wishes to demonstrate its willingness to shoulder (limited) international responsibilities, China sent out mixed signals at the London summit. It might have disappointed enthusiasts who had expected Beijing to come forward with a more generous gesture of support for a new global economic order, but what mattered to China was the defense of its national interests bottom line.

China's behavior at the G-20 summit in Pittsburgh in September 2009 was a variation on the same theme: demonstrating willingness to cooperate while fiercely guarding Chinese core interests. On the eve of the Pittsburgh summit, President Hu Jintao announced at the United Nations that China would invest heavily in clean energy and reduce the carbon intensity of its economy. Although Hu did not accept any mandatory emission caps for China, his announcement was greeted positively by the international community, which was eager for global leadership on the eve of the UN Copenhagen Conference on Climate Change scheduled for December 2009. On China's pet issue of a new super-sovereign international reserve currency, Beijing exhibited a less combative stance. Its senior financial officials barely mentioned the issue before the Pittsburgh summit. China also displayed its customary restraint when the Obama administration announced, on the eve of the G-20 summit, antidumping tariffs on China-made tires. While Washington's action clearly annoyed Beijing and made the Obama administration look weak on free trade, China retaliated with relatively minor measures, such as antidumping tariffs on American-made auto parts and chicken products. The last thing Beijing wanted was a major disruption in the all-important Sino-American trade ties before an important international gathering.

Beneath this surface of restraint and self-effacement, however, China defended its key interests tenaciously. As a rising power underrepresented in multilateral international financial institutions, China showed, whenever the opportunity arose, its impatience with the slow pace of reform that would give large developing countries, such as China, India, and Brazil, commensurate representation in these bodies. So on the eve of the Pittsburgh summit, senior Chinese officials reiterated Beijing's call for transferring voting power as well as senior executive positions in the World Bank and the IMF held by developed nations to developing countries.[27] The tactic apparently had to objectives: putting the West on the defensive and making China appear as the champion of the interests of developing countries.

A more vital area of concern to China at the Pittsburgh summit was the issue of global imbalances. Since China's external surplus in 2008 was the largest in the world both in absolute terms and as a share of GDP, Beijing has been blamed for contributing to the credit bubble. A key topic on the agenda of the Pittsburgh summit, put forth by the United States, was global imbalances and sustainable development. The Chinese government was not prepared to leave even such implicit charges against its macroeconomic policy unanswered. Sounding a bit defensive, the Chinese foreign ministry flatly rejected criticisms of China's economic policy. It insisted that "global economic imbalance is a special phenomenon in the process of economic globalization and due to many complex factors." Implicitly, Beijing did not want its high savings, low consumption, and trade surpluses blamed as causes of the global imbalances. How President Hu Jintao and his retinue fought to defend China's reputation and macroeconomic policy at the Pittsburgh summit remains unknown. But judging by the pronouncements of the summit, they must have been quite effective and successful. There were no critical references to the key elements of China's macroeconomic policy, most importantly its undervalued currency. With the support of the Europeans, American President Barack Obama presented a modest proposal suggesting a peer-review process overseen by the IMF to tackle global imbalances.

With its economy rebounding at a faster rate than expected, China could afford to dig in its heels at the summit. While all the other major economies were mired in recession or showed weak recoveries, China's growth returned to its double-digit pace in the second quarter of 2008, a development credited with boosting commodity prices and confidence around the world. Flaunting its economic success, China uncharacteristically seemed to enjoy basking in flattering global spotlight. Premier Wen Jiaobao cited China's aggressive stimulus package as the key to China's rapid recovery and flatly rejected the notion of an "exit strategy"—reducing fiscal and monetary stimulus so that a more sustainable growth cycle could return. On September 10, two weeks before the Pittsburgh summit, Premier Wen vowed that China "cannot and will not" abandon its monetary or fiscal stimulus anytime soon.[28] Intended to counter Western criticisms that China's mammoth stimulus had distorted its economy and fueled new asset bubbles, such statements also convey an unmistakable message about the superiority of the Chinese system and its effectiveness in responding to crisis.

Conclusion

To the extent that China has fared much better than all the other major economies, it has definitely seen its strategic positions strengthened. Martin Wolf, the insightful columnist for the *Financial Times*, pronounced that "China has emerged as the most significant winner from the global financial and economic crisis" (Wolf 2009). No doubt, this statement is true as far as the facts go. Compared with its main trading partners, China has indeed weathered the global economic tsunami in remarkably good shape: its growth rate has recovered fast (though not to the pre-crisis double-digit pace); its financial institutions boast strong balance sheets (though a huge amount of bad credit looms in the future due to the relaxation of credit standards during the crisis).[29] Most important, what matters for China is the perception, shared nearly universally, that the new Middle Kingdom has turned the crisis into an opportunity to accelerate its ascendance.

Without a doubt, the China model has emerged from the crisis an apparent winner as well. This should not be a surprise. If anything, the China model, which is essentially a statist development model, is ideally suited to a massive negative demand shock, as one produced by this crisis. With a combination of luck (China entered the crisis with a relatively strong fiscal balance sheet and a recapitalized banking system), decisive policymaking (which a one-party state is known for), and direct control of the banks (all the largest banks in China are majority-owned by the state and their executives appointed by the Chinese Communist Party), China had the resources, the decision-making mechanisms, and the institutional instruments to pump enormous public resources into the economy when the crisis hit. However, it may be premature to declare that the China model has proved its efficacy and will endure. A statist approach to economic crisis is normally more effective than a purely market-based approach. But one should not confuse crisis management with sustainable development. No doubt, the China model has proved effective in fighting the global crisis, but Beijing's performance during the crisis, however impressive, should not be taken as an indication that the same statist approach will work as well in addressing deeply embedded structural problems and long-term developmental challenges, such as inequality, domestic economic imbalances, weak social safety nets, and inadequate government services. Since many of these problems are themselves the results of a statist developmental strategy, it is difficult to imagine that the same approach will provide effective solutions.

On the external front, the question of whether China is ready to act as a responsible great power committed to a more expansive and cooperative role in global affairs remains unresolved. The four case studies illustrate that, by and large, China continues to set its national and international agenda according to the precepts of realism. In the case of designing and implementing a massive domestic stimulus package, China was primarily concerned with its short-term objective of reviving economic growth, even at the risk of worsening structural imbalances and thereby fueling trade tensions with the West in the future. China's quest for natural resources continued apace during the crisis as well, reflecting its strategic desire to seek secure access to the critical raw materials needed for its modernization. This case only serves to underscore China's continuing lack of faith in the global commodities market or an international cooperative regime that will provide such secure access. The principle of self-help thus predominated the thinking of Chinese policymakers. The two other cases—China's call for a new international reserve currency and Chinese behavior during the G-20 summits in the crisis—provide a more mixed picture of Chinese intention. While Chinese behavior clearly did not deviate from their habitual desire to protect and advance China's national interests, it nevertheless reflected a more cooperative attitude. In neither case did China genuinely try to press for strategic advantages at the expense of the United States or the West. By calling for a new international reserve currency, a proposal that echoed positively among many Western, though non-U.S., officials, China put on the agenda an important policy item that merits serious consideration. Of course, China would have strengthened its case enormously by taking substantive steps to reform its own currency management regime. The fact that China did not do so again raised doubts about the true intent of China's action. Perhaps the most heartening example of China's evolving stance on international cooperation was its participation in the three G-20 summits. Even though it did not exert leadership or make an extraordinary gesture to show its readiness to assume greater global responsibilities, China nevertheless underscored its (rhetorical) commitment to such responsibilities and its purchase of $50 billion IMF bonds served as a first step in this direction.

Of course, the crisis is not over, and Beijing can conceivably make new commitments or undertake additional initiatives to demonstrate its leadership in the global economy and indicate a clear break with its realpolitik approach to international affairs. But based on the evidence so far, the signals from Beijing are decidedly mixed.

Notes

1. See the report by an independent task force sponsored by the Council on Foreign Relations 2007.
2. A good summary of the key features of the China model might be found in Ramo 2004.

3. The best summary of China's internal and external imbalances is Nicholas Lardy's 2006 policy brief, "China: Toward a Consumption-Driven Growth Path."

4. "China's 4 Trillion Yuan Stimulus to Boost Economy, Domestic Demand." *Xinhua*, November 9, 2008.

5. See Atkinson 2008.

6. "China's $586-Billion Stimulus Plan Could Boost World Economy," *Los Angeles Times*, November 9, 2008.

7. "China Unveils Sweeping Plan for Economy," *The New York Times*, November 9, 2008.

8. "China Seeks Stimulation," *The Economist*, November 10, 2008.

9. World Bank 2008.

10. "Poll Shows China's Growth Surge Expected to Slow," *The Wall Street Journal*, July 22, 2009; "Recovery Picks Up in China as U.S. Still Ails," *The New York Times*, September 18, 2009.

11. "Asia Rebounding Rapidly, Bank Reports," *The New York Times*, September 22, 2009.

12. See analysis by the IMF, July 23, 2009, available at www.imf.org/external/np/tr/2009/tr072309.htm.

13. Also see Pritchett's chapter in this book on the related subject.

14. U.S. Treasury. 2009.

15. As the party can no longer legitimize its rule on the basis of the Marxist ideology, it justifies its authority by its ability to deliver a rising standard of living to the Chinese people. That is why growth is of paramount importance to the party.

16. Quoted in *Caijing*, March 30, 2009.

17. *Wall Street Journal.* June 29, 2009. "Beijing Formalizes Call for New Reserve Currency."

18. Russia Today, January 28, 2009. "Putin's Speech at Davos World Economic Forum." Available at www.russiatoday.com/Top_News/2009–01–28/Putin_s_speech_at_Davos_World_Economic_Forum.html

19. Roy 2009.

20. See Alden 2005.

21. Director of National Intelligence 2009.

22. The International Crisis Group 2008; Zweig and Jianhai 2005

23. *International Business Times,* June 12, 2009, Available at www.ibtimes.com.au/articles/20090612/china-039minmetals-seals4-bln-minerals-deal.htm.

24. "China's Shopping Spree." *The Independent,* March 18, 2009, www.independent.co.uk/news/business/analysis-and-features/chinas-shopping-spree-1647378.html.

25. "China's Zhongjin gets OK for Australia mine stake." China Mining Association, February 6, 2009. Available at www.chinamining.org/Investment/2009-02-06/1233887240d21300.html.

26. Xinhua News Agency. 2009. "China Calls for Full-scale Financial System Over-

haul." Available at http://en.chinagate.cn/features/2009g20/2009–03/26/con tent_17528198.htm; Xinhua News Agency. April 3, 2009 . "Hu Calls for Further Support to Developing Countries to Combat Crisis. Available at http://en .chinagate.cn/features/2009g20/2009-04/03/content_17548074.htm.

27. Xinhua News Agency. September 25, 2009. "Summary of Pittsburgh G20 summit participants' views." Available at www.china.org.cn/business/2009-09/25/ content_18599542.htm#.

28. Bloomberg News. September 22, 2009. "China Stimulus Delays Economy Restructuring, ADB Says (Update3)." Available at http://bloomberg.com/apps/ news?pid=20602014&sid=aKNJbNHyc9oI.

29. Based on their published financial statements, China's state-owned banks report strong earnings. Their non-performing loans amount to a small share of their outstanding credit, usually under 2 to 3 percent (except for the Bank of Agriculture). Whether such data are credible is a debate among analysts. Particularly questionable would these banks' loan-loss provisions because of their exposure to risky investments in China's real estate sector.

References

Alden, Chris. 2005. "China in Africa." *Survival* 47(3): 147–64.

Atkinson, Caroline. 2008, December 18. Regular Press Briefing, Director, External Relations Department. Washington, DC: International Monetary Fund. Available at www.imf.org/external/np/tr/2008/tr121808.htm

Batson, Andrew. 2009. "Wen Voices Concern over China's U.S. Treasurys." *The Wall Street Journal,* March 13.

Bergsten, Fred. 2008. "A Partnership of Equals." *Foreign Affairs* 87(4): 57–70.

Christensen, Thomas. 1996. "Chinese Realpolitik." *Foreign Affairs* 75(5): 37–52.

Cook, Sarah, and Wing Lam. 2009. "The Financial Crisis and China: What Are the Implications for Low Income Countries?" Institute of Development Studies. Available at www.ids.ac.uk/index.cfm?objectid=C3B5CC41-B423-2546-A7FC 8E2A7E4CB850.

Council on Foreign Relations. 2007. *U.S.-China Relations: An Affirmative Agenda, a Responsible Course.* New York: Council on Foreign Relations.

Deng, Yong. 2008. *China's Struggle for Status: The realignment of International Relations.* Cambridge, UK: Cambridge University Press. Director of National Intelligence. 2009. "The National Intelligence Strategy of the United States of America."Available at www.dni.gov/reports.

Foot, Rosemary. 2001. "Chinese Power and the Idea of a Responsible State." *The China Journal* 45(January): 1–19.

Huang, Yiping. 2009. "China's New Policy Strategy and the G20." *East Asian Forum.* Available at www.eastasiaforum.org/2009/03/29/g20-chinas-new-policy-strategy/.

Hulbert, Matthew. 2009. "Enter the Dragon: Economic Turmoil and Resource Acquisition." Center for Security Studies. Available at www.isn.ethz.ch/isn/Cur

rent-Affairs/Security-Watch/Detail/?ots591=4888CAA0-B3DB-1461-98B9-E20E7B9C13D4&lng=en&id=97476.

International Crisis Group. 2008. "China's Thirst for Oil" Available at www.crisis group.org/home/index.cfm?id=5478&l=1;

Johnston, Alastair Iain. 2008. *Social States: China in International Institutions 1980–2000.* Princeton: Princeton University Press.

Kent, Ann. 2007. *Beyond Compliance: China, International Organizations, and Global Security.* Stanford: Stanford University Press.

Krugman, Paul. 2009. "China's Dollar Trap." *New York Times*, April 2.

Lardy, Nicholas. 2006. "China: Toward a Consumption-Driven Growth Path." Washington DC: The Petersen Institute for International Economics.

Lynch, Daniel. 2009. "Chinese Thinking on the Future of International Relations: realism as the Ti, Rationalism as the Yong?" *The China Quarterly* 197(March): 87–107.

Ramo, Joshua Cooper. 2004. *The Beijing Consensus.* London: The Foreign Policy Centre.

Roy, Denny. 2009. "China's Democratised Foreign Policy." *Survival* 51(2): 25–40.

Sohn, Injoo. 2008. "Learning to Co-operate: China's Multilateral Approach to Asian Financial Co-operation" *The China Quarterly* 194(June 2008): 309–26.

Swaine, Michael D., and Ashley Tellis. 2000. *Interpreting China's Grand Strategy.* Santa Monica, CA: Rand.

U.S. Department of the Treasury. 2009. "Major Foreign Holders of Treasury Securities." www.treas.gov/tic/mfh.txt.

Wang, Hongying. 2007. "Linking Up with the International Track": What's in a Slogan?" *The China Quarterly* 189(March): 1–23.

Wolf, Martin. 2009. "Wheel of fortune Turns as China Outdoes West." *The Financial Times,* September 13, 2009.

World Bank. 2008a. "China Quarterly Update, December 2008," Washington, DC: World Bank.

World Bank. 2008b. "China's Stimulus Policies are Key for Growth in 2009 and an Opportunity for More Rebalancing," *World Bank Update,* November 25, 2008. Available at http://web.worldbank.org/WBSITE/EXTERNAL/COUNTRIES/EAST ASIAPACIFICEXT/CHINAEXTN/0,,contentMDK:21989619~pagePK:1497618~p iPK:217854~theSitePK:318950,00.html.

Yanping, Li. 2009. "China 'Super Currency' Call May Signal Dollar Concern (Update1)." Available at www.bloomberg.com/apps/news?pid=newsarchive&sid= acneRCVQY09Y

Zhen, Cao. 2009. "China Speeding up Overseas Acquisitions." *Caijing.* Available at http://english.caijing.com.cn/2009-02-24/110073365.html.

Zimin, Chen. 2005. "Nationalism, Internationalism, and Chinese Foreign Policy." *Journal of Contemporary China* 14(42): 35–53.

Zweig, David, and Bi Jianhai. 2005. "China's Global Hunt for Energy, *Foreign Affairs* 84(5): 25–38.

CHAPTER 6

Latin American Development after the Global Financial Crisis

José Antonio Ocampo

A REVISION of development thinking had been going on in several Latin American countries before the global financial crisis. In this sense, after leading the enthusiasm for economic liberalization since the mid-1980s—since the mid-1970s in the Southern Cone countries of Argentina, Chile and Uruguay—in the 2000s Latin America also became a leader of the return of state control of economic and social affairs. Two political shifts led this process: a more radical left-wing movement in Venezuela, Bolivia, and Ecuador and a more social-democratic one in Brazil, Uruguay, and Chile and, more recently, in Paraguay and El Salvador. Aside from these movements, right-wing politics also moved somewhat to the center. This trend toward stronger state intervention is likely to continue and will now take place in the context of a broader acceptance of the increased role of the state at the global level.

The basic reason for the early Latin American shift to greater state interventionism was frustration with the effects of market reforms, both in social and economic terms. In social terms, the sense in several, if not most, countries was that liberalization had worsened the endemic inequality of wealth and income distribution that has historically characterized the region and had created new forms of insecurity and exclusion. It is, of course, paradoxical that the shift took place in a period in which income distribution actually started to improve, thanks at least in part to state activism (discussed further below). In economic terms, with a few exceptions, economic growth was frustrating after liberalization. The exception was the 2004–8 boom, which was based on a combination of extremely positive external shocks (booming world finance and trade, high commodity prices, and increasing remittances). Even then, Latin America lagged behind other regions in the developing world.

As of early 2010, it still remains risky to talk of an "after" in relation to the global financial crisis, as some of its effects continue to dominate global economic trends. Although the "Great Recession" may now belong to history, two major uncertainties remain: there may be a new global slowdown in the immediate future (a "double dip") and, particularly, dynamic medium- and long-term period of world economic growth may not follow the recovery. In the past, severe financial crises have led to slow *long-term* economic growth in many countries. This, by the way, was true of Latin America after its "lost decade" of the 1980s. The basic assumption in this chapter is, therefore, that we are at the beginning of a longer period of slower economic growth, certainly in the industrialized world but even in the dynamic parts of the developing world (China itself may be unable to settle on stable basis around a 10 percent growth rate). Particularly critical in this regard is what will happen to world trade, which, as we will see, was the strongest casualty of the current crisis.

In this chapter, I concentrate on the implications of this scenario for Latin America. First I examine the nature of the crisis, as seen from Latin America, and the room to maneuver allowed for countercyclical macroeconomic policies that the region partially espoused this time. Second, I look at long-term growth and, specifically, the future of the orthodox export-led growth model that Latin America has embraced for the past quarter century. Then I explore the topic of equity and particularly one of the dimensions of equity that was already subject to heated debates before the crisis: universal versus targeted social policies.

In discussing these issues, I will try to answer three basic questions: (1) has Latin America finally learned to implement countercyclical macroeconomic policies? (2) will Latin America revisit the orthodox brand of export-led growth that it has followed? and (3) will Latin America finally embrace universal social policies? In normative terms, the view of the author is that all these questions should be answered positively, and this is what rebuilding a stronger state for a new phase of development means.[1] But the answers may be negative in practice, and herein lay some of the major problems ahead.

It remains to be said that many of the views espoused in this chapter are those that have been disseminated over the past two decades by the United Nations Economic Commission for Latin America and the Caribbean, or

ECLAC, which the author himself led for six years. It is time for these views to be broadly heard and embraced.

Has Latin America Finally Learned to Implement Countercyclical Macroeconomic Policies?

The crisis hit Latin America hard, with diversity across the region, with some surprises.[2] ECLAC estimates indicate that the regional GDP fell by 1.9 percent in 2009. The country most strongly affected was Mexico, but most economies in the region faced either negative or at best small positive growth. Indeed, in strict terms, this crisis is worse than those of 1990 and 2002 but still better than that of early 1980s (see figure 6.1). Thanks to the strong recovery of several South American countries, notably Brazil, the 2010 per capita GDP will exceed that of 2008 by a small margin, but there are important exceptions to this pattern, notably Mexico and Venezuela, as well as most Central American countries, where GDP per capita will continue to be lower than in 2008.

The transmission of the shock had some surprises. In the case of remittances, the initial reduction was unexpectedly moderate, but it speeded up since the second quarter of 2009.[3] The major surprise was the much weaker

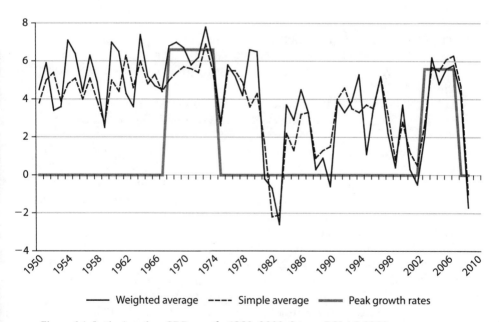

Figure 6.1 Latin America: GDP growth, 1950–2009. Source: ECLAC 2009a.

financial shock vis-à-vis similar episodes in the past.[4] Spreads and yields on sovereign and, particularly, corporate bonds went up since mid-2008 and sharply so with the global financial meltdown of September and October 2008, but then fell sharply since the second quarter of 2009. By mid-2009, yields had come back to levels close to those experienced during the boom years, except in countries where "political risk" factors were present. Financial flows were sharply cut, and there were some outflows and losses in derivate markets at the worst of the crisis, but inflows also came back since early 2009 and, particularly, the second quarter of the year. This was also reflected in exchange rate pressures: strong initial depreciation pressures after the September 2008 meltdown, followed by renewed appreciation since the second quarter of 2009. Reserve losses were minimal (from $435 billion in September 2008 to $411 billion in February 2009 for the seven major economies of the region) and stock markets stabilized at the worst point at double the dollar values that had prevailed before the boom, the best performance in the world. Recovery in both areas, particularly in stock markets, has been strong since the second quarter of 2009.

Thus, in strict financial terms, this is the weakest crisis that Latin America has faced over the past three decades. So, the severity of the Latin American recession can hardly be explained in purely financial terms. A better explanation is the magnitude of the trade shock. According to the data provided by the CPB Netherland Bureau for Economic Policy Analysis (CPB 2010), world exports fell during the first half of 2009 by 31.0 percent versus the same period in 2008 in value, and 18.1 percent in volume terms. Although there has been a recovery in international trade since mid-2009, in the first quarter of 2010, the value and volume of world exports still remained 13.4 and 4.5 percent below the levels of the first half of 2008.[5] The United Nations (2010) has estimated a reduction in world trade volumes of 13.1 percent in 2009, with only a partial recovery (7.6 percent growth) in 2010.

This veritable collapse of world trade was transmitted to Latin America, where exports fell in the first half of 2009 by 30.9 and 15.3 percent in value and volume terms, respectively, versus the first half of 2008 (ECLAC, 2009b, table II.2). According to CPB (2010), during the last quarter of 2009, Latin American exports were still 5 percent below the first half of 2008 but started to exceed that level during the first quarter of 2010—though not in value terms. It must be added that Latin America benefited from the commodity price boom of 2004–8 and was severely hit by the collapse of commodity prices that started in mid-2008 and accelerated after September of that year. Although commodity prices recovered since the second quarter of 2009 and continued to be high by historical standards, particularly in the case of minerals, they also remained below the peak reached during the first quarter of 2008.

What this means is that for Latin America this has been a trade crisis rather than a financial crisis. This implies that, although the region has been able to reduce its financial vulnerabilities, this advance has not compensated for the high trade vulnerabilities that characterize today the region's more open economies. It also means that the possibility of exporting itself out of the crisis—the typical pattern of how Mexico overcame its 1994–95 crisis and how Latin America as a whole partly overcame the 1998–2002 crisis—cannot be the basis of a strong recovery this time, which has to depend, much more than during the recent past, on domestic demand. Beyond the short term, this trade crisis has deep implications for the export-led strategy that the region has followed for a quarter century, an issue to which I will return in next section of this chapter.

The reduced intensity of the financial shock is associated with both external and domestic factors. The former are reflected in the early return of risk taking, thanks to the strong and successful Keynesian policies in place throughout the world—a factor that was absent during the emerging country crises of recent decades. In domestic terms, and in sharp contrast to previous crises, Latin America avoided the need to adopt procyclical policies during the current turmoil, particularly the need to increase domestic interest rates and fiscal austerity packages. Beyond that, there was some room to maneuver for countercyclical macroeconomic policies, particularly expansionary monetary and credit policies (including, in the latter case, active use of development banks) and, in fewer countries, expansionary fiscal policies, mainly additional government spending. In any case, domestic credit slowed down sharply after the global financial meltdown (ECLAC 2009a).

The reasons behind the unexpected strength of the Latin American economies are subject to debate. An element of consensus is that part of the resilience is associated with stronger domestic financial systems, a result of both better regulation adopted after previous crises and the success in developing domestic bond markets, which reduced the need for external financing, particularly by the public sector. In macroeconomic terms, there is, however, considerable discussion about the source of the additional space for countercyclical macroeconomic policies. This discussion involves two major interlinked issues. The first is whether the additional improvement is the result of a shift in the region toward countercyclical policies during the previous boom. The second is whether the improved resilience is due to improved domestic policies (e.g., fiscal austerity and the shift of central banks toward inflation targeting regimes) or to external factors.

The answer to the first question is close to an unequivocal no. The word "countercyclical" has become part of the accepted jargon during the crisis, but it was rather infrequently used and practiced during the previous boom (IADB 2008; Ocampo 2007). This is clearest in the case of fiscal policy. Among the larger countries, Chile stood alone in implementing a truly countercyclical fiscal policy rule, which targeted a small structural fiscal surplus and transferred excess fiscal revenues to stabilization funds held abroad. Aside from this and the case of a couple of Central American countries (El Salvador and Guatemala), fiscal policy was procyclical, in the sense that primary fiscal spending grew faster than long-term and ever short-term GDP growth (Ocampo 2009). Actually, the fiscal responsibility laws adopted around 2000 by several countries were redrafted to allow for some additional spending, and some were eliminated altogether (Jiménez and Tromben, 2006). Overall, therefore, the source of improved fiscal accounts was booming revenues (particularly in countries that derive fiscal revenues from natural resources), not countercyclical fiscal policies.

Central banks did adopt some countercyclical policies during the boom, but they were rather moderate. Among the major central banks of the region, Chile and Peru followed (though less than fully) the upward trend of U.S. Federal Reserve intervention rates from mid-2004 to mid-2006, but Brazil and Mexico reduced their rates during this period and Colombia kept them constant. Colombia stood alone in its attempt to cool down the domestic effects of the euphoria generated by booming capital inflows from mid-2006 to mid-2007. It was thus only rather late, during the acceleration of inflation in 2008, that most central banks adopted some (generally moderate) contractionary monetary policies. If anything, this implies that inflation targeting actually biased central bank policies, by making them less reluctant to respond to expansionary pressures if the latter were not reflected in higher inflation rates and, therefore, that they did not generally counteract the expansionary pressures coming from booming capital inflows, as the exchange rate appreciation generated by those inflows had favorable effects on domestic inflation.

The answer to the second question on the macroeconomic debate is, again, almost unequivocally that exceptional external factors were the dominant factor and improved external balance sheets the major source of additional strength (Izquierdo et al. 2008; Ocampo 2009). As we have seen, fiscal policies were generally procyclical during the boom and monetary policies at best moderately countercyclical. Although the region as a whole tended to run a current account surplus in its balance of payments, this was essentially a reflection of booming terms of trade. Once adjusted by this factor, there was actually a persistent deterioration in the current account balance. In other words, if governments spent additional fiscal revenues, countries generally spent the terms of trade boom (Ocampo 2009).

The external balance sheet improved in all major countries of the region as a result of two basic factors: rising foreign exchange reserves (including resources held in stabilization funds) and moderate public sector borrowing abroad. The first reflects the heavy interventions in foreign exchange markets by central banks, particularly during periods of booming capital inflows (Ocampo 2007, 2009). Heavy interventions in foreign exchange markets indicate that floating, when in place, was dirty, except in the case of Mexico (which, in any case, started to intervene heavily in that market during the recent crisis). The second reflects, as we have seen, booming public sector revenues and the development of domestic bond markets. As figure 6.2 indicates, the mix of these two factors led to a sharp reduction in the net external debt ratio, which fell from around 30 percent of GDP in 1998–2000 to around 6 percent in 2008. One way of looking at this trend is that, during the recent boom, Latin America finally overcame the debt crisis that had continued hanging on as a threat to its development for a quarter of a century.

Will the current rhetoric lead Latin America to fully move into a countercyclical macroeconomic policy framework? It remains to be seen. In the case of fiscal policy, the main challenge is how to avoid the political economy issues that affect fiscal policy during booms: the difficulty in explaining to their national parliaments and their citizens that fiscal policy has to become austere largely to counterbalance private sector euphoria, since this mix has strong distributive implications (Marfán 2005). In the case of monetary policy, the crucial issue is whether orthodoxy favoring inflating targeting will be replaced by a more balanced view according to which central banks have multiple objectives: not only inflation but also economic activity, financial stability, and orderly foreign exchange markets. The lack of recognition of these multiple objectives has allowed in the past for monetary policies that have not been consistently countercyclical, in particular the revealed reluctance to cool down booms when inflation was not at risk.

Will Latin America Revisit the Orthodox Brand of Export-Led Growth That It Has Followed?

Orthodox export-led growth has been at the center of the development strategy followed by Latin America over the past quarter century. By the adjective "orthodox," I differentiate this strategy from that which is equally export-led but involves state intervention in the production sector

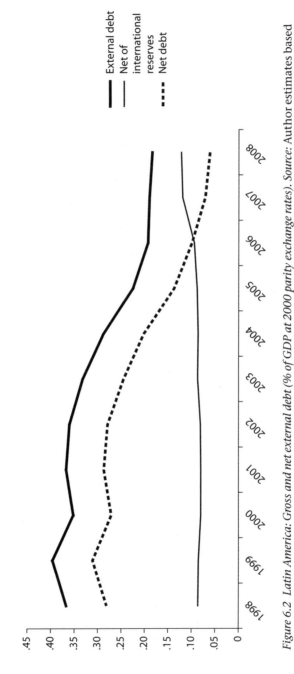

Figure 6.2 Latin America: Gross and net external debt (% of GDP at 2000 parity exchange rates). Source: Author estimates based on ECLAC data. In the case of Chile, reserves include stabilization funds.

and active exchange rate management, which has been more characteristic of East Asia, including in recent decades of China. Such interventions include industrial or, more generally, production sector policies (as they do not focus strictly on manufacturing as in the past) and, in some countries, active technology policies. In export-led economies, such interventions are aimed at improving export "quality," meaning by this concept the technological contents and domestic value added of export activities. The essential criterion of orthodox export-led growth followed by Latin America has, therefore, been the "neutrality" of incentives, which means that state intervention has refrained from promoting specific economic activities. The major exceptions to neutrality have been free trade agreements, which eliminate neutrality in the treatment of trading partners, and some subsidies (such as income tax exemptions) to foreign direct investment and export processing zones.

This strategy was proposed as the alternative to the perceived inefficiency associated with state-led industrialization (generally called import-substitution industrialization, a name that emphasizes only one aspect of the policies that were typical of the past, and not necessarily the most important one). In this view, the essential problem of the old Latin American strategy was the fact that it generated not only static inefficiencies but also negative effects on technical change and, thus, on economic growth.

The objective of accelerating economic growth through orthodox export-led growth generally failed in Latin America. It did lead to faster export growth but *not* to faster GDP growth. Figure 6.1 indicates that, on average, growth was slower and much more unstable over the past two decades than it was in 1950–80. As figure 6.3 indicates, labor productivity (GDP per worker) grew at a slower pace in most Latin American countries in 1990–2008 than in 1950–80. The only major exceptions were Chile and the Dominican Republic; two other countries show a similar but poor performance in both periods, El Salvador and Uruguay. For the region as a whole, GDP per worker grew at a 0.7 percent per year since 1990 versus 2.7 percent in 1950–80. Estimates of total factor productivity indicate a similar poorer comparative performance in recent decades.

What went wrong? First and foremost, the orthodox view ignored the fact that the there is a link between growth and production structures, associated to the very different technological content of alternative economic activities.[6] Second, it ignored that domestic linkages matter in terms of the multiplier effect of export growth on domestic economic activity. In the case of exports, this means that pure export processing (*maquila*) may give rapid export growth but limited GDP growth, if anything because GDP is nothing else but domestic value added. Indeed, it is peculiar that some of the major subsidies that have been granted during the export-led growth

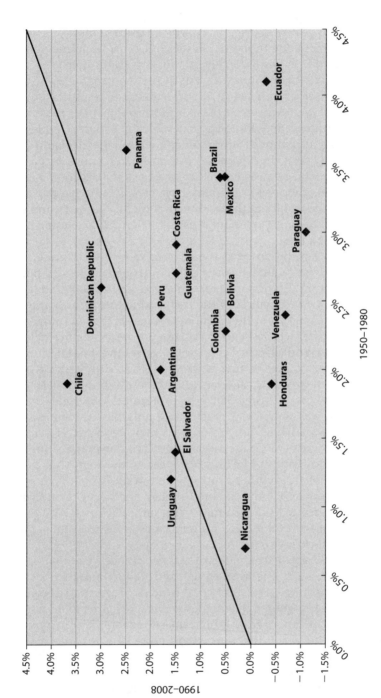

Figure 6.3 GDP per worker: 1990–2008 versus 1950–1980. Source: Author estimates based on ECLAC data.

era have *reduced* rather than increased domestic value added (e.g., income and other tax exemptions for export processing zones and foreign direct investment). The net result was a bias toward poor export quality and to weak linkages between export and GDP growth. This is in sharp contrast with East Asia, where exports have a rising technological content and are part of a regional technological cluster, so that even if the technological content in a specific location is low, the regional content is high.

Furthermore, the leading economic activities and firms were unable to absorb the labor force, including workers who became idle due to the contraction of previous protected activities that were unable to survive under the new economic conditions. As ECLAC has put it, the net result was increased dualism: reforms have led to the creation of highly productive "world class" firms and activities but also to rising labor market informality (see, for example, ECLAC 2000). Indeed, the major assumption of orthodox thinking that failed to materialize was that of full employment, as a large (and even an increasing) share of the labor force has remained in low-productivity (informal) sectors, dragging down overall productivity.

The collapse of global trade added another dimension. Now even the weak engine of growth that Latin America depended on in recent decades may run at low gear. Under these conditions, will Latin America continue to bet on this strategy? And, if not, what will replace it?

There are three possible ways out of the current impasse—which could be adopted in variable mixes, since they are not incompatible—and a complementary macroeconomic policy. The first is to shift more in the direction of active production sector policies. The second would be to strengthen the links with the new dynamic poles of the world economy, particularly China. The third would be a greater focus on domestic markets, which at the regional level means strengthening the regional integration processes. The complementary macroeconomic policy would pay greater attention to competitive exchange rates.

If more active production sector policies are followed, the associated strategies may continue to be export oriented; in that case, it would be more efficient if they were part of a regional technology cluster, as in East Asia. The essence of this strategy is the emphasis on technological innovation, through a mix of directly supporting technological innovation and encouraging productive branches, firms, and exports with higher technological contents. The essential instruments are a strong development bank and research and development subsidies. Brazil has clearly moved in that direction, partly followed by Chile and Colombia. Among the smaller countries, Costa Rica also took this path, but only indirectly, through the attraction of a global player in technology-intensive exports (INTEL). The rest of Latin America still falls significantly behind, though there are now seeds of a new strategy in several countries, in many cases as local rather than national strategies.

It is important to emphasize that this strategy does not necessarily mean renouncing the comparative advantages associated with natural resources, if a Scandinavian (but also an Australian or a New Zealand) route is followed of adding technological content to natural resource intensive exports. Terms of trade trends are also important in this regard. The twentieth century tended to confirm the Prebisch-Singer hypothesis of a long-term fall in real commodity prices, though more as a result of abrupt downward shifts than of a persistent deterioration (Ocampo and Parra 2003). The twenty-first century opened with a boom of commodity prices, though more of mineral (including energy) than agricultural prices (Ocampo 2009, table 1). Two factors have been running in the direction of high commodity prices, reproducing late nineteenth- rather than twentieth-century patterns: the dynamic growth of China, which is a major mineral importer, and the link between high energy and agricultural prices through biofuels (see World Bank 2009 for more on this and broader commodity issues). In any case, although the crisis cut short the commodity boom, and it is now difficult to disentangle long-term trends from short-term volatility, commodity prices continue to be high by the standards of recent decades. Thus, long-term trends may actually work in favor of commodity, particularly mineral, producers. This is, of course, a complement, not a substitute, for a shift toward a technology-oriented policy.

The second strategy, growing integration with the dynamic parts of the world economy, mainly China, has already been followed by several countries, particularly in South America. Indeed, China is now the first (in the case of Brazil and Chile) or second (in the case of Argentina and Peru, as well as of Costa Rica and Cuba) export destination for several Latin American countries (ECLAC 2009b, table I.4). But this strategy implies also an emphasis on the diversification of the export basket, which is still dominated by a few commodities (oil, soybeans, copper, and mineral iron) and lacks, therefore, the broader export diversification that Latin America has been able to achieve since the late twentieth century (Gallagher and Porzecanski 2009).

The third strategy is refocusing on the domestic market and, more broadly, on regional markets. A strict focus on the domestic market is viable for Brazil, which in a sense already adopted it through the strategy of "consumption of the masses" of the Lula administration, and perhaps partly for Argentina and Colombia, but not for other countries. Strengthened regional integration is, therefore, more appropriate for the region as a whole. Its basic advantage, as ECLAC has emphasized for several decades, is that intraregional trade has a much larger share of manufactured goods and, particularly, of manufactured goods with higher technological content (see again, ECLAC 2009b, chapter 3). It also gives broader opportunities to small and medium-sized firms. But this strategy must overcome its two major problems: a procyclical bias and the strong political divisions within the region that have already considerably weakened one of the major integration processes (the Andean Community). A strong emphasis on regional integration must also be accompanied, as has been recognized, by improvements in the regional infrastructure, particularly highways, regional electricity grids, and oil and gas pipelines. Indeed, a major push in integration infrastructure could be a key both to dynamic investment and intraregional trade, contributing on both sides to dynamic economic growth.

A complement to a strategy that mixes in variable ways these three components would be greater attention to exchange rate competitiveness. The reason, in this case, is that there is considerable evidence that a strong current account and a stable and competitive exchange rate help accelerate economic growth (see, for example, Rodrik 2007 and Frenkel and Rapetti 2010). This has two major implications. The first relates to macroeconomic policy and indicates that central banks should place exchange rate management at the center of their strategies, but also that fiscal policy should complement central bank efforts in this area during booms. This is an accepted doctrine in several parts of East Asia but runs counter to orthodox inflation targeting. In a sense, one of the essential contradictions of the orthodox export-led strategies followed by Latin American countries is that they place export growth at the center but then subject it to the instabilities associated with exchange rate volatility. Another implication is that central banks may need more instruments to manage broader objectives, including returning to more active management of the capital account (Brazil already took steps in that direction by adopting a tax on portfolio capital inflows in late October 2009). The additional implication is, of course, that this may require that countries take minimal steps at exchange rate policy coordination, particularly if deeper regional integration is part of the strategy. Divergent exchange rate regimes were a major reason behind the collapse of Argentine-Brazilian trade in the late twentieth century. These differing exchange rate policies also affected Andean trade during the current crisis.

Revisiting the orthodox export-led model that Latin America has followed over the past quarter century makes sense, as its performance has been weak and may be even weaker in the near future, but doing so requires stronger state intervention in several areas. Given the ideological dominance that the orthodox paradigm still maintains, it is possible that the shift will take place as a result of a series of pragmatic decisions taken as a result of political pressures in the face of weak economic growth. This is, in fact, how the shift toward more inward-oriented policies took place in the 1930s and 1940s, not through the adoption of an alternative paradigm, which came at the end rather than the beginning of the process. But an alternative paradigm does now exist. Since the 1990s, ECLAC led regional thinking on how to revisit the role of production sector policies for the now open economies of the region (see, for example, ECLAC 1990, 2000, 2008a, and 2008b). It is time for its views to be heard more broadly in the region. And, it is time for the multilateral development banks to embrace those views, particularly in the case of the World Bank, which played a central role in disseminating the orthodox trade strategies that are now in place in Latin America.

Will Latin America Embrace Universal Social Policies?

The endemic inequality that characterizes Latin America has generated the greatest demands for reform, including the call in Washington circles for a second wave of reforms with a strong focus on equity (see, among others, Birdsall et al. 2001 and Kuczynski and Williamson 2003).

Interestingly, the consensus on the need to focus on equity came as Latin America started to experience an unprecedented reduction in poverty levels. According to ECLAC (2009c), the poverty headcount ratio fell from 44 percent in 2002 to 33 percent in 2008. This is an outstanding reduction by any historical standard and was associated with both rapid growth and an improvement in income distribution. The latter was fairly broad based and followed two decades of deterioration (ECLAC 2009c; Gasparini et al. 2009).

Gasparini et al. (2009) and Cornia (2010) include dynamic employment generation and reductions in rural-urban gaps during the recent boom among the factors that facilitated the reversal in income distribution trends. This was due in the latter case to improved commodity prices and the reversal of the rising skill premia that characterized the period of structural reforms, which also benefited from a significant and widespread reduction in inequality in access to education (though not to university education). Other social policies, particularly transfer payments to poor households and rising minimum wages in some countries, also contributed to this result—though the effects of conditional cash transfers as such were generally small. In any case, part of the improvement was due to the reversal of the worsening income distribution that had characterized the crisis of the late 1990s in several countries and the favorable external conditions that characterized the boom.

The current crisis may thus interrupt this favorable trend. This raises question regarding the nature of the economic and social policies necessary to sustain this remarkable improvement. There are many dimensions to this debate, but I focus here on important dimension that came back to the center of regional debates in recent years: that between universalism versus targeting in social policy.

Universalism goes back to the roots of the conceptions on which modern welfare states were built in industrialized countries (with some exceptions). In Latin America, the development of the welfare state started in the early twentieth century in a few countries and on a broader basis during the period of state-led industrialization. However, its development never paralleled the welfare states of industrialized countries, particularly in terms of creating ambitious tax and transfer system to reduce income inequality. For most Latin American countries, social security came late and was restricted in scope, due to its association with formal employment and its corporatist tones. The result was a segmented and incomplete welfare state that irradiated its benefits to middle sectors of society but tended to marginalize the poor, particularly in rural areas.

The market reforms of the 1980s and 1990s initially placed social policy in a subordinate status. This is reflected, for example, in the lack of any special mention of social policy in the ten principles of the "Washington consensus," as summarized by Williamson (1990), except as a priority for public sector spending. As in other areas, the World Bank played a central role in spreading new views of social policy during the reform period, which can be best summarized in terms of three instruments: targeting, demand subsidies to facilitate a more competitive system with private sector participation, and decentralization.[7] The first focused at making social policy consistent with limited fiscal resources while spreading some benefits to the poor. The other two instruments focused on rationalizing the state apparatus. In short, the emphasis was on efficiency in the use of limited amounts of social spending, not on equity.

The application of the new principles was uneven throughout the region. In educational policy, the focus on demand subsidies led by Chile was not generally followed and the focus of most countries was on the reorganization and increased access to public sector schools. In health and, particularly, in pension reforms, the systems did allow in several countries for broader participation by private agents and even for the total privatization of the pension system, though these trends were far from generalized. Targeting had its best manifestation in the development of conditional cash transfer programs, a system that was led by Brazil and Mexico but spread throughout the region. Decentralization advanced more in countries with a strong federal tradition (Argentina and Brazil) as well as in two countries with a centralist state but a de facto federalist system (Bolivia and Colombia).

The return of universalism as a paradigm in social policy was closely

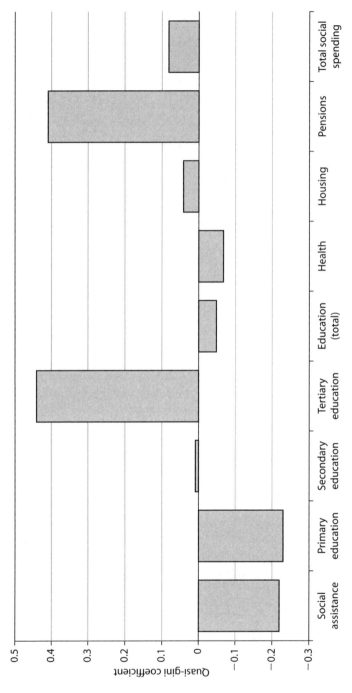

Figure 6.4 Redistributive effect of social spending. Source: ECLAC (2007), tables II.16 to II.19.

tied to the concepts of social rights and social citizenship. The more precise formulation came from ECLAC (2000), which put forward four principles of social policy: universalism, solidarity, efficiency, and integrality. The paradigm of social citizenship obviously leads to the discussion of the relation between entitlements and the capacity to provide them, which is linked to the level of economic development. This led to the concept of "basic universalism" that was proposed by a team at the Inter-American Development Bank led by Molina (2006). This concept implies that social policies should focus on the provision of a basic set of entitlements and risk-mitigating instruments that can be made available to the whole population, with homogenous quality standards and provided on the basis of the principles of citizenship.

This paradigm also aimed at overcoming the problems associated with targeting, which include political capture, administrative costs and errors, and the stigma that is associated with receiving money from the state (Mkandawire 2007). It also includes the need to face the broader challenge of segmentation. Indeed, targeting by itself leads to segmentation and creation of dual structures and may actually enhance segmentation in labor markets—a reason why some of its promoters have now called for a return to some form of universal social policies (Levy 2008).

The virtues of universal social policies can be better understood with a reference to the distribute effects of different policies. Figure 6.4 summarizes the quasi-gini coefficient of different types of social spending, which fluctuates between –1 (perfect targeting of spending to the poor) and 1. The most redistributive areas of spending include social assistance as well as those programs that have achieved universal or close to universal coverage, particularly primary education and some basic health programs. A second category includes services with an intermediate level of coverage, such as secondary education and housing (which includes water and sewage). In this case, spending is, on average, not too far from equi-distribution. Health spending lies between the first two categories and its quasi-gini is, on average, slightly negative. A third category includes tertiary education and pensions, where spending benefits high-income groups to a larger extent. Even in these cases, however, the distribution of spending is generally better than that of primary income and thus has some redistributive effects.

Only social assistance programs confirm the views of the defenders of targeting. As we have seen, the best examples are conditional cash transfers but there are also highly redistributive policies, such as nutrition programs and those that focus on early childhood development. However, the redistributive effect of social assistance spending is limited, as it concentrates only a small fraction of total social spending (less than a fifth, according to ECLAC 2007, table II.20). Thus, the most important redistributive effect—as

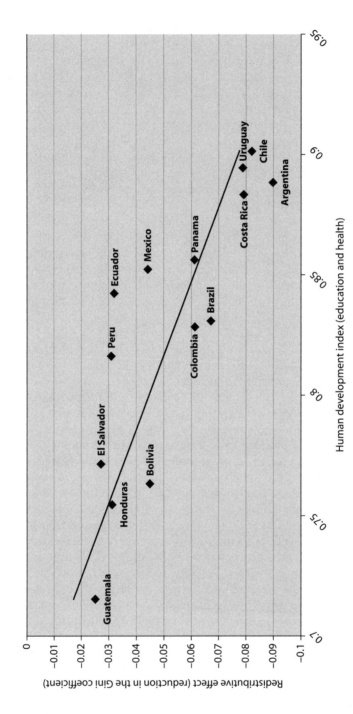

Figure 6.5 Links between human development and the redistribute effects of social policy. Source: Human Development Index according to UNDP (data for 2007). Reduction in the Fini coefficient according to ELCAC (2007), tables II.16 to II.19.

estimated by the implicit addition to the income of low-income quintiles—is associated with education and health programs of universal or close to universal coverage. Furthermore, for all programs, the *marginal* spending associated with increased coverage is highly redistributive, a fact that is missed in traditional estimates, such as those reproduced in figure 6.4. This implies that the marginal redistributive effects of social spending may be as high in the second as in the first category and even for those areas of social spending that are included in the third.

It is important to emphasize that the limited progressiveness of social security spending is due to its very close association with formal employment. The solution therefore lies in the design of a solidarity pillar financed with general government revenues (ECLAC 2006). Such pillar would be highly progressive, as already reflected in the noncontributory part of the pension systems of Argentina, Bolivia, and Brazil.

The conclusion that can be derived form this analysis is clear: the progressiveness of social spending is closely associated with the coverage of services, not with the use of targeting instruments. In this sense, the best targeting is a universal social policy. This view is confirmed when we look at the association between the degree of development of social policy (as reflected in the social components of the Human Development Index of the United Nations Development Program) and the redistributive impact of social spending. This is shown in figure 6.5. This figure indicates that the largest redistributive effect of social spending is achieved in those countries that had an early development of more universal systems of social policy: Argentina, Chile, Costa Rica, and Uruguay. Countries with a somewhat lower level of development—Brazil, Colombia, and Panama—also have a more intermediate level of redistribution from social spending, which is even more limited in countries with an even lower level of development of their social policies—Bolivia, El Salvador, Honduras and Guatemala. Some countries in the second category—Ecuador, Mexico and Peru—have limited redistributive effects of their social spending relative to other countries in the region.

Although universal coverage of basic social services should therefore be the essential objective of social policy, targeting can play a subsidiary role in three specific areas. First, social assistance (conditional cash transfers, nutrition programs, state pensions for the elderly poor) could be seen a complement to a universal system. A basic requirement is that the associated programs should aim at the universal coverage of the targeted population. Second, targeting can also be used to enhance the access of the poor to universal social programs. This is indeed a particular advantage of the recent conditional cash transfers: that they ties assistance to access of the population to universal programs of education and health. And third, targeting can also be used to differentiate the type of programs for specific groups of population, particularly to the indigenous peoples. In the last two cases, targeting is used as an instrument of universalism and not as its substitute.

The data provided by figure 6.5 concentrate on secondary income distribution and leave aside one of the basic advantages of universal systems: their contribution to a better primary distribution of income. This can be illustrated in relation to industrialized countries by the fact that countries of Continental Europe, which have more universal welfare systems, have a better distribution of income than those countries that use more means testing (targeting) in their social policy, the Anglo-Saxon countries (Alesina and Glaeser 2004). Causality goes both ways in this case: more equal societies demand more universal systems of social policy, but the latter contribute in turn to equality. On the contrary, the extensive use of means testing has led to what Korpi and Palme (1998) have called the "paradox of redistribution": the more we target, the less we are able to reduce poverty and inequality. One basic reason for this is, as I have pointed out, that targeting leads by itself to segmentation.

A further advantage of universal social policies is their political appeal and particularly their appeal to the middle classes, which is essential to get the political backing for the public sector resources necessary to make universal policies effective. Indeed, in this regard, the fight of the middle classes to have access to social benefits should be seen as a positive feature and not in the negative light with which it is usually depicted in the literature on targeting—which sees this phenomenon as the politically connected depriving the poor from access to social services. On the contrary, access by middle sectors to social services was the route to the development of universal welfare states in the industrialized world. The access of the middle classes to social services can also be seen as evidence and guarantee that social policy provides high-quality services (Grynspan 2006).

Furthermore, it should be borne in mind that the true "middle classes" of Latin America (or, rather, middle segments of the income distribution) are relatively poor. This is reflected in the fact that in countries with lower per capita income (Bolivia, Honduras, or Nicaragua), part of the population of the third and fourth quintiles of the income distribution has incomes below the poverty line, defined by ECLAC according to the cost of a basic food basket, and most of them earn incomes below two poverty lines, . In turn, in countries with intermediate levels of income (Colombia or the Dominican Republic), most of the households in those quintiles have incomes below three poverty lines.

The major constraint to a universal social policy is, of course, its strong demand for public sector resources. In this sense, one of the advantages of targeting is that it demands fewer resources. But it was politically naïve to think that it was possible to reduce spending aimed at middle income groups to give it to the poor. In practice, some rationalization of this sort took place but social spending tended to increase again since the 1990s, as a result of the democratic wave that swept the region. Reactions to redistributing spending from the middle classes to the poor show that democracy does not work by reducing the benefits to the middle classes but rather by extending those benefits to the poor while simultaneously aiming at more and better services to the middle classes.

The major demand is therefore on the fiscal regime.[8] The crux of the matter is therefore the "Fiscal Covenant" required by Latin America, as expressed by ECLAC (1998) a decade ago. And the crucial issue in this regard is the low income tax of Latin America, particularly from personal income taxes, as pointed out by ECLAC and, more recently, by the World Bank (2006) and OECD (2007). The capacity to raise taxes—and, particularly, more redistributive taxes—to achieve more universal systems of social spending is thus the domain where the battle of equity will be fought in the future.

Universal policies are thus a better route to overcoming the endemic inequalities that characterize Latin America and to rebuild the social covenant under the strong distributive conflict that are already evident in the region and that may expand during a period of weak economic performance. But this will not be possible without a new fiscal covenant, perhaps the area of greatest need in the process of rebuilding stronger states for the new phase of development. But there is no alternative route to building more equitable societies in Latin America other than exercising the strong redistributive role of the state.

Conclusion

In this chapter, I argue that a revision of development thinking had been going on in Latin America prior to the global financial crisis, reflecting frustration with the effects of market reforms in social and economic terms. The broader acceptance of a stronger role for the state is likely to continue in the face of the similar trend at the global level unleashed by the crisis. In Latin America such a stronger role should involve three pillars.

The first is the final acceptance of the role of countercyclical macroeconomic policies, which should be consistently applied during booms as well as busts. This implies not only a change in fiscal rules—following, for example, the Chilean model of targeting structural fiscal balance—but also a recognition by central banks of the multiple objectives of monetary policy. These objectives include, aside from inflation, smoother business cycles, financial stability, and stable and competitive exchange rates—necessary for the success of the second pillar of this policy package.

This second pillar would be a movement away from the orthodox export-led growth policies that have prevailed since the reform period toward equally export-led but more active development strategies. The latter would involve production sector policies aimed at improving the technological contents and domestic value added of export activities, strengthening the links with the new dynamic poles of the world economy—particularly China, though with a diversified export basket—and enhancing regional integration. The last element of this strategy—regional integration—requires overcoming the political divisions that are currently blocking this process and emphasizing new dimensions of integration, particularly infrastructure.

The third pillar would be the adoption of policies to combat the endemic inequality that characterizes the region, which would reinforce the positive trends that have been experienced in this area prior to the crisis. A major contribution, in this regard, would be a definite move toward universal social policies. This will not be possible, however, without a new fiscal covenant, which would give states the resources needed to deepen redistributive policies. Here lies the weakest link in the chain of rebuilding stronger states and the area in which it would be shown whether the commitment to improve equity has gone beyond mere rhetoric.

Notes

I thank the editors of the volume for useful comments to a previous version of this chapter.

1. It is not easy to match the implicit model I recommend with the typologies proposed by Mitchell Orenstein and Arvind Subramanian in other chapters of this volume. The closest is Orenstein's "European social market" model, though with stronger macroeconomic and production sector interventions than are typical in Europe. In terms of Subramanian, it is certainly far from his "foreign finance fetish," whose rejection I agree with, but in a sense shares some features of the types of interventions that he identifies with the "export fetish," a concept that I find imprecise.

2. See, among the many analyses, ECLAC (2009a), IADB (2009), Jara et al. (2009) and Ocampo (2009).

3. For Mexico, Colombia, Ecuador, and several Central American countries for which data are available, remittances fell 5.2 percent in the last quarter of 2008, 6.7 percent in the first quarter of 2009, and 15.8 percent in the second quarter of 2009 versus the same period one year before. For those countries for which information is available for the third quarter, the reduction was 16.6 percent.

4. See a close analysis of all of the indicators that follow in Ocampo (2009).

5. Statistics available at the WTO Web site (www.wto.org) give only slightly different figures for the value of world exports: a contraction of 31.5 percent during the first quarter of 2009 versus the same period in 2008 and of 23.5 percent in the third quarter of 2009 versus the first quarter of 2008.
6. See, among many others, ECLAC (2008a and 2008b), Cimoli et al. (2006) Hausmann et al. (2006) and Ocampo et al. (2009).
7. To these we must add specific projects aimed at managing the social costs of structural reforms, the most important of which were the social emergency funds in the 1980s.
8. See Peter Heller's chapter in this volume for more on the fiscal challenges that have emerged from this crisis.

References

Alesina, Alberto, and Edward L. Glaeser. 2004. *Fighting Poverty in the US and Europe: A World of Difference.* Oxford: Oxford University Press.

Birdsall, Nancy, Augusto de la Torre, and Rachel Menezes. 2001. *Washington Contentious: Economic Policies for Social Equity in Latin America.* Washington, DC: Carnegie Endowment for International Peace and Inter-American Dialogue.

Cimoli, Mario, Analissa Primi, and Maurizio Pugno. 2006. "A Low Growth Model: Informality as a Structural Constraint." *CEPAL Review* 88(April).

Cornia, Giovanni Andrea. 2010. "Income Distribution under Latin America's Center-Left Regimes." *Journal of Human Development and Capabilities* (February).

CPB Netherlands Bureau for Economic Policy Analysis. 2010. *World Trade Monitor: May 2010,* July 26. Available at www.cpb.nl/eng/research/sector2/data/trademonitor.html

ECLAC (United Nations Economic Commission for Latin America and the Caribbean). 1990. *Transformación productiva con equidad.* Santiago, Chile: ECLAC.

———.1998. *The Fiscal Covenant: Strengths, Weaknesses, Challenges.* Santiago, Chile: ECLAC.

———. 2000. *Equidad, desarrollo y ciudadanía,* Bogotá: ECLAC and Alfaomega (English edition of the original version is also available).

———. 2006. *Shaping the Future of Social Protection: Access, Financing and Solidarity.* Santiago, Chile: ECLAC.

———. 2007. *Social Panorama of Latin America 2007.* Santiago, Chile: ECLAC.

———. 2008a. *La transformación productiva 20 años después: Viejos problemas, nuevas oportunidades.* Santiago, Chile: ECLAC.

———. 2008b. *Progreso técnico y cambio estructural en América Latina.* Santiago, Chile: ECLAC.

———. 2009a. *Economic Survey of Latin America and the Caribbean, 2008-2009,* Santiago, Chile: ECLAC.

———. 2009b. *Panorama de la inserción internacional de América Latina y el Caribe 2008-2009.* Santiago, Chile: ECLAC.

————. 2009c. *Social Panorama of Latin America 2009*. Santiago, Chile: ECLAC.

Frenkel, Roberto, and Martin Rapetti. 2010. "Economic Development and the International Financial System." In *Time for a Visible Hand: Lessons from the 2008 World Financial Crisis,* edited by Stephany Griffith-Jones, José Antonio Ocampo and Joseph E. Stiglitz. Oxford: Oxford University Press.

Gallagher, Kevin P., and Roberto Porzecanski. 2009. "China and the Latin America Commodities Boom: A Critical Assessment." *Working Paper No. 192*, Political Economy Research Institute, University of Massachusetts, Amherst.

Gasparini, Leonardo, Guillermo Cruces, Leopoldo Tornarolli, and Mariana Marchionni. 2009. "A Turning Point? Recent Developments on Inequality in Latin America and the Caribbean." Research for Public Policy, Human Development, HD-02–2009, New York: UNDP, Regional Bureau for Latin America and the Caribbean.

Grynspan, Rebeca. 2006. "Universalismo básico y Estado: principios y desafíos." In *Universalismo básico: Una nueva política social para América Latina*, edited by Carlos Gerardo Molina, 75–81.Washington, DC: Banco Interamericano de Desarrollo and Editorial Planeta.

Hausmann, Ricardo, Jason Hwang, and Dani Rodrik. 2006. "What You Export Matters." *Journal of Economic Growth* 12(March): 1–25.

IADB (Inter-American Development Bank). 2008. *All That Glitters May Not Be Gold: Assessing Latin America´s Recent Macroeconomic Performance.* Washington, DC: IADB.

————. 2009. *Policy Trade-offs for Unprecedented Times: Confronting the Global Crisis in Latin America and the Caribbean.* Washington DC: IADB.

Izquierdo, Alejandro, Randall Romero, and Ernesto Talvi. 2008. "Booms and Busts in Latin America: The Role of External Factors." Inter-American Development Bank, Research Department, Working Paper No. 631. Washington, DC: IADB.

Jara, Alejandro, Ramón Moreno, and Camilo E. Tovar. 2009. "The Global Crisis and Latin America: Financial Impact and Policy Response." *BIS Quarterly Review* (June).

Jiménez, Juan Pablo, and Varinia Tromben. 2006. "Política fiscal y bonanza: Impacto del aumento de los precios de los productos no renovables en América Latina y el Caribe." *Revista de la CEPAL* 90 (September).

Korpi, Walter, and Joakim Palme. 1998. "The Paradox of Redistribution and Strategies of Equality: Welfare State Institutions, Inequality and Poverty in the Western Countries." *American Sociological Review* 63: 661–87.

Kuczynski, Pedro-Pablo, and John Williamson, eds. 2003. *After the Washington Consensus: Restarting Growth and Reform in Latin America.* Washington, DC: Institute for International Economics.

Levy, Santiago. 2008. *Good Intentions, Bad Outcomes: Social Policy, Informality, and Economic Growth in Mexico.* Washington DC: Brookings Institution.

Marfán, Manuel. 2005. "Fiscal Policy, Efficacy and Private Deficits: A Macroeconomic

Approach." In *Beyond Reforms: Structural Dynamics and Macroeconomic Vulnerability*, edited by José Antonio Ocampo. Palo Alto and Santiago: Stanford University Press and Economic Commission for Latin America and the Caribbean.

Mkandawire, Thandika. 2007. "Targeting and Universalism in Poverty Reduction." In *Policy Matters: Economic and Social Policies to Sustain Equitable Development*, edited by José Antonio Ocampo, K. S. Jomo, and Sarbuland Khan, 305–33. Himayatnagar, London, and Penang: Orient Longman, Zed Books, and Third World Network.

Ocampo, José Antonio. 2007. "The Macroeconomics of the Latin American Boom." *CEPAL Review* 93 (December).

———. 2009. "Latin America and the Global Financial Crisis." *Cambridge Journal of Economics* 33(June).

Ocampo, José Antonio, and Mariángela Parra. 2003. "The Terms of Trade for Commodities in the Twentieth Century." *CEPAL Review* 79(April).

Ocampo, José Antonio, Codrina Rada, and Lance Taylor. 2009. *Developing Country Policy and Growth: A Structuralist Approach*. New York: Columbia University Press.

OECD Development Centre. 2007. *Perspectivas Económicas de América Latina 2008*. Paris: OECD.

Rodrik, Dani. 2007. "The Exchange Rate and Economic Growth: Theory and Evidence." *Processed* (July), John F. Kennedy School of Government, Harvard University, Cambridge, MA.

United Nations. 2010. *World Economic Situation and Prospects as of mid-2010*. New York: United Nations, May.

Williamson, John. 1990. "What Washington Means by Policy Reform." In *Latin American Adjustment: How Much Has Happened?* edited by John Williamson. Washington, DC: Institute of International Economics.

World Bank. 2006. *Poverty Reduction and Growth: Virtuous and Vicious Circles*. Washington, DC: World Bank Latin American and Caribbean Studies.

———. 2009. *Global Economic Prospect 2009: Commodities at the Crossroads* Washington, DC: World Bank

CHAPTER 7

The International Financial Crisis

Eight Lessons for and from Latin America

Liliana Rojas-Suarez

OVER THE PAST CENTURY, Latin America has not been short of ideas about development models. Indeed, some analysts have concluded that the region has tried it all: from a focus toward exports as a growth engine to massive tariffs and an inward bias, from large government interventions to a free market approach, and from autocracy to democracy. In spite of all these different approaches, Latin America has demonstrated a repeated pattern of intense economic volatility.

To be more exact, since the beginning of the twentieth century, there have been three distinct economic models for development. Two models have been overthrown, and the present model has been under intense criticism during the current decade. The trend of these overarching paradigms has been simple. An economic crisis has led to a new paradigm that slowly expanded its influence and universality; soon this paradigm took hold of the region, delivered marginal growth to countries, and generally began to show chronic problems; those problems turned into a crisis, which spurned a new paradigm shift. Now the most recent economic model—that of open and deregulated markets—has been tested by the severe international financial crisis and several conclusions can be reached from that experience. In contrast to previous crisis episodes, however, the region shows no intention of abandoning its most recent paradigm.

A brief history of the evolution of growth models in Latin America helps us understand current choices made by policymakers and to derive lessons for future decisions.[1]

The first model, known as the export-led model, was adopted during the period before the 1930s, when a swift progression of industrialization abroad translated into a greater global demand for Latin America's primary goods, like silver, copper, wool, cotton, coffee, grain, and later oil. Based on the hypothesis that the region should specialize in the production of primary commodities, public policy was directed to protect the interests of exporters with disregard for improvements of local social services, such as health and education.[2] The model delivered growth during the 1920s. But as Latin American economies began to heavily specialize in specific raw materials, the model began to reveal weaknesses. The lack of diversification left the health of Latin American economies at the mercy of fluctuating commodity—food and raw material—prices. These issues became chronic and irreversible when the Great Depression occurred and the demand for primary goods abroad collapsed. As a result, external demand could no longer power the economic activity of the region. Policymakers began to look inward to their own domestic economy.

The next paradigm was import substitution industrialization, or ISI. Under this new model, championed by Raul Prebisch, Latin America shifted its focus toward industrial production, with its own domestic market as the economic motor. The primary goals for ISI were gaining economic independence, reducing vulnerability to external shocks like the great depression, and creating more employment at home. During this period, tariffs were raised on imported goods, and governments implemented industrial stimulus to spur the formation of factories and more sophisticated commercial industries.

This model was initially successful in that manufacturing grew as a percentage of the gross domestic product until the 1970s. But import substitution did not satisfy its goals, and it eventually failed for three reasons. First, Latin America was still dependent on the so-called first world. Instead of buying finished manufactured goods, Latin America imported intermediate goods used for capital accumulation. And the region's economies were still significantly trading primary goods to industrialized countries. Second, ISI did not create enough jobs. Latin America countries did not integrate with each other effectively, and domestic demand was insufficient to allow for a dynamic market for manufactured products. Also states ran the industrialization, which meant limited innovation; this hampered industrial growth and employment. Third, governments progressively accumulated large amounts of debt to finance the industrialization, especially during the 1970s, when the rise in oil prices motivated international banks to lend more aggressively to developing countries. During the 1970s, Latin

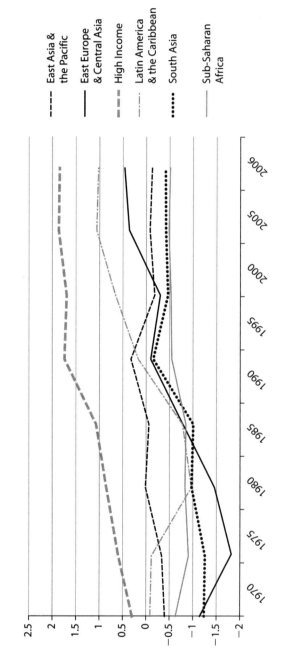

Figure 7.1 *Financial openness in Latin America. Source:* Chinn and Ito (2007)

East Asia &
the Pacific

East Europe
& Central Asia

High Income

Latin America
& the Caribbean

South Asia

Sub-Saharan
Africa

America's foreign debt rose from $27 billion to $231 billion. In the 1980s, oil prices dropped, and Latin America lost the foundation that permitted such aggressive lending. In 1982, Mexico was the first to announce that it could no longer sustain its floating interest burden, and thus began the debt crisis of the 1980s and the well-known "lost decade" of the region.

The debt crisis that occurred in the 1980s marked the region's next economic shift, which was to the model of financial openness and deregulation. The crisis caused a maelstrom of problems for the Latin American people: hyperinflation, decreased income per capita, paralyzed markets, and minimal liquidity. Latin American economies could no longer sustain their debt burdens; a number of governments had defaulted on their loans, and they needed to negotiate with advanced industrialized economies, namely the United States, in order to minimize the economic damage. A solution was found in the Brady plan (which began in 1989 in Mexico), that allowed for the securitization of governments' external debt liabilities and for the creation of a highly liquid market for international bonds and other securities issued by the region. Debt securitization facilitated the region's increased access to international markets but was by no means a panacea.

With very low domestic saving ratios and extremely volatile terms of trade (resulting from export concentration in commodities), most Latin American countries liberalized their capital accounts seeking to support their development efforts with capital inflows, especially with foreign direct investment. In sharp contrast with the ISI model, the private sector was seen as the motor of growth. Also, distinct from both the export-led and the ISI models, the central role of the government was to facilitate competition and the workings of the market economy rather than picking winners (primary commodities under the export-led model or the manufacturing sector under the ISI model).

But, under the new paradigm, greater financial openness implied a policy decision to let market forces, through the behavior of the international capital markets, assess the performance of the economy. This in turn required that macroeconomic stability needed to be maintained *at all times*, since deterioration in investors' perception about a country's credit-worthiness would result in a quick reversal of capital inflows. Moreover, the sustainability of financial openness required adequate regulation and supervision of the domestic financial system to avoid excessive risk-taking activities that might have compromised the maintenance of both financial and macroeconomic stability.

The process of financial liberalization continued and, as shown in Figure 7.1, by the early 2000s Latin America was the most financially open region in the developing world, second only to industrial countries.[3]

However, during the 1990s the requirements for sustainable open capital accounts were not followed in a number of countries in the region. Lacking adequate financial supervision and macroeconomic stability, a fresh round of economic and financial crises plagued the region. These started with Mexico's tequila crisis in the mid-1990s, when unsustainable macroeconomic conditions induced a sharp reversal of capital flows. Crisis countries also included Colombia (1998), Argentina (1994, 2001), Venezuela (1994), Brazil (1999), Ecuador (2001), Uruguay (2001), and Dominican Republic (2002). The few countries, like Chile and Peru, that managed to avoid deep economic imbalances also did not experience economic and financial crises. To the critics of the open capital account model, these crises revealed the weakness of subjecting countries to the vagaries of international capital markets.

But rather than abandoning the new paradigm of growth based on liberalized capital accounts, the crises of the 1990s and early 2000s led most governments in the region to improve the policies that would allow for the sustainability of this model. There were (and are) some well-known exceptions, notably Ecuador and Venezuela.[4]

Supported by improved policies and a positive international environment, Latin American economies grew once again starting in 2003 and this time for five consecutive years at annual average regional rates above 4 percent, an outcome not seen since the 1970s. Not even a return to high growth was able to induce strong support for further comprehensive market-based reforms. An important reason behind this reticence was that large segments of the population did not feel included in the benefits from growth. The result of this thinning of patience with the current growth model has been a significant slowdown of the process of structural reforms in most countries in the region.

Notwithstanding these developments, reports of a generalized political backlash against the market economy and market-oriented reforms need to be taken with caution. Although some countries have elected leftists or center-leftists leaders, there are drastic differences in ideology and governance between for example the current government of Venezuela and that of Brazil and Uruguay. Also, the coalition in Chile has successfully been able to deal with social demands.

As the recent international crisis erupted in 2007 and later progressed during 2008–9, Latin American countries with open capital accounts did not impose capital controls to the outflows, even though the reversal of inflows from the region was severe. At the time of this writing, the generalized assessment about Latin America's management of the crisis was quite positive, albeit with important caveats.[5]

The rest of this chapter presents lessons derived from the experience of Latin America during the recent international crisis. As the title indicates, some are lessons *for* the region, but others are lessons *from* Latin America to other developing countries that might seek to achieve growth in the context of greater integration to the international capital markets, such as Eastern Europe now and maybe Africa in the future. Based on the Latin American experience, countries tend to abandon development paradigms that prove to be economically, politically and socially unsustainable. Given the good performance of Asian countries during the recent international crisis (and the quick recovery of the region during its own crisis in the late 1990s), a shift of Asian countries toward a very open financial system à la Latin America is quite unlikely in the foreseeable future.[6]

Although there are many lessons from the crisis, the analysis here focuses on eight selected ones, all of them related to the central issue of this chapter: the sustainability of the open capital account model of growth in Latin America. Some lessons are not new but are newly reinforced by the crisis. An example is the imperative need for export diversification in the region; this lesson is a century old. Some others break with myths, such as the region's inability to undertake countercyclical policies. Yet others reveal some new aspects of the region's development process, such as a renewed assessment of the roles of domestic public banks and foreign banks. All of them taken together bring a new sense of optimism toward the region.

LESSON I. **Because of a shifting geo-economic international landscape accentuated by the crisis, it is more important than ever for Latin American countries to increase their trade diversification, not only in products but also in partners.**

For quite a long time, the strong economic interconnections between Latin America and the United States have been characterized in a poignant saying: "If the United States gets a cold, Latin America gets pneumonia." However, while the United States is still a key trading partner for Latin America (and the most important contributor of foreign direct investment to the region[7]), its share in total exports has declined significantly over the last 15 years. This demonstrates the increasing importance of new economic powers, as a number of Latin American countries have increased exports to new regions, especially China and other Asian countries.

Table 7.1 shows this trend by comparing the direction of exports by Latin American countries between 1992 and 2007. With the exception of Mexico (which has increased its share of exports to the United States) and Venezuela (which has kept this share constant), Latin American countries have favored a larger participation of Asian or intraregional trade.[8]

Based on this pattern, it is not surprising that Mexico is the most affected by the international crisis with a projected negative growth rate of

Table 7.1. Direction of exports by trading partners (1992–2007) in percentages

	Latin America		United States		Europe		Asia		Rest of the world	
	1992	2007	1992	2007	1992	2007	1992	2007	1992	2007
Argentina	33.52	41.37	10.75	7.58	34.60	21.18	13.35	21.37	7.79	8.50
Bolivia	39.88	62.39	16.02	8.82	41.10	11.17	1.67	14.26	1.33	3.35
Brazil	22.43	24.10	19.34	15.58	32.64	29.47	18.93	19.71	6.66	11.14
Chile	17.33	16.88	15.37	13.01	32.10	26.36	33.11	41.02	2.10	2.73
Colombia	27.20	36.04	36.19	35.28	28.87	19.33	4.74	6.00	3.01	3.35
Costa Rica[a]	22.06	26.10	41.33	33.91	29.04	15.53	1.86	21.86	5.71	2.61
Ecuador	19.00	32.98	45.65	43.12	17.09	16.57	15.89	2.83	2.37	4.50
El Salvador[b]	48.95	65.85	30.54	19.57	16.20	11.32	1.66	1.97	2.66	1.30
Guatemala[b]	41.05	53.13	37.30	25.38	13.29	7.47	4.32	8.38	4.03	5.64
Honduras[b]	11.23	29.97	55.96	42.66	26.74	20.61	4.34	4.20	1.73	2.56
Mexico	5.01	6.03	80.71	82.28	7.82	5.41	3.07	2.79	3.39	3.49
Nicaragua[b]	29.52	48.15	41.41	27.49	17.53	14.93	0.64	2.97	10.91	6.46
Paraguay[c]	48.43	59.51	5.33	3.27	36.44	19.82	4.75	5.55	5.05	11.84
Peru	19.02	20.93	20.70	18.02	34.34	27.32	20.49	25.72	5.45	8.01
Uruguay[b]	51.02	40.72	9.07	10.97	22.82	24.02	14.60	11.32	2.49	12.97
Venezuela	17.97	23.46	52.31	52.40	11.25	13.18	3.84	2.01	14.63	8.95

Source: Inter-American Development Bank 2005.
[a] The information for the year 1992 corresponds to the year 1994
[b] The information of the year 1992 correspond to the year 1993
[c] The information of the year 2007 corresponds to the year 2006

Table 7.2. Export concentration index, 2006

Exporting region or country	Herfindahl-Hirschman Index
Latin America	31
Chile	39
Venezuela	91
East Asia	21
Eastern Europe	13

Source: Foxley 2009 based on World Bank 2008.
Note: The Herfindahl-Hirschman Index is a measure of the degree of export concentration within a country. The values of the Herfindahl-Hirschman Index range between 0 for no concentration and 100 for maximum concentration.

over 7 percent in 2009. With respect to trade partners, Mexico is by far the most concentrated country in the region: over 80 percent of its exports are directed to the United States.

The most diversified countries in the region in terms of trade partners are Brazil, Costa Rica, Chile, and Peru. Brazil, Chile, and Peru in particular are actively seeking new bilateral trade partners in Asia and within Latin America. As discussed by Birdsall and Rojas-Suarez (2004), both the movement toward open regionalism and the inclusion of Asian partners grant these countries greater access to the global system. Diversification has served these countries well during the international financial crisis.

Unfortunately not all Latin American countries favor free trade. The leaders of a group of countries have raised their voices against globalization and have increased impediments to global trade with measures such as increased tariffs and other protectionist measures. The key countries in this group (Argentina, Ecuador, and Venezuela) each have differing degrees of protectionist measures and antimarket policies. Economic indicators for these countries before the international crisis show a very poor performance, with extremely high inflation in Argentina and Venezuela and severe fiscal problems in Ecuador. For this group of countries, it is fair to say that the international crisis simply exacerbated economic fragilities already rooted in the pre-crisis period.

While many Latin American countries are diversifying trade partners, they are not sufficiently diversifying the products to be exported. Table 7.2 presents an indicator of export concentration: the Herfindahl-Hirschman Index. As noted by Foxley (2009), exports in Latin America remain highly specialized in primary goods, with the extreme being Venezuela, which basically exports a single commodity: oil. In contrast, East Asian and Eastern European countries have been able to achieve greater diversification, moving forward in the value added chain by increasing their production

Exchange rate in Brazil (BRL per USD)

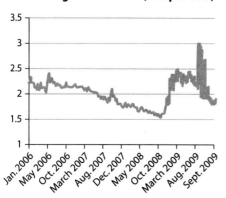

Exchange rate in Chile (CLP per USD)

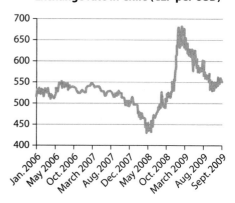

Exchange rate in Colombia (COP per USD)

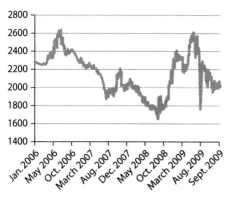

Mexico (%)

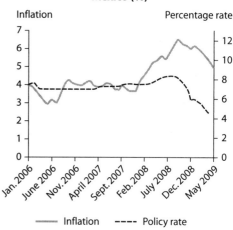

Inflation   Percentage rate

——— Inflation   - - - - Policy rate

Exchange rate in Peru (PEN per USD)

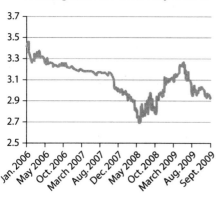

Figure 7.2 Exchange rate behavior in selected Latin American countries.
Source: JP Morgan and Central Bank.

of manufacturing goods. In the case of Latin America, increased diversification into both manufacturing and services is highly desirable.[9]

Although diversification in export partners has helped Latin America to deal with the current international crisis, the region has not yet learned a central lesson from previous crises, namely that the high volatility of commodity prices makes the region extremely vulnerable to external shocks. After all, the export-led model of the beginning of the last century was abandoned precisely because of plummeting commodity prices during the Great Depression, and the debt crisis of the 1980s was preceded by a collapse in the price of oil (a commodity exported by a number of countries in the region). This time around, Latin America's terms of trade fell sharply at the peak of the crisis in early 2009. Had that trend continued, the emphasis of the discussion in this chapter would have been different.

LESSON 2. **Increased flexibility of exchange rates in the context of inflation targeting is the right policy choice for Latin America.**

Unlike previous crises episodes over the past three decades, contagion from the global financial crisis of 2007–9 did not result in exchange rate crises across Latin American countries. Central banks were not forced to abandon their announced exchange rate regime after costly and ineffective efforts to defend an established exchange rate parity or exchange rate band. Just recall the sharp devaluations of the early 1980s throughout the region that ended with periods of extremely high or hyperinflations, or the abandonment of Brazil's "crawling" peg of its currency in 1999 following contagion from the Russian crisis, or the dramatic abandonment of Argentina's ten-year-old currency board in 2002.

For a change, there was no drama on the exchange rate front in Latin America during the late 2000s global crisis. This in spite of nominal exchange rate depreciations of around 30 percent in a number of countries (such as Chile, Colombia, and Brazil) during the peak of the crisis (see figure 7.2).

What was different? The answer is that by the early 2000s a large number of countries in Latin America had adopted more flexible exchange rate regimes. In addition, a number of central banks had chosen to combine this greater flexibility with inflation targeting.[10] The truth of the matter is that after recurrent episodes of crises, most Latin American countries learned an important lesson: having chosen to maintain a liberalized capital account, it is extremely difficult to simultaneously have both an independent monetary policy and a fixed exchange rate system. This derives from the well-known proposition of the so-called impossible trinity (i.e., the impossibil-

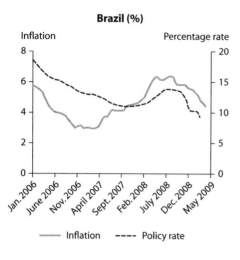

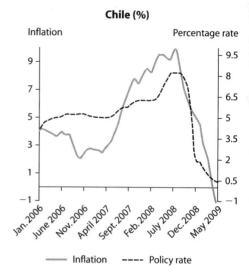

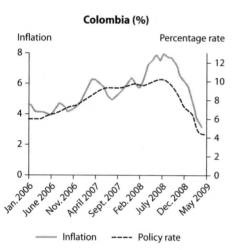

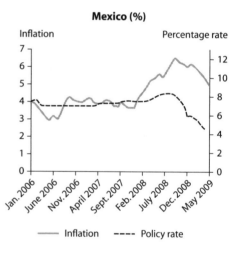

Figure 7.3 Inflation and interest rate in
selected Latin American countries.
Source: Central Bank.

ity of simultaneously fixing the exchange rate, setting domestic interest rates, and having perfect capital mobility).

Actually, most of the previous exchange rate crises of the 1990s in Latin America followed a similar pattern. An external adverse shock materialized (such as a deterioration in the region's terms of trade or an increase in the external funding costs). This was followed by a sharp reversal of capital inflows to the region, which put upward pressure on the exchange rate. To defend the peg, central banks increased interest rates and allowed foreign exchange reserves to decline. Because debt ratios were high in the region (see discussion above), it was straightforward for speculators to conclude that the country would have to abandon the exchange rate peg and, therefore, to sharply bet against the maintenance of the announced peg.[11] The speculation itself led to further losses of foreign exchange reserves to a point where it was clear to governments that they could not longer sustain the exchange rate peg. This process was known as "one-sided bet," implying that speculators always won in the bet against the parity.

No one-sided bets took place during the recent global financial crisis.[12] Since most countries in the region were not committed to a peg or a band, central banks let the exchange rate depreciate when capital inflows to the region reversed sharply in late 2008 to early 2009. Most important, because monetary policy was not restricted by the behavior of the exchange rate, most central banks were able to undertake countercyclical monetary policies. Thus, in sharp departure from their behavior in previous crises episodes, central banks lowered interest rates significantly in the midst of the crisis (figure 7.3). The expansionary monetary policies helped to provide necessary liquidity to domestic financial systems and therefore helped to ameliorate the adverse impact of the shock on local credit. Because the external shock implied a contraction in global demand, the expansionary monetary policies were consistent with the maintenance of the low inflation targets in many countries in the region.[13]

This lesson from Latin America is applicable to other countries in the developing world, especially those in Eastern Europe. Having liberalized their capital account, a number of countries in this group were among the most affected during the crisis precisely because they were committed to fixed exchange rate systems (Latvia, Ukraine, and Belarus are vivid examples of this problem).

LESSON 3. **Lacking the capacity to issue hard currencies, accumulating large stocks of international reserves and implementing other forms of insurance against volatility is highly desirable.**

To economists, a policy of pursuing both flexible exchange rates and the accumulation of foreign exchange reserves appears contradictory. After all, the idea is that in a flexible exchange rate system, movements in prices (the exchange rate) and not in quantities (foreign exchange reserves) do the adjustment following a shock (positive or negative). This assessment is correct and that is why the previous lesson talks about increased rather than pure flexibility of exchange rates. The restrictions imposed by the volatility of capital inflows to Latin America imply that a pure flexible exchange rate system cannot adequately contribute to economic and financial stability.

A major reason is that when foreign inflows to Latin America suddenly cease, even a sharp depreciation of the exchange rate cannot generate sufficient resources (through export revenues) quickly enough to meet due external amortization and interest payments. Now, if we were talking about industrial countries with the capacity of issuing fully tradable and liquid currencies (like the U.S. dollar, the yen, the euro, the British pound, etc.), the countries would issue liquid external liabilities that would be used to service debt payments (at a depreciated exchange rate, of course). But developing countries in general, and Latin America, in particular, cannot issue hard currency; that is, currency that is fully tradable and highly liquid in the international capital markets (such as the euro, the yen, or the U.S. dollar). Thus it is fully appropriate to accumulate large amounts of foreign exchange reserves in good times to deal with the vagaries of international capital markets.[14]

This is what many Latin American countries did in the years prior to the international financial crisis. A good measurement of the adequacy of net foreign exchange liquidity is the ratio of short-term debt to international reserves. The lower the ratio is, the greater a country's ability to meet due external payments in the presence of an adverse shock. Table 7.3 shows this ratio for a number of emerging market economies. By 2008, Poland and Hungary displayed the highest ratio among the countries in the sample and were, therefore, the most vulnerable countries to an external shock, according to this indicator. In contrast, most countries in Asia and Latin America displayed much lower ratios and were, therefore, in a better footing to face the crisis.[15]

A related lesson, learned by most Latin American countries before the crisis, but not by countries in Eastern Europe, is that large current account deficits tend to be unsustainable in countries that cannot issue hard cur-

Table 7.3. Short-term external debt/international
reserves (%) in selected countries

Country	2007	2008
Argentina	85.33	75.21
Brazil	21.57	23.01
China	14.42	14.70
Colombia	24.63	26.04
Ecuador	59.89	31.36
Hungary	88.00	81.92
India	11.43	17.89
Indonesia	28.67	30.72
Malaysia	13.81	24.95
Mexico	45.08	49.24
Peru	20.97	19.71
Philippines	23.93	21.49
Poland	74.71	82.68
Taiwan	30.80	32.22
Venezuela	27.29	22.09

Source: Deutsche Bank.

rencies (unless they hold extremely high stocks of foreign exchange reserves, with a punitive opportunity cost). The lesson learned from recurrent balance of payments crisis in Latin America is that it does not matter significantly if the large current account deficit is generated by the public or private sector. If an adverse external shock leads investors to increased risk aversion, emerging markets with large current account deficits will face significant problems in rolling over existing maturing debts and in acquiring new ones. As explained above, a central reason is that, lacking the capability to issue a liquid international currency, investors' increased risk aversion will induce a portfolio shift away from emerging markets' debt and toward the holding of liabilities issued by safer issuers. At this point, experience shows that to avoid large private sector bankruptcies governments will absorb important fractions of private sector debt in their books. That is why in emerging markets private debt is often a contingent liability of the public sector.[16]

Table 7.4 illustrates the sharp differences in balance of payment positions between the various emerging markets regions of the world. While Latin America and East Asia faced the beginning of the international crisis with positive current account balances, Eastern Europe's external position was extremely fragile. While countries in Eastern Europe built up large stocks of external debt, in the years previous to the crisis a number of Latin American countries bought back expensive debt and improved the maturity profile of their debt obligations. As noted by Foxley (2009), East-

Table 7.4. Current account and debt ratios by regions and selected countries

Region	Current account as percentage of GDP (annual average)		Ratio of external debt to GDP, 2008 (%)
	2003–7	2008–10	
Eastern Europe	−9.2	−7.2	89.4
Bulgaria	−13.61	−13.42	66.46
Czech Republic	−3.73	−2.92	n/a
Hungary	−7.58	−5.07	95.36
Latvia	−15.72	−8.45	113.32
Poland	−2.95	−4.63	37.15
Romania	−9.46	−8.89	45.32
Slovak Republic	−6.95	−5.67	49.20
Latin America	2.7	−0.9	26.6
Argentina	2.80	1.39	57.03
Brazil	1.09	−1.81	18.19
Chile	2.32	−3.94	32.90
Colombia	−1.56	−3.33	25.88
Ecuador	0.77	−1.15	39.94
Mexico	−0.70	−2.04	19.15
Peru	0.86	−3.26	30.49
Venezuela	13.83	5.32	24.54
East Asia	7.5	6	32
Philippines	2.75	2.14	51.31
Indonesia	1.91	−0.34	35.90
Malaysia	14.23	13.67	34.86
Taiwan	7.33	−4.63	n/a

Sources: Current account information source is International Monetary Fund 2009. Ratio of external debt source is World Bank World Development Indicators 2008, data.worldbank.org/data-catalog/world=development-indicators, and Foxley 2009.
Note: The regional averages do not correspond to the average of the few selected countries in each region. Figures from 2010 are estimates.

ern European countries' accession to the European Union gave them a false sense of security regarding their ability to enjoy continuous access to international capital markets. Self-insurance through accumulation of foreign reserves was extremely low when the crisis started.

But it is important to note that, while a large accumulation of foreign exchange reserves is a good mechanism for self-insurance against highly volatile capital flows, it is a very costly alternative, and ideally countries would have access to other mechanisms that would substitute partially for reserves.[17] There are a number of other market instruments that could help countries acquire much-needed hedging. These instruments include contingent lines of credit with foreign private financial institutions and issuance of indexed bonds, either to GDP or commodity prices. Perry (2009) recommends that multilateral organizations help developing countries issue these types of instruments. At this juncture, however, we cannot say that this sensible recommendation has been a lesson learned from the recent global financial crisis (more of this in lesson 8).

LESSON 4. **Fiscal stabilization funds are a must, especially in democratic and unequal Latin America.**

In contrast to the effective countercyclical monetary policies undertaken by a number of countries in the region during the crisis, Latin America had difficulty implementing countercyclical fiscal policies. Only Chile and to some extent Peru were able to undertake fiscal stimulus without concerns about jeopardizing the dynamism and sustainability of their public debt. Even in Brazil, where an important fiscal expansion took place, there were serious concerns about the ability of policymakers to reverse fiscal stimulus at the appropriate time (i.e., avoiding turning a countercyclical policy into a steady-state one), especially in the context of upcoming presidential elections in 2010.

Mexico was clearly incapable of undertaking countercyclical fiscal policies, which was demonstrative of most Latin America countries. Sharply affected by the global crisis, Mexico's fiscal revenues deteriorated significantly, exposing unfunded financial needs. Efforts to support local governments affected by the recession took place in 2009 through the issuance of government bonds. These bonds further compromised the future fiscal stance as amortization and interest payments became due. Lacking a solid fiscal stance and facing a potential downgrade of its debt by the international credit ratings (which would increase external financing costs), the Mexican government submitted to its congress a fiscal proposal that included a severe fiscal adjustment.[18] Thus, to a large extent, the Mexican government implemented a procyclical fiscal policy in 2010.

In sharp contrast, Chile was capable of undertaking an active countercyclical fiscal policy without affecting its financing and its credit-worthiness to international capital markets. This is because Chile follows a fiscal rule that allows it to save during good times (in the so-called Economic and Social Stabilization Fund—FEES) and increase expenditures during a crisis. The fiscal rule calls for achieving a targeted "structural fiscal balance," where a structural balance is defined as the difference between structural fiscal revenues and observed fiscal expenditures. Structural fiscal revenues are defined as the level of revenues that would have occurred if the output were at its potential level and the price of copper and derivatives were at their long-run level.[19] This allows for a smoothing of fiscal revenues. In the years previous to the crisis, when the price of copper was high and output was growing fast, the fiscal authorities targeted a structural fiscal surplus. In 2009, when economic conditions deteriorated, the Chilean authorities were able to move to a structural fiscal deficit that was financed by past savings under the FEES.

Chile also used fiscal countercyclical resources to recapitalize the state-owned Banco Estado, Chile's Development Agency (CORFO), and the Insurance Fund for Small Enterprises (FOGAPE) to support credit to exporters, small enterprises, and consumers. That is, the government was able to partially offset credit reductions from the private sector by channeling government funds through public banks. This encouraging development requires further analysis that goes beyond the scope of this chapter, but there is a potential lesson from the Chilean experience. Public banks can play a crucial role in the direct provision of credit when the private banking sector needs to take a cautionary position due to adverse external circumstances and the extension of credit by public banks is fully funded. It is too early however, to come to long-term conclusions, as a return to good times would need to be accompanied by a retrenching of credit activities by public banks to avoid crowding out private sector financial institutions.[20]

LESSON 5. **Sound banks are a key shield against external shocks, but domestic rather than foreign banks might play a greater stabilizing role.**

A lesson learned the hard way by most Latin American countries is that weak banking systems are not compatible with open capital accounts. The 1980s and 1990s witnessed a large number of banking crisis episodes ignited by a sudden reversal of capital inflows to the region. As discussed above, a sudden stop of external funding leads to a depreciation of the exchange rate. It also exerts a downward pressure on economic activity as important projects (both from the public and private sector) meet funding constraints. The past has shown that these developments expose existing fragilities in the regions' banking systems.

Because of lax regulatory and supervisory frameworks during the 1980s and the 1990s, banks in many countries took excessive credit risk in good times. A rapid deceleration of economic activity in the face of a reversal of capital inflows resulted in a proliferation of bad loans and sharp losses of capital in already undercapitalized banking systems. Moreover, exchange rate depreciations exposed important currency mismatches in the system. In particular, a phenomenon known as "liability dollarization" was present in many countries in the region where both the U.S. dollar and the local currency were used for financial transactions.[21] Liability dollarization

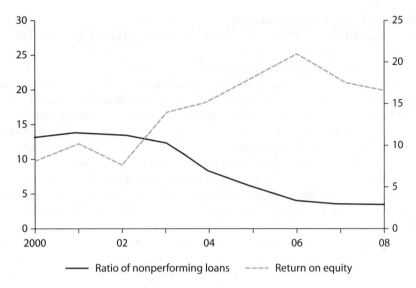

Figure 7.4 Financial soundness indicators in Latin America. Source: Regional Economic Outlook Western Hemisphere—IMF (2009).

meant that banks were extending U.S.-dollar denominated loans to borrowers whose income was denominated in local currency (most individuals and firms working in non-tradable sectors). A sharp depreciation of the exchange rate implied that these borrowers were not able to service their debts. The Argentina and Uruguay crises of the early 2000s were vivid examples of the problems associated with liability dollarization.

During the recent international crisis, exchange rates depreciated significantly (see lesson 2 above), and most countries faced recession. But breaking with the region's pattern, no banking crisis emerged. The fundamental reason for this was a combination of improved regulatory and supervisory standards (see lesson 6), along with improved risk-assessment mechanisms in a number of large banks in the region. Thus, as shown in figure 7.4, indicators of financial solvency in Latin America improved significantly in the 2000s.[22] However in spite of these improvements, confidence in many of the region's financial systems has been far away from being restored. As a result, the ratio of deposits to GDP have remained extremely low in most countries (the regional average is below 30 percent) and this is consistent with the low private savings ratios observed throughout the region (see lesson 7).

But a new, important lesson has also emerged from the recent crisis: banks that contribute to financial stability do not have to be foreign banks.

To many readers, this could appear as an obvious statement. But as those familiar with the process of internationalization of the banking system in Latin America can testify, it is not.

The significantly increased participation of foreign banks in Latin America started in the mid-1990s as a result of two factors, depending on the country. The first was that the process of liberalization of domestic financial systems together with the privatization of public banks drew foreign investment into local banking systems. The second was that the need to recapitalize banking systems, in the context of severe banking crises, involved efforts to attract foreign capital into local banking systems. Albeit sharp differences between countries, participation of foreign banks in Latin America has been high. By 2007, foreign banks accounted for over 85 percent of total assets of the banking systems in Mexico and El Salvador, and the median value for the region was about 40 percent.[23]

Foreign banks have brought significant benefits to the region. As documented in IADB (2005), the evidence shows that the increased participation of foreign banks has been associated with greater efficiency and improvements in risk-assessment techniques. However, while at the beginning of the process of internationalization foreign banks displayed better financial indicators than local banks, that is not longer the case. By 2008, in many countries it was difficult to distinguish between domestic and foreign banks with respect to their financial soundness indicators, such as capitalization and liquidity ratios, return on assets and operating costs.

Moreover, a recent study by Galindo, Izquierdo, and Rojas-Suarez (2010) shows that for most of the 2000s the response of bank credit to changes in economic activity has been as equally procyclical in both foreign banks and domestic banks. This has also been true during the recent international crisis. Facing a sharp reduction in economic growth, both foreign and domestic banks have reduced the expansion of credit. Thus, there appears to be some convergence in behavior between domestic and foreign banks.[24]

However, evidence also shows that foreign banks respond differently than domestic banks to *external financial shocks*. The results from Galindo, Izquierdo, and Rojas-Suarez (2010) suggest that in the presence of an adverse external financial shock foreign banks reduce real credit growth and increase real interest rates more than domestic banks and in the presence of positive external financial shocks, they do the opposite. That is, foreign banks tend to amplify the impact of foreign financial fluctuations on domestic variables. Interestingly enough, the study also shows that origin matters and that Spanish banks behave more like domestic banks and do not amplify the impact of foreign shocks on credit and interest rates.

These results need to be taken with caution, especially since there are large differences across countries in the region. The challenge for policymakers is twofold. First, they must encourage entry to the system of sound banks without a bias favoring foreign banks.[25] Second, they must implement policies that preserve the gains of greater financial integration obtained through foreign banks while avoiding the excessive transmission of foreign financial shocks into domestic economies. The establishment of letters of agreement between domestic and foreign supervisors is a must. These agreements have already been signed with Spain but have been difficult to obtain from a number of other industrial countries.

LESSON 6. Financial regulation in Latin America needs to be designed to meet the particular features of the region, not those of industrialized countries.

Lesson 5 stressed the absence of severe banking difficulties in Latin America during the recent international crisis and attributed that result, at least partly, to improved regulation. But what type of financial regulation was (and is) in place in the region? Certainly not the international accord for bank capital requirements, better known as Basel II, since most supervisors were concerned about the complexities of the accord and were moving very slowly toward its implementation. This policy decision served the region well, especially since Basel II faced intense criticisms during the crisis by analysts in industrial countries. Some even listed Basel II (implemented in Europe) and Basel I (the result of a 1988 meeting in Basel and still the standard in the United States) as major culprits for the eruption of the crisis.

The argument was that regulatory capital requirements were unable to improve banks' solvency but instead increased banks' incentives to take excessive risk.[26] Two examples stand out: The first example is that Basel I created incentives for excessive mortgage securitization by banks in the United States because mortgage loans kept in bank's balance sheets carried a higher capital requirement than securitized loans kept off balance sheets. The second example relates to the intensive use of credit rating agencies in Basel II. These agencies severely overvalued the quality of structured products and, therefore, played a major role in the build-up of the crisis.

Following the eruption of the financial international crisis, the Basel Committee for Banking Supervision initiated a process of revising Basel II and by 2010 some new proposals have been advanced (the so-called Basel III). As with Basel II, however, most of Latin American countries are not rushing to change their banking laws to accommodate the recommendations of Basel III. Ideally, regulation on banks should converge across countries to avoid regulatory arbitrage; namely, the shifting of bank operations toward those countries with less stringent regulation. In practice, however, the degree of development matters for the adequate design of adequate regulation.[27] And that is an important lesson that needs to be learned from the international crisis.

Something else to consider is that in the least developed Latin American countries (such as many in Central America and Paraguay), solid accounting and reporting standards are not in place and enforcement of contracts is extremely weak. In this environment, capital requirements become meaningless. This is because simple non risk-weighted bank capital is calculated by subtracting liabilities from assets. If, for example, nonperforming loans were not adequately estimated, the calculated value of capital would also be wrong. Also in several of these countries, capital markets are incipient or nonexistent; thus, there are no market signals that can complement the role of supervisors in assessing the quality of banks. For this group of countries, efforts need to be focused on establishing the appropriate legal, judicial, and accounting frameworks before placing high expectations on the effectiveness of capital standards.

Second, for the relatively most developed countries in Latin America, where capital requirements can indeed be a useful supervisory tool, the challenge is to design the standard that works best for those countries, and Basel II does not seem to fit the bill. Neither the use of credit rating agencies nor the heavy reliance on the banks' internal models for risk assessment is useful. There is no regulation for credit rating agencies in these countries and supervisors do not have sufficient tools to evaluate the quality of banks' internal models. For this group of countries, a simple leverage ratio needs to be at the core of capital requirements.

Will the international setting bodies arrive at this kind of conclusions when revising their proposed regulations? One can just hope that the increased role of the G-20 in the global landscape will play an important role in ensuring adequate recommendations for financial regulation in developing countries and that Latin America will benefit from that.

LESSON 7. **As in previous episodes of adverse external shocks, the global international crisis once again demonstrated that low savings rates are an important constraint for Latin America's development model.**

When comparing different development models, a number of analysts question the desirability of relying on foreign capital inflows as a key engine for growth. As I hope has become evident throughout the discussion in this chapter, it has not been easy for Latin American countries to ensure the sustainability of their market-led financially open model.[28] Nor has it been cheap, as accumulating large amounts of foreign exchange reserves entails important financial costs. However, as discussed in the beginning of this chapter, most Latin American countries have no intention to deviate from their chosen model. The fundamental reason is that domestic savings are extremely limited.

As the analysis in Birdsall and Rojas-Suarez (2004) shows, financing development relies on three major pillars: foreign financial flows, export revenues and domestic savings. The lack of diversification of export products implies that the region is subject to large terms of trade shocks mostly because of the large concentration on commodity exports, whose prices are extremely volatile. Thus Latin America cannot rely on export revenues to provide a steady source of finance.[29]

Latin America has made important progress toward maximizing the benefit from external sources of finance and toward minimizing the adverse consequences of a sudden reversal of inflows. But the region has not been successful in improving domestic savings ratios. Figure 7.5 shows a disheartening development. By 2006, the region as a whole displayed a ratio of national savings to GDP that was comparable to levels reached in the 1970s. While this regional ratio typifies well the representative Latin American country, there are two exceptions. The first is Chile, whose savings ratio has significantly increased. The second is the Central American region, with declining national saving ratios.[30]

Like the catalyst crises seen before, the recent global financial crisis once again demonstrated the constraints on development imposed by holding low national savings ratios. Prior to this recent crisis, the absence of deep and liquid financial and capital markets in most Latin American countries induced large corporations to find sources of finance abroad with cheaper rates and better overall conditions. This was a natural development of globalization that benefitted local companies in the period from 2003–7. But during the crisis, when international capital markets dried up, many corporations suffered serious constraints in access to finance. As a result, external debt default rates rose for corporations from Mexico and Brazil. Undoubtedly, in both boom and bust periods, Latin America's growth and development efforts would be in a better footing if the region enjoyed higher national savings ratios.

However, this is easier said than done, since there is no consensus in the empirical literature regarding the direction of causality between national savings and economic growth.[31] Notwithstanding this debate, it is important to differentiate between private and public savings.

With regard to private savings, growth is an important determinant but it is not the only one. In many countries in the region, memories are still fresh regarding individuals' major losses in the real value of their wealth resulting from deep and recurrent financial crisis (see lesson 5 above). Re-

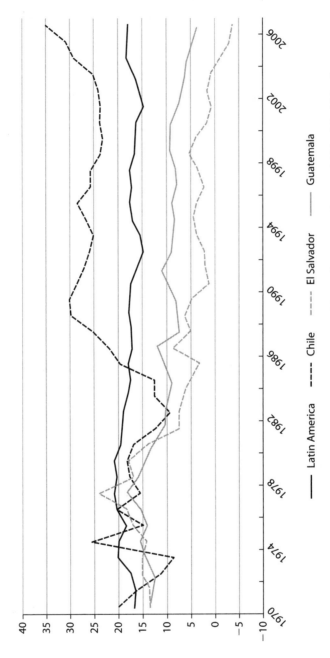

Figure 7.5 National savings over GDP in Latin America. Source: World Development Indicators 2008—World Bank.

— Latin America   ---- Chile   ---- El Salvador   —— Guatemala

gaining full credibility in the stability of the financial system takes a very long time, but is a necessary condition for private savings ratios to increase on a sustainable basis.

In addition, as explained in Loayza et al. (2000), demographic differences also matter. High young-age dependency ratios (population younger than 15 years old as a percentage of working-age population) have a negative effect on private savings rates, and this can partly explain low private saving ratios in Latin America. Moreover, Chile shows that a fully funded pension scheme allows private savings to increase without completely offsetting declines in public savings. Not many countries in the region have been able to successfully finance the fiscal cost of the transition to such a system, which requires support from general government revenues. The deep fiscal problem in Bolivia that resulted from the establishment of private pension funds is a case in point. Also, as coverage has remained extremely limited, private pension funds have not been able to induce increased savings for large segments of the population.

Improving public savings (the difference between government revenues and government spending) is a much more direct and accessible policy goal than increasing private savings. Before the crisis, a number of Latin American countries had increased public saving by running primary fiscal surpluses. However, as recognized in Birdsall et al. (2008), efforts to improve public savings need to focus on improving the collection of taxes and on a better allocation of government expenditures. While financing the development needs of Latin America requires increased revenues, there is a minimum level of expenditure on the provision of public goods, especially in the social areas. Many countries in the region are below that minimum. The reader is directed to Birdsall et al. (2008) for specific policy recommendations for improving tax systems in the region.

LESSON 8. **Because the likelihood of large and unexpected international shocks will be there in the foreseeable future, multilateral organizations need to stand ready to provide liquidity to developing countries, including those in Latin America.**

In the period before the emergence of the international financial crisis, the International Monetary Fund had significantly reduced its balance sheet. In 2006 Mervyn King, governor of the Bank of England, stated that the role of the IMF as a lender of last resort was going to become less and less important as corporations and governments were finding cheaper and larger sources of finance in the international capital markets.[32] This view had achieved nearly consensus at the time.[33] In Latin America, demand for new IMF resources had practically vanished. By the end of 2006, Uruguay, one of the smallest countries in the region, was the second-largest IMF borrower (Turkey was the largest).

The global nature of the recent international financial crisis completely reversed views among the role of the IMF and other multilateral organizations. Large contagion from industrial to developing countries proved that, in a globalized world, full decoupling is almost impossible to achieve. This was certainly true in financially open Latin America. As capital inflows, especially trade finance to the region dried up, the liquidity needs of many countries mounted. The extension of credit lines by the U.S. Federal Reserve to Brazil, Mexico, and other emerging markets eased some of the liquidity constraints, but the IMF, the obvious institution for liquidity provision, was not ready, lacking both the funding and the instruments. It was only in the second quarter of 2009 that the G-20 agreed to capitalize the IMF and that an adequate liquidity facility, involving fast-track disbursement, the Flexible Credit Line was created. Colombia and Mexico quickly applied to obtain this credit line.

An important lesson from the crisis is that the stability of the global financial system and that of Latin America needs the IMF as a lender of last resort and other multilateral organizations as complementary sources of funding. While essential (as explained in lessons 3 and 4), all type of self-insurance mechanisms (like accumulation of foreign exchange reserves and fiscal stabilization funds) as well as market-based insurances (such as contingent lines of credit with international banks or GDP-indexed bonds) might prove insufficient in the presence of a large adverse shock. As discussed above, the fundamental reason is that Latin America and the rest of developing regions do not issue hard, liquid currencies but use them in financial and trade transactions. This feature is not going to change any time soon.

Conclusion

The international financial crisis that erupted in developed countries in 2007 adversely affected all developing regions of the world; albeit with very different degrees of intensity. In contrast to previous crises episodes, Latin America fared relatively well: domestic banking systems remained stable and no runs against the local currencies took place. The crisis, however, exposed the strengths and weaknesses of the current paradigm of development in the region, which is based on liberalized capital accounts and significantly improved macroeconomic conditions.

On the strength side, increased (but not pure) flexibility of exchange rates in the context of inflation targeting proved extremely valuable to ride the storm since—in sharp departure from the past—countries were in a position to lower interest rates and provide needed liquidity to firms when financing from the international capital markets dried up. Moreover, in the years before the crisis, the region understood that self-insurance mechanisms through the accumulation of foreign exchange reserves and an improved term structure of external liabilities favoring longer maturities were essential tools for countries lacking the capacity to issue hard currencies.

On the weakness side, the crisis showed that two chronic maladies in the region, its lack of exports diversification and its very low savings ratios, have the propensity to work against the sustainability of Latin America's development model. While the former implied that the region was exposed to a sharp deterioration of the terms of trade at the peak of the crisis, the latter severely constrained the availability of domestic credit.

But beyond weaknesses and strengths, the crisis has opened up new issues and challenged some established beliefs in the region. Of particular importance are the role of the state during systemic crises generated abroad and the relevance of international financial regulations. During the crisis, a number of countries, including Chile (the best performer in the region), found out that, when adequately managed and fully funded, public banks can partially offset the sharp reduction of credit from private banks. It is however too early to derive long-term conclusions about this policy decision as the return to good times would need to be accompanied by a retrenching of credit activities by public banks to avoid crowding out of private sector financial institutions.

Regarding international financial regulations, many analysts in the region are now celebrating the slow pace taken by regulators in implementing Basel II, the proposed regulation for bank capital requirements. Basel II has been blamed as a major culprit for the eruption of the crisis in industrialized countries. In this chapter, I have discussed a number of alternatives that Latin American countries can consider in designing regulations that are adequate for the degree of development of their financial systems. One can only hope that the G-20 and multilateral organizations take note of this experience and abandon the prevailing view that leveling the playing field in global financial markets implies similar financial regulations for countries regardless of their level of development.

Notes

The author is grateful for the valuable comments and suggestions by Nancy Birdsall, Seth Colby, and Francis Fukuyama and for the excellent research support from Veronica Gonzales and Ed Collins. The usual disclaimer applies.

1. See Shixue (2001) and Sanchez-Anochea (2007) for further discussion of these development models.
2. This model resulted in a dual economy, with a modern export sector and a severely underdeveloped "traditional sector" producing art crafts in the urban areas and non-export agricultural products in the rural areas.
3. The index of financial openness by Chinn and Ito (2007) takes higher values the more open the region is to cross-border capital transactions.
4. Argentina also belonged to this group for a long time; but at the time of this writing the country is trying to get renewed access to the international capital markets, including through negotiations to deal with unresolved issues from the debt default of the early 2000s.
5. In late 2009, inflows to a number of Latin American countries recovered. Facing uncertainties about the sustainability of the recovery and the potential excessive appreciation of the real exchange rate, Brazil imposed limited controls on short-term portfolio inflows (foreign direct investment constitutes the lion's share of inflows to Brazil and this form of inflows was not subjected to controls). At the time of this writing it was too early to make an assessment about the effectiveness of the controls or the government's timeline regarding the maintenance of the controls.
6. In the view of the author, there is no such a thing as an ideal development model for all regions of the world as economic and political conditions differ significantly across regions. Moreover, existing paradigms evolve over time as those conditions change. Although a comparison between different development models is way beyond the scope of this chapter, there are neither signs no incentives for important convergence between the Asian model (high saving ratios, less open capital account) and the Latin American model. While, most likely, both regions could benefit from certain aspects of the alternative model, an adequate assessment of that issue requires a separate paper.
7. See ECLAC 2009.
8. Uruguay has slightly increased the U.S. share in its exports, but from very low levels.
9. Recent evidence shows that the effects of exchange rate changes on the profitability and competitiveness of the manufacturing sector are similar to the effects on services (see, for example, Baggs et al. 2008). The fundamental reason is that firms engaged in the production of services rely on manufacturing and primary goods inputs. In Latin America, the export of tourism and tourism-related services is a good example.
10. Exceptions to the movement toward increased exchange rate flexibility are Ecuador, El Salvador, and Panama, which have adopted dollarization, and most other Central American countries that actively manage their exchange rate.
11. The depletion of foreign exchange reserves reduced the country's capacity to repay its outstanding external obligations. This was compounded by increased

domestic interest rates to defend the exchange rate parity since higher interest rates also increased the financing cost of domestic debt.

12. Ecuador and El Salvador, two of the dollarized countries in the region suffered important pressures on their exchange rate systems. Discussions about a possible abandonment of dollarization are now an important component of the economic debate in Ecuador.

13. Not all countries in the region have been able to keep inflation low, Argentina and Venezuela being the most noticeable examples. In these two cases, however, inflation rates were on an upward trend even before the start of the global financial crisis, and, thus, mostly reflect important macroeconomic imbalances.

14. A policy of accumulating foreign exchange reserves implies that pure floating is not possible. Instead, managed floating is the recommended policy option. This involves a combination of rules and limited discretion. An important rule is that central banks cannot intervene to continuously smooth exchange rate fluctuations. The discretion is that, sporadically, central banks can intervene in the foreign exchange market to manage their international liquidity position. See Rojas-Suarez (2003) and Goldstein (2002) for further elaboration on this issue.

15. Chile and Mexico were in intermediate positions between the best and the worst self-insured countries. By the end of 2008 and the beginning of 2009, Chile corrected its deficiency of foreign exchange reserves by sharply intervening in the foreign exchange market, inducing a sharp depreciation of its exchange rate.

16. Although the recent large bailouts of private financial and non-financial corporations in the United States and other industrial countries suggests the statement is valid not only for emerging markets but in the recent case even for the world's most credit-worthy countries.

17. As noted in Rojas-Suarez (2003), the benefits of accumulating foreign liquidity as a buffer to unexpected shocks need to be balanced against the cost of holding these assets, which are characterized by low returns. Indeed, an important problem in the consolidated government and central bank balances is the large interest rate differential between their debt liabilities and their liquid assets. As an additional policy to deal with unexpected shocks, in the 2000s many Latin American countries changed the profile of their external financial obligations, buying back expensive debt with near-term maturity and improving the overall term structure of their external debt. During the 1990s, Chile lengthened the average term of external liabilities by taxing short-term inflows more heavily than long-term inflows.

18. In November 2009, Fitch downgraded Mexico's sovereign debt by one notch.

19. For a full description of how the Chilean rule operates see IADB (2005).

20. In Brazil, the authorities also extended credit through the Brazilian Development Bank (BNDES). However, this is not surprising in this country since public banks play a large role in the financial system. In contrast, in Chile, public banks typically act as second tier banking.

21. The use of U.S. dollars in many Latin American countries started in the 1980s when huge devaluations and high or hyperinflation resulted in large losses in real wealth by holders of assets denominated in local currency.
22. See IMF (2009) for a comprehensive discussion of these issues.
23. The two clear exceptions are Ecuador (4.5%) and Venezuela (1.8%).
24. As discussed in lesson 4, this development led governments from some countries to promote the expansion of credit by public banks.
25. In the past, efforts to attract foreign banks were fully justified given the performance of domestic banks.
26. See, for example, a 2007 statement of the U.S. Shadow Financial Regulatory Committee. Available at www.aei.org/docLib/20071210_ShadowStatement253 .pdf.
27. See Rojas-Suarez (2001, 2004) for a detailed discussion on the constraints faced by developing countries in their use of capital adequacy standards as a supervisory tool.
28. Arvind Subramanian's chapter "The Crisis and the Two Globalization Fetishes" provides further discussion on the risks of relying heavily on foreign financial flows.
29. Although it is important to recognize that diversification in terms of trade partners is a move in the right direction.
30. In the case of Central America, recent studies show that remittances have had a positive impact on private consumption, but an adverse effect on economic growth and savings. See, for example, the paper by Cáceres and Saca (2006) for the case of El Salvador. Thus, in Central America, remittances add to other factors explaining low savings ratios.
31. See Carroll and Weil (1993) and Gavin et al. (1997) for evidence that growth causes savings and Gutierrez (2007) for mixed evidence about the direction of causality in Latin America. An important recent paper by Aghion et al. (2009) provides theoretical background and empirical evidence showing that increased domestic savings might be needed to generate economic growth in developing countries that lag in the implementation of technological innovations. Their cross-country regression shows that lagged savings are positively associated with productivity growth in poor countries but not in rich countries.
32. See www.bankofengland.co.uk/publications/speeches/2006/speech267.pdf.
33. I, among others, was among those not subscribing to this view. See www.cgdev .org/content/opinion/detail/6438/.

References

Aghion, Philippe, Diego Comin, Peter Howitt, and Isabel Tecu. 2009. "When Does Domestic Saving Matter for Economic Growth?" Working Paper 09–80. Harvard Business School, Boston, Massachusetts. Available at www.hbs.edu/research/ pdf/09-080.pdf.

Baggs, Jen, Eugene Beaulieu, and Loretta Fung. 2008. "Are Service Firms Affected by Exchange Rate Movements?" Paper presented at the Midwest International Economic Meetings, May 1–3, University of Iowa, Iowa City.

Birdsall, Nancy, Augusto de la Torre, and Rachel Menezes. 2008. *Fair Growth: Economic Policies for Latin America's Poor and Middle-Income Majority.* Washington, DC: Center for Global Development and Inter-American Dialogue.

Birdsall, Nancy, and Liliana Rojas-Suarez, eds. 2004. *Financing Development: The Power of Regionalism.* Washington, DC: Center for Global Development.

Cáceres, Luis René, and Nolvia N. Saca. 2006. "What Do Remittances Do? Analyzing the Private Remittance Transmission Mechanism in El Salvador." IMF Working Paper WP/06/250. Washington, DC: International Monetary Fund.

Carroll, C., and D. Weil. 1994. "Savings and Growth: A Reinterpretation." *Carnegie-Rochester Conference Series on Public Policy* 40 (0): 133–92.

Chinn, Menzie D., and Hiro Ito. 2007. "A New Measure of Financial Openness." La Follette School Working Papers. University of Wisconsin, Madison, Wisconsin.

Economic Commission for Latin America and the Caribbean (ECLAC). 2009. *La Inversión extranjera directa en America Latina y el Caribe.* Santiago, Chile: ECLAC.

Foxley, Alejandro. 2009. *Recovery: The Global Financial Crisis and Middle-Income Countries,* Washington, DC: Carnegie Endowment for International Peace.

Galindo, Arturo, Alejandro Izquierdo, and Liliana Rojas-Suarez. 2010. "Financial Integration and Foreign Banks in Latin America: How Do they Impact the Transmission of External Financial Shocks", CGD Working Paper no. 203. Washington, DC: Center for Global Development, Washington, DC.

Gavin, M, R. Hausmann, and E. Talvi. 1997. "Saving Behavior in Latin America: Overview and Policy Issues." Working Paper R-346.Washington, DC: Inter-American Development Bank.

Goldstein, Morris. 2002. *Managed Floating Plus. Policy Analysis in International Economics* 66. Washington, DC: Institute for International Economics.

Gutierrez, Mario. 2007. "Savings in Latin America after the Mid 1990s: Determinants, Constraints and Policies" *Serie Macroeconomía del Desarrollo 57.* Santiago, Chile: ECLAC. Available at www.eclac.org/publicaciones/xml/9/27899/LCL2662_P .pdf. Inter-American Development Bank (IADB). 2005. "Foreign Banks." In *Unlocking Credit: The Quest for Deep and Stable Bank Lending,* Economic and Social Progress in Latin America, edited by Arturo Galindo, 129–60. Washington DC: IADB.

International Monetary Fund. 2009. *Regional Economic Outlook: Western Hemisphere.* Washington, DC: International Monetary Fund. Loayza, Norman, Humberto Lopez, Klaus Schmidt-Hebbel, and Luis Serven. 2000. "Savings in Developing Countries: Overview." *World Bank Economic Review* 14: 91.

Perry, Guillermo. 2009. "Beyond Lending: How Multilateral Banks can Help Developing Countries Manage Volatility." Washington, DC: Center for Global Development.

Rojas-Suarez, Liliana. 2001. "Can International Capital Standards Strengthen Banks in Emerging Markets?" Working Paper WP01–10. Washington, DC: Institute for International Economics.

———. 2003. "Monetary Policy and Exchange Rates: Guiding Principles for a Sustainable Regime." In *After the Washington Consensus: Restarting Growth and Reform in Latin America,* edited by Pedro Pablo Kuczynski and John Williamson, 123–55. Washington, DC: Institute for International Economics.

———. 2004. "International Standards for Strengthening Financial Systems: Can Regional Development Banks Address Developing Country Concerns?" In *Financing Development: The Power of Regionalism,* edited by Nancy Birdsall and Liliana Rojas-Suarez, 137–64. Washington, DC: Center for Global Development.

———, ed. 2009. *Growing Pains in Latin America: An Economic Growth Framework as Applied to Brazil, Colombia, Costa Rica, Mexico and Peru.* Washington, DC: Center for Global Development.

Rojas-Suarez, Liliana, and Sebastian Sotelo. 2007. "The Burden of Debt: An Exploration of Interest Rate Behavior in Latin America." *Contemporary Economic Policy* 25(3): 387–414. Sanchez-Ancochea, Diego. 2007. "Anglo-Saxon Structuralism versus Latin American Structuralism in Development Economics." In *Ideas, Policies and Economic Development in the Americas,* edited by E. Perez-Caldentey and M. Varengo, 208–27. New York: Routledge Studies in Development Economics.

Shixue, Jiang. 2001. "Evolution of the Latin American Development Models in the 20th Century: Lessons and Implications for Other Developing Countries." *Asian Journal of Latin American Studies* 14(1): 173–97.

Part III • International Institutions

CHAPTER 8

Toward Strengthened Global Economic Governance

Kemal Derviş

THE GREAT CRISIS of 2008–9 was a stark reminder of global economic interdependence. A crisis that started in a segment of the U.S. financial sector spread across sectoral and national borders and threatened to engulf the world economy as a whole. The demonstration of this interdependence was also a wake-up call for strengthened and reformed global economic governance. For progress to be possible, both political will and an overall strategic design are needed. In this chapter, I try to distinguish between the respective roles of informal (G-20) and formal (IMF, World Bank, UN, WTO) governance mechanisms and discuss the specific areas of focus for each of the major institutions. The discussion focuses on functional delineation, not on the important governance reforms needed by each of the institutions themselves, largely because piecemeal institutional reforms without an overall organizing framework had become very difficult, often adding to existing duplication and confusion of roles.

Regarding informal governance, now the G-20 meetings take place at the level of leaders rather than finance ministers and other officials and offer the hope that functional delineation with regard to international organizations can be clarified. The natural and inherent bureaucratic rivalries can be much more easily dealt with at the level of political leaders than at the level of sectoral ministers. Whether the momentum for overall reform created by the crisis will endure remains to be seen. The continuing cross-border challenges posed by global current account imbalances, the harmonization of financial sector policies, the need for coordination in monetary policies, the need for mutually consistent macro and fiscal policies and the need to deal with climate change, will remain and grow.

Historical Background

The twentieth century saw two major attempts at building strong global governance. The first took place after the devastation of World War I with the creation of the League of Nations. It was thoroughly unsuccessful, with the United States never joining the League. A little more than a decade after the first Great War, the world experienced the Great Depression, with a level of massive unemployment never seen in modern times. Failure to coordinate economic policies and prevent "beggar thy neighbor" trade and exchange rate measures contributed to the global pain and hopelessness of the Great Depression. At the end of the dismal 1930s, with extreme totalitarian ideologies having risen to power in many countries, World War II started. It would inflict even greater devastation and misery on tens of millions of human beings. The Holocaust, the biggest and most systematic of historical crimes, showed how far human evil could go, at a time when the world descended into generalized violent conflict, racism, and extreme nationalism.

Even before the end of that nightmare, when the final victory of the allied forces seemed assured, efforts began to design a system of global governance that would replace conflict with cooperation and build global institutions to help humanity preserve peace and manage global collective action. At the center of the institutional design were the United Nations and the Bretton Woods institutions, including the International Monetary Fund and what would become the World Bank. An international trade organization, envisioned by John Maynard Keynes, could not be agreed on at that time. Nonetheless the GATT (General Agreement on Tariffs and Trade) supported a process of liberalizing trade and formulating a body of international trade law.

The radical ideological antagonism between the "West," led by the United States, and the communist bloc, led by the Soviet Union, made it impossible for the world to become a community of nations unified in a cooperative structure of global governance, as hoped for by the founding fathers of the UN and of the Bretton Woods institutions. The Soviet Union and its allies stayed in the United Nations, because of the Soviet veto at the Security Council. Most communist countries did not, however, participate in the Bretton Woods institutions, where they would have been unable to block decisions. These financial institutions developed as fully "Western" led organizations.

For four decades, from the early 1950s to the early 1990s, the post–World War II system continued to function with only relatively minor alterations. On many issues the United Nations was deadlocked, with the Soviet Union and the United States each able to block decisions at the Security Council with their vetoes. The Bretton Woods institutions, often called the IFIs (international financial institutions), developed independently of the United Nations and were not hampered down by a deep ideological division and a frequent recourse to the equivalent of a veto by any one power.[1] Both the Bretton Woods Articles of Agreement and the UN Charter had required the two institutional structures to cooperate. The UN created ECOSOC, the Economic and Social Council, to coordinate the UN's economic and social programs, subsidiary bodies and specialized agencies, including the IFIs which had been launched in theory as part of the broad UN system. In 1947, the World Bank and the IMF formally became specialized UN agencies. This did not, however, amount to more than the most superficial, sporadic, and entirely voluntary cooperation. The Bretton Woods institutions did not have any political or peacekeeping mandate. So there was no conflict or overlap in that area. But the UN did develop activities in the economic field, which in theory were to be coordinated with those of the IMF and the World Bank by the ECOSOC. In fact the two structures operated in parallel and sometimes at cross purposes.

The fall of the Berlin Wall in 1989 and the ensuing collapse of the Soviet bloc, as well as the world market oriented development of the People's Republic of China that had gathered momentum already in the 1980s, changed the international system quite radically.[2] By the early 1990s, the deep ideological division of the world had, de facto, ended.[3] Those years marked another momentous historical change that could have provided an opportunity for deep reforms in global governance. Thankfully, this time the epochal change did not follow a worldwide catastrophe. That also meant, however, that while there was an opportunity for change, there was no great sense of crisis or urgency. The collapse of the Soviet Bloc was a relatively "soft" shock, thanks to the remarkably peaceful way it occurred.[4] The United States, having reached the peak of its power and dominance compared to the rest of the world in the 1990s, did not use that opportunity to take the initiative to try to reshape global governance in any fundamental way. The formerly communist countries did join the Bretton Woods institutions and cooperation within the UN did improve. The GATT was strengthened and became the WTO in 1995, and many formerly communist countries also started to join the WTO. Despite the expanding membership, there was little fundamental reform in the individual institutions or in their interaction. The governance and mode of operation of the Security Council, of the General Assembly, or of the IFIs did not change. Moreover, the institutional structures of the IFIs and of the UN did remain separate over the next two decades. There was no attempt to design a more integrated form of global economic governance. It is therefore with this dual structure, alongside the WTO and with overlapping institutional mandates, that the world found itself at the beginning of the great economic and financial crisis of 2008–9.

While the immediate cause of the crisis was the failure to regulate and supervise subprime mortgage lending in the United States, the development of large global payment imbalances, and the lack of international macroeconomic policy coordination and of strong regulatory harmonization in the financial sector across borders were clearly contributing factors. At the end of the first decade in this new century, it appears we have encountered another historical moment that might encourage substantial institutional reform in global economic governance. The economic crisis has been sufficiently deep and widespread to shock the system. Moreover, it came at a time when the scientific evidence that climate change was posing a serious threat to the long-term future of the planet had become stronger and more widely accepted. Neither the threat of economic and financial instability, nor the longer-term climate threat, is of a purely national or local nature. The combined effect these threats are having on political perceptions and priorities in many countries may open up another window of opportunity for strengthened global economic governance. This chapter attempts to provide an overview of the prospects for better functional delineation between the various global processes and institutions.

Increasing Complementarities between Formal and Informal Governance

When thinking of prospects for global economic governance, it is important to distinguish between the formal and informal intergovernmental processes and institutions that have developed over time and how they can evolve in the future. The formal part of the system consists of the treaty-based organizations and their governing bodies, such as the IMF, the World Bank, the UN organizations, and the WTO. The informal part of the intergovernmental system consists of the various G-N meetings. These meetings started with the G-5, conceived by then French President Valery Giscard d'Estaing in the mid-1970s, quickly became the G-7, and then grew to take various shapes, from the G-8 (the G-7 plus Russia) to the G-20, the G-20 plus, and various other in-between G-N's.[5] The July 2009 meeting of the

G-8 in L'Aquila, Italy, witnessed a bewildering combination of groups: the G-8, the G-8+5+Egypt, G-8+5+7 international organizations, meetings with the Major Economies Forum, and lastly, the G-8 and Algeria, Angola, Egypt, Ethiopia, Libya, Nigeria, Senegal, South Africa, and the African Union Commission, with the addition of leaders from a whole string of international organizations: IEA, IBRD, IMF, ILO, OECD, WTO, and UN!

It is not useful to argue endlessly about the relative advantages of the formal and informal processes. Both are needed. The informal gatherings can be more flexible, they can allow leaders or ministers to develop closer personal relationships. This setting allows relatively bold proposals to be made, knowing that they will be reviewed and fine-tuned in the governing boards of the formal institutions and will take their final shape after such reviews. This is in fact what happened with the G-20+ meetings that met in London and Pittsburgh in April and September of 2009. Important principles were agreed upon relating to the lending capacity of the IMF, the way its resources would be augmented, the issuance of special drawing rights, international approaches relating to cross-border taxation and tax havens, support for the poorest countries (to be led by the World Bank and monitored by the UN), and work by the International Labour Organization (ILO) on the employment and social protection content of recovery policies. The fact that the G-20+, at leaders level, agreed on these proposals allowed an accelerated process of bringing these proposals to the decision-making bodies of the formal institutions. Many of these proposals were then formally endorsed by the governing bodies.[6]

Looking forward, the G-N informal meetings can and should be viewed as a facilitating initiative. They allow for the building of relationships and for top leaders to be engaged with global issues and the challenges of global collective action, in a setting that is conducive to both a reasonably high level of ambition and to working together in a context that is outside the usual domestic political domain.

The great economic crisis of 2008–9 led to the emergence of G-20 meetings at leaders level as the most important and visible of G-N meetings. The L-20, where L stands for leaders, met three times in less than a year. It may be useful to distinguish the leaders-level meeting from the ministerial meetings of the G-20 by calling it an L-20 or L-20+. The London and Pittsburgh meetings, in particular, eclipsed the July G-8 meeting. This preeminence of the L-20 combined with the demonstrated necessity the G-8 felt to augment their own meeting (by inviting a large number of other countries), showed that the G-8 is increasingly becoming an anachronism. In the final communiqué of the Pittsburgh meeting the L-20+ was endorsed by participants as the "premier forum for [our] international economic cooperation." The G-7 or G-8 will probably continue to meet in various formats, because the country chairing the G-N in any particular year may want it to meet,[7] and the G-7 (rather than the G-8) still feel as a "like-minded group," but the center of attention has shifted to the L-20.

This emergence of the L-20 has significant implications for the formal governance track of the international system, particularly for the Bretton Woods institutions. Table 8.1 below compares the countries present at the L-20+ meeting in London and Pittsburgh, to the membership of the IMFC (the international monetary and financial committee) during the Istanbul meetings of the IMF and the World Bank in the fall of 2009 and to the composition of the IMF Executive Board. The last two memberships are not identical, both chairs come from the same constituencies but the chair in the IMFC and the executive director at the board do not necessarily come from the same country.

There is considerable overlap. The major emerging market economies were not present in the G-7 or G-8 meetings; they are now present in the L-20, which is closer in composition to the IMFC and the IMF Board. In both cases there is still an overrepresentation of Europe, when compared with such variables as global population and global GDP. In both cases the smaller and poorer countries of the world are not strongly represented, although here one can argue that they are underrepresented more in relation to their sheer number than with respect to their share in the world's population or GDP. Despite valid arguments about exact composition and membership, however, the kind of gap that exists when comparing the old G-7 to the governance bodies of the more formal institutions has narrowed in the case of the L-20+. In the old days, the G-7 often used to take informal decisions among themselves, and then, having agreed, they would more or less impose these decisions on the formal governance bodies of the Bretton Woods institutions. Today, nothing prevents the G-7 from trying to coordinate in the same way. The fact is, however, that the active involvement and sound preparation of emerging market leaders in the L-20+ means that the process of consultation now involves them and that, in turn, means less "capture" of the Bretton Woods institutions' decision making process by the G-7 countries.

The quotas and voting weights in the governing organs of the Bretton Woods institutions remain an issue of course. Brazil has a weight of 1.4 percent of total votes at the IMF, compared with 2.1 percent for Belgium. India has a weight of 1.9 percent compared with 0.9 for Austria, larger, but not at all reflecting the weight of these two countries on the global scene. The fact that Brazil and India are "equal" participants in the L-20, while Belgium and Austria are not present (except indirectly through the presence of the EU), makes these anachronistic weights at the IMF and the World Bank a little easier to bear. This is not to say that these voting weights can stay fro-

Table 8.1. The L-20 and IMF governance

Country	L-20	IMFC members	Executive directors
Algeria		x	
Argentina	x	x	x
Australia	x		
Belgium		x	x
Brazil	x	x	x
Canada	x	x	x
China	x	x	x
Egypt		x	x
Ethiopia[a]	x		
European Union	x		
France	x	x	x
Gabon		x	
Germany	x	x	x
India	x	x	x
Indonesia	x	x	
Iran			x
Italy	x	x	x
Japan	x	x	x
Korea		x	x
Mexico	x		
Netherlands	x	x	x
Russia	x	x	x
Rwanda			x
Saudi Arabia	x	x	x
Sierra Leone			x
South Africa	x	x	
South Korea	x		
Spain	x	x	x
Sweden		x	x
Switzerland		x	x
Thailand[a]	x		x
Turkey	x		
United Arab Emirates		x	
United Kingdom	x	x	x
United States	x	x	x

Sources: www.imf.org and www.londonsummit.gov
Note: IMFC membership and ED chairs as of summer 2009. The Egyptian minister of finance participated in the London meeting as the representative of the managing director of the IMF. He is the chairman of the IMFC but was not invited in that capacity or in his national capacity. IMFC = International Monetary and Financial Committee. L-20 = leaders of G-20 countries.
[a]Representing ASEAN and NEPAD, not members of L-20 as such.

zen. The problem has to be solved for the Bretton Woods institutions to be able to realize their full potential. Actual decisions are taken by the governing organs of the treaty-based organizations, not by informal gatherings, despite them being at leaders level. However, the active participation of the major emerging market countries in the L-20+ meetings and in preparation for these meetings has definitely increased the "ownership" of the international system by those countries, increased the pressure for reforms in the formal governance bodies, and improved the chances for these reforms to be implemented.[8]

The emergence of the L-20+ could also have a positive effect on the relationship between the UN system and the IFIs. As discussed in the beginning of this chapter, the postwar rivalry between the Soviet Union and the West meant that the Soviets and their allies did not join the IFIs but were active in the UN where the Soviet Union had the right to veto Security Council decisions. Moreover, not only the Soviet Union but also the developing countries had greater influence on the UN General Assembly, where the one-country, one-vote rule meant that the G-7 were often in a clear minority. Over the decades, this led to a dual structure in global economic governance. On one side, there were the IFIs, clearly dominated by the G-7 and having most of the financial resources available for collective action or development assistance. On the other side, there was the UN system, somewhat orphaned when it came to financial resources for the economic and social domain but active conceptually and having the advantage of greater perceived legitimacy rooted in greater universality and less dominance by the richest nations. This often has led to duplication, overlap, and a general sense of inefficiency for the global system as a whole. The disappearance of the Soviet bloc and of the deep ideological antagonisms that existed until the early 1990s, coupled with the recent emergence of the L-20+ could mean that the factors that have kept the UN system and the IFIs so far apart may finally weaken. There is less reason for the developing countries as a whole to consider the IFIs as beyond the reach of their influence and there is more reason for the advanced countries to seek the use of the legitimacy and universality of the United Nations, without fearing systematic obstruction from a "structurally" antagonistic power and its allies.

This is not to say that all animosities and cleavages have disappeared, far from it, unfortunately. First of all, the rebalancing of the voting weights in the IFIs has only started in a very modest way and the growing influence of the L-20+ process cannot replace the need for change in those formal voting weights. At the UN, the old cleavage between the Soviet bloc and the West and its allies has disappeared, but Russia, with the veto power it has inherited from the Soviet Union, has increasingly charted a course that has been different from that of the United States and, often, also different from the other European countries and Japan. The developing countries continue to act as a separate bloc, the G-77, to which China formally belongs, hence the title of "G-77 and China." These cleavages often divide and immobilize the United Nations. Nonetheless, they are not as deeply ideological and systematic as the divisions of the Cold War era had been. Moreover, the Obama administration in the United States has signaled that it wants to engage with the United Nations system, that it recognizes the need for dialogue with all countries, and that legitimacy and international law are valid national and global objectives, however imperfect the world may still be. This in itself is a huge structural shift coming from the most powerful country in the world.

At the same time, the challenges requiring global collective action are daunting. The economic crisis has shown how the world narrowly escaped what could have been a real worldwide financial meltdown with much worse consequences on prosperity than what occurred in 2008–9. At least part of the cause of this narrowly averted catastrophe was insufficient international macroeconomic policy and regulatory cooperation. Climate change provides another huge challenge for collective action in the economic and social domain. The international trading system, with its body of international law having gradually grown and strengthened over decades, has resisted protectionist pressures triggered by the economic crisis rather well. But climate change in particular, and the differential pricing of carbon that is implicit in the differentiated role of the developed and the developing countries, has the potential for greatly disrupting the cooperative mechanisms around the WTO.

In view of these challenges, this should be the time to take advantage of the relative convergence of formal and informal governance processes, of the absence of Cold War–type deep ideological antagonisms dividing the major nations, and of the opportunity of a U.S. administration that clearly rejects unilateralism and calls for a "multi-partner" world,[9] to shape the new economic governance structures appropriate for the first half of the twenty-first century.

A Broad Outline for a Renewed Structure of Global Economic Governance

A renewed broad functional structure for global economic governance, building on the informal processes and reformed formal institutions, could be envisioned in the manner outlined below. This chapter focuses on the "functional architecture" of global economic governance, not on the governance arrangements for the individual institutions themselves.[10] It should be understood, however, that functional reform and clarity will need to be accompanied by major political governance reforms of the various institutions themselves, for the "system" of global economic governance to be more successful as a whole.[11]

An Institutionalized L-20+ at the Center of the System

The L-20+, more or less as it met in London, in Pittsburgh, in Toronto, and is scheduled at the time of this writing to meet in Seoul in November 2010, could function as a broad global "council" that oversees, in an informal way, global economic governance as a whole. It would meet once a year, with the host country having some leeway in influencing the exact format. It would consist of the leaders of about 20 systemically important large countries, representing about 80 percent of world GDP and about 65 percent of world population. It would also include, however, in a more formalized way than has happened so far, three or four representatives of regional groupings that would bring to the meeting the voice of smaller countries not individually present. These could be elected by the regional geographical groups at the United Nations or designated by regional organizations such as the African Union and ASEAN.[12] Moreover, the L-20+ meeting would also include the leaders of the major international organizations, starting with the secretary-general of the United Nations, as the "primum inter pares" among them, and including the managing director of the IMF, the president of the World Bank, the director-general of the WTO and the director-general of the ILO. Depending on the priorities of a meeting at a particular time, the leaders of other organizations could also be invited. In 2009–10, employment has been a major challenge, and therefore it was natural to invite to the director-general of the ILO to the Pittsburgh meeting. Employment will remain a huge priority in the foreseeable future and the ILO's presence will remain essential. The same is true for trade and the WTO. If there was a particularly serious global health concern, the director-general of the WHO could be invited to participate in the leaders-level forum. Again, some host country discretion will to continue to be useful.

Some also argue for the presence of regional organizations at this institutionalized L-20+. Including them, in addition to the representatives of the regional country groupings, would lead to considerable enlargement of the group and does not appear feasible or desirable. The secretary-general of the OECD may become an exception, as the OECD becomes much more global in the coming years.

Such a composition would lead to having about 30 principals around the table. It would be a group that can deal with key global issues. The inclusion of the heads of the major international organizations has already been an indirect way of increasing the global legitimacy of these meetings. It will also help to make the meetings more relevant to the problem-solving processes for which these organizations have mandates and staff.

The L-20+ would be a central but informal channel of global economic governance. Formal global governance, resulting in internationally binding decisions, can only come from institutions that function under treaty-based mechanisms. It is within a treaty-based framework that sovereign nation states can commit themselves to certain policies, dispute resolution mechanisms, or to financial burden sharing arrangements. The informal meetings would play a complementary role to this formal channel. An L-20+ would have a comprehensive perspective on world affairs, provide a unique forum to deal with a broad agenda, and allow key leaders to meet and interact on a personal level. One should not expect more from the institutionalized informal meetings, as global governance that results in internationally binding agreements and practices must come from the formal channel.

A Renewed IMF

As envisioned by Keynes, the IMF would be central among the formal treaty-based organizations in the economic and financial domain.[13] The IMF would continue to systematically collect macroeconomic and financial data and engage in macroeconomic and financial sector research and analysis, offering this "knowledge" as a public good for all to use. The IMF would also continue to provide "exceptional" or "work-out" finance to countries experiencing an acute crisis in their balance of payments. This "extraordinary" finance would continue to become available provided there is agreement with the IMF on appropriate policy responses to overcome the crisis.

These two functions have been those of the IMF for a very long time. In addition, however, the renewed IMF would provide access to precautionary finance on an ongoing basis to a large number of countries that prequalify on the basis of agreed criteria.[14] The flexible credit line (FCL), adopted in early 2009, could be the basic instrument for this precautionary finance, provided the interpretation of access criteria is adjusted to post-crisis conditions. The FCL was adopted as a response to the dire conditions facing the world economy in the fall of 2008, and as a revised version of earlier unsuccessful attempts starting with the contingent credit line (CCL) agreed to by the IMF board as early as 1999.[15] The FCL is still not fully what a precautionary facility should be. The code of conduct required for prequalification should be defined more clearly and should allow sufficient policy space to member countries. The IMF's precautionary finance should essentially be an insurance fund for all member countries that agree to follow some broadly acceptable macroeconomic policies. Allowing policy space cannot mean that *any* set of policies would be acceptable. Rather, it must mean that policies are not dictated by one narrow school of thought and that observed "results," such as growth performance, levels of debt and the demonstrated ability to conduct countercyclical fiscal policies, would have to count for more than the particular instruments countries use to achieve these results. The difference between precautionary and "work-out" finance is similar to the difference between the liquidity a national central bank routinely makes available to banks, and special "rescue" loans that may be needed in exceptional crisis circumstances. For example, all banks that satisfy the basic criteria for banking regulation qualify for the rediscount window. Banks in crisis, however, may or may not obtain a special rescue package from their national central bank.

Last but not least, the renewed IMF would encourage and facilitate international macroeconomic policy coordination, building on the ad hoc multilateral surveillance consultations that began very timidly in 2006. It is time the IMF again becomes "global" in its surveillance role, rather than being an institution to which the developed countries pay no attention. This does not mean that the IMF becomes a global regulator and bank supervisor. Most countries are unwilling to grant it such a role, and the democratic process implies that many decisions will have to be made by colleges of regulators, with the aid of discussions in the Financial Stability Board, rather than a universal multilateral organization such as the IMF. Indeed the Financial Stability Board, enlarged to include G-20 members among emerging market economies, is already playing a very important complementary role. However, countries can and should agree that the IMF—sometimes in cooperation with others—has the function of providing impartial assessments of a country's macroeconomic and financial policies and that these assessments will be discussed in a multilateral setting with the mandatory participation of those called upon by the IMF to participate. The G-20 has agreed to systematize such arrangements, which is a large step forward for global economic governance. If implemented as announced, this would transform the IMF into a much more "legitimate" institution, whose advice and, when appropriate, conditionality would be politically more acceptable because of its truly global role.[16]

The World Bank and the Regional Development Banks

There is no doubt that the bulk of capital that will flow from the developed to the developing countries will be private capital in search of profitable investment opportunities. Public capital flows, coming from public institutions such as the multilateral development banks, can only play a complementary role. That role remains very important, however, and needs to incorporate the key objectives of countercyclical stability and the financing of global public goods more explicitly, in addition to the more traditional poverty reduction objective. The system of multilateral development banks, with the World Bank at its center, would have four essential functions.

The multilateral development banks (MDBs) would continue to systematically collect economic, social, and environmental data and conduct research and analysis on all topics relating to sustainable economic development and offer the results as a public good for all to use. As is the case for the IMF in the area of macroeconomics, the value of the knowledge and the data accumulated and organized should not be underestimated and the economies involved in collecting information in a somewhat centralized and systematic manner are substantial.

The MDBs would also provide increased volumes of stable development finance, with particular attention to both compensating for the cyclical nature of private flows and crowding-in private capital through the use of guarantees, insurance services, and other forms of financial product development,[17] including the use of the highly successful International Finance Corporation (IFC) and its regional counterparts.[18] The MDBs would continue to provide concessional loans and grants to the poorest countries and fight extreme poverty, particularly but not only in the poorest countries. There is some ambiguity in the way the poverty eradication objective of all MDBs is translated into financing. Half of all the more than one billion extremely poor people in the world actually live in lower-middle income and middle-income countries,[19] yet it is only the poorest countries that receive concessional resources. The underlying political and ethical assumption is that the middle-income countries have enough national resources internally to channel to their own extremely poor. Official development assistance is reserved for the poorest countries that cannot fight extreme poverty on their own. Given that official development assistance goes mostly to governments, this is probably an unavoidable and understandable feature. There is no global progressive income tax or global social safety net that channels resources from the richest to the poorest individuals directly. The sovereign states largely remain the intermediaries for official assistance, and it is understandable, therefore, that concessional resources are channeled to the governments of the poorest countries. Some direct "individual-to-individual" redistribution takes place through private philanthropy, complementing official channels and reaching the extremely poor, some of which are in middle-income countries.

In addition to the three traditional functions of MDBs described above, there is now a fourth objective for MDBs that has greatly gained in importance: the financing of global public goods. The huge increase in concern about climate protection should be instrumental in clarifying and building up this fourth function of the MDBs, which is related, but distinct from their other objectives. The protection of the Brazilian or Indonesian rain forests, for example, constitutes a global public good. Both countries are middle-income countries and do not qualify for any significant amounts of concessional assistance in relation to their size. And yet, asking them to bear the entire financial burden of providing the world with the global public good of protecting their forests, so that they can absorb carbon and reduce global warming, would be clearly unfair and politically unacceptable to them. There is an obvious need for concessional or grant resources coming from the rich countries to, for example, Brazil and Indonesia, not for the purpose of poverty eradication but to meet the global objective of climate protection. The same can be said for helping India develop its energy sector with due regard to controlling carbon emissions, for example. The fourth major objective of the MDBs should be, therefore, the concessional financing of global public goods, including in the middle-income countries. The climate debate has added further emphasis and urgency to this need, which traditionally has been recognized in the context of infectious disease control.

The amount needed for the adequate provision of global public goods will reach hundreds of billions of dollars annually, providing the MDBs with a huge challenge and a big role, even if only a fraction of these resources is made available through the MDBs themselves. The MDBs have started to help in that area by administering trust funds that rich countries place in their custody and ask them to disburse.[20] These funds are extremely segmented, have very complicated governance arrangements and lead to large transaction costs. It would be much more efficient to streamline that whole system by formally recognizing that the MDBs have a mandate to finance global public goods, to raise and pool concessional resources for that purpose in a coordinated way, similar to what is done for concessional resources in the framework of the International Development Association, and to cover the incremental cost arising from global public goods provision in a transparent and multilaterally accepted manner.

The United Nations and Global Economic Governance

What role is there for the United Nations in global economic affairs? Some have long argued that the IFIs should be the instruments of the international community in the economic domain and that the United Nations' role should be confined to political, security, and humanitarian matters. This argument could gain further strength if the overall reforms outlined in this chapter are implemented. The emergence of the L-20+, with a strong presence of middle-income countries as well as reforms of IFI governance that strengthen the voice and share of developing countries, could over-come the historical perception that the IFIs "belong" to the rich countries and that the UN system is the counterweight needed by the developing countries. If the developing countries do indeed begin to perceive such a change in the "ownership" of the IFIs, with, in a few years and just as a pos-sible scenario, a South African president of the World Bank or an Indian managing director of the IMF, they might no longer insist on a substantial role of the UN system in the economic domain.

A better and less "ideologically" determined delineation of the role of the UN and the IFIs would be desirable and could lead to greater efficiency in resource use. A total marginalization of the UN in the economic domain would not be desirable, however. First, precisely because of its preeminent role in peacekeeping and humanitarian action, the UN will remain deeply involved in many developing countries. It retains strong moral author-ity and legitimacy, partly because of this peacekeeping and humanitarian role. The secretary-general embodies and symbolizes that moral authority across the world, despite the many weaknesses and failings of the UN sys-tem. There are other reasons for a continued role of the UN in global eco-nomic affairs. Small countries, developed and developing, will never feel entirely satisfied in structures such as the L-20+ or the IMF board, even if sig-nificant governance reforms take place, because by logic and necessity the bigger countries will play a more dominant role in these structures. Small countries have been and will continue to regard UN organizations as more responsive to their small country needs and sensitivities. The Funds and Programmes of the UN and the Specialized Agencies benefit from special skills and experience that are not always available elsewhere. While they deal with special "sectoral" problems such as health, education, agricul-ture, labor, and so on; these have relevance to more general economic pol-icy issues. Finally, some "competition" in this domain, particularly in the realm of ideas, has actually been valuable in the past and should continue. The concept of "global public goods," which is proving so critical in today's global collective action discussions, was largely developed and popularized by the UN Development Programme (UNDP).[21] The "Human Development Reports" of the UNDP have provided the best intellectual competition to the World Bank's "World Development Reports." The ILO's analysis of labor markets developments set a standard in that area. These are just some of the examples of the UN system's intellectual contributions over past decades, taking place in an environment much more constrained by resources than that of the IFIs.[22]

To play a continued and perhaps in some ways even strengthened role, the UN system should pursue the "coherence" reforms launched over the last few years. Fragmentation, duplication, and bureaucratic obstacles within the system should be reduced drastically. One key reform that would help to streamline the UN in development would be to make the executive head of UNDP, who already chairs the UN Development Group, into a second deputy secretary-general for economic and social affairs.[23] The secretary-general will always be too busy with pressing political and peacekeeping matters to personally manage the economic and social domain of the UN. One deputy secretary-general is needed to help with political matters, to manage the UN internally, and to represent the secretary-general in various meetings and forums. The UNDP administrator could become a second deputy to help manage the vast economic and social domain and be the key interlocutor of the IFIs as well as the UN's own specialized agencies in that domain. This is what already has, to some degree, taken place in practice over the past few years. It should be formalized and clarified for the benefit of the system as a whole. The additional title of deputy secretary-general for development would not give the UNDP administrator any new "line authority" over other UN agencies, but it would elevate her or his status in the overall global governance system, notably in the International Monetary and Finance Committee of the IMF and the Development Committee of the World Bank. This would allow for stronger coordination both within the UN system and between the UN and the IFIs.

The UN system would provide intellectual leadership and stimulate debate on development issues, competing in that with the MDBs, and it would provide functional and sectoral technical and capacity building assistance, with a strong emphasis on national and local governance in all its forms, including the building of democratic institutions and public service delivery. The UN would also have the leading role in post-conflict transition assistance and in the strategic integration of peacekeeping, governance development, and post-conflict or post-disaster reconstruction, building on its peacekeeping presence and political mediation expertise.

The World Trade Organization

Despite the great difficulties in concluding various trade rounds, notably the Doha round that was launched on November 14, 2001; the WTO has been a rather successful part of the global economic governance system. More than in other domains, there is now a body of accepted international trade law.[24] Strong protectionist pressures appeared with the great crisis of 2008–9, but they did not get out of hand, due precisely to the rules that have been accepted as part of the WTO membership and process. No doubt the personal technical expertise on trade matters and the respect that the director-general enjoys in the world has been particularly important for the

WTO, given the very few resources it has at its disposal as an organization and the key intellectual catalytic role the director-general has to play personally in trade negotiations. As for other organizations, an open, merit-based, competitive process for designating the director-general will also be essential for the WTO in the future.

The key danger facing the WTO and the global public good of an open and rules-based trading system in the next decade is likely to come from the fact that trade rules and agreements get overburdened with other global collective action objectives. The issues surrounding global climate protection policies provide an example of that danger.[25]

The fundamental principle with respect to burden sharing that has been accepted by climate negotiators is that developing countries and developed countries have differentiated responsibilities for climate protection. The details have not been agreed upon and there is ongoing controversy on how this principle will translate into practice. It *is* agreed, however, that while there can be no lasting climate protection without participation in mitigation of the rapidly growing emerging market economies, the initial burden of mitigation that (in one way or the other) takes the form of a higher price for carbon, will not be borne equally by the richer and poorer countries. For quite some years, the carbon price implicit in various policy measures such as emission ceilings, carbon intensity of GDP measures, or explicit taxation of carbon will be lower in the developing countries than in the developed ones. This may not be efficient from a worldwide optimal allocation of resources point of view, but it is dictated by accepted distributional considerations. The efficiency problem can be, to some degree, reduced by the cross-border trading of emission permits, the use of offsets whereby the rich countries pay for and earn credit for mitigation in poorer countries and concessional financial flows covering the incremental cost of mitigation, as discussed in the section on the MDBs role in financing global public goods above.

Some in the rich countries want to use "trade policy" to force developing countries to participate in climate protection policies, as there have been demands to use trade policy for other objectives, including political or human rights objectives in the past. When evaluating these demands in connection to climate protection objectives, it is important to keep the following firmly in mind. As long as countries sign up to an overall deal on climate protection, as negotiated under the UNFCC or possibly some other framework, the use of trade policy to achieve climate-related objectives that are different from what is agreed on in the climate protection negotiations would be inconsistent and totally inappropriate. This would hold in particular with respect to the explicit or implicit carbon price a country would practice domestically. It would clearly be totally inconsistent to agree with a country on a particular regime for carbon emissions that would have certain consequences for the price of carbon in that country and then argue that there should be border-adjustment duties on carbon-intensive products imported from that country because the cost of carbon in the country in question is lower than in the domestic economy! And yet this kind of reasoning is present in some draft legislation of certain rich countries. It is a different question to ask whether trade measures of some form could be taken against countries that simply refuse to cooperate in global climate protection. That is conceivable and could be logically consistent, though not necessarily desirable. But one cannot negotiate a global deal allowing different carbon prices across countries based on differential burden sharing and then ask for trade policies that require equal pricing.

This very critical and timely example illustrates two problems. Trade policies and the WTO process can easily be overburdened with other objectives, because in most cases trade retaliation provides powerful leverage that the large, rich countries, in particular, can use. Clearly, this characteristic of trade measures has to be used sparingly, otherwise it will deadlock the trade negotiations and undermine the primary role of the WTO, which is to provide the world with the global public good of an open multilateral trading system and protect it from "beggar thy neighbor" policies. Second, the example from the climate protection area shows why there is need for overall coordination in global economic governance, across functional areas and particular institutions. The L-20+ should take up the intersection of climate protection and trade policies and formulate a coherent framework that would prevent climate negotiations and trade negotiations from contradicting each other. The WTO and UNFCC process could then take place within that coherent framework.

Conclusion

The discussion above attempts to provide a broad functional geography of the kind of global economic governance that could emerge from the great crisis of 2008–9 and could respond to the pressures arising from global interdependence and from the increased urgency to provide global public goods, particularly in the area of climate protection. It is encouraging that despite the recovery from financial panic in the second half of 2009, the L-20 deepened their work and launched a process of IMF-facilitated consultations that could result in a much more serious attempt at policy coordination among the major economies. The system will evolve from where it has arrived at the end of the first decade of the twenty-first century, rather than be redesigned from scratch. Each one of the components has to be strengthened and renewed, but there is also a pressing need for overall coherence and increased efficiency and legitimacy. The process will remain intergovernmental and peer-review driven, rather than supranational, and there will be no significant "enforcement" powers given the IMF. But the facilitating role of the IMF, made more effective by courageous and innovative analytical work, could go a long way in fostering greater policy coherence. Some, including myself, had called for a formal "leaders-level global council" to oversee the entire architecture of global economic governance within the United Nations and based on a system of constituencies and rotation, at the leaders level.[26] That may still be an ideal objective, but it is probably more practical to make the L-20+ into something resembling such a global council while keeping it informal. The reforms of the formal institutions could be guided and inspired by the L-20+. The formal decisions would have to be made by the reformed governance bodies of the treaty-based organizations, with much greater coherence, notably between the functions of the UN system, the IFIs, and the WTO. As the economic crisis of 2008–9 has again shown us, we can only imperfectly predict from where and how dangers to the prosperity and security of the world might arise. We know, however, that global interdependence has increased greatly and that there are large benefits to collective action. The economic crisis provided an impetus for reform. The rebalancing of the world economy with the rising weight of the emerging market countries has accelerated. For global collective action to become more effective, a better functional delineation of the processes and institutions of global economic governance should accompany rapid reforms in governance.

Notes
1. Amendments to the Articles of Agreement within the Bretton Woods institutions require at least three-fifths of members, representing 85 percent of the total voting power, in order to become effective. A country's voting power is weighted according to shares of both basic votes (where each country receives equal amounts) and voting shares, much more important in the overall weighting, based on a formula that considers a country's GDP, openness, variability, and official reserves. The United States is the only single country that has a "veto power" on some decisions because it currently holds 16.7% of total voting power. At the UN Security Council, however, decisions on substantive matters require approval from at least four nonpermanent members and all five permanent members who vote. Hence the five permanent members (China, France, UK, U.S., and Russia) each hold a "veto power" that the nonpermanent members do not.
2. The People's Republic of China had joined the Fund membership on April 17, 1980.
3. Fukuyama (1989) had predicted the end of "that" history in his prescient article published several months before the fall of the Berlin Wall.

4. There were exceptions, such as the violent disintegration of Yugoslavia.
5. The informal part of the global governance system also includes meetings and interactions between officials and professionals from various countries, as well non-state actors and civil society. These interactions are very important as emphasized by authors, see, for example, Slaughter (2004, 2009). This chapter focuses more narrowly on the informal high-level meetings among leaders or ministers.
6. See the various communiqués from the G-20 meetings.
7. President Sarkozy of France had argued for a series of G-8 plus 6 meetings in parallel to the L-20 meetings. At the Pittsburgh meetings, France supported the final communiqué endorsing the G-20+/L-20+. France will host the leaders-level meeting in 2011.
8. A process of governance reform started at the annual meetings of the IMF and the World Bank in Singapore in 2006 and continues with significant changes in voting weights expected to be ready for implementation in 2010 or 2011.
9. See Clinton (2009).
10. For a good discussion of governance issues themselves, see Martinez-Diaz and Woods (2009).
11. For an analysis of institutional governance, see Woods and Lombardi (2006).
12. The practice so far has been to let the host country decide on regional representation. It would be better in the future to formalize the process of selection, although letting the host choose has had the advantage of bringing politically less controversial figures to the table.
13. As early as 1943, Keynes had proposed a very central role for his "International Clearing Union," which, albeit in weakened form, became the IMF: "We need a central institution, of a purely technical and non-political character, to aid and support other international institutions concerned with planning and regulation of the world's economic life" Keynes (1969).
14. For a discussion of the IMF and precautionary financing, see Derviş (2009a, 2009b).
15. The FCL was preceded by the Short-Term Lending Facility (SLF), which was approved in October 2008, for which, however, no takers ever materialized.
16. These changes in the role of the IMF—and others—would have to be accompanied by much more substantial changes in the formal governance arrangements than those that have been possible so far.
17. The cyclical nature of private capital flows has been very clearly demonstrated over the last decades. See, for example, Reinhart, Kaminsky, and Vegh (2004) and Reinhart and Reinhart (2008). For an excellent early example of analysis of cross-cutting themes in Article IV Consultations, see IMF (2009).
18. On the need for countercyclical development finance, see, for example, Ocampo and Griffith-Jones (2008).
19. See PovCalNet Online Poverty Analysis Tool, worldbank.org.

20. The total amounts of such trust funds have reached tens of billions of dollars for the MDB system as a whole.
21. See Kaul, Conceição, Goulven, and Mendoza (1998 and 2003) and Carbone (2007).
22. For an excellent presentation of the UN's conceptual contributions, see Emmerij, Jolly, and Weiss (2001).
23. The high-level panel on coherence convened by then Secretary-General Kofi Annan in 2006 did recommend that the UNDP administrator officially become the "development coordinator" of the UN system, something very close to what is recommended here, see United Nations (2006).
24. See Hoekman and Mavroidis (2007).
25. On this, see several excellent papers in Brainard and Sorkin (2009).
26. See Derviş (2005).

References

Brainard, L. and Sorkin, I., eds. 2009. *Climate Change, Trade, and Competitiveness: Is a Collision Inevitable?* Washington, DC: Brookings Institution Press.

Carbone, M. 2007. "Supporting or Resisting Global Public Goods? The Policy Dimensions of a Contested Concept." *Global Governance* 13: 179–98.

Clinton, H.R. 2009. *Foreign Policy Address at the Council on Foreign Relations*. Speech, Council on Foreign Relations. Washington, D.C. Available at www.state.gov/secretary/rm/2009a/july/126071.htm.

Derviş, K. 2005. *A Better Globalization: Legitimacy, Governance, and Reform, Center for Global Development*. Washington, DC: Brookings Institution Press.

———. 2009a. *Precautionary Resources and Long Term Development Finance: The Financial Role of the Bretton Woods Institutions after the Crisis*. Center for Global Development's Richard H. Sabot Lecture.

———. 2009b. "A Way Forward: Formal and Informal Aspects of Economic Governance." In *Dialogue on Globalization: Re-defining the Global Economy*, 25–32.New York: Friedrich-Ebert-Stiftung.

Emmerij L., Jolly R. and Weiss T.G. 2001. *Ahead of the Curve? UN Ideas and Global Challenges*. United Nations Intellectual History Project Series. Bloomington: Indiana University Press.

Fukuyama, F. 1989. The End of History. *The National Interest* 16: 3–18.

Hoekman, B. M., and Mavroidis, P. 2007. *The World Trade Organization: Law, Economics and Politics*. London: Routledge.

International Monetary Fund. 2009. *Cross-Cutting Themes in Major Article IV Consultations*. Washington, DC: IMF.

Kaul I., I. Grunberg, and M. Stern , eds. 1999. "Introduction" and "Defining Global Public Goods." In *Global Public Goods: International Cooperation in the 21st Century*, edited by I. Kaul, I. Grunberg, and M. Stern. Oxford: Oxford University Press.

———. 2003. *Providing Global Public Goods: Managing Globalization*. Oxford: Oxford University Press.

Keynes, J. M., to Montagu Norman. 1941. *Collected Writings of John Maynard Keynes*, 25:98–99. Oxford: Oxford University Press.

———. 1969. "Proposals for an International Clearing Union." In *The International Monetary Fund 1945–1995: Twenty Years of International Monetary Cooperation*, edited by J. Keith Horsefield, 3:19–36. Washington, DC: IMF. Originally published 1943.

Martinez-Dias, L., and Woods, N. 2009. *Networks of Influence: Developing Countries in a Networked Global Order*. Oxford: Oxford University Press.

Ocampo, J. A., and Griffith-Jones, S. 2008. "A Counter-cyclical Framework for a Development-Friendly International Financial Architecture." In *Macroeconomic Volatility, Institutions and Financial Architecture: The Developing World Experience*, edited by J. M. Fanelli. Houndmills, United Kingdom: Palgrave/Macmillan.

Reinhart, C., Kaminsky, G. and Vegh, C. 2004. "When It Rains It Pours: Procyclical Capital Flows and Macroeconomic Policies." NBER Working Papers 10780. Cambridge, MA: National Bureau of Economic Research.

Reinhart, C., and Reinhart, V. 2008. "Capital Flows Bonanzas: An Encompassing View of the Past and Present." NBER Working Paper 14321. Cambridge, MA: National Bureau of Economic Research.

Slaughter, A. 2004. *A New World*. Princeton: Princeton University Press.

———. 2009. America's Edge: "Power in the Networked Century." *Foreign Affairs* 88(1): 94.

United Nations. 2005. *Delivering as One*. Report of the High-Level Panel on System-wide Coherence. New York: United Nations.

Woods, N., and Lombardi, D. 2006. "Uneven Patterns of Governance: How Developing Countries Are Represented in the IMF." *Review of International Political Economy*.

Part IV • After the Crisis

CHAPTER 9

The Financial Crisis and Organizational Capability for Policy Implementation

Lant Pritchett

DRAMATIC EVENTS, particularly those that contradict expectations, elicit the demand for "lessons"—how could the conventional wisdom have gone so wrong? Certain events become associated with the apexes and nadirs of intellectual tides. The beginning of the end of the popularity of "import substitution" policies can be dated to August 1982 when Mexico was unable to service its debts, which occasioned a reexamination of debt-financed big push industrialization through import substitution. The dramatic collapse of Argentina's hyperorthodox approach to pegging its currency to the dollar in December 2000 dates the end of the popularity, at least in some circles, of policies that attempted to wring all government discretion out of macroeconomic policymaking.[1] Therefore it seems natural that events as dramatic as the financial and economic crisis of 2008 must have "lessons" and mark the end of at least some of the ideas that created the conditions for such dramatic and negative events to occur.

I address the question not of lessons from the financial crisis generally, but rather, are there lessons for the financial crisis for *development* thinking? This is a more difficult question than the lessons about financial and asset markets in the advanced countries that were the epicenter of the crisis, as the developing countries generally played no essential role in causing the crisis. I argue that the three main lessons from the financial crisis of 2008 for development thinking are indirect, but important: (1) it is not policies that matter but policy implementation, (2) the capability for policy implementation is a key determinant of success, and (3) this capability is not a fixed fact but varies under pressure and with nonlinear dynamics capacity can be hard to build but easy to destroy.

This chapter follows that threefold structure. The first section defines and empirically illustrates the difference between "policy" and "policy implementation." The second section discusses what capability for policy implementation is and its centrality for success using the paradigm examples of the Spartans, Paper Tigers, and the Keystone Cops. The last section introduces the notion of the risks for policy implementation capability of premature or excess load bearing, that is, that while the building of capability for policy implementation is usually a long drawn-out process of incremental change, a lesson of this financial crisis is that excess pressure on policy implementation—financial, political, technical—can cause sudden collapses. I argue that, while this may be a small part of the lessons of the crisis, it is a huge lesson for development. The practice of encouraging development has been riddled with examples of destroying capabilities through premature load bearing on organizations and of institutions being built that appear isomorphic to functional institutions but which in fact have weak capability. Risking yet another metaphor, it is reminiscent of building papier-mâché replicas of bridges and then driving heavy trucks over them. Before I dive into a substantive discussion of organizational capability as it relates to development, we should first look at the Paper Tiger that prompted this whole discussion in the first place, the financial regulators of the United States.

Yes, Even Here

The conventional wisdom in pre-crisis development thinking was that prosperity came from good policies and "good institutions": "good institutions" that created and facilitated markets (e.g., property rights), "good institutions" that prevented rapacity and arbitrary actions by the state (particularly the executive), "good institutions" that made governments capable of smoothing the rough edges of capitalism by providing a modest amount of regulation, some needed services that were state responsibilities (e.g., infrastructure), and some services (e.g., education, health, safety nets).

Simon Johnson, formerly a chief economist of the International Monetary Fund (IMF), has popularized the view that the financial crisis in America is a simple case of elite capture of the institutions of governance (Johnson 2009). This elite capture facilitated the emergence of the bubble both directly and indirectly by allowing puzzlingly irresponsible regulation of financial markets. The obvious solutions to the crisis—nationalizing the banks for instance—were also not pursued for the same reasons. As Johnson put it in a widely read article in a popular magazine, if any other country came to the IMF for assistance and proposed to do what the United States was doing, that country would be told to go home and come back when it was serious about tackling its underlying problems of elite capture.

While it is hard to gauge what the "general" opinion among economists is, I would guess that nearly all of my close colleagues believe the financial crisis reveals the deep susceptibility of the U.S. organizations responsible for regulating key markets to political influence. Put another way, many believe that, in the face of the pressure the large-scale financial institutions (commercial banks, Wall Street investment banks, and quasi-private organizations like Fannie Mae) were able to bring to bear, the organizations and institutions responsible for regulating financial markets proved to be Paper Tigers. Economists find it easy to point to a variety of decisions made about the way in which banking regulation was implemented or the rating of commercial paper was handled that are appear to be example of the organizations responsible caving into to political pressures.

Let me say, first, I am not entirely convinced by this view, and second, I am no expert on the U.S. financial industry or its regulation. That said, this concept is a by no means implausible. If we assume that this account of events is true, then a major lesson of the financial crisis is that the organizations responsible for implementing financial regulation both in the United States (and throughout large parts of the rich industrial world) were incapable of implementing technically sound policies because of the pressures that could be brought to bear by the financial institutions. If this narrative of the financial crisis is true, what are the implications for development thinking?

Development practice of the past decade has been built around the notion of liberalized markets and strengthened institutions, both political (the expansion of democracy) and administrative (establishing professionalized civil services with high levels of individual capacity).[2] But what if the right lesson from the financial crisis is that U.S. organizations were not robust to the degree of pressure liberalized capital markets created? The United States has had over 200 years to develop democratic institutions, independent judiciary, and institutionalized checks and balances on executive function with legislative oversight. The country has a nearly 100-year-old tradition of civil service. The main organizations responsible for regulation of financial markets, the Federal Reserve Bank system and the Securities and Exchange Commission were established in 1913 and 1933 respectively and hence have over 70 years of organizational history. The United States has a professionalized cadre of economists around which a professional identity is formed among many who move in and out of positions of responsibility. The country has a free press, laws promoting transparency in public policymaking, campaign finance reform, and on and on. And I only use the United States because I live here. The crisis was just as deep and handled perhaps even more weakly in countries like the United Kingdom or in some other European countries (there is lively debate on this of course).

If, with these long and deep historical conditions and organizational capabilities and individual capacities the United States is, as Johnson asserts, just another country suffering from elite capture, then what does one make of advice to other countries to liberalize markets and strengthen the institutions to regulate those markets?[3] If the lesson of the crisis for the United States is that the size, sophistication, and complexity of financial markets exceeded the organizational capability of the country's regulatory apparatus, then what is the lesson for, say, Algeria or India or Indonesia or Mexico? That their problem is that they have "weak institutions"? These questions are not rhetorical but are pressing to pursue as the origins of the crisis becomes clearer.

Policy and Policy Implementation

A problem with discussing the lessons from the crisis is that words like "policies" and "institutions" have been used in so many ways by so many people, both across disciplines and even within disciplines. It is less than clear what people mean when they talk about "policy failures" or "weak institutions." Before discussing lessons about capability for policy implementation I must introduce a few key definitions, with illustrations.

A policy is a mapping from states of the world to actions by an agent of an organization. This is an articulation of the commonsense notion of policy but already clarifies that the difference between a "policy action" and a "policy" (which is roughly that between a real function and a real number). Some mistakes in "policy" are not that the mapping is incorrect but that the state of the world is not correctly identified so that the policy action is a mistake. When different people say "policy" it is not clear whether people are even talking about the same type of thing, as people commonly conflate a specific policy action (raising the interest rate in a particular circumstance) with a notional policy (managing interest rates to stabilize economic activity), with a realized policy (the sequence of policy actions resulting from the implementation of a notional policy).

Since a policy is a mapping, there are several elements to a completely specified policy beyond just the statement of the rule or notional policy. I wish to highlight two. A completely specified policy has to specify what organization or body or individual has the authority to declare the juridical and hence administratively relevant state of the world (and how, if at all, this declaration can be challenged and overturned). So while a policy of a "10 percent flat rate income tax" may sound like a simple policy, as the mapping from the state of the world (taxable income) to the action of the agent of the state (collect 10 percent of that amount) is simple, policy implementation is complex as there have to be a set of rules that define what "income" is for tax purposes (which may or may not agree with commonsense notions of what income is) and who gets to declare what income is. This declaration of the state of the world may, or may not, be separated in policy implementation from the agents or organization responsible for other actions in policy implementation. This conceptual distinction of declaring the state of the world is important as it is immediately obvious there is no interesting policy without de facto discretion.[4] Even if the mapping appears to have no discretion (e.g., if the state of the world is X, you must always do Y) the declaration of whether the state of the world is X automatically creates discretion as what matters for policy is not the simple common sense notions of state of the world but the juridically declared state of the world and if the appropriately specified body declares, for the purposes of policy implementation, that night is day then night *is* day.

The second key concept is that there may be little or no connection between the *notional* policy as specified on paper in the laws and regulations and the *realized* policy. The realized policy is not a choice of any given individual or agency but rather is the endogenous outcome of the operation of a complex set of incentives and motivations that face the individual agents responsible for implementation. These depend on the direction organizations of implementation and on the background conditions in which the organizations and frontline agents are embedded (e.g., existence of effective legislative or judicial oversight, social norms of behavior, etc.).

In the context of the United States, these roles are usually quite clear. The tax code constitutes the "notional policy"—the mapping between states of the world (income) and taxes owed. The Internal Revenue Service (IRS) is the designated organization responsible for implementation, giving it the responsibility to both declare the juridical state of the world (what any taxpayer's taxable income is) and to act to collect the corresponding tax through its frontline workers. The IRS is embedded in a complex set of "institutions" ranging from accountancy that influences bodies of professional practice and creates codes of conduct of those who interact with the IRS as well as legislative oversight of IRS functioning and possibilities of judicial review of IRS conduct or, in some cases, decisions. In the United States, one generally feels the gap between notional policy and realized policy is present, but manageable and not sufficient to thwart the actual intent of the notional policy. In some sense what one means by "strong

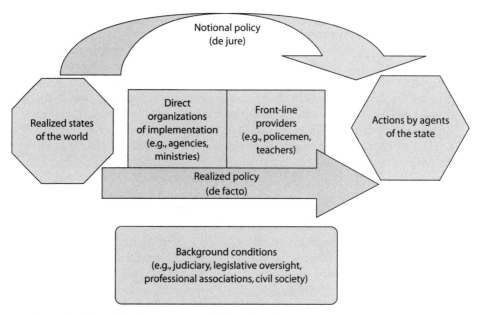

Figure 9.1 Distinction between notional (de jure) and realized (de facto) policy depends on organizational capability, influenced by background institutions. Source: Based on Pritchett (2005).

institutions" is that the average policy implementation capability of the designated organizations is high.

This is in stark contrast to developing countries where the gap between notional and realized policy is first order. An empirical example from India will illustrate this idea. A study examined a program to reduced absences among nurses in Rajasthan (Banerjee, Duflo, and Glennerster 2008). The study examined the impact of introducing better tracking of the attendance of nurses with a potential to dock their pay if their attendance was not at least 50 percent (note already the low baseline and target). Since the program was implemented in cooperation with a nongovernmental organization (NGO) that had long experience in the state, there was enormous attention to accuracy in assessing the seemingly very simple state of the world of whether the nurse showed up for work or not. They instituted an automated time recording system that was then independently "ground truthed" by the NGO doing spot checks on both the machines and the physical presence of the nurses. In the end after 18 months of implementation the program had no impact on *presence*—even of the newly hired people even on the monitoring days—but recorded "absences" were no higher than they ever were. How? One exception to the attendance rule was if the nurse's presence was required elsewhere for other duty so that as a juridical matter, even if nurses were not there, their absences were not considered an absence for administrative purposes. This then created a sufficient loophole. So the notional policy that "if you are absent more then 50 percent of the time (state of the world), your pay will be docked (action by the state)"—which seems like a wholly nondiscretionary policy conditioned only on hard facts—was subverted to a *realized* policy of getting untruthful but nevertheless administratively compelling excuses for absences and nonattendance.

The first lesson of the crisis is that whether or not a "policy" will be effective depends not only on whether the notional policy would be effective if it were to be implemented (which is often a technical matter of the relevant causal model) but also whether the policy is capable of being implemented in the political and administrative environment. Why this is a lesson of the crisis we will come back to below, but across the developing world there is an increasing realization that in many domains the capacity for policy implementation is in fact the key constraint. Changing the policy may or may not have any impact on anyone's behavior where the de jure and de facto policies have diverged. Conversely, one need not change the de facto policy to achieve substantial differences in policy implementation, either strengthening or weakening the impact of the same notional policy (see figure 9.1).

Organizational Capability: Spartans, Paper Tigers, and Keystone Cops

The battle of Thermopylae, at which a small force of Spartans (and others) held off a massive invading force from Persia, fighting to the last man, resonates through the ages. It is remarkable that a relatively obscure battle over 2,000 years ago inspired (another) recent Hollywood movie (and a spoof). There are of course a variety of reasons why this battle is so famous, but the reason I want to focus on is that the Spartans illustrate the robustness of organizational capability for policy implementation to countervailing pressures.

Drawing on the definitions above of policy and policy implementation, I can define organizational capability for policy implementation as some measure of the distance between outcomes from the *ideal* set of actions conditional on realized states of the world that would maximize the organization's objectives and the *actual* set of actions undertaken by the agents of the organization, appropriately integrated over states of the world. Public sector organizations—ministries of education, police forces, militaries, cen-

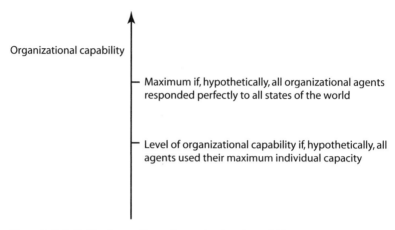

Figure 9.2 Individual capacity and organizational capability.

tral banks, tax collection agencies—have *stated* objectives. One can define their organizational capability as the extent to which the agents of the organization, both leadership and frontline agents, undertake the actions that would, contingent on the states of the world, pursue the organizations objectives.

The first important distinction to make is that the individual capacity of the agents is one, but only one, element of organizational capability. Figure 9.2 begins constructing the graphs that illustrate the points of this chapter. On the vertical axis is the extent to which the agents of the organization if they were to act at their maximum individual capacity would fulfill the organization's objectives.

While individual capacity plays a role in organizational capability, it is far from the only factor. As we all know there is many a slip twixt the cup and the lip, and the ideal of individual agents using their maximal individual capacity at all times to pursue their organization's objectives is only a thought experiment. In fact, agents have their own interests, goals, and objectives, and agents choose their actions to pursue those objectives. This is not to say those objectives are pecuniary exclusively or even primarily as intrinsic motivation or commitments to professional identities or desires to help their comrades or not "lose face" certainly play important roles. But there are pressures on agents to pursue other objectives and these can be less or greater. Let us first illustrate these with a military analogy.

On the vertical axis in this case is an army's ability to inflict damage on an enemy. One can imagine how large this capability would be if the army itself were under no countervailing battlefield pressure and all agents (from officers down) were operating at their maximum individual capacity. This might be larger or smaller depending on the size of the force, the equipment at their disposal, the level of training, and so on. But every military leader knows that this definition of organizational capability is irrelevant. The more important question is the robustness of that capability to pressure from the opponent. How quickly does the ability of a fighting force to act to inflict damage on the capability of the opponent degrade under actual battlefield conditions?

The U.S. Marine Corps official doctrine *Warfighting* (1997) is publicly available and makes for interesting reading. For the U.S. Marines "war is an interactive social process" in which one force attempts to impose its will on the other. Hence, the overwhelming emphasis of their war fighting doctrine is not destroying the opposing force in material terms (casualties or equipment) but rather destroying the opposing force's will to fight. Their goal is to sufficiently disrupt the opposing forces' organizational coherence such that its individual agents cease to act as a coherent purposive body and begin to pursue their own immediate interests. At this point, the organizational capability of forces, even with huge numbers of personnel and massive equipment, disintegrates.[5] Roughly, turn the opposing army—an (social) organization capable of directed action—into a mob of individuals.[6]

One element of this process, and which makes military history fascinating, is that the process is sharply nonlinear. That is, in battlefield situations the degradation of organizational capability often does not follow a linear process in which incremental units of battlefield pressure yield constant units of degradation of capability. At least at times, a small action can cause a ripple effect in which soldiers believe their position is untenable, lose the will to defend it, and a battle becomes a rout (or conversely, a single action prevents the loss of a position that would cause a rout).

These considerations of the robustness of organizational capability with respect to pressure and potentially nonlinear dynamics lead to figure 9.3, which contrasts three paradigm cases: Spartans, Paper Tigers, and Keystone Cops.

The Keystone Cops were a staple of early silent film comedies and were a platoon of policemen who, with great fanfare and flurry of activity would rush around completely incompetently. This is an example of an organization (or disorganization) in which even under ideal conditions is incapable of accomplishing anything and hence has low organizational capability over all ranges of pressure.

A contrast to the Keystone Cops is a Paper Tiger. A Paper Tiger is an organization that appears to have high capability—it has trained people with the individual capacity to, in principle, to recognize states of the world and

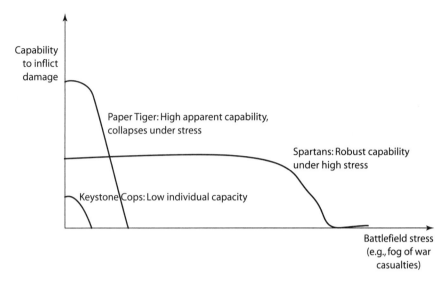

Figure 9.3 Patterns of the robustness of capability to pressure: Spartans, Paper Tigers, Keystone Cops.

respond to them—and has the materials with which to work and has, again at least in principle, modes of command and control of the organization that allow it to operate. But, when put under battlefield stress, the capability collapses as the individuals cease to pursue the organizations interests and the organizational integrity and coherence necessary for capability disappears—a large army that looks fantastic in parades becomes a mob on the battlefield.

This brings us back to the Spartans. Part of the point of Spartan training (indeed Spartan society itself) was to create individuals with high capacity (e.g., knew how to execute the individual skills), but another part—a part of all military training—was devoted to maintaining that capability as an organization even under the greatest duress when the actions of the individual put their lives at risk in order to maintain the overall organizational integrity and coherence.

All of this discussion of militaries is in part relevant, because militaries are large public sector organizations given responsibility for aspects of policy implementation. But primarily they serve as a useful analogy of more general issues that affect all elements of policy implementation, from direct service provision (e.g., education, health, agricultural extension) to "obligation imposition" (e.g., policing, tax collection) to the implementation of economic policies from the macro (e.g., central banks) to the micro (e.g., prudential regulation).

Let me give another empirical example from detailed research that illustrates the gap between individual capacity and organizational capability and hence the potential for Paper Tiger organizations. Das and Hammer (2005) did a detailed study of providers of medical care in New Delhi by starting not from a list of licensed providers but from a user survey. Hence the providers included both public sector doctors who had the standard Indian training and the variety of private providers from high quality doctors to "Bengali doctors" who were, euphemistically, "less than fully qualified" (some substantial fraction of private providers had less than a high school education). The study first assessed the individual capacity of providers by asking them to respond to a series of researcher-prepared vignettes in which study participants were trained to present with sets of diagnostic conditions and the providers (knowing these were hypothetical) attempted to diagnose and recommend therapeutics. Not surprisingly, this aspect of the study revealed a substantial amount of "Keystone Cops," as the median provider was just below the standard of "do no harm," which is scary but not the most interesting part for present purposes.

The study then followed up with the same providers by observing their actual clinical practice, with the providers knowing they were being observed. This created a measure of the application of individual capacity in a variety of organizational settings. Figure 9.4 differentiates by three types of settings: private providers, government-operated primary health clinics (PHCs), and government hospitals. There are three striking findings. First, there was almost perfect alignment in the private sector between what they knew in theory and what they did in practice—if anything, the incentives were to overtreat (the study shows that they do substantial amounts of overprescribing of needless therapy). Second, in the government PHCs there is an enormous gap between what they know in theory and what they do in practice. There is a huge "effort deficit" as, even when these doctors are in the clinic (and other studies have shown that absenteeism among health providers in India is rampant), they simply do not perform. Third, interestingly, in public hospitals the "effort deficit" is not nearly as large as in the clinics.

This empirical work illustrates the concepts. The stated objective of the notional policy of the government is to provide clinics to expand availability of health care services. The implementation of this policy requires that public sector agents (e.g., frontline health care providers) make the correct mapping between "states of the world" (e.g., disease conditions) and the appropriate action by the agent of the state (e.g., recommend therapy). Suc-

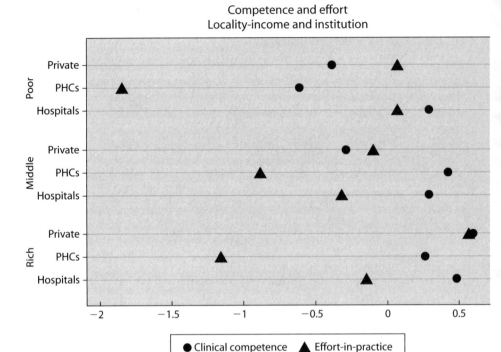

Figure 9.4 The gap between individual capacity and organizational capability in public
sector clinical care in Delhi, India. Source: Adapted from Das and Hammer (2005).
PHC = primary health clinics

cessful policy implementation requires both individual capacity—the ability of the agents to make the correct assessment of the state of the world and
how to respond as evidence by ability to correctly diagnose and treat—and
that this individual capacity be embedded in an organization with capability—the material conditions and overall setting in which individuals exercise their capacities to further the (notional) objectives of the organization.
This evidence suggests that large parts of the government run health care
system in India is a Paper Tiger: on paper there are clinics, in the budget
there are medicines, on the payroll there are nurses and doctors, but under
the actual everyday pressures in which individuals face incentives the organizational capability of the system is a small fraction of its notional or
apparent capability.

Lessons about Institutions and Organizational Capability from the Crisis

Prior to the financial crisis, the conventional wisdom in development economics was tending toward the view that "institutions rule" in explaining long-run growth and levels of economic prosperity.[7] If one could crudely caricature the stages of general slogans of development, there was an "accumulation" phase in which the key problem of development was framed as the rapid accumulation of human and physical capital.[8] A second phase was a "policies" phase in which economists confronted the puzzle of low growth in spite of accumulation of physical and human capital. A good example of this is when economists encountered the debt crisis of the early 1980s in which the Volker shock of sudden increase in rates and decrease in availability of capital flows revealed that the debt accumulation had not created sufficient capability for production and, in particular, export capability to service those debts. The shorthand for the conventional wisdom of the macro-policies was the "Washington consensus."

This led to the third phase of either (1) "good institutions" were needed to implement the "good policies" (the World Bank conventional wisdom was to pair "good policies and institutions") or (2) the more radical "institutions rule" view that if countries had sufficiently "good" institutions they would either muddle along even without particularly good policies or that these institutions themselves would eventually produce the equivalent of good policies in practice. In either case, prior to the recent crisis the view that long-run development required not just good policies but also organizations capable of policy implementation and "building institutions" was the conventional wisdom.

What has the crisis taught us about those ideas? Two things, it has highlighted the dangers of putting institutions under stress, particularly in the development context of premature load bearing and it has challenged the notion of "good institutions."

Organizations, Institutions, and Premature Load Bearing

One of the pressing difficulties of development is that we know very little about building organizational capability but we increasingly realize we know a lot about destroying it.

Given the definitions above of organizational capability, it is clear that "building organizational capability" can mean one of two things. The predominant way in which the development literature, and even more especially development assistance organization's practice, has conceived of building organizational capability is pushing up the vertical axis of indi-

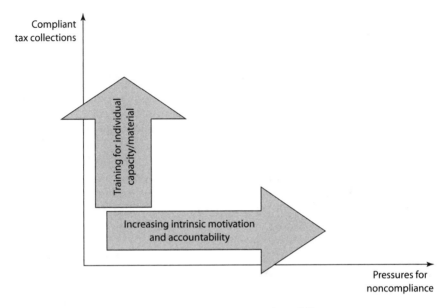

Figure 9.5 Alternative ideas for building organizational capability.

vidual capacity and organizational design (see figure 9.5). The robustness to stress was often not a key consideration. Take an example of an agency responsible for collecting taxes—a custom's agency for instance. Their organizational job is to map from a juridical state of the world—the dutiable value of an import—to an action—collecting the appropriate tax. This requires the agents of the customs agency to carry out these actions. One can think of building capacity of the organization by "training" the agents so that they know the legal tariff code and how to apply it in specific circumstances. One can also think of strengthening the organization's apparent stress-free capability through material support—for example, computerization or making the code updates available.

Alternatively, one can conceive of the expansion of organizational capability as the increase in the willingness of the organization's agents to perform under pressure. That is, it may well be that the agent's of the organization already know what it is they ought to be doing but are simply failing to do it. One reason the studies of absenteeism cited above are so telling is that it is very difficult to attribute absenteeism to a lack of individual capacity: everybody knows what day it is. If the problem is that, when an organization is a Paper Tiger that has collapsed under stress and is already performing far below its existing apparent capability, it is doubtful that expanding individual capacity is a fruitful strategy.[9]

The links between organizational capability and institutions comes to the fore in plans to expand organizational capability, in three ways: overall accountability through the background institutions in which organizations are embedded, intrinsic motivation through professional identities, and available organizational strategies.

Accountability is an omnibus term for mechanisms that induce agents to pursue the interests of principals—in this case public sector organizations tasked with policy implementation. The World Bank's *World Development Report 2004* (I was part of the team that produced that report) emphasized that accountability is a system and that there are multiple channels through which agents have to be held accountable. One can imagine various ways in which the management of public sector organizations can expand capability. But, as the old saying goes, "just because the tire is flat does not mean the hole is on the bottom."[10] Just because tax collectors are wildly corrupt does not mean the problem is with the *management* of the tax agency. It could well be that the relationship between the citizens and the state (taken as the executive control of the administrative apparatus of the state), the relationship of accountability we called "politics," is so weak that the state is predatory and benefits from corrupt and rapacious tax collectors. Alternatively, it could be the control of the executive or legislative apparatus of the state over its implementing organizations is so weak the leadership of public sector organizations themselves feel no responsibility for performance.

Organizational capability is not formed in a vacuum but is, at least in part, dependent on the country's and societies' background institutions: How well does the polity work to represent the interests of citizens? Is there an independent judiciary? Is there a tradition of civil service? Is there legislative oversight? Figure 9.6 shows the four primary relationships of accountability.

A second element is that in many functional organizations it is not extrinsic accountability through the threat of punishment or the promise of reward but intrinsic motivation that accounts for at least some measure of performance. This is far too complex a topic to address, but professional identity almost certainly plays a role in framing many people's behavior. Even in organizations that are otherwise dysfunctional and in which there are no high powered (or even low powered) incentives, one often finds people toiling away at their jobs because this is just what people like them (e.g., teachers, doctors, military officers) do.

There is also a rich literature on "social capital" in which individuals'

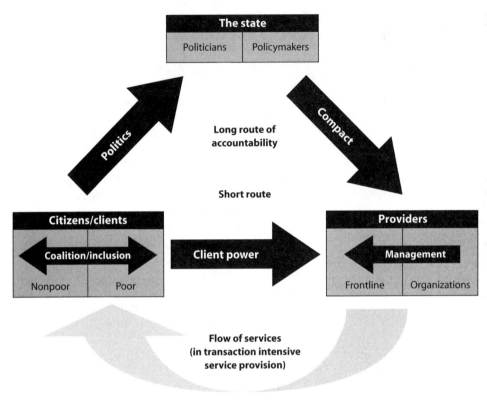

Figure 9.6 The accountability triangle and the four relationships of accountability.
Source: Adapted from World Bank 2004.

behavior is shaped by their embeddedness in a rich set of relationships with an intrinsic element of development (Fukuyama 2001, 2004). This behavior continues to play a role in the performance of public sector organizations even in developed economies that are notionally completely "modern" states. Often organizations function because of their social capital, in that individuals in organizations perform not because of outside threats but rather that, because of their relationships within the organization, individuals are more satisfied when performing well (and trust that others will do their part). Again, the analogy to the military literature is strong, as it has long placed enormous stress on "unit cohesion." Tendler (1998) shows how important the construction of the social conditions conducive to governance reforms is to the ability of reforms to actually change behavior.

A third point about the "background institutions" is that they constrain the possibilities available to various organizational types. That is, publicly traded private sector firms can offer high-powered incentives to employees based on stock market valuation—as these sets of institutions exist and function. Ministries of education cannot offer teachers explicit high-powered incentives.

Building organizational capability is therefore an extremely complex and problematic task. The naïve view that organizational capability is the sum of individual capacities and that "training" and material support through assets and budgets are the key to organizational capability is untenable. Building the robustness of organizations so that they can withstand pressure and induce their agents to utilize their capacity involves both a wide variety of determinants, many of which are not under the control of organizational leadership. So while organizational capability for policy implementation is central to successful development, there are few generalized lessons about how to build capacity.

In contrast, it is increasingly obvious how to destroy organizational capability: premature load bearing. While I know nothing about how to build the capability of an army I know exactly how to destroy that capability—put it into battle against a force capable of generating pressure and it will disintegrate.

This leads to a central emerging issue in development thinking: the dangers of what is known as *isomorphic mimicry*—copying actions of an organization that you wish to emulate—which repeats for the third time the key mistake of development. The first time was to say, "Rich countries have more stuff (e.g., bridges, factories) than poor countries, hence accumulating stuff is the key to development." The second time was to say, "Rich countries have good policies (e.g., open to trade), hence adopting good policies is key to development." The charming third time is to say, "Rich countries have good institutions, hence promoting good institutions is the key to development."

The problem is defining "good institutions." If these are defined in form, then it is relatively easy to transplant organizations and institutions. Countries can easily adopt the legislation that establishes the forms: independent central banks, outcome-based budgeting, procurement practices, electricity regulation. However, having the *forms* does not automatically create the organizational capability to carry out the *functions*. Isomorphism (DiMaggio and Powell 1991) is the securing of organizational legitimacy, not by actual functionality but by imitating the forms other organizations that are successful. The evolutionary analogy is to nature's mimics, such as insects that adopt the coloration of other insects that are poisonous even though they themselves are not.

Difficulties come in allocating to the isomorphic organizational forms

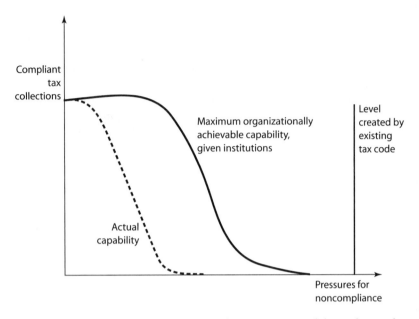

Figure 9.7 Premature load bearing: Pressure from organizational demands exceeds maximal organizational resistance.

the high pressure functions these organizations perform in rich countries after they have developed high and robust organizational capability. For instance, Dubash (2008) describes the adoption of an "independent regulator" to set electricity tariffs in India. The transplantation of the exact legislation and organizations of the "independent" regulation of electricity from other countries did not lead at all to the expected results, when, of course, none of the background institutions, conditions, and history that made this successful in its original environment were present in the Indian states adopting the form. Figure 9.7 illustrates a hypothetical case in which the existing tax code—because of its complexity, level of rates, or definition of base—creates pressure for individual agents to deviate from compliance that exceed, not only what the organization is capable of but the *maximum* organizational capability even if those elements under control of leadership (the "management" elements of accountability) were optimally designed.[11]

An empirical example perhaps helps illustrate the point of premature load bearing. There have been two major approaches to measuring the "investment climate" and how government regulations do or do not inhibit business growth. One is the "doing business" surveys that record the de jure regulations. The other sources are the "enterprise" surveys that ask firms what they actually do. In some cases these overlap so that the doing business survey records what compliance with regulations would entail while businesses tell of actual practice. Figure 9.8 (Hallward-Driemeier and Pritchett 2009) shows one such example in which we compare the doing business estimates of the days of the number of days it would take to import something with the distribution across all firms with the actual days the firms report their last import of that object took them. Each box whisker is the distribution of the firm's enterprise survey responses, which provides an estimate of the typical but also the time taken in the worst cases. The striking thing about this figure is that *all* of the increase in the doing business reported number of days to import is associated with the *gap* between de jure and de facto—actual days taken, even among the firms reporting the worst delays—do not appear to increase days reported taken for import at all. For instance, compare the country with the de jure regulations that take 32 days to comply. The median is less than 10 days but the 90th percentile is actually roughly full compliance (30 days). In contrast, the country where the de jure regulations imply it would take 95 days to import, the median is still less than 10 and the 90th percentile firm by reported delay takes only 21 days. While there are obviously a number of interpretations of this figure,

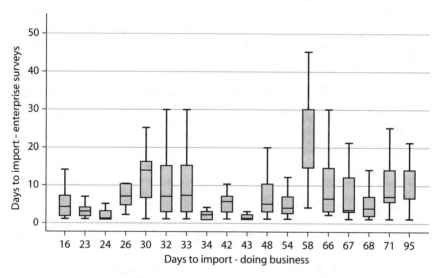

Figure 9.8 Comparing doing business days (days estimated) with enterprise survey (actual) days to import an item. Note: Excludes outside values. Source: Author calculations.

one interpretation is that when de jure regulations exceed the organization capability, maximum compliance simply breaks down and outcomes are deal by deal. Once a policy implementing organization has passed the threshold into collapsed Paper Tiger all else is irrelevant.

The usual interpretation of the doing business results is that the regulations that create such long delays for importing, are overly restrictive of economic activity. In this interpretation it may well be that the non-compliance is in fact a positive thing, because if the firms actually had to comply with the de jure regulation, it would freeze up economic activity entirely. There is certainly a sense in which, if one has bad policies, weaker implementation can be a blessing. However, once organizational capability has collapsed, one has to consider what impact regulatory reform would have. Even if the new regulations are substantial reductions over the existing ones, they may still require greater implementation capability than the organizations possess and hence result in the similar gaps between de jure and de facto. Once you are in a submarine whether the water is 10 or 100 feet deep is not a huge issue.

So, a first lesson is that putting organizations (whose capability depends at least in part on the background institutions on which it can draw to create accountability on the one hand and intrinsic motivation on the other) under duress before they have developed sufficient not just apparent capability but also robustness to pressure is a recipe for disaster. To bring back analogies I used earlier in the chapter, this is like building a papier-mâché model of a bridge a then driving a truck over it or like throwing green troops into a rout. The developing world is in fact now riddled with agencies delegated responsibilities for implementation of policy regulations in which the de jure policy and the stated organizational objectives have no normative or positive traction on the behavior of the agents of the organization. While this is perhaps a good thing if the policies themselves are overly restrictive, organizational disability spills over into capability to enforce even desirable regulation.

Specific Lessons for Development

There are a variety of reactions to the problems with the strains placed on organizational capability for policy implementation by the pressures of overly complex, detailed, and "high stakes" policies when the de jure and de facto realities diverge.

One is to adopt the view that we should all become "libertarians of necessity."[12] Many argue that development policy advisers and supporters should admit that, while it would be nice if it were the case that optimal policies *could* be implemented, they cannot. The question is then whether it is better to just admit the incapability and not pretend to regulate as that regulation itself can create negative pressures. That certainly was an argument made to support liberalization of import policies in the 1980s and 1990s: it didn't matter whether or not there was, in principle, an empirical case for "infant industry" protection; in practice one would get rent seeking. The fact that the U.S. regulatory apparatus was not Spartan but, at least at the pressures applied, a Paper Tiger suggests that no country will be able to regulate financial transactions to guarantee the absence of crisis. The "libertarian of necessity" argument would suggest that being guarded by a Paper Tiger is worse than no protection at all (as Paper Tigers do eat).

While this argument that "none is better than weak" might have been an attractive argument about trade policy, one can hardly take the same view with respect to say the responsibilities of the state for security, or law enforcement, or contract enforcement—all of which require large degrees of organizational capability. Not to mention other key developmental functions of the state—infrastructure, public health (*not* curative services), or basic education.

The alternative to "standing back and letting it all be" will be a rather thorough-going rethinking of how development is to be achieved. From a variety of different angles (including both "left" and "right" politics) people are pointing out that the expectations placed on the contemporary developing country states and their organizations of implementation far exceed those placed on the now developed countries when they had similar levels of income (Chang 2003; Hall and Leeson 2007). This is perhaps most obvious in the "state building" exercises the United States and its allies are promoting in Afghanistan in which gains in democratic practice and administrative capability acquired over centuries in the historical experience of the United States are expected to be "short-run" goals. Fukuyama (2004) has begun the exploration of what state building looks like in the post "end of history" world, but this is a daunting task. Most development efforts are grounded in a practice of development as what my colleagues and I call accelerated modernization through transplanted best practice, which emphasizes form over function. Placing more emphasis on allowing the robust capability of policy implementation to emerge gradually contextually under performance pressure (which will be against all instincts of most "big development" practice) is one way of avoiding the problems of premature load bearing.

Conclusion

I propose three lessons highlighted by, and some directly stemming from, the "Great Recession."

First, policies are only as good as the organizational capability for policy implementation, as the outcomes are produced by realized policy and not by what is on the books.

Second, organizational capability is not a constant but itself depends on the countervailing pressure under which policy is implemented. Some organizations are like Spartans and can withstand enormous amounts of pressure without buckling. Some organizations are Keystone Cops and have no capability even under ideal conditions. In between are the Paper Tigers that appear on paper to have all of the right designs and resources and perhaps even individual capacities but the organizational capability is not robust to pressure. So Spartan on paper becomes Keystone Cop in practice.

Third, premature load bearing is asking organizations to take on tasks of greater complexity or countervailing pressure than the organization can withstand. Years, or even decades, of "capacity building" or "institution building" can disappear if a nonlinear dynamic of organizational demoralization is set in motion. On this score the lesson of the financial crisis for the United States is that "it can happen here" and the lesson for the rest of world of that "it can happen there" should be sobering indeed.

Notes

1. This phenomenon extends beyond economic policy of course, as the U.S. loss in the Vietnam War, the collapse of the Soviet Union, and the events of 9/11 are used to draw "lessons" and to date the shifts in intellectual tides.
2. One way of interpreting Fukuyama's (1992) famous "end of history" argument is that "democracy" as a mode of organizing polities was the final condition to which historical evolution had been (inevitably?) headed and that "development" was merely an accelerator in this process.
3. The financial crisis is perhaps the power crisis in California writ large. As California's system was apparently the "model" of separation of generation and delivery with regulated markets being promoted, it did raise some pretty fundamental questions about the needed capacity to implement. Whatever you think of California, if I were a Moroccan or Indonesian policymaker, the fact that California could mess up so badly would give me pause.
4. Other than the policy of doing the exact same thing in all states of the world, which is not a very useful policy in any domain.
5. None of this is particularly original, as these are the ideas of B. Liddell Hart, transmuted into the German army's application of blitzkrieg in which the deep penetration of rapidly moving armored units sufficiently disrupts the ability of the opposing army to respond such that the capability of the opposing army disappears, often with small casualties or materiel loss. The German conquest of France in World War II is perhaps the paradigmatic example.

6. Using the example of an army is hardly original; Wilson's classic *Bureaucracy* (1989) opens with a martial example.

7. Rodrik, Subramanian, and Trebbi (2004) have the title "institutions rule" arguing for the primacy of institutional indicators over measures of "policy" and "geography" in explaining economic growth. Easterly and Levine (2003) argue that countries' endowments affect income through institutions. Hall and Jones (1999) decompose levels of income into observed accumulated factors and what they call "social capability" finding that most of income differences are due to this "social capability." The massively influential paper of Acemoglu, Johnson, and Robinson (2000) argued that institutions were important (and that they could empirically identify the causal impact of institutions using settler mortality, but that controversial claim was subsidiary to the real point that institutions cause prosperity). Economic historians Sokoloff and Engerman(2000) argued that factor endowments affected long-run productivity by influencing the development of the institutions necessary to support prosperous market economies (again, the view that institutions are essential to prosperity is essential, whether or not these are affected by factor endowments is a separate point).

8. As an aside, in spite of the myth to the contrary there never was a "physical capital" phase that was displaced by a "human capital" phase among development thinkers. All of the early writers on development (e.g., Arthur Lewis, Gunnar Myrdal, etc.) emphasized the importance of accumulating human capital. Myrdal's book *Asian Drama* written in the late 1950s takes the point about the importance of schooling as the settled conventional wisdom. It perhaps received less attention because success on this front seemed less problematic—as governments would take care of it—rather than that economists thought it was less important.

9. For instance, in the example above with medical care providers, one can estimate the connection between existing years of formal training and actual performance and ask the hypothetical: "how many years of additional training of public sector doctors would it take before their performance in practice (at the existing patterns of behavior) matched that of the private sector?" The connection between capacity and performance is so weak the answer is roughly that doctors would have to spend their entire careers in training—clearly "individual capacity building" and "organizational capability building" are not synonyms.

10. I learned this aphorism from Robert Solow in connection with labor markets and unemployment, but cannot find any source so perhaps he made it up.

11. The example of customs is not random. In my earlier work with Geeta Sethi, we demonstrated that as the official *ad valorem* tariff rate on items went up the *actual* ratio of officially reported revenue collected to officially reported import value stagnated and at the same time the variance across items with the same ad valorem rate increased. This strongly suggested that, beyond a certain ad va-

lorem rate (around 30–40 percent), the demands for undermining collections overwhelmed organizational capability.

12. As much as I wish this were my phrase, it is the working title of a paper by Melissa Thomas now entitled "Great Expectations: Rich Donors and Poor Country Governments" (2009).

References

Acemoglu, Daron, Simon Johnson, and James Robinson. 2000. "The Colonial Origins of Comparative Development: An Empirical Investigation." *The American Economic Review* 91(5): 1369–1401.

Bertrand, Marianne, Simeon Djankov, Rema Hanna, and Sendhil Mullainathan. 2007. *"Obtaining a Driving License in India: An Experimental Approach to Studying Corruption."* Quarterly Journal of Economics 122(4): 1639–76.

Banerjee, Abhijit, Esther Duflo, and Rachel Glennerster. 2008. "Putting a Band-Aid on a Corpse. Incentives for Nurses in the Indian Public Health Care System." *Journal of the European Economics Association* 6(2–3): 487–500.

Chang, Ha-Joon, 2003. *Kicking away the Ladder: Development Strategy in Historical Perspective.* London: Anthem Press.

Das, Jishnu, and Jeffrey Hammer. 2005. "Money for Nothing: The Dire Straits of Medical Practice in Delhi, India." World Bank Policy Research Working Paper no. 3669, Washington, DC: World Bank.

DiMaggio, Paul, and Walter Powell. 1991. *The New Institutionalism in Organizational Analysis.* Chicago: University of Chicago Press.

Dubash, Navroz. 2008. "Institutional Transplant as Political Opportunity: The Practice and Politics of Indian Electricity Regulation." CLPE Working Paper 31. Toronto: Comparative Research in Law and Political Economy.

Easterly, William, and Ross Levine. 2003. "Tropics, Germs, and Crops: How Endowments Influence Development" *Journal of Monetary Economics.* 50(1): 3–39.

Fukuyama, Francis. 1992. *The End of History and the Last Man.* Simon and Schuster.

———. 2004. *State Building: Governance and World Order in the 21st Century.* Ithaca, NY: Cornell University Press.

Hall, Joshua, and Peter Leeson. 2007. "Good for the Goose but Bad for the Gander: International Labor Standards and Comparative Development." *Journal of Labor Research* 28: 656–78.

Hall, Robert, and Charles Jones. 1999. "Why Do Some Countries Produce So Much More Output per Capita Than Others?" *Quarterly Journal of Economics* 114(1): 83–116.

Hallward-Driemeier, Mary, Gita Khun-Jush, and Lant Pritchett. 2009. "Deals versus Rules: Uncertainty in Policy Implementation in Africa." Working paper RWP10–027, Kennedy School of Government, Harvard University.

Johnson, Simon. 2009. "The Quiet Coup." *The Atlantic Monthly* (May).

Pritchett, Lant. 2005. "Reform Is Like a Box of Chocolates: An Interpretive Essay on Understanding the Pleasant and Unpleasant Surprises from Policy Reform." Kennedy School of Government, Harvard University. Available at www.hks. harvard.edu/fs/lpritch/reform%20is%20like%20a%20box%20of%20choco lates.pdf.

Rodrik, Dani, Arvind Subramanian, and Fransico Trebbi. 2004. "Institutions Rule: The Primacy of Institutions over Geography and Integration in Economic Development." *Journal of Economic Growth.* 9(2): 131–65.

Sokoloff, Kenneth, and Stanley Engerman. 2000. "History Lessons: Institutions, Factor Endowments, and Paths of Development in the New World." *Journal of Economic Perspectives* 14(3): 217–232.

Tendler, Judith. 1998. *Good Governance in the Tropics.* Baltimore: Johns Hopkins University Press.

U.S. Marine Corps. 1997. *Warfighting.* Available at www.dtic.mil/doctrine/jel/service _pubs/mcdp1.pdf

Wilson, James Q. 1989. *Bureaucracy: What Government Agencies Do and Why They Do It.* New York: Basic Books.

Woodside, Alexander. 2006. *Lost Modernities: China, Vietnam, Korea and the Hazards of World History.* Cambridge, MA: Harvard University Press.

World Bank. 2004. *World Development Report, 2004: Making Services Work for the Poor.* Washington, DC: World Bank.

CHAPTER 10

The Democratic Recession

Before and After the Financial Crisis

Larry Diamond

HARD ECONOMIC TIMES are supposed to be hard on democracy, particularly new and fragile democracies. This is one of the cardinal principles of empirical democratic theory. As Seymour Martin Lipset argued in his 1960 classic *Political Man*, when democratic regimes lack intrinsic legitimacy (what is often now called democratic "consolidation"), they depend precariously for their existence on effective performance, primarily in economic terms. Weakly legitimate democracies may muddle along in the absence of crisis for some time, but when they lose their effectiveness, they collapse—as did Germany, Austria, and Spain in the 1930s, following the onset of the Great Depression (Lipset 1960). In fact, the economic disarray of the late 1920s and 1930s swallowed up a number of other democracies as well in Europe and Latin America, even though the origin of the "first reverse wave" of global democratization can be traced to Mussolini's March on Rome in 1922 (Huntington 1991).

During the second half of the twentieth century, there was a strong relationship between economic performance and the survival of regimes, particularly democracies. Analyzing data from 1950 to 1990, Adam Przeworski and his colleagues found that when democracies face a decline in income, they are three times more likely to disappear than when they experience economic growth. Looking at longer-term trajectories, the impact of economic performance became even more striking: "The chance that a democracy will die is 1 in 135 when incomes grow during any three or more consecutive years, and 1 in 13 when incomes fall during any two consecutive years" (Przeworski et al. 2000). More than two-thirds of all the democratic failures that Przeworski et al. documented in their forty-year period of analysis were accompanied by a fall in income in one or both of the preceding years. Thus, "deaths of democracies follow a clear pattern: They are more likely when a country experiences an economic crisis, and in most cases they are accompanied by one" (Przeworski et al. 2000).[1]

Yet the current period in world history defies these patterns. By all accounts, the global financial crisis that began in September 2008 has triggered the worst economic downturn since the Great Depression. Yet, as I argue below, it appears to have had little effect on the survival of democracy so far, for three reasons. First, the countries hardest hit economically by the financial crisis (at least in the first year or so following the onset) have mostly been the wealthy, industrialized democracies or the new European market economies. As Przeworski and his colleagues also showed, democracy has never broken down in a wealthy country, and after many decades of successful functioning, these democracies are now consolidated and deeply institutionalized.

The post-communist democracies of Central and Eastern Europe that have recently been admitted into the European Union (and would face enormous economic costs for abandoning democracy) also now appear to be consolidated. Second, in the newer and weaker democracies (including both the upper-middle-income ones in Eastern Europe and the less developed ones), where the economic turbulence has been felt the effect has been the defeat of democratically elected governments, not the demise of democracy. And third, the breakdowns of democracy that have been occurring largely predate the onset of the global recession and are due to bad internal governance, not unfavorable global conditions. In fact, in a surprising number of instances, democratic breakdowns occurred amid pretty decent aggregate rates of economic growth.

The analysis that follows should not be read as implying that economic circumstances do not matter for the fate of fragile democracies. Indeed, the quantitative data over recent decades suggest that they matter *especially* for younger and lower-income democracies.[2] But where governance is bad—in particular, where corruption and abuse of power are rampant, and where inequality is extreme and intensifying—it may not much matter much for democracy that the economy as a whole is expanding. To the extent that democracies depend for their survival on the support or at least acquiescence of the governed, bad governance undermines that support and inclines them toward calamity. Both survey data and objective trends suggest that in the short run, political factors may be more important than economic ones in determining the fate of new and fragile democracies. Thus, even if the world economy recovers quickly and vigorously from the current recession, more democracies will fail if they do not improve the quality of governance and rein in abuse of power. The "new idea on development" that emerges from this analysis, then, is not about global economic structure, rules, or flows, it is about governance. If the established democracies and international institutions do not find ways to induce and support better governance, the democratic recession will deepen, whether the global economic recession ends or not.

The Global (Political) Recession of Democracy

One of the most remarkable features of the growth of the "third wave" of global democratic expansion that began in 1974 has been its persistence. Unlike the relatively short "second wave" that began after World War II, the third wave has not yet met with a decisive "reverse wave" of democratic breakdowns. Yet, as I have argued elsewhere, there are worrisome signs of a democratic rollback in the world.[3] First, the number of democracies in the world leveled off in the mid-1990s at about 120 and has not changed dramatically since then; according to Freedom House, there were 119 electoral democracies at the beginning of 2009 (Puddington 2009). Since 1995, the percentage of states that could be called electoral democracies has oscillated within a narrow margin, between about 60 and 63 percent of all the independent states of the world.

Second, the incidence of democratic breakdown has been increasing in the world during this long third wave. If we count not only blatant reversals of democracy—by either military or executive coup—but also incremental degradations of the democratic process that drag a system eventually below the threshold of electoral democracy, then by my count (which is very close to that of Freedom House), one of every five democracies that has existed during the third wave has been reversed. This is a significantly higher percentage than is generally appreciated, but more importantly, it is a significantly higher percentage than was the case just a few years ago, because the incidence of democratic reversals has been rising. In fact, the vast majority of all the democratic reversals (29) that have occurred during the 35 years of the third wave have occurred in this past decade, and eight just in the last three years (table 10.1). I would not yet term this a clear "reverse wave," but when we look at the developments through 2009, it does appear now that the number of transitions away from democracy is exceeding the number to democracy. And note that recent breakdowns have also occurred in large and strategically important states, such as Russia, Nigeria, Venezu-

Table 10.1. Breakdowns of democracy during the third wave of global democratic expansion (1974–2009)

Type of breakdown	Number of such breakdowns	Percentage of all democracies (150)[a] during third wave	Countries with dates of democratic breakdown and renewal
Breakdown with subsequent return to democracy	10	6.6	India (1975–1977) Turkey (1980–1983) Ghana (1981–2000) Nigeria (1983–1999)[b] Fiji (1987–1997) Thailand (1991–93)[c] Peru (1992–2001) Lesotho (1994–2002) Zambia (1996–2001) Bangladesh (2007–8)
Breakdown with no return to democracy by 2007	19	12.7	Lebanon (1975) Sudan (1989) The Gambia (1994) Pakistan (1999) Fiji (2000) Kyrgyzstan (2000) Russia (2000) Nepal (2002) Nigeria (2003) Venezuela (2005) Thailand (2006)[c] Solomon Islands (2006) Philippines (2007) Kenya (2007) Georgia (2008) Mauritania (2008) Honduras (2009) Madagascar (2009) Niger (2009)
Total	29	19.3	

[a]This counts all the democratic regimes that existed between April 1974 (the beginning of the third wave) and August 2009, as follows: 40 democracies already existed, 102 countries made transitions to democracy during this period, and eight of those countries (Ghana, Nigeria, Thailand, Peru, Lesotho, Zambia, Central African Republic, and Bangladesh) suffered a breakdown and then a return to democracy in this same period, thus, those seven are counted twice.

[b]Nigeria had two democratic reversals in this period: the military coup of 1983 and the massively rigged elections of 2003.

[c]Thailand had two democratic breakdowns in this period. It suffered military coups in 1991, leading to a return to democracy in 1992, and in 2006, with a less than democratic system still in place by September 2009.

ela (all three oil-dependent states), Pakistan, Thailand, the Philippines, and Bangladesh.

The third worrisome indicator is that the level of freedom in the world, as measured annually by Freedom House, is now also in decline—for several consecutive years. For many years after 1995, levels of civil and political freedom continued to expand, even as the number of electoral democracies leveled off. Every year except one between 1996 and 2005, the number of countries improving their freedom score (on either political rights or civil liberties or both) exceeded the number of countries declining in freedom— and usually by a large margin. However, 2006, 2007, and 2008 were the first three consecutive years since the end of the Cold War in which the number of countries declining in freedom exceeded the number gaining. Nearly four times as many countries declined as improved in freedom in 2007, and during the year 2008 well over twice as many declined as improved.

Of course, the second and third trends are related. First, obviously, when democracy is lost, freedom levels decline. But there is also the fact that virtually all of the democracies that have broken down since 1999 were illiberal, and a number of them had gradually been getting more so over time (table 10.2). Moreover, these democracies were poorly governed, with levels of corruption, rule of law, and effectiveness of state administration that compared quite unfavorably with other democracies. What we observe, in other words, is an apparent correlation between bad governance and democratic vulnerability. By contrast, overall economic performance does not seem to have been a consistent culprit here, as many of these failed democracies of the past decade had positive economic growth rates in the year or two before their collapse, which we can also see in table 10.2. In fact, some of the democracies had quite good, even startlingly good, economic performance, around the time they failed, with annual economic growth rates over (or well over) 6 percent. This table also reveals a pattern. Generally, those democracies that were extinguished as a result of the mounting executive abuses of power were experiencing robust economic growth at the time. This was particularly true of the oil countries, where rising oil prices produced growth rates in the year before and the year of democratic demise of 6.4 and 10 percent in Russia, 10.3 and 21.2 percent in Nigeria, and 18.3 and 10.5 percent in Venezuela, but the same was true to a lesser extent of the Philippines and Kenya (while in Georgia and Niger growth was outstanding in the year before the reversal but slight in the year of it). In the case of the oil countries, it is even plausible that the booming oil economies added to the incentive to strangle democracy. To be sure, it is hard to locate the demise of democracy precisely in time when it is due to a gradual process of decay rather than a discrete event like a coup, but the

Table 10.2. Recent cases of loss of democracy (1999–present)

Country and year of democratic reversal	Freedom scores, year before reversal	Per capita GDP in PPP, year of reversal, 2009 U.S.$ (IMF)	Economic growth rate	
			Year of reversal	Year before reversal
Pakistan 1999	4,5	1,698	3.7	2.6
Fiji 2000	2,3	3,332	–1.8	9.2
Kyrgyzstan 2000	5,5	1,339	5.4	3.7
Russia 2000	4,5	7,646	10.0	6.4
Nepal 2002	3,4	832	0.1	5.6
Nigeria 2003	4,5	1,598	21.2	10.3
Venezuela 2005	3,4	9,992	10.5	18.3
Solomon Islands 2006	3,3	2,480	6.9	5.4
Thailand 2006	3,3	7,410	5.2	4.6
Bangladesh 2007	4,4	1,315	6.3	6.0
Philippines 2007	3,3	3,380	7.1	5.3
Kenya 2007	3,3	1,677	7.1	6.4
Georgia 2008	4,4	4,869	2.0	12.3
Mauritania 2008	4,4	2,055	1.0	2.2
Honduras 2009	3,3	4,275	–2.0	4.0
Madagascar 2009	4,3	996	7.1	–0.4
Niger 2009	3,4	740	1.0	9.5

Source: Economic data are from the World Bank and the IMF *World Economic Outlook Database,* October 2009, www.imf.org/external/pubs/ft/weo/2009/02/weodata/index.aspx.
Note: Growth rates for 2009 are projected. Freedom scores are from the annual surveys of "Freedom in the World," by Freedom House, www.freedomhouse.org, for the year before the democratic breakdown. Scores range from 1 to 7, with 1 being most free and 7 most repressive. The number before the comma indicates the score for political rights; the score after the comma indicates civil liberties. PPP = purchasing power parity

pattern is striking. Even in some countries where the military intervened, like Thailand and Bangladesh, the economy was clearly growing, even in per capita terms. Only in a few countries—Nepal in 2002 and more recently Mauritania, Honduras, and Niger—did growth expire or swing negative in per capita terms in the year of reversal.[4]

What has consistently plagued the failed and failing democracies of the past decade has been bad governance. Table 10.3 presents data (in percentile scores) for four indicators of the quality of governance (as measured by the World Bank) in the year before the breakdown of democracy. Most of these countries were in the bottom third of the distribution on most of these indicators around the time their democracy was overthrown or strangled by executive abuse. Of the 17 countries on this list, only two countries (Fiji and Thailand) were above the median on the rule of law, and only four on corruption. More typical was Kenya, which was in the 17th percentile on

Table 10.3. Percentile scores on World Bank (WB) governance rankings, year before democratic reversal

Country and year of democratic reversal	WB political stability	WB government effectiveness	WB rule of law	WB control of corruption
Pakistan 1999	10.6	25.1	23.3	21.4
Fiji 2000	75.5	53.1	56.7	64.1
Kyrgyzstan 2000	42.3	44.5	30.0	30.6
Russia 2000	21.2	39.8	20.5	20.9
Nepal 2002	24.5	41.2	44.3	43.2
Nigeria 2003	5.8	10.4	4.8	2.4
Venezuela 2005	13.0	16.6	9.5	14.6
Solomon Islands 2006	55.3	29.9	18.1	58.3
Thailand 2006	28.4	66.4	55.7	54.4
Bangladesh 2007	9.1	25.1	25.2	4.9
Philippines 2007	12.0	54.5	44.8	21.4
Kenya 2007	16.8	28.4	21.0	18.4
Georgia 2008	23.6	55.5	41.0	48.8
Mauritania 2008	30.8	26.5	35.2	38.6
Honduras 2009	32.5	34.1	20.6	20.8
Madagascar 2009	30.1	33.2	40.2	55.1
Niger 2009	20.6	20.9	22.5	20.3

Note: For WB indicators, survey was carried out biannually until 2002. For Fiji, Kyrgyzstan, Russia, and Nepal, data from two years prior to reversal are used.

political stability, the 28th percentile in government effectiveness, the 21st in rule of law, and the 18th in control of corruption—in other words, stuck in the bottom quarter of the most poorly governed states (a category mainly containing authoritarian regimes).

To summarize, the troubled and failed democracies of the third wave have shared a few key characteristics. First, they tend (with a few exceptions like Russia, Venezuela, and Thailand) to be poor or lower-middle-income, with per capita incomes (in purchasing power parity dollars) under $5,000. Second, they are poorly governed (as measured by the World Bank). Most of the current democracies that could be said to be severely at risk, if they are even still democracies in some cases (countries like Bolivia, Burundi, East Timor, Ecuador, Haiti, Liberia, Malawi, Nicaragua, and Sierra Leone), fall into the bottom third of states in the world in controlling corruption. In addition, their governments are not very effective in terms of the quality and independence of the civil service and of public services and policy formulation and implementation more generally.[5] Third, they are politically unstable, with significant levels of politically motivated violence, a recent history of such that has not been put to rest, or a more general diffuse sense that the government is fragile and could be overthrown. Fourth, they are deeply polarized on class, ethnic, or other lines of cleavage (sometimes, as in Bangladesh, deeply rooted in enmity between parties), which is one reason why they suffer civil wars and high levels of political violence. Fifth, executive power is seriously abused.

Executive abuse of power has been in the key factor in the demise of democracy in places like Russia, Venezuela, Nigeria, the Philippines, Georgia, Honduras, and Niger, and it certainly played a role in others like Pakistan and Kenya. Kapstein and Converse (2008) find in their quantitative analysis that "effective constraints on executive power substantially increase the chances that democracy will survive" in post-transition and fragile circumstances. Several of the current democracies that are most at risk have presidents with grandiose political projects that they believe require them to concentrate and aggrandize power. For Evo Morales and President Rafael Correa in Ecuador, it is to remake the country along populist-left policy lines, while redistributing wealth and power to the countries' historically dispossessed indigenous majorities (and to themselves and their supporters). For their fellow leftist Daniel Ortega in Nicaragua, it seems to be to restore the dominance of his Sandinista party and movement, as well as his own revolutionary authority and legacy—while digging into the same national trough of corruption at which previous presidents of the country have fed. For President Abdoulaye Wade of Senegal, it is to dominate the country's institutions and pass power on to his son. In Sri Lanka, having finally defeated the Tamil Tigers in a civil war, the victorious president seems determined to promote an ethnic chauvinist agenda for Sinhalese dominance, which would squander the opportunity of the end of the war to forge reconciliation and more enduring basis for peace.

Significantly, none of these narratives of democratic struggle and crisis is mainly about the stresses of imploding economic growth or spiraling unemployment. Certainly, economic and social injustice forms the backdrop for the crises of social and political polarization that have been gathering in the Andean region of South American and in parts of Central America (like Nicaragua, Honduras, and Guatemala) for quite some time. But as we see in table 10.4, some of these fragile democracies—like Bangladesh, Burundi, Liberia, Malawi, Sierra Leone, and Sri Lanka—appear to be only lightly affected by the global recession. That is also true of a number of other African democracies that appear more liberal or look less vulnerable, like Ghana, Benin, Mali, and Zambia.[6] Mostly, these are poor countries not that well integrated into world markets. In a few other vulnerable low-income countries, like Ecuador, Guatemala, Haiti, Nicaragua, and Senegal, economic growth is plunging below population growth rates, meaning negative per capita income growth. But in Nicaragua and Senegal, this could just as likely undermine as advance the hegemonic ambitions of presidents

Table 10.4. Selected low-quality and at-risk electoral democracies, 2009

Country	Freedom scores		World Bank governance			Per capita GNP 2008 PPP$	GDP growth rates (%)			
	2008	2005	Control of corruption percentile	Political stability percentile	Government effectiveness percentile		2007	2008	Est. rate 2009	Est. rate 2010
Bangladesh	4,4	4,4	10.6	9.6	22.7	1,440	6.3	6.0	5.4	5.4
Bolivia	3,3	3,3	38.2	14.8	19.0	4,140	4.6	6.1	2.8	3.4
Burundi	4,5	3,5	15.9	10.0	10.4	530	3.6	4.5	3.2	2.6
Ecuador	3,3	3,3	22.7	20.1	15.2	7,760	2.5	6.5	-1.0	1.5
Guatemala	3,4	4,4	27.5	25.4	37.4	4,690	6.3	4.0	0.4	1.3
Haiti	4,5	7,6	6.8	11.5	9.0	1,180	3.4	1.2	2.0	2.7
Liberia	3,4	4,4	33.3	17.2	7.6	300	9.4	7.1	4.9	6.3
Malawi	4,4	4,4	33.8	46.4	30.3	830	8.6	8.7	5.9	4.6
Nicaragua	4,3	3,3	21.3	31.1	15.6	2,620	3.2	3.2	-1.0	1.0
Senegal	3,3	2,3	38.6	36.8	51.2	1,760	4.7	2.5	1.5	3.4
Sierra Leone	3,3	4,3	12.6	25.4	11.4	750	6.4	5.4	4.0	4.0
Sri Lanka	4,4	3,3	54.1	2.9	46.9	4,480	6.8	6.0	3.0	5.0

Note: Freedom scores are from the annual surveys of "Freedom of the World," by Freedom House, www.freedomhouse.org. Scores range from 1 to 7, with 1 being most free and 7 most repressive. The number before the comma indicates the score for political rights; the score after the comma indicates civil liberties. PPP = purchasing power parity who have already pretty much revealed their undemocratic intentions. In Ecuador and Bolivia, by contrast, it could reinforce the leftist, anti-globalist narratives of populist authoritarian presidents. In short, it is much too early to dismiss the global economic downturn as a factor that could undermine the stability of low- and lower-middle-income democracies, but at most its effects seem likely to be secondary, reinforcing other negative trends.

Where the Global Recession Is Hitting Harder

Needless to say, not all developing and emerging market economies have been spared from the harsh impact of the world's most severe economic downturn since the Great Depression. Most countries have been experiencing some kind of economic downturn, and in a great many of the more mature or middle-income, emerging market countries, the IMF reported negative (expected) economic growth rates for 2009, though in most cases this was expected to recover to at least modest positive growth for 2010. In some cases, the impact at the end of 2008 was brutal enough to obliterate economic growth even that year. As we see in table 10.5, the downturn—from quite brisk or even vigorous economic growth rates in 2007—was quite severe in a number of countries, such as the Baltic States (Latvia, Lithuania, and Estonia), Poland, Romania, Ukraine, Argentina, Brazil, Colombia, Uruguay, South Africa, Botswana, Korea, and Taiwan. Among the selected developing and emerging market democracies in table 10.5, it has generally been the least developed ones (e.g., Indonesia, Ghana, Mali, and Zambia) that have experienced the lightest impact. But within Africa, South Africa and Botswana have experienced a sharp downturn in growth.

What has been the political impact on democracy of the financial crisis and the consequence global recession on these harder-hit countries? So far, surprisingly little: that is, governments have come and gone, but democracy remains stable. Both effects have been quite surprising. Among this group of democracies that have been harder hit by the recession but that are more strongly rooted as democracies, incumbents have often taken an electoral beating. In fact, ruling parties (of incumbent presidents or prime ministers) were defeated in about two-thirds of the elections (9 of 15) where power was up for grabs in presidential or parliamentary contests during the period October 2008 through January 2010 (see table 10.6 for a listing of election results). My strong hunch is that this is a higher rate of incumbent defeat than is normal in emerging market democracies, but certainly not unexpected given the tough economic times. The image of hard times for incumbents is exacerbated by the severe setbacks ruling parties encountered in midterm elections in the presidential systems in Argentina and Mexico.

A good example of electoral punishment came in Bulgaria, where in

Table 10.5. Economic growth rates (actual and expected), 2007–10

Country	2007	2008	2009 expected	2010 expected
Central and Eastern Europe				
Albania	6.3	6.8	0.7	2.2
Bulgaria	6.2	6.0	–6.5	–2.5
Estonia	7.2	–3.6	–14.0	–2.6
Hungary	1.2	0.6	–6.7	–0.9
Latvia	10.0	–4.6	–18.0	–4.0
Lithuania	8.9	3.0	–18.5	–4.0
Poland	6.8	4.9	1.0	2.2
Romania	6.2	7.1	–8.5	0.5
Serbia	6.9	5.4	–4.0	1.5
Slovakia	10.4	6.4	–4.7	3.7
Turkey	4.7	0.9	–6.5	3.7
Ukraine	7.9	2.1	–14.0	2.7
Latin America				
Argentina	8.7	6.8	–2.5	1.5
Brazil	5.7	5.1	–0.7	3.5
Chile	4.7	3.2	–1.7	4.0
Colombia	7.5	2.5	–0.3	2.5
Mexico	3.3	1.3	–7.3	3.3
Uruguay	7.6	8.9	0.6	3.5
Asia				
Bangladesh	6.3	6.0	5.4	5.4
India	9.4	7.3	5.4	6.4
Indonesia	6.3	6.1	4.0	4.8
Korea	5.1	2.2	–1.0	3.5
Taiwan	5.7	0.1	–4.1	3.7
Africa				
Benin	4.6	5.0	3.8	3.0
Botswana	4.4	2.9	–10.4	4.1
Ghana	5.7	7.3	4.5	5.0
Mali	4.3	5.1	4.1	4.5
South Africa	5.1	3.1	–2.2	1.7
Zambia	6.3	5.8	4.5	5.0

Source: International Monetary Fund 2009.

the July 2009 parliamentary election incumbent Prime Minister Sergey Stanishev's Socialist Party was able to garner only 17.7 percent of the vote, down from 34 percent in 2005. Sofia mayor Boiko Borisov, a burly, 50-year-old former bodyguard, won nearly 40 percent of the votes, and came close to an outright majority of seats, on the strength of two campaign pledges: to mount a fierce assault on corruption and to tackle the economic downturn. It is quite possible, however, that the first mattered more than the second; in 2008, "Bulgaria lost access to more than 500m euros (£430m) of

EU funding for failing to deal with corruption and organized crime."[7] This underscores a continual theme of democratic elections across the troubled landscape of the global recession: Particular national factors, often political, mattered as much as or more than economic distress. And often, the economic distress was a serious aggravating factor, but not the sole cause of electoral alternation.

In Panama, Ricardo Martinelli, a multi-millionaire businessman, recaptured the presidency for the political right with a thumping victory of the ruling party, which finished nearly 10 percent points down from its performance in 2004. The left-of-center ruling coalition had "struggled to rein in crime and high prices," amid a sharp economic downturn that had slashed economic growth from 9.2 percent in 2008 to an estimated 1.8 percent in 2009.[8] Martinelli, leading a three-party coalition, won by the biggest margin (24 percentage points) since the restoration of democracy in 1989. The right of center also made gains in other post-communist elections in 2009, tossing out the former communists in presidential elections in Mongolia and in Macedonia, where the ruling Social Democratic Union went down to a crushing defeat, with barely a third of the vote and down nearly a quarter of the vote from its performance in 2004. In both countries, economic growth plummeted about 10 percentage points into steep negative territory during the year of the election, 2009. In Moldova, the cause of the (still rather unreformed) Communist Party's decline at the polls in mid-2009 was partly due to the parliamentary deadlock over the choice of a president, but this was part of the fallout of an intensely disputed and allegedly fraudulent election three months earlier, in which that ruling party had expanded its majority despite poor governance and a plunging economy (Mungiu-Pippidi and Munteanu 2009). A free and fair election might have booted the Communists out of power.

In Chile, after two decades in the political wilderness following the exit of right-wing military dictator Augusto Pinochet and the restoration of democracy in 1990, the political right finally triumphed again. After losing to Concertación candidate Michelle Bachelet, billionaire businessman Sebastián Piñera finally triumphed in a January 2010 run-off election, defeating Christian Democratic former President Eduardo Frei. Particularly striking was the improvement in Piñera's first round vote in December 2009 over the 2005 first-round vote, from 30 to 44 percent. To be sure, the long-ruling center-left coalition had achieved impressive results. "Booming copper revenues and prudent fiscal policies," along with innovative and dedicated antipoverty programs, had "helped the government reduce poverty from 45 percent in 1990 to 13 percent today," while lifting per capita income to the level of a middle-income country, at about $14,000. The incumbent, President Bachelet (who was barred from reelection) was personally popu-

Table 10.6. Election results in emerging-market democracies, post–September 2008

Country and type of election	Date of election	GDP growth rate in year of election	Change in % points from previous year	Ruling party % of vote	Change from last election	Ruling party % of seats	Change from last election (%)
Lithuania, parliamentary	10/12–10/26/08	3.0	-5.9	9.0[a] D	-19.4	7.1[a]	-20.6
Romania, parliamentary	11/30/08	7.1	0.9	18.6[b] D	—	19.5	1.6
Ghana, legislative presidential	12/07/08	7.3	1.6	49.7 D	-2.8	46.9	-8.7
Bangladesh, parliamentary	12/20/08	6.0	-0.3	33.2 D	-8.2	10.0	-54.3
El Salvador, presidential	3/15/09	-2.5	-5.0	48.9 D	-8.8		
legislative				39.0	0	38.0	0
Slovakia, presidential	4/04/09	6.4	-3.8	55.5	-4.4		
Macedonia, presidential	4/05/09	-4.0	-11.5	36.9[c] D	-23.7		
Moldova, parliamentary	4/05/09	-9.0	-16.2	50.0	4.0	59.4	4.0
parliamentary	7/29/09			44.7	-4.7	47.5	-11.9
Indonesia, legislative	4/09/09	4.0[d]	-2.1[d]	20.9	13.4	26.8	16.8
South Africa, parliamentary	4/22/09	-2.2[d]	-5.3[d]	66.0	-3.8	65.9	-3.8
India, parliamentary	4/09–5/09	5.4[d]	-1.9[d]	28.6	2.0	37.9	11.2
Panama, presidential	5/03/09	1.8[d]	-7.4[d]	37.7 D	-9.7		
legislative				40.6	-8.4	38.0	-19.6
Mongolia, presidential	5/24/09	0.5[d]	-9.1[d]	47.4 D	-12.2		
Argentina, legislative[e]	6/28/09	-2.5[d]	-9.3[d]	30.8		37.0	-23.0
Albania, parliamentary	6/28/09	0.7[d]	-6.1[d]	47.0		50.0	-7.1
Bulgaria, parliamentary	7/05/09	-6.5[d]	-12.5[d]	17.7 D	-16.3		
Mexico, legislative	7/05/09	-7.3[d]	-8.6	28.0	-5.4	29.4	-11.8

Indonesia, presidential	7/08/09	4.0[d]	-2.1[d]	60.8	0.2
Romania, presidential	11/22/09	-8.5[d]	-15.6[d]	50.3	-0.9
Chile, presidential	12/13/09-1/10	-1.7[d]	-4.9[d]	48.4 D	-5.1
Ukraine, presidential	1/10	-14.0[d]	-16.1[d]	5.5 D	-34.4[f]

D = ruling party or incumbent loss of power. Source for economic growth data, see table 10.5.

[a] The Lithuanian election was extremely complicated, as the ruling coalition consisted of many parties. The largest party, Labor, is treated here as the "ruling" party, and it declined from 39 to 10 seats, although the party of the prime minister, the Social Democratic Party, gained five seats but lost the prime minister's post, as power shifted from a left to a right coalition. The presidential election results are not listed because both the current and former presidents ran as independents.

[b] Election results for former Prime Minister Popescu-Tariceanu's National Liberal Party (also supporting the incumbent president) are used, and for the lower house. Senate elections showed similar results.

[c] Second round vote total.

[d] Estimate.

[e] Only 127 of 257 seats were contested in Argentina's midterm elections. The figures are for the ruling Peronist party.

[f] Yuschenko probably won more than the officially announced 39.9% of the vote in the October 31, 2004, first-round voting for president, and in the final run-off he won 52%, so his real decline in vote strength was even greater.

lar—with a stunning 78 percent approval rating—and admired for her competent and effective economic management.[9] But there was still considerable unease over the maldistribution of wealth, and the election was poorly timed for the ruling coalition, as Chile's GDP was projected to decline by 1.7 percent in 2009, after a number of years of mainly 4 to 6 percent annual economic growth.

The post–financial crisis electoral gains were not only for the right, however. In El Salvador, the ruling Arena party was toppled from the presidency in March 2009 by a moderate leftist after four terms and 20 years in power. Arena lost nearly 9 percentage points off its previous vote. While the economy sunk into negative growth in 2009, it had recorded at least modest growth (averaging about 3 percent) in preceding years, as "each successive Arena administration worked hard to improve the delivery of public services" (Colburn 2009). But economic inequality remained severe while poverty was reduced at only a modest pace. Moreover, the left had been gaining at the local level for some time, and many observers expected it to win the presidency once it transcended its divisions and fielded a less radical candidate. Arena's 2009 defeat was particularly stunning because it marked the first democratic and "peaceful turnover of power since the nation-state became independent in 1821," and because it brought to power the party, the FMLN (Farabundo Martí National Liberation Front), that had once been "a coalition of guerrilla groups that fought a bitter insurrection in the hope of ushering in revolutionary change" (Colburn 2009). But the victory probably owes more to long-term and short-term political factors than to the immediate economic downturn. In Mexico, the ruling right-of-center party, PAN, was also handed a setback in midterm legislative elections, falling from 40 percent of the seats in the lower house to less than 30 percent, amid mounting problems of drug violence and an economy expected to shrink by over 7 percent in 2009.

Elsewhere in 2009, left-of-center governments that had performed well or remained popular with voters were rewarded with strong votes of confidence. With India feeling the global recession only lightly and the country coming off several years of exceptional economic growth under a very capable prime minister, Manmohan Singh, the Congress Party defied expectations and substantially increased its share of seats in parliament (by more than a third). With the vote choice still polarized along racial lines and the African National Congress still carrying the mantle of liberation from apartheid, the ANC managed to hold on to nearly a two-thirds majority in parliament. And with Indonesia enjoying greater stability and more even governance than it had know since the fall of Suharto, incumbent President Susilo Bambang Yudhoyono coasted to reelection with over 60 percent of the vote on the first round in July 2009, a few months after his once-small party nearly tripled its share of the legislative vote. The ruling party in Ghana was not so fortunate. After eight years in power, and with the incumbent stepping down, the New Patriotic Party suffered an excruciatingly narrow election defeat to the former ruling party (of former authoritarian strongman Jerry Rawlings). It would be difficult to blame the economy for this setback, as Ghana was still enjoying some of its best economic performance since independence. Rather voters seemed to be reacting against the familiar problem of rising corruption and arrogance in power.

What do we learn from this review of electoral politics in a time of global economic turmoil? If there is a common thread that runs through all these cases, it is the resilience of democratic politics. Voters punished incumbent leaders and parties who performed poorly, either because they were dragged down into the global economic undertow or because they had otherwise done a poor job of meeting voters' expectations for good governance (or both). In most cases where economic downturns were sharp, with the economic growth rate in the election year plummeting by at least 7 percentage points (Macedonia, Panama, Mongolia, Argentina, Bulgaria, Mexico, and Ukraine), incumbent parties took a beating. Nowhere was the fate of an incumbent president more humiliating than in Ukraine, where President Viktor Yushchenko fell from a reported 40 percent of the first-round vote (and possibly a real first-round majority) in October 2004, and 52 percent in the run-off election that year, to a pathetic 5.5 percent in the January 2010 election. In the 2010 election, the not very reconstructed former Communist Party boss, Victor Yanukovych, the villain of the Orange Revolution in 2004, finished well ahead of the pack, with 35 percent of the first-round vote, to 25 percent for the incumbent prime minister, Yulia Tymoshenko, who had been Yushchenko's partner in the Orange Revolution and then fell into conflict with him. No doubt voters were punishing the incumbents in large measure for corruption and internal bickering, but the country's disastrous economic plunge in 2009 (see table 10.6) also played a big role. Even in Chile, where incumbent president Michelle Bachelet remained personally very popular, fatigue with the long-ruling left-of-center coalition, the Concertación, and unease with the more modest but nevertheless fall-off in economic growth into negative territory, conspired to produce the first presidential election victory for the political right since the country's return to democracy in 1990. The only ruling party that defied this trend was the rather unreconstructed Communist Party in Moldova, which probably rigged the vote. One could also cite the narrow presidential election victory of the incumbent president in Romania in late 2009, but that came in a semi-presidential system where governing power had shifted to a different ruling coalition after parliamentary elections the previous year.

The summary data can be viewed in table 10.7, which takes each election

Table 10.7. Economic performance and the fate of incumbents, post-financial crisis elections in emerging-market democracies

	Economic growth declines < 3%	Economic growth declines 3–7%	Economic growth declines > 7%	Total
Incumbent victory	3	3	2	8
Incumbent defeat or setback	3	3	7	13
Total	6	6	9	21

in table 10.6 as a separate case. I sort the cases into two outcomes—whether the incumbent party gained (or retained power) in an election or whether it lost power (or suffered a midterm legislative defeat)—and into three groups: modest impact, with economic growth declining (or estimated to decline) in the election year by less than 3 percentage points from the previous year, moderate impact (3 to 7 points decline), and severe economic impact, with growth declining from the previous year by more than 7 percentage points. In most cases of severe impact (7 of 9), the incumbents lost—probably eight of ten if one counts Moldova. In the other two classes of economic impact, the results were about evenly split between incumbents winning or losing. Altogether, these rough economic times were predictably a bad time for incumbents: almost two-thirds of them (13 of 21) lost or were suffered setback in national elections following economic decline of any degree. Save for the case of Moldova, where democracy has been of very low quality and is arguably expired, democratic elections have performed as intended, providing a safety valve that punishes incumbents while preserving the system as a whole.

Future Prospects

I have offered a relatively sanguine view of the impact of the global economic recession, but a concerned view about the global state of democracy. On the former count, I hardly mean to argue for complacency. If the world were to descend into a genuine depression, lasting many years and wreaking much more severe economic damage on countries, all bets would be off. At a minimum, illiberal populist and even extremist political parties could be expected to garner much more electoral support, even in a number of the post-communist countries that have entered the European Union. In some of these countries, the principal obstacle in the way of democratic breakdown might then be the EU itself, with its political conditionality and its economic transfers to buffer economic dislocation and social pain. Elsewhere, in parts of Asia, Latin America, and Africa, the pace of democratic breakdowns would surely accelerate and possibly gather into a potent and undeniable reverse wave, driven not only by the spread of economic crisis but also by the much deeper symbolic loss of prestige for democracy in an era—were to come—where the rich, established, capitalist democracies proved powerless to turn back the tide of economic misfortune.

Fortunately, however, there are already signs that the United States is slowly emerging from the recession, and the more seriously affected countries will probably follow it as global demand gradually increases. But if this scenario plays itself out and the United States and the industrialized world are able to avoid a "double-dip" recession, then we will return to the "normal," pre-September 2008 trend line. And that is not a reassuring trend. If the good news is that emerging democracies are weathering an economic storm that is not of their own making, the bad news is that they are too often yielding to governance deficiencies that are largely endogenous to their deficient political institutions and norms.

If there is a "new idea in development" that emerges from this analysis, it is that we need to think much harder about the kinds of incentives that can induce politicians and governments in emerging democracies (and non-democracies) to govern more accountably and responsibly. We know, broadly, what needs to be done to control corruption and abuse of power. It requires much more than good intentions or seemingly benign or idealistic leaders. It requires institutional change. Legislatures must be strengthened and empowered to monitor and check the executive branch. Judiciaries must be elevated in their capacity and professionalism and made, constitutionally (by their appointment and functioning), truly independent of the executive and political parties and interests more broadly. Other agencies of "horizontal accountability"—audit agencies, countercorruption commissions, ombudsmen, electoral commissions, other regulatory bodies—must be given the resources, leadership, and statutory autonomy to monitor, control, and punish wrongdoing, and to ensure a reasonably open, honest, and level electoral playing field.[10] Economic transfers and "development assistance" must be tied to serious and lasting institutional changes in these regards, and political assistance flows must work to strengthen these institutions and the demand for these institutional reforms in civil society. This is not really a new idea, in that the field of development assistance has been gravitating in this direction for much of the past decade. But the gravitation is slow and is clearly being outrun and outmaneuvered by negative political trends on the ground. If we do not become more resolute in setting expectations for better governance and more effective in allying with advocates for good governance reforms in these societies, many more democracies will fail in the next decade, whether the world economy recovers or not.

Notes

1. More recently, with a different data set (1960–2004) and methodology, Ethan Kapstein and Nathan Converse found a similar effect for young and therefore fragile democracies: higher GDP growth, particularly averaging over five years, "is significantly associated with a reduced probably of democratic reversal" (Kapstein and Converse 2008, 60).
2. That is the implication of the findings of both Przeworski et al. (2000) and Kapstein and Converse (2008). As the latter show, for example, older and more economically developed democracies have greater ability to withstand the negative effects of poor economic performance.
3. For elaboration, see Diamond, *The Spirit of Democracy*, chap. 3.
4. In these cases, it is hard to know which was cause and which effect. It is possible, in other words, that the sudden implosion of political stability might have contributed to the economic downturn (via the familiar route of loss of investor confidence).
5. The explanation for these measures of governance can be found in Kaufmann, Kraay, and Mastruzzi (2009).
6. As of October 2009, the IMF expected these economies to record positive per capita income growth in 2009, with overall GDP growth generally expected to top 4 percent in 2009 and perhaps hit 5 percent in 2010.
7. "Bulgaria Opposition Wins Election," BBC News, July 6, 2009. Available at http://news.bbc.co.uk/2/hi/8134851.stm.
8. "Panama Election: Supermarket Millionaire Ricardo Martinelli Wins Presidency," *The Telegraph* (London), May 4, 2009.
9. "Billionaire Beats Rivals in Chile's Presidential Election," CBC News, December 13, 2009. Available at www.cbc.ca/world/story/2009/12/13/chile-election.html?ref=rss.
10. See Diamond (2008), chap. 13, and Schedler, Diamond, and Plattner (1999).

References

Colburn, Forrest D. 2009. "The Turnover in El Salvador." *Journal of Democracy* 20 (July): 143–52.

Diamond, Larry. 2008. *The Spirit of Democracy: The Struggle to Build Free Societies throughout the World.* New York: Times Books.

Huntington, Samuel P. 1991. *The Third Wave: Democratization in the Late Twentieth Century.* Norman: Oklahoma University Press.

International Monetary Fund. 2009. *World Economic Outlook 2009.* Washington, DC: International Monetary Fund.

Kapstein, Ethan, and Nathan Converse. 2008. *The Fate of Young Democracies.* Cambridge, UK: Cambridge University Press.

Kaufmann, Daniel, Aart Kraay, and Massimo Mastruzzi. 2009. "Governance Matters VIII: Aggregate and Individual Governance Indicators, 1996–2008," World Bank Policy Research Working Paper No. 4978. Washington, DC: World Bank.

Lipset, Seymour Martin. 1981. *Political Man: The Social Bases of Politics.* Baltimore: Johns Hopkins University Press. Originally published in 1960.

Przeworski, Adam, Michael E. Alvarez, Jose Antonio Cheibub, and Fernando Limongi. 2000. *Democracy and Development: Political Institutions and Well-Being in the World, 1950–1990.* Cambridge: Cambridge University Press.

Puddington, Arch. 2009. "The 2008 Freedom House Survey: A Third Year of Decline." *Journal of Democracy* 20(April): 98.

Schedler, Andreas, Larry Diamond, and Marc F. Plattner. 1999. *The Self-Restraining State: Power and Accountability in New Democracies.* Boulder, CO: Lynne Rienner Publishers.

CHAPTER 11

The Labor Mobility Agenda for Development

Michael Clemens

WHERE YOU ARE BORN, not how hard you work, is today the principal determinant of your material well-being. A person born to a family living at the United States national poverty line enjoys ten times the living standard of the *average* person born in the least developed countries defined by the United Nations.[1] The project of global development policy has been that of extending the prosperity of people born in countries where the industrial revolution has deeply taken root to people born in countries where it has yet to arrive.

That is, the project of global development policy has been to encourage convergence between the living standards of people from rich countries and those of people from poor countries. Convergence is not the only possible criterion of global development; even if one country is being left behind by others, it could still be getting richer than it once was. But accepting a world without convergence is accepting a world where some groups of people are permanently poorer than others.

So far, the principal tool of this convergence project has been that of removing international barriers to the movement of things that affect workers' productivity and earnings. Removing these barriers is the traditional development agenda. It is a worthy goal; 45 countries in sub-Saharan Africa *collectively* have an economy that is smaller than the economy of the U.S. city of Chicago (Birdsall 2006). Just as it is unclear how Chicago could remain prosperous if it were shattered into 45 isolated nations, so it is unclear how Africa might become rich without building greater international linkages.

Rich countries have therefore rightly sought to reduce international barriers to the movement of things that might raise the productivity and living standards of people born in poor countries. These include various forms of financial capital, goods, services, technologies, and institutions. Rich countries' traditional development agenda—give aid, encourage investment, extend trade preferences, transfer technologies—is roughly an effort to lower international barriers to the movement of various factors of production.

Many of those barriers are indeed tumbling. Private capital is far more mobile today than 30 years ago (Caselli and Feyrer 2007; Giannone and Lenza 2009), and foreign aid flows have reached an all-time high, topping $100 billion per year (OECD 2009). Trade barriers remain but have fallen enormously in the past few decades (Bergin and Glick 2007; Clemens and Williamson 2004). Access to schooling has spread massively: Net primary school enrolment in sub-Saharan Africa went from 50 percent to over 70 percent in the past 20 years, and net secondary school enrollment in Latin America doubled during the same period (World Bank 2009). Finally, institutions and technologies from rich countries have spread rapidly to poor countries. In 2008, the world had 50 more countries that were electoral democracies than in 1989 (Freedom House 2009). Access to technologies like vaccines and cell phones has skyrocketed, even in the poorest corners of the world.

The Big Hole in the Traditional Development Agenda

If the traditional development agenda of removing these barriers has delivered global convergence of living standards, the global financial crisis that began in 2008 should raise special concern beyond the immediate downturn. Many have asked whether or not some of these barriers that have been falling might rise again. Certainly the global financial crisis of the late 1920s caused most countries to sharply restrict international trade and financial flows (Eichengreen and Irwin 2009; James 2001). So if the traditional development agenda has worked, development advocates should be gravely concerned about the resurgence of barriers. It would mean that gaps in living standards might be expected to stop converging and start diverging.

But if the traditional development agenda has *not* been causing global convergence of living standards, the crisis should inspire a different type of thinking. Without clear evidence that the traditional agenda has been delivering convergence, we should take the crisis not as an occasion to fear for the traditional agenda but as an occasion to remake it. This chapter is a call to replace the old development agenda with one that includes the only form of international linkage that the old agenda has largely ignored: labor mobility.

How's That Working Out for You?

Dr. Phil McGraw, an American television show host and author of self-help books, poses a famous question to people who sustain unhelpful behavior: "How's that working out for you?" It is time to ask whether the traditional development agenda is sufficient to cause convergence in productivity and earnings. If it is not, we need fundamental changes in the traditional development agenda if we desire convergence.

The answer is, generally: no. Although the traditional agenda has succeeded in greatly increasing international linkages, the convergence of

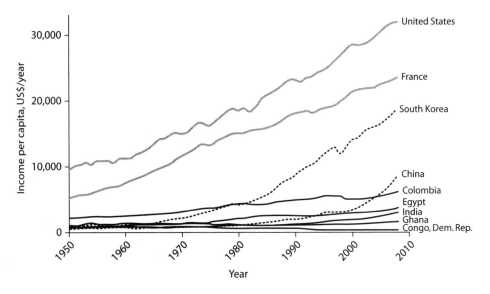

Figure 11.1 Long-run divergence of GDP per capita, with a few exceptions. Note: Incomes measured at 1990 purchasing power parity-adjusted U.S. dollars. *Source:* 1950–2003 numbers from Maddison 2003. 2004–8 numbers take growth rates from the Penn World table 6.3 (University of Pennsylvania 2010) and apply them to the Maddison 2003 figure.

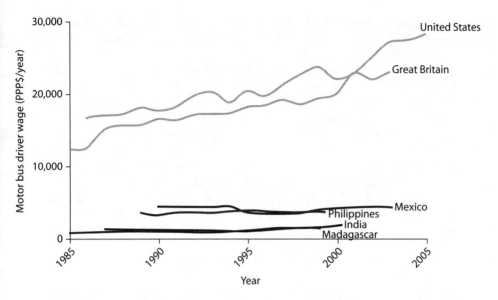

Figure 11.2 Divergence of low-skill wages. Source: Occupational Wages around the World (OWW) database. Wages shown are average monthly wages for a "motor bus driver" (occupation code 111, wage "x4wuus"), converted to current U.S. dollars at purchasing power parity using the purchasing power parity (PPP) conversion factor (GDP) to market exchange rate ratio (PA.NUS.PPPC.RF) from the World Bank's *World Development Indicators 2008*. For a description of the underlying wage data see Freeman and Oostendorp (2001).

incomes is generally not occurring. It is true that for people born in certain developing countries, incomes have converged toward those typical of the richest places over the last few decades. This has happened in South Korea, Singapore, China, and to a less dramatic degree in Botswana, Mauritius, Chile, and Tunisia. But living standards in many developing countries have risen little in decades, and even most of those growing the fastest are merely keeping pace with the richest countries rather than growing fast enough to someday meet them.

Figure 11.1 shows the course of average real incomes in several countries, highlighting the typical experience of non-convergence contrasted with exceptional convergence experiences. Average incomes conceal broad differences in income distribution, of course, so figure 11.2 shows the trajectory of the earnings of a typical low-skill worker—a bus driver—in several countries in the latter years of the twentieth century. Despite convergence on education, health, and other development indicators, the big story of income trajectories across the world has been one of divergence (Kenny 2005; Pritchett 1997).

This does not mean that the traditional development agenda has failed to mitigate the divergence that has occurred. Henry and Sasson (2009) show, for example, that freer movement of capital into developing countries rapidly causes increases in real wages there. McCaig (2009) shows that Vietnamese provinces with a one standard-deviation greater exposure to large bilateral U.S. tariff cuts in the early 1990s experienced an 11–14 percent greater decrease in poverty rate, and there is other evidence (Slaughter 1997) that trade opening has caused there to be less income divergence than there would have been without it. But as a whole the evidence does suggest that traditional efforts—given the extent to which they have been realized and their effects on income convergence—have been overwhelmed in magnitude by forces leading to divergence.

And the mere fact that the traditional development agenda has so far failed to produce generalized convergence of incomes does not mean that it has no merit. The global spread of education, for example, has inherent value beyond its potential to make workers more productive. But it does mean that the old agenda of encouraging international movements of capital, education, technology, and institutions has not been adequate as a strategy for convergence of earnings. Why it has not is an old and major question in economics (e.g., Clark 1987). But the fact remains that it has not. The traditional development agenda is incomplete.

Why the New Development Agenda Needs Labor Mobility

It is time to add labor mobility to the traditional development agenda. To understand why, we need to examine the silent assumption that the goal of development is for *places* to develop. Most mainstream definitions of "development" regard it as a change in the lives of people, without necessary regard to places.

The leading undergraduate textbooks on development economics define "development" clearly around people. Ray (1998, 7) defines development as an increase in "the income, well-being, and economic capabilities of peoples." Perkins, Radelet, and Lindauer (2006, 12 and 40) define it as a rise in "per capita income and product" along with "improvements in health, education, and other aspects of human welfare" affecting people's "freedom to live the lives they desire." For Todaro (2000, 16), economic development occurs when three aspects of people's lives improve: "sustenance" or basic needs of food, shelter, health, and protection; "self-esteem" or a sense of not being used by others as a tool for their own ends, stressed by Denis

Goulet; and "freedom" or the ability to choose freely without constriction by material conditions or servitude, emphasized by Sir Arthur Lewis.

Likewise, Nobel laureate Amartya Sen (1999, 36) has influentially argued that the "expansion of freedom" is "the primary end and the principal means" of development. This means, first, that increases in substantial freedoms are valuable to the extent that they cause generalized increases in income per capita or decreases in child mortality. But they are also, simultaneously, valuable unconditionally as they constitute a form of development.

Nothing in these definitions suggests that improvements by people in one place inherently constitute development to a greater degree than those made by the same people in another place. If we reflect for a moment, a free choice to move from one place to another in order to secure better living conditions—comprising the large majority of all migration from poor to rich countries—fits every aspect of these definitions. Such migration constitutes development.

But this simple fact remains far outside mainstream development thinking. For most people, the clearest indicators of "development" in a country might be the average per capita income of people who reside in that country and the number of people residing in that country who live in poverty. The problem is that indicators like these, fashioned exclusively according to place, define international movement to constitute something other than development, except to the extent that it affects the incomes of those who do not move. A construction worker who experiences a 50 percent higher living standard by moving from rural Kenya to Nairobi has contributed to Kenya's development, but if the same worker achieves a 300 percent higher living standard by moving to London, this is considered irrelevant to Kenya's development unless that person happens to send money to people who did not leave. If one were to ask this Kenyan which one of these options contributed more to his or her well-being and freedom, the answer might well be the move to London.

But standard development statistics define international movement per se to have no effect at all on development. Clemens and Pritchett (2008) construct a concise development measure focused on people rather than places, "income per natural." This is the average per capita income of people born in each country on earth, regardless of where they reside. This statistic, unlike traditional income per resident, captures income gains from all sources, both those realized domestically and those realized through international movement. There is a big difference between income per natural and income per resident. The average income per Guyanese person, for example, is 50 percent higher than the average income of people residing in Guyana. About 1.1 billion people live in a group of countries whose income per natural collectively is 10 percent higher than GDP per resident.

It gets worse: standard, place-based poverty statistics can actually define an increase in one person's income to constitute a *rise* in poverty if that increase arises from international movement. Suppose a Ghanaian earning $7/day in Ghana at U.S. prices triples his real income by moving to the United States and earning $21/day. He came from far above Ghana's poverty line of roughly $3/day (measured as purchasing power at U.S. prices), but he ended up below the U.S. poverty line of about $30/day for a single adult (Clemens 2009). Thus there is one less person in Ghana who is "not poor," and one more person in the United States who is "poor." The result of his move is that the fraction of people in poverty in both countries rises, even though all that has happened to anyone's income is that one person's income tripled.

Many people are suspicious of viewing migration unambiguously as a form of development. Migration sometimes imposes severe costs on migrants and their families, so how can we know that those costs do not outweigh the benefits? We can know that because for the vast majority of international migrants, migration is a free choice. It is implausible that the armed guards who actively block migration at rich countries' borders know more about what is good for the welfare of migrants and their families than migrants do. It is reasonable to believe that small shares of migrants have no idea what they are getting into—despite the vast proliferation of communications technologies through the developing world—and it is reasonable to believe that small shares of migrants do not grasp the harm that their absence does to their loved ones. But it is not reasonable to presume, without overwhelming evidence, that most migrants take actions that on balance harm themselves and their families.

Paternalist thinking about migrants echoes disgraceful, paternalist thinking about other groups of workers from our own past. Many in the 1950s held the notion that American women who chose to work outside the home did terrible damage to their unattended husbands and "latchkey" children, rendering it unclear whether society benefited from allowing women to work. This has since been replaced with the more enlightened conventional wisdom that women make decisions about labor force participation based on a better understanding of the trade-offs involved for their families' welfare than anyone else has, or can have. It is high time that we respected migrants enough to believe that the vast majority of them take important decisions with the best interests of themselves and their families at heart—like most people everywhere.

These ideas are dangerous to traditional thinking. Once one begins thinking of international movement as an unambiguous form of development and poverty reduction, there is an immediate and unsettling consequence: if migration is a form of development, then blocking migration reverses development. "Repatriating" Guatemalans out of Tijuana or Nigerians out of the Canary Islands actively suppresses development for the people who have chosen to move. While difficult to ponder, it is nonetheless true by any mainstream definition of development—just as surely as blocking developing countries' trade or technology adoption hinders development.

This per se is not a sufficient reason to refrain from blocking movement. The regulation of movement has a range of other costs and benefits beyond the specific cost of interrupting development for migrants. But a good starting point would be to appreciate this cost for what it is: development in reverse.

Place-based development made sense back in the 1950s when relatively few people moved internationally and when the traditional development policy agenda was fashioned. Today, well over 200 million people live outside their countries of birth. A vision of development that defines this movement to be irrelevant or pernicious to development is anachronistic and should be scrapped. The economic crisis that began in 2008 may yet inspire resurgence of isolationist—and thus place-based—thinking about development, but as of this writing there are few major trends in that direction.

Obstacles to a Labor Mobility Agenda for Development

In every rich country, development is nearly absent from the mainstream migration policy debate. And migration is largely off the development agenda.

Migration policy is seen as a strictly domestic issue: People in rich countries often ask, *Do they take our jobs? How can our industry get the labor it needs? Will they become like us or stay like themselves?* Politicians, researchers, and journalists very rarely ask how rich countries' migration policy can contribute to global development. And the development policy debate in rich countries is about how people born in poor countries can have more money, trade opportunities, political freedoms, stability, health, and other amenities enjoyed by the vast majority of people born in rich countries, but only if those needs are realized somewhere outside rich countries. Every aspect of globalization for development is on the table except labor mobility. It is the unexplored continent of globalization for development.

I propose three big reasons that labor mobility has been off the development agenda. First, few believe that enough migration can occur to be an important part of the solution for so many millions of poor people. Second, many believe that if many migrants greatly raise their living standards, living standards must fall in the places they arrive. Third, many believe that higher levels of migration would destroy societies and therefore can never be politically feasible. New research gives insight into each of these questions.

Can Migration Do Much to Help Development?

Migrants can gain enormously from the act of migrating. Clemens, Montenegro, and Pritchett (2008) estimate the income gains to moving from a developing country to the United States. They compare data on 1.5 million workers in 42 developing countries to data on people from the same countries working in the United States, using a variety of methods to adjust for observable and unobservable differences between migrants and nonmigrants. They conservatively estimate that the average annual wage gain to a 35-year-old male with 9–12 years of education moving from a developing country to the United States is $10,000 to $15,000 in additional annual income—that is, double or triple the annual income per capita of the developing world as a whole. Guatemalan immigrants raise their real earning power by roughly 200 percent just by stepping into the United States, Filipinos experience a 250 percent wage increase, Haitian immigrants reap a 680 percent increase.

These income gains vastly exceed the gains feasibly wrought by any known development policy intervention in situ, that is, without movement. No known schooling intervention, road project, anti-sweatshop campaign, microcredit program, investment facility, export promotion agency, or any other in situ development program can surely and immediately raise the earning power of a large group of very poor people to anywhere near this degree.

It is nevertheless common to believe that the power of human movement to increase living standards across the developing world is weak, an entertaining sideshow to "real" development work. This common feeling might arise from any of three objections.

First, there is the objection that "not everyone can come here." It is certainly true that moving to the United States is not a feasible poverty reduction strategy for every poor person in Mexico: some of those people would not choose to migrate even if they could, and the gains to migration might decrease markedly if everyone who wished to migrate could do so. Both of these issues are hard to measure quantitatively with existing evidence.

But even if 100 percent of poor people cannot benefit from a policy, this alone is not a reason to dismiss that policy. The fact that it is impossible for every black American to be the CEO of a corporation does not justify actively preventing even one black American from a becoming a CEO. The fact that it would be impossible for the entire unemployed population of the United States to find a job in Manhattan does not justify actively blocking even one job-seeker from entering Manhattan. Instead we have open institutions that punish anyone who regulates access to jobs or neighborhoods based on traits irrelevant to a person's fundamental ability to contribute to society, traits such as being born black or being born outside Manhattan.

Asking whether a policy can benefit every last poor person is the wrong question. Suppose I want to know if a school built in the inner city was effective. The last question I would ask would be whether every last child in all the inner cities of America could hypothetically attend *that* school. The first question I would ask would be how children who attended that school fared relative to those who did not. For example, if a large fraction of the inner-city children from that metropolitan area who continued to college went through the school in question, that would start to suggest that that the school was effective. To assess the value of the school to children, it is much more important to know whether that school has been an important part of advancement for children in the real world than to know whether that school could hypothetically advance every last child.

We can ask a closely related question about migration. Rather than asking how many Mexicans who are poor would not be poor in a hypothetical world where everyone left Mexico, we could ask what role migration has played in the poverty reduction that has actually happened for Mexicans. It turns out that migration has been at the heart of real poverty reduction for real Mexicans.

Suppose we set a conservative poverty line of $10/day per person of purchasing power at U.S. prices (about one third of the true poverty line in the United States). How many Mexicans who ever rose above this poverty line did so by migrating? Clemens and Pritchett (2008) show that, out of the 23 percent of all the Mexicans living either in Mexico or the United States who have emerged from poverty and live on more than $10/day, a very large share did so by leaving Mexico. Forty-three percent of those people live in the United States. If we were to add in the Mexicans who live in Spain and other rich countries, we would find that roughly half of all Mexicans who have ever emerged from poverty—by this poverty measure—did so by leaving Mexico. Thus, even if it is the case that migration cannot lift every Mexican out of poverty, it is nevertheless the case that migration has been the principal escape from poverty for Mexicans who have done so.

And this estimate is conservative, because it doesn't account for the fact that emigration from Mexico has caused earnings to rise in Mexico for those who did not leave. This happened both because emigrants pushed up wages in Mexico by reducing the labor supply (Mishra 2007) and because many emigrants helped people in Mexico to emerge from poverty by sending remittances. The estimate is also conservative because there is no evidence of "positive selection" of migrants out of Mexico; that is, there is no evidence that people who emigrated would have made systematically more in Mexico if they had not migrated than people who did not migrate (Clemens, Montenegro, and Pritchett 2008).

Clemens and Pritchett (2008) also show that by the same measure, 27 percent of all Indians who have escaped poverty, and live either in the United States or in India, did so living in the United States. For Haitians, the same figure is 82 percent. Migration has gone hand in hand, on a massive scale, with poverty reduction—the real poverty reduction that has occurred, not the hypothetical poverty reduction we wish for in situ but cannot find a way to accomplish. While it might be nice to imagine other things that could happen in Haiti that would hypothetically bring people out of poverty without necessitating departure, the fact is that those things have not happened.[2]

This does not mean that migration, if added to the traditional development agenda, will magically cause the incomes of people in Haiti to converge with those of people in the United States. But it does mean that migration has been a principal cause of convergence, to date, between the incomes of Haitians and Americans. No one should doubt the power of migration to achieve income convergence. Migration thus deserves a sizeable seat at the table of development policy.

Second, there is a common objection that migration must not be worth the costs, because so many migrants from developing countries face conditions at the destination that rich-country observers view as deplorable. Many migrants live in the shadows as undocumented workers, many work very long hours in difficult conditions for low wages, and many spend long periods separated from their families. Observers in rich countries often find it difficult to believe that migration of this sort could bring substantial benefits to developing country workers and attribute migration choices to murky, irrational forces like a "migration mentality."

The evidence is enormously against ideas of this sort. The opportunity to migrate from poor to rich countries is vastly oversubscribed. In 2007, for every one visa the United States granted through its annual Diversity Visa Lottery, there were 200 applicants. For each of the past several years, the U.S. Department of Homeland Security has reported roughly 400–500 deaths occurring in the process of crossing the U.S. border with Mexico. In 2008, the waiting list for naturalization applications to the United States stood at 2.5 million people.

This tremendous unmet demand for migration means that whatever conditions migrants face at the destination, either they are far better than the migrants' best available alternative, or migrants either generally are irrational or generally are completely misinformed about what they are getting into. No serious research suggests that migrants are systematically less rational than nonmigrants. And the only highly rigorous study comparing migrants earning expectations to actual earnings—taking advantage of New Zealand's randomized visa lottery, so that each person's ex post increase in earnings is uncorrelated with his or her ex ante expectation of the increase—shows that poor migrants from Tonga expect to earn about 50 percent less than they actually do earn, not more (McKenzie, Gibson, and Stillman 2007).

Especially in today's world of very cheap international calling cards and voice-over-Internet calls, it is fantastic to think that migrants generally receive little information about the conditions that await them at the destination. Rather, a principal reason why many rich-country observers find it difficult to imagine that migrants are made enormously better off by arriving at difficult working conditions in the destination might be related to difficulties they face in imagining what it is like to live on $2, $5, or $10 per day at U.S. prices, which is the best available alternative for many migrants from developing countries.

Third, there is the objection that the positive effects of emigration on migrants from developing countries might be counteracted by negative effects on people who do not migrate. Two common forms of this idea are the concern that migration causes poor political institutions by providing an escape valve for those who would otherwise exert pressure for reform at home (e.g., Li and McHale 2009) and the concern that skilled emigrants erode the human capital base required for development at home (e.g., Bhagwati and Dellalfar 1973). A profound difficulty with arguments of this type is that stopping migration, by itself, does little to address the complex underlying causes of poor institutions and poor incentives for human capital accumulation in developing countries. If emigration per se greatly damages institutions and public services, then stopping emigration per se—removing the emigration choice, forcing people to live in a place they prefer not to live, per se—must greatly raise the quality of institutions and public services. If movement substantially causes the problem, stopping movement must substantially solve the problem *by itself*.

But that is not credible. Why is it that no one would contemplate raising the incentive for better public policies in inner-city neighborhoods of the United States by forcing people to live there and pressure for reform? Why is it that no one would consider improving conditions in those neighborhoods by forcing the smartest inner-city children to remain there? Such policies are off the table because it is intuitive to many people that inner-city neighborhoods have complex underlying problems, of which the desire of many people to leave those neighborhoods is a symptom, not the fundamental cause. And if the problems of the inner city are complex, the problems of the world's poorest countries are far more complex.

Migration is a choice, a choice of where to live. And if migration greatly harms development, free choice must harm development, so that the removal of choice—forcing people to live where they would rather not—must greatly help development. The burden of proof should lie on anyone making this very strong claim (Clemens 2009). For example, even the African countries that have lost vastly more health professionals relative to their populations than others have no worse health indicators—in fact, they have more health professionals at home and *better* health indicators (Clemens 2007). The burden of proof should lie on anyone making the strong claim that highly trained, tertiary-care health professional emigration affects Africans' health to any significant degree relative to the numerous other large influences on Africans' health unrelated to emigration. These include the skewed geographic distribution of health professionals within countries, poor efforts at disease prevention, lack of proper pharmaceuticals, warfare, corruption, inadequate or absent performance incentives, and a long list of other factors of which health professional emigration is a symptom.

Up to this point, this discussion has not even touched on remittances, an aspect of migration that really does bring tremendous benefits to poor *places*. This omission is deliberate; one goal of this text is to try to refocus the discussion on people rather than places. But there is little doubt that remittances greatly benefit people who do not migrate. Globally, remittances are now several times larger than global flows of foreign aid. Remittances are much maligned as simply contributing to useless consumerism and reducing labor force participation by the recipient household. Yang (2008) uses a careful research design, using sudden currency devaluations during the Asian Financial Crisis to separate the true effect of changes in remittances from the problematic correlations analyzed by many studies. He shows that increases in remittances cause households in the Philippines not to engage in wanton consumption but rather to invest in children's education and entrepreneurial activity.

And while many studies show a correlation (a relationship that may not be causal) between increased remittance receipts and decreased labor force participation (e.g., Görlich et al. 2007), there is no reason to criticize this phenomenon from a development perspective. The ability to consume leisure and time at home is something that expands people's freedoms and therefore constitutes development if it does not greatly harm others. Why is it that when a spouse in a rich country no longer feels compelled to work because his or her partner earns enough to support the household, this is seen as a sign of success, but when migration allows the same thing to happen in a developing country it is a disturbing sign of failure? If development includes an expansion in people's ability to do what they wish with their time, as by any reasonable definition it must, then decreased labor force participation by remittance-receiving households is nothing more than a further sign of the development benefits of migration.

Must People in the Destination Countries Suffer?

Large numbers of people in migrant destination countries believe that migrants from poor countries must do great economic and social harm to voters at the destination who set migration policy (GMFUS 2009). There is research to support this view: Borjas (2003) finds that all immigration to the United States between 1980 and 2000, both authorized and unauthorized, cumulatively caused the wages of the average American worker to decrease by 3.2 percent. Borjas (2007) also calls proposals to use migration policy as a development tool "hopelessly naïve," warning of "very ugly political consequences." Should development advocates ignore migration and promote development for places rather than people, because it is in the very act of keeping poor people out of prosperous places that they have been made prosperous?

Start with Borjas's estimate of the wage impact wrought by immigrants. Suppose that the many millions of immigrant arrivals in the United States at the end of the twentieth century caused, over 20 years, wages of the average American-born worker to end up about 3 percent lower than they otherwise would have been. This means that blocking immigration would have an effect equivalent to granting the average American-born worker a 3 percent raise at the end of 20 years. This is the same as an annual raise of 0.15 percent over what he or she otherwise would have earned—a tiny fraction of one percent, each year. By comparison, as discussed above, the average wages of a Haitian man arriving in the United States *immediately* increase almost 700 percent. It is ethically difficult to forcibly prevent immense gains for the extremely poor from fear of miniscule losses to people who are far wealthier.

Apart from this, Borjas's estimate is controversial and is the most pessimistic figure that has emerged from careful economic research. Ottaviano and Peri (2008) find that the *cumulative* effect of all immigration to the United States between 1990 and 2006 was to lower average native-born workers' wages by just 0.4 percent. This suggests that blocking all immigration during that entire period would have given the average native-born worker an annual salary raise of 0.025 percent. The difference between their result and Borjas's arises from recognizing that native-born high school dropouts (who compete most directly with low-skill immigrants) turn out to be close substitutes in the labor market for those with only a high school degree and from recognizing that immigrants are not quite perfect substitutes for native-born workers with the same skills: immigrants tend to take different jobs and do them differently than native-born workers, decreasing the competition between them.

And this effect is all but washed away by price changes. Cortes (2008) shows that two decades of immigration lowered prices for things like child care, cleaning services, and construction in the United States to such a degree that the typical consumption basket got 0.3 percent to 0.4 percent cheaper. If immigration reduced Americans' earnings, it also raised the purchasing power of those earnings to a degree that balances Ottaviano and Peri's estimate of the earnings effect.

Ottaviano and Peri also note that both their figure and Borjas's are short-run effects; the long-run effect they show is a gain in average wages of 0.6 percent, as native-born owners of capital and labor adjust their investments to the presence of immigrants. This means that those same workers that in Ottaviano and Peri's work had lower wages than they would have otherwise due to immigration between 1990 and 2006, also had higher wages than they otherwise would have due to immigration that occurred in years prior to that period.

We must keep these figures in perspective: The grand academic debate is whether massive immigration causes a cumulative, short-run decrease in average native-born wages of 3 percent or half a percent, after decades of many millions of arrivals. On the one hand, the entire range of careful estimates is therefore approximately zero. On the other hand, the gains to immigrants from developing countries, as discussed above, are on the order of 200 percent to 300 percent of average incomes in the developing world. Immigration is very, very far from being a zero-sum game of "their poverty or ours." Within ranges that even slightly resemble current migration levels, it is rather simply "their poverty or their prosperity," while we remain prosperous.

Both of the above studies find that immigration reduces the wages of the least-educated Americans by more than it reduces the wages of the average American. About 20 years of immigration cumulatively reduced the wages of high school dropouts by 9 percent according to Borjas, and about 2 percent according to Ottaviano and Peri. This fact is often cited by immigration opponents who seek support among Americans concerned with U.S. inequality.

For several reasons, this is an illegitimate reason to block the movement of low-income people. First, exactly the same argument could have justified trapping black Americans in the South during the Great Depression. Movement of blacks out of the South and into urban formal sector jobs traditionally held by whites—the post–World War I phenomenon known as the "Great Migration"—was a major cause of convergence between black and white earnings (Bailey and Collins 2006). There can be little doubt that this movement exerted downward pressure on wages of urban white Americans, particularly the least educated urban white Americans, compared with what would have happened if that movement had been stopped. Yet few today would consider this a legitimate basis for forcibly preventing blacks from leaving rural Mississippi or from taking formal employment alongside urban whites.

Second, if blocking immigration would indeed raise the wage returns to dropping out of high school relative to completing high school, such a policy is directly contradictory to other policy efforts to encourage disadvantaged kids to stay in school. A range of national government, local government, and community efforts are dedicated to raising the incentives for U.S. high school completion (Smink and Reimer 2005). Many people concerned about U.S. inequality would support such efforts; it would be odd for them to simultaneously support immigration limits that undo those efforts by lowering the relative rewards of staying in school. High school dropout rates have steadily declined in the United States over the past 20 years, at all income levels and for all ethnic groups (Cataldi et al. 2009). If immigration sped that process by decreasing the rewards to dropping out of school, this is an added benefit of immigration.

Third, the rise in inequality in the United States over the past 30 years has happened mostly at the top of the wage distribution, far from the earnings of low-skill migrants. It owes much more to an increase in the wage premium for college graduates relative to high school graduates, than it owes to changes in the wage premium for high school graduates relative to high school dropouts (Goldin and Katz 2007). This type of inequality is exacerbated not by allowing immigration but by limiting immigration of a particular kind: high-skill workers. In 2007, temporary "specialized occupation" (H-1B) U.S. visas were so tightly rationed that the whole year's quota was exhausted on the first day applications were accepted. Most users of H-1B visas are from developing countries. Limits of this type tend to prop up the earnings of the most educated and highest-earning workers already here, tending to raise U.S. inequality.

Fourth, even after all that immigration may have modestly depressed their earnings, high school dropouts in today's America enjoy living standards vastly better than high school dropouts in large parts of the world. The median high school dropout in the United States earns $24,000 per year (Cataldi et al. 2009). This is roughly five times the average living standard enjoyed by people in developing countries, after adjusting for differences in the cost of living. A high school dropout moving to the United States from Ghana, Cambodia, India, or Ecuador immediately raises his living standard by well over 300 percent (Clemens, Montenegro, and Pritchett 2008).

This means that the economic suffering alleviated by migration is vastly greater than the economic suffering caused by it. Suppose Borjas's estimate is correct, and high school dropouts in the United States saw their wages reduced by 9 percent cumulatively over 20 years due to immigration—thus less than one-half of one percent per year. Why is it that a high school dropout born in the United States, who is immensely richer than one born in Ghana, has a right to be protected from a losing 0.5 percent of his earnings next year, by a policy that directly prevents another high school dropout from increasing hers by 300 percent?

Not one person on earth chose where he or she was born. Blocking migration, thereby doing enormous harm to some in the name of tiny assistance to others, is very far from enlightened social policy. It rests on the arbitrary decision that certain people born in certain places have an inborn right to high living standards, while those born elsewhere have a right only to stay in poverty, regardless of their effort, talent, or character. This idea is an ugly sibling of the idea that people born white or born male have an inborn right to high living standards, regardless of *their* effort, talent, or character. Few consider these ideas compatible with American values of equal opportunity.

Is It Politically Impossible for Destination Countries to Allow More Migration?

Many people share Borjas's concern with the "very ugly political consequences" of increased immigration. Immigrants are often accused of causing social disintegration, cultural corruption, increased welfare spending, and crime. There is extensive evidence that refutes each of these notions, showing for example that immigrants typically contribute as much to public coffers as they take out (e.g., Auerbach and Oreolpoulos 1999; Lee and Miller 1998) and that they obey the law at least as much—apart from immigration-related infractions—as the native born (e.g., Riley 2008, 193–97; Clemens and Bazzi 2008). Simply put, even recent increases in labor mobility have not managed to change the fact that today the major migrant destination countries remain the world's wealthiest countries, the world's strongest democracies, and the world's most comprehensive welfare states with the firmest rule of law.

But even if past levels of labor mobility have not destroyed the destinations' societies, might greater mobility in the future wreck those societies yet? Current rates of immigration to the United States, relative to its size, are at or below decades-long rates of pre-1914 immigration that the country absorbed with great success—despite religious and linguistic differences between those immigrants and natives (table 11.1). The critical national

Table 11.1. Comparing recent immigration rates to historical rates

Country of origin	Period	Permanent resident arrivals Total over period	per year	Average U.S. population during period	Annual arrivals per 1,000 population
Ireland	1840–59	1,695,626	84,781	23,751,163	3.6
Germany	1840–89	4,282,190	85,644	36,819,922	2.3
Italy	1895–1914	3,335,263	166,763	83,825,250	2.0
Russian empire	1895–1914	2,760,987	138,049	83,825,250	1.6
Mexico (includes unauthorized)	1990–2008	9,265,517	487,659	278,226,682	1.8

Sources: Permanent arrivals from Ireland, Germany, Italy, and Russian empire are from Bureau of the Census (1975: Series C89-119, pages 105–6). Estimated authorized arrivals from Mexico, 1990–2008, are from DHS (2009: table 2, page 6). Estimated unauthorized arrivals from Mexico, 1990–1999, are from DHS (2003: table B), and for 2000–2008 from Passel and Cohn (2008: table 3). Annual estimates of population of the United States from Maddison (2009).

social conflict of that period, the Civil War plus Reconstruction, was unrelated to these immigration flows. The U.S. economy is enormously bigger, stronger, more diverse, and vastly less dependent on agriculture now than it was then, meaning that its ability to absorb new workers without conflict over scarce resources is greater now than it was when there was an agricultural frontier. Britain's total removal of all barriers to labor mobility from Poland, Lithuania, and six other transition countries in 2004 has neither wrecked Britain's economy and social services, nor led to major social conflict (e.g., Blanchflower and Shadforth 2009).

Many fear that large-scale immigration must lead to levels of social diversity that undermine the social contract (such as Goodhart 2004), eroding support for redistributive programs such as Medicaid or unemployment insurance. This requires the simplistic view that the social contract depends on an altruistic willingness to redistribute income to people "like ourselves," one that can be broken if too many people unlike ourselves show up. But support for redistributive social programs can be based on many desires other than altruism: a desire to reduce crime, prevent insurrection, and create a safety net if we ever need one ourselves—all desires that could increase with greater immigration. Australia and Canada sustain robust social programs despite having roughly double the foreign-born population share of the United States. About half the population of Toronto is foreign-born, and 43 percent of its population from racial minorities, while Toronto remains a society under law and offers some of the world's finest social services. Today Sweden has the same foreign-born share as the United States, about half of which come from outside the EU, and it would be difficult to claim that Swedes' support for the welfare state is nearing collapse (Legrain 2006).

But there is an even greater example of free movement without social catastrophe, an example on a much larger scale and involving utterly different populations. It is little discussed. Today in downtown Johannesburg, South Africa, black African faces fill the sidewalks. How did they get there? Not by accident: the white population of South Africa made the policy decision to allow them free access. Until the early 1990s, a complex system of laws strictly limited the ability of black South Africans to enter, live in, and work in rich areas such as downtown Johannesburg. A 1970 law, the Black Homelands Citizenship Act, stripped most black South Africans of their citizenship and made them citizens of other, very poor countries known as "homelands" (an act not recognized by the international community, but locally enforced). An elaborate and difficult procedure was necessary for black to work in high-income areas, particularly in certain professions, a procedure closely analogous to limited work visas.

It is not difficult to imagine the fear that many white South Africans in the 1980s felt as they pondered eliminating these restrictions. Most black South Africans were very poor and unskilled, were profoundly different culturally and linguistically from their white counterparts, and were enormously more numerous. In terms of the relative numbers, incomes, and cultural differences, the opening of the rich portions of South Africa to unfettered movement and work by black South Africans is analogous to the opening of the United States to the entirety of Latin America or the opening of the United Kingdom to free immigration from all of Nigeria. Many American or British people would contemplate these scenarios with horror, and surely many white South Africans pondered with equal horror the unthinkable elimination of restrictions on black's movement and economic activity.

But the astonishing thing—and it is one of the most notable events of the twentieth century—is that precisely this happened. South Africa did not just ease restrictions on blacks' movement and economic participation, it went all the way and eliminated all of the barriers, dropped them completely, and added in full permanent citizenship and voting rights for good measure.

How did this grand experiment come out? Was there civil war, cultural disintegration, economic catastrophe? Nothing resembling any of these, nothing that is even a shadow of many people's fears, took place. Crime has certainly increased somewhat. But the principal consequence of this opening has been that goal that has eluded achievement by the traditional development policy agenda: convergence. Bhorat, van der Westhuizen, and Goga (2007) show that poverty headcounts among black households decreased from 55 percent to 27 percent between 1993 and 2005, while the same welfare measure showed no decrease at all for whites, but rather a slight improvement.[3] They show, in fact, that whites' economic welfare has risen since 1993 at all levels of the distribution, from the poorest 10 percent of whites to the richest 10 percent.

In other words, the opening of South Africa's white areas to free movement and labor market participation by a vastly poorer and less educated population six times greater in size was insufficient to reduce white South African's living standards by even a tiny amount after over a decade. Meanwhile, it allowed living standards of the poor to sharply converge toward those of the rich. The elusive goal of moving toward income convergence has been achieved, and none of the worst fears of those favoring continued restrictions on movement have been realized.

Is it outlandish to draw analogies between the world at large and South Africa? The left side of figure 11.3 shows the relative populations and per capita income of the poor black areas and the rich white areas of South Africa at the end of apartheid. The right side of the figure shows the same numbers for the developed countries of the world and the developing countries today, as defined by the World Bank. The people to whom South Africa granted not just free movement and labor-force participation, but full citizenship, were relatively neither less poor nor less numerous than today's entire population of the developing world relative to the developed world. Why, then is our natural presumption that the consequences to rich countries of even a total opening with full citizenship for all, as South Africa did, must be worse than what has occurred in South Africa? We must not take this analogy too far, but these questions are legitimate.

This said, no serious policy proposal for using increased facilitation of international movement as a development tool contemplates anything remotely close to a total opening—with full citizenship—as the rich areas of South Africa did. Even a tripling of work visas allowing greater labor mobility between poor and rich countries, certainly not requiring anything like immediate full citizenship in rich countries for the entire developing world, would not approach the magnitude of what South Africa did. To the extent that there have been any negative impacts in the white areas of South Africa, then, the impacts of any global easing of labor mobility that is seriously being contemplated should be far smaller.

Conclusion

The idea that labor mobility is sufficient for income convergence is an old one. Over decades of research, Hatton and Williamson (2005) have shown that labor mobility in the long nineteenth century was crucial to

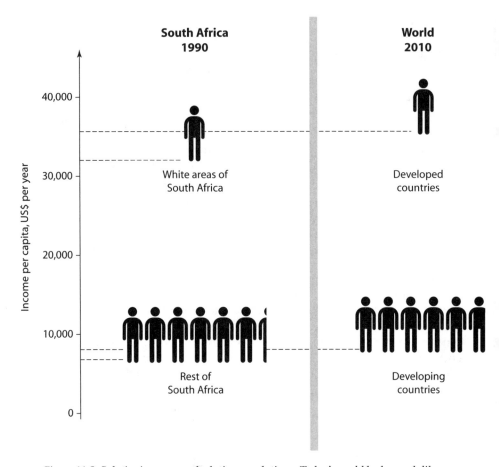

Figure 11.3 Relative incomes and relative populations: Today's world looks much like South Africa did just before apartheid ended. Sources: INCOME: Income figures are all in 2005 US$ at purchasing power parity, or PPP (reflecting the amount that would be necessary in the United States to purchase the same standard of living). White areas of South Africa 1990: PPP$31,502, rest of South Africa: PPP$3,977. High-income OECD: PPP$35,650, developing countries: PPP$5,319. Per-capita income figures for South Africa in 1990, measured in 2000 rand, are from van der Berg and Louw (2004), table 1. The ratios of these figures for "black" (6,008 rand), "colored" (11,404 rand), and "white" (51,951 rand) to the national "total" (12,903 rand) are then applied to the national figure for GDP per capita in 1990, measured in 2005 US$ at PPP, from the *World Development Indicators 2009* (PPP$7,824), to estimate GDP per capita by racial group. The "white areas" figure is estimated as the "white" estimate of GDP per capita, and the "rest of South Africa" figure is estimated as a population-weighted average of the estimates of GDP per capita for "black" and

income convergence among the rich countries of the Atlantic economy and then-poor countries like Ireland, Sweden, and Greece. In the late twentieth century we have tested whether labor mobility is *necessary* for income convergence, by building an international system of development policy that has attempted to foster global linkages of all kinds *except* labor in the name of development.

And we have come up short. Incomes are not converging toward those in rich countries, for most people in most developing countries. It is possible that the lesson of this failure is that labor mobility is, in fact, necessary to convergence. Development is about people, not places; the development benefits of labor mobility are enormous; and the costs of greater labor mobility, sorely feared, are often exaggerated. The next step for global development policy might be to take labor mobility seriously as a powerful weapon in the fight to give all people on earth the same opportunities that most readers of this chapter now enjoy.

Are Americans capable of considering migration policy a tool for development policy? Yes, absolutely, because they already do and they have for centuries. If we conceive of development as improving the living standards of people rather than places, then development has stood at the center of America's immigration policy from the beginning. Generations have admired the Statue of Liberty as a symbol of America's tradition of using migration policy to help people born all over the world to better their lives through movement. In the common at Cambridge, Massachusetts, stands a proud monument to the role of U.S. immigration in fighting the poverty resulting from the Great Irish Famine. At least one in five Americans has known an immigrant in their own family—that is, about 22 percent of the

---

"colored." "Indians" are excluded for simplicity. Per-capita income figures for high-income OECD countries and low and middle income ("developing") countries for 2008 come from the World Bank's *World Development Indicators 2009*, and estimates for 2010 are created by applying to the 2008 figures the estimated growth rates in 2009 and 2010 for "advanced economies" and "emerging and developing economies" found in the International Monetary Fund's *World Economic Outlook* for September 2009, table 1.1. POPULATION: There were 31.6 million "black" and "colored" South Africans in 1990, and 5.0 million "whites," thus 6.3 blacks and coloreds for each white (van der Berg and Louw 2004). There were 5.62 billion residents of low and middle income countries, and 0.97 billion residents of high-income OECD countries in 2008, thus 5.8 developing-country residents for each high-income OECD resident (from the World Bank's *World Development Indicators 2009*), a ratio that would not substantially change between 2008 and 2010.

U.S. population is either an immigrant, or has an immigrant parent, or has an immigrant grandparent.[4] Today the country hosts over 365,000 refugees and asylum seekers from across the globe (UNHCR 2007), more than the entire population of Pittsburgh. This policy would be inexplicable if Americans did not deeply feel that migration policy can transform the well-being of people thrown into unfortunate circumstances through no fault of their own.

In fact, migration could be a more politically palatable development tool than other tools, such as foreign aid. Foreign aid is costly and requires government to actively coerce taxpayers to fund payments abroad. Allowing immigration saves money because it is much cheaper to allow than to prevent. Blocking migration can be much more costly than aid: The United States spends $15 billion per year on border enforcement (Hanson 2009), but spends just $6 billion on year on aid to the least developed countries (OECD 2009, p. 217). And unlike taxing to fund foreign aid, allowing immigration requires no active coercion by the government; on the contrary, allowing immigration requires reducing active coercion by the government.

The clearest step toward a migration policy that includes development, and a development policy that includes migration, is for rich countries to greatly raise the number of temporary work visas available to people from developing countries. Even working for limited periods in rich countries can offer spectacular earning opportunities to developing-country employees (Clemens, Montenegro, and Pritchett 2008). And all of the alternative policies are bad. Setting aside the ethical problems of forcibly limiting movement, trying to stop migration in a mobile world helps create hundreds of thousands of clandestine migrants per year and deters people from leaving who fear the risks of returning (Clemens and Bazzi 2008). Allowing permanent migration while blocking temporary migration might greatly limit the number of people born in a poor country who ever get the chance to work in a rich country, if voters fear those who come to stay more than those who come for a while and go (Pritchett 2006). A focus on permanent migration also ignores the reality, revealed as the European Union slowly opens to migration from its poorest new member nations, that many people seeking work in richer areas seek it as a temporary opportunity before soon returning home (Clemens and Bazzi 2008).

The economic crisis that began in 2008 will not end migration. U.S. unemployment was as high in 1981 as it was in 2009, and the increases in U.S. immigration that came before 1981 simply continued thereafter toward today's record immigration levels. The global nature of this latest crisis means that times are hard everywhere, raising the pressure to migrate. And as international wage divergence continues, the incentive to migrate only grows, regardless of temporary slowdowns at the destinations. Migration is here to stay.

The question is not whether more migration will occur after this crisis, but whether we will take the opportunity offered by the crisis to remake development policy to include migration. We can do this now, or wait another 50 years to see if the traditional development agenda will deliver the generalized wage convergence it has so far denied us. If you are in a position to influence development policy, talk about development as improvements in the welfare of people, and the role of migration will emerge naturally. If you are in a position to influence migration policy, talk about its tremendous influence on opportunity. Americans will intuitively understand you, because greater opportunity through migration is at the very heart of the nation's identity.

Notes

1. The U.S. poverty line for a single adult is $10,830 per year (Department of Health and Human Services 2009), thus $29.67/day. GDP per capita at purchasing power parity (that is, measured as purchasing power at U.S. prices) in the UN-defined least developed countries was $1,111/year in 2006, or $3.04 per day.

2. These statistics represent a correlation between movement and poverty reduction, not strictly and entirely the effect of movement on poverty reduction. It is possible, for example, that a number of the Haitians living above $10/day in the United States would be living above that line if they had been forced to stay in Haiti. That said, it is implausible that a large fraction of Haitians living in the United States would be earning $10/day ($3,650/year) in Haiti. First, only 1.4 percent of the Haitian population lives on greater than $10/day (Clemens and Pritchett 2008). Second, that 1.4 percent mostly comprises the most educated people in Haiti, but the large majority of Haitians who go to the United States are not those with the highest levels of education. Only 27.5 percent of Haitian-born adults in the United States have a bachelor's degree or higher, and some substantial fraction of those would not have attained higher education if they had remained in Haiti. That is, it is likely that just roughly a fifth or less of the Haitians who are in the United States would have had a bachelor's degree or higher if they had not left Haiti. Forty percent of Haitians working in the United States are employed in basic service occupations (U.S. Bureau of the Census 2007, American Community Survey 1-Year Estimates). The evidence is very weak that, controlling for education level, Haitians who leave Haiti earn more than 50 percent more than Haitians who do not leave Haiti (Clemens, Montenegro, and Pritchett 2008). In short, the most plausible conclusion is that migration itself was the cause of leaving poverty for some very large share of the 82 percent of Haitians above $10/day who live in the United States, even if it was not the cause for all of them.

3. The poverty line they use is the 40th percentile in 1993 of the government's Comprehensive Welfare Index, an aggregate of income, education level, assets, and access to government services.
4. U.S. Bureau of the Census 2009, table 39, estimates the foreign-born fraction of the population as 12.5 percent. Lee and Miller (1998, 187) estimate that for every foreign-born person there in an additional 0.77 person who has either at least one foreign-born parent, or at least one foreign-born grandparent, or both. Thus 12.5 percent × 1.77 = 22.2 percent of the U.S. population is two generations or fewer from an immigrant. This estimate is conservatively low because it does not count U.S.-born children who have a foreign-born sibling.

References

Auerbach, Alan J., and Philip Oreopoulos. 1999. "Analyzing the Fiscal Impact of US Immigration." *American Economic Review* 89(2): 176–80.

Bailey, Martha J., and William J. Collins. 2006. "The Wage Gains of African-American Women in the 1940s." *Journal of Economic History* 66 (3): 737–77.

Bergin, Paul, and Reuven Glick. 2007. "Global Price Dispersion: Are Prices Converging or Diverging?" *Journal of International Money and Finance* 26 (5): 703–29.

Bhagwati, Jagdish, and William Dellalfar. 1973. "The Brain Drain and Income Taxation." *World Development* 1 (1Ð2): 94Ð101.

Bhorat, Haroon, Carlene van der Westhuizen, and Sumayya Goga. 2007. "Welfare Shifts in the Post-Apartheid South Africa: A Comprehensive Measurement of Changes." DPRU Working Paper 07/128. Cape Town: University of Cape Town.

Birdsall, Nancy. 2006. "Overcoming Coordination and Attribution Problems: Meeting the Challenge of Unfunded Regionalism." In *The New Public Finance: Responding to Global Challenges*, edited by Inge Kaul and Pedro Conceição. Oxford: Oxford University Press.

Blanchflower, David G., and Chris Shadforth. 2009. "Fear, Unemployment, and Migration." *Economic Journal* 119 (535): F136–F182.

Borjas, George J. 2003. "The Labor Demand Curve *Is* Downward Sloping: Reexamining the Impact of Immigration on the Labor Market." *Quarterly Journal of Economics* 118(4): 1335–74.

———. 2007. "Immigrants Are People Too," The Borjas Blog, comment posted September 7, 2007. Available at http://borjas.typepad.com/the_borjas_blog/2007/09/immigrants-are-.html.

Caselli, Francesco, and James Feyrer. 2007. "The Marginal Product of Capital." *Quarterly Journal of Economics* 122 (2): 535–68.

Cataldi, Emily Forrest, Jennifer Laird, Angelina Kewal Ramani, and Chris Chapman. 2009. *High School Dropout and Completion Rates in the United States: 2007.* Washington, DC: National Center for Education Statistics, U.S. Department of Education.

Clark, Gregory. 1987. "Why Isn't the Whole World Developed? Lessons from the Cotton Mills." *Journal of Economic History* 47 (1): 141–73.

Clemens, Michael A. 2007. "Do Visas Kill? Health Effects of African Health Professional Emigration," CGD Working Paper 114. Washington, DC: Center for Global Development.

———. 2009. "Skill Flow: A Fundamental Reconsideration of Skilled-Worker Mobility and Development," Human Development Research Paper 2009/08. New York: United Nations Development Program.

Clemens, Michael A., and Samuel Bazzi. 2008. "Don't Close the Golden Door: Making Immigration Policy Work for Development." In *The White House and the World: A Global Development Agenda for the Next U.S. President,* edited by Nancy Birdsall. Washington, DC: Center for Global Development.

Clemens, Michael A., Claudio E. Montenegro, and Lant Pritchett. 2008. "The Place Premium: Wage Differences for Identical Workers across the U.S. Border." CGD Working Paper 148. Washington, DC: Center for Global Development.

Clemens, Michael A., and Lant Pritchett. 2008. "Income per Natural: Measuring Development for People Rather than Places." *Population and Development Review* 34 (3): 395–434.

Clemens, Michael A., and Jeffrey G. Williamson. 2004. "Why Did the Tariff-Growth Correlation Reverse after 1950?" *Journal of Economic Growth* 9 (1): 5–46.

Cortes, Patricia. 2008. "The Effect of Low-Skilled Immigration on U.S. Prices: Evidence from CPI Data." *Journal of Political Economy* 116 (3): 381–422.

Eichengreen, Barry, and Douglas A. Irwin. 2009. "The Slide to Protectionism in the Great Depression: Who Succumbed and Why?" Working Paper 15142. Cambridge, MA: National Bureau of Economic Research.

Freedom House. 2009. *Freedom in the World 2009.* Washington, DC: Freedom House.

Freeman, Richard B., and Remco H. Oostendorp. 2001. "The Occupational Wages around the World Data File." *International Labour Review* 140 (4): 379–401.

German Marshall Fund of the United States (GMFUS). 2009. *Transatlantic Trends: Immigration.* Washington, DC: German Marshall Fund of the United States.

Ginannone, Domenico, and Michele Lenza. 2009. "The Feldstein-Horioka Fact." Working Paper 15519. Cambridge, MA: National Bureau of Economic Research.

Goldin, Claudia, and Lawrence F. Katz. 2007. "Long-Run Changes in the Wage Structure: Narrowing, Widening, Polarizing." *Brookings Papers on Economic Activity* 2: 135–65.

Goodhart, David. 2004. "Too Diverse?" *Prospect* January 22.

Görlich, Dennis, Toman Omar Mahmoud, and Christoph Trebesch. 2007. "Explaining Labour Market Inactivity in Migrant-Sending Families: Housework, Hammock, or Higher Education." Kiel Working Paper 1391. Kiel, Germany: Kiel Institute for the World Economy.

Hanson, Gordon H. 2009. *The Economics and Policy of Illegal Immigration in the United States.* Washington, DC: Migration Policy Institute.

Hatton, Timothy J., and Jeffery G. Williamson. 2005. *Global Migration and the World Economy: Two Centuries of Policy and Performance.* Cambridge, MA: The MIT Press.

Henry, Peter Blair, and Diego Sasson. 2009. "Capital Market Integration and Wages." NBER Working Paper 15204. Cambridge, MA: National Bureau of Economic Research.

Huntington, Samuel P. 2005. *Who Are We? America's Great Debate.* London: The Free Press.

James, Harold. 2001. *The End of Globalization.* Cambridge, MA: Harvard University Press.

Kenny, Charles. 2005. "Why Are We Worried about Income? Nearly Everything That Matters Is Converging." *World Development.* 33 (1): 1–19.

Lee, Ronald D., and Timothy W. Miller. 1998. "The Current Fiscal Impact of Immigrants and Their Descendants: Beyond the Immigrant Household." In *The Immigration Debate: Studies on the Economic, Demographic, and Fiscal Effects of Immigration,* edited by James P. Smith and Barry Edmonston Washington, DC: The National Academies Press.

———. 2000. "Immigration, Social Security, and Broader Fiscal Impacts." *American Economic Review* 90 (2): 350–54.

Legrain, Philippe. 2006. *Immigrants: Your Country Needs Them.* Princeton: Princeton University Press.

Li, Xiaoyang, and John McHale. 2009. "Emigrants and Institutions," Working Paper. Galway, Ireland: National University of Ireland.

Maddison, Angus. 2009. "Statistics on World Population, GDP and Per Capita GDP, 1–2006 AD." *The World Economy: Historical Statistics*, Paris: OECD. Extension of data presented in Angus Maddison. 2003. Available at www.ggdc.net/maddison.

McCaig, Brian. 2009. "Exporting out of Poverty: Provincial Poverty in Vietnam and US Market Access." CBE School of Economics Working Paper 2009–502. Canberra: Australian National University.

McKenzie, David, John Gibson, and Steven Stillman. 2007. "A Land of Milk and Honey with Streets Paved with Gold: Do Emigrants Have Over-Optimistic Expectations about Incomes Abroad?" Discussion Paper 2788. Bonn: Institute for the Study of Labor.

Mishra, Prachi. 2007. "Emigration and Wages in Source Countries: Evidence from Mexico" *Journal of Development Economics* 82 (1): 180–99.

Organisation for Economic Co-operation and Development (OECD). 2009. *Development Cooperation Report 2009.* Paris: OECD Publishing.

Ottaviano, Gianmarco I. P., and Giovanni Peri. 2008. "Immigration and National Wages: Clarifying the Theory and Empirics." Department of Economics Working Paper. Davis: University of California, Davis.

Passel, Jeffrey S., and D'Vera Cohn. 2008. *Trends in Unauthorized Immigration: Undoc-*

umented Inflow Now Trails Legal Inflow. Washington DC: Pew Hispanic Center. Available at http://pewhispanic.org/files/reports/94.pdf.

University of Pennsylvania. 2010. Penn World Tables. Available at http://pwt.econ.upenn.edu/php_site/pwt_index.php.

Perkins, Dwight H., Steven Radelet, and David L. Lindauer. 2006. *Economics of Development,* 6th ed. New York: W.W. Norton.

Pritchett, Lant. 1997. "Divergence, Big Time." *Journal of Economic Perspectives.* 11 (3): 3–17.

———. 2006. *Let Their People Come: Breaking the Gridlock on Global Labor Mobility* Washington, DC: Center for Global Development.

Ray, Debraj. 1998. *Development Economics* Princeton, NJ: Princeton University Press.

Riley, Jason L. 2008. *Let Them In: The Case for Open Borders.* New York: Gotham Books.

Sen, Amartya. 1999. *Development as Freedom* New York: Anchor Books.

Slaughter, Matthew J. 1997. "Per Capita Income Convergence and the Role of International Trade." *American Economic Review* 87 (2): 194–99.

Smink, Jay, and Mary S. Reimer. 2005. *Fifteen Effective Strategies for Improving Student Attendance and Truancy Prevention.* Clemson, SC: Clemson University National Dropout Prevention Center.

Todaro, Michael P. 2000. *Economic Development,* 7th ed. New York: Addison-Wesley.

United Nations High Commission for Refugees. 2007. *UNHCR Statistical Yearbook 2007.* Geneva: United Nations High Commission for Refugees.

U.S. Bureau of the Census. 1975. *Historical Statistics of the United States: Colonial Times to 1970, Bicentennial Edition.* Washington, DC: U.S. Government Printing Office.

———. 2009. *Statistical Abstract of the United States 2009.* Washington, DC: Government Printing Office.

U.S. Department of Health and Human Services. 2009. "Annual Update of the HHS Poverty Guidelines." *Federal Register.* 74 (14): 4199–4201.

U.S. Department of Homeland Security. 2003. *Estimates of the Unauthorized Immigrant Population Residing in the United States: 1990 to 2000.* Washington, DC: U.S. Department of Homeland Security. Available at www.dhs.gov/xlibrary/assets/statistics/publications/Ill_Report_1211.pdf.

———. 2009. *Yearbook of Immigration Statistics 2008.* Washington, DC: U.S. Department of Homeland Security.

van der Berg, Servaas, and Megan Louw. 2004. "Changing Patterns of South African Income Distribution: Towards Time Series Estimates of Distribution and Poverty." *South African Journal of Economics* 72 (3): 546–72.

World Bank. 2009. *World Development Indicators 2009.* Washington, DC: World Bank.

Yang, Dean. 2008. "International Migration, Remittances, and Household Investment: Evidence from Philippine Migrants' Exchange Rate Shocks." *Economic Journal* 118 (April): 591–630.

CHAPTER 12

Global Economic Crisis and Demographic Change

Implications for Development Policy

Peter S. Heller

THIS CHAPTER WAS WRITTEN in the context of a global economy in which low-income countries (LICs)[1] will have to reformulate their strategies for development and growth in coming years. The characteristics of this economy are certainly not of their choosing and its nature is by no means certain. Some of the dimensions of the global economy of the future have been well recognized for years but have not been taken seriously with respect to forcing significant policy changes. But others are only now being recognized as a consequence of the recent economic crisis. Like a building with many a hidden flaw, it has taken a serious tremor to reveal their severity and the sources of potential vulnerability that could threaten the stability and sustainability of the structure. Equally important, we can only guess whether, how, and by how much these structural weaknesses will be addressed by policymakers and the policy implications for LICs of the ways in which these weaknesses are dealt with. Nevertheless, such uncertainties are now a fact of life that LICs will have to take into account as they consider the appropriate set of economic policies for coming years.

In this chapter, I first describe how the consequences of the recent economic crisis may interact with forthcoming structural developments linked to demographic trends and existing policy frameworks and how they may pose considerable uncertainties for the global economic environment that will prevail in the next decade or so. I suggest some changes in the development policy paradigm, offering ideas on how LICs may need to reorient their policy frameworks, both to exploit the probable future global economic environment and to obtain adequate flexibility to respond to the uncertainties that will characterize it.

The Interaction of the Global Economic Crisis with Key Structural Trends in the Global Economy

Even before the onset of the global economic crisis in late 2007, many economic analysts warned of the challenges that the world economy would face in coming decades, first with the aging of the industrialized country populations and then with the subsequent aging of the Chinese population and some other important emerging market economies (EMEs), particularly in Asia. In part, the challenges derived from past failures by many advanced economies to prepare the ground for these developments, both in policy reforms in the social insurance field and in fiscal consolidation efforts. But the recent financial crisis has thrown a further monkey wrench into the economic policy environment. It has substantially enlarged public sector debts, created the possibility of a lengthy period of lost incomes and lower productivity, dramatically reduced the wealth of many households in some key industrial economies, and raised questions about the growth engines that will drive many industrial economies in the future.

Why Does This Matter for the LICs?

Before discussing the various tensions that now characterize the global economic environment, and the heightened uncertainties that these now create, it is important to underscore what might be obvious, namely why these issues matter so much for LICs. The most obvious reasons relate to how much their economies depend on the pace and structure of global economic growth. Naturally, in their export of goods and services, LICs benefit when the pace of global economic growth is rapid, whether in the form of primary commodities, manufactured goods, or tourism receipts (the so-called linkage phenomenon). A robust global economy, particularly among the more advanced economies, also generates the savings that can fuel capital flows as well as direct foreign investments in LICs, fostering a climate where investors are open to taking risks and obtaining the potential profits from investment in LICs. With robust growth, unemployment levels are low and the demand by individual countries for migrant workers from LICs is high, facilitating the substantial and, for many of these countries, vital flow of remittances that can support consumption and investment, both among their poorest households and in the broader economy. Furthermore, when industrial economies' fiscal positions benefit from strong growth, they are more open to meeting, and possibly increasing, their commitments to expand overseas development assistance.

The recent recession substantially highlighted the impact of a weakening of these various linkages, as reflected in the significant slowdown in exports, tourism from advanced economies, lost jobs among migrant workers, and the resulting fall in remittance receipts. For LICs, this has meant reduced foreign exchange earnings, a loss in the foreign exchange reserve cushions that had been built up in preceding years, higher public debt levels as they have pursued countercyclical fiscal policies, increased recourse to IMF loans, and a significant downward adjustment in imports.

Much has also been made of the extent to which the "linkage" between industrial and EMEs has been a dominant factor of this recession, namely, whether the slowdown in the former has had a similar impact on the latter. Here the evidence appears mixed, as the strong fiscal stimulus package implemented by China has lessened the impact on EMEs from the industrialized country economic recession. Such a partial delinking has limited the extent of the global slowdown, supported recent evidence of a modest recovery, and provided an independent source of demand for LIC exports. But even if there has been some delinking, the weight of the industrial economies in global GDP is sufficiently large that their growth has largely determined the global economic growth rate and will do for many years to come.

Some Key Sources of Vulnerability to the Global Economic Superstructure

Nine of the sources of vulnerability that are now emerging as a consequence of the current crisis, as well as from forthcoming demographic and environmental developments, and what they might presage about the global economic environment of coming years are listed below and a discussion of each one follows.

1. Significant loss of wealth by many households in industrialized countries
2. Loss of income associated with the current crisis
3. Incipient fiscal pressures associated with demographic and structural policy trends
4. High fiscal deficits and public debt levels associated with the stimulus packages and financial sector restructuring efforts
5. Uncertain sources of economic growth in the United States

6. Continuing large global current account imbalances
7. Looming demographic pressures facing China
8. Prospect of continued vulnerabilities in the financial sector
9. Consequences of climate change.

1. *Significant loss of wealth by many households in industrialized countries.* The combination of the loss in asset portfolio values by many households and institutions and the drop in real estate values in some key industrialized countries have created an important structural break in the pattern of savings and consumption behavior. The need for a rebuilding of assets will dampen the prospects for debt-financed consumption as a major source of aggregate demand growth in many industrialized countries for a number of years.

2. *Loss of income associated with the current crisis.* In addition to a loss in wealth, real output levels have fallen in most advanced economies and are only now starting to pick up again. The rate at which unemployment and economic output levels are restored to pre-crisis levels in industrialized countries is highly uncertain. Current estimates of the time it will take to get back to speed range from several years to a decade. The sustained rate of diminished demand is a serious risk for LICs.

3. *Incipient fiscal pressures associated with demographic and structural policy trends.* The fiscal costs of tending to aging population are huge. If entitlement structures are left as they are, these costs will consume ever-larger portions of countries' GDP, diverting funds away from other kinds of consumption and investment.

4. *High fiscal deficits and public debt levels associated with automatic stabilizers, the stimulus packages, and financial sector restructuring efforts.* Government fiscal stimulus programs and automatic stabilizers are now the major bulwarks supporting aggregate demand growth in industrial and emerging market economies. All analysts recognize that the impact of these programs will be a significant addition to the stock of public debt, raising their ratios to GDP significantly—perhaps by as much as 20 to 40 percentage points. As a consequence, the magnitude of fiscal retrenchment required to achieve budget sustainability will be even larger and politically more difficult to achieve.

Points one through four raise the obvious issue of what are likely to be the key sources of aggregate demand growth in the advanced economies. If industrial governments are constrained and households become conservative in their consumption behavior, then aggregate demand growth can only arise from an intensified pace of investment or expanded exports. But the former is likely to be heavily linked to prospects for higher consumption or exports. And a significantly higher growth in exports would need to entail an important change in relative exchange rates for countries with substantial current account deficits.

5. *Uncertain sources of future economic growth in the United States.* A far more speculative issue is the contribution the United States will make to global economic growth. The current crisis has revealed dramatic weaknesses in the housing, financial, and automobile sectors; an unemployment rate reaching levels not seen since the Great Depression; and a significant overleveraging of American households and many businesses. If health sector reform proves successful in terms of cost cutting, this would dampen growth in another one of the heretofore "dynamic" sectors of the economy.

6. *Is there a prospect for past global current account imbalances to be reduced?* In considering the global economic environment looking ahead, the obvious question looms as to whether the large global imbalances characterizing the pre-2008 global economy will be reduced. The crisis will cause large consumer countries like the United States to save more. Many economists believe that the needed corollary to this is that countries with higher savings rates, like China, Germany, and the oil exporters, should consume more. In the wake of the crisis, none of the countries with excess savings— or large current account surpluses—have signaled that they are willing to restructure their economies to consume more and save less. This raises the concern that global economic balances might tilt further toward the "excess savings" and low real interest environment that characterized the pre-2008 global economy. Such a possibility offers both potential opportunities and dangers to LIC policymakers.

7. *The looming demographic pressures facing China.* China is aging rapidly. Given the limited social insurance framework, households are understandably likely to persist in maintaining a high savings rate to accumulate funds for their retirement years. Thus, one can question whether China will be a major source of additional global aggregate demand growth in the coming decade or so. Only after 2030 might one see China forced to run higher government deficits to finance an adequate social safety net and now nascent and newly developing social insurance programs.

Once China's older population does begin to rise, its absolute size will put enormous pressures on its labor market. This may simply mean that Chinese workers will continue to participate in the labor market far beyond what would be the normal retirement age, given the insufficiency for many of accumulated savings—for, in spite of its high savings rate, many Chinese people live in poverty and cannot save adequately for retirement—or government retirement transfers. But it might make China more open to immigration of workers from other countries, particularly where these workers can offer skills that are in demand. This will favor those LICs willing and able to exploit this opportunity for exporting labor to enhance receipts from remittances.

8. *The prospect of continued vulnerabilities in the financial sector.* The recent crisis has revealed the potential difficulties that can confront regulators in addressing the structural weaknesses that have been revealed in the financial sector. Two implications emerge. First, it would be dangerous for LICs to assume that the practices that almost brought down the financial system in 2007–8 will not recur, particularly with the prospect of a savings glut and a low interest rate environment continuing. Second, LICs and EMEs need to take stock of the factors that allowed some countries to avoid heavy exposure of their financial systems to a seizing up of liquidity in the most recent crisis. The possibility of another bursting of asset bubbles and dampening of global growth cannot be minimized (though it would likely happen differently next time).

9. *Climate change.* There is a final structural change that will influence the economic policy environment of LICs. The fact of climate change and its potential future impacts are not likely to have a dramatic impact on the global economic environment itself, but for many LICs, climate change already has economic implications. These effects will become even more serious in the future. This is not the place for an extended discussion of these effects—suffice it to say that it would be an enormous error for countries located in equatorial regions to ignore the higher temperatures, changing precipitation patterns, and increased sea level effects that will be felt increasingly in coming years.

Paradigm Shift I: LIC Policymakers Should Explicitly Consider Alternative Medium-Term Scenarios in Formulating Their Development Strategies

LICs should develop models that contemplate different scenarios and account for the different factors that are likely to affect global growth as well as the sources of that growth. Such models would prove a useful tool for policymakers weighing the costs and benefits of policies in a highly uncertain world. The preceding discussion underscores some of the uncertainties that characterize the global economy looking ahead. The pace of global growth will impact the demand for LIC exports, the employment levels of their workers in advanced industrialized countries, remittances levels, demand for tourist services, and the demand for primary commodities (starting with oil but extending to other primary mineral and agricultural products as well). One can equally speculate about the sources of global growth. While past growth rates have obviously been most rapid in China and India, in other emerging market economies, and in some developing economies, the dominant role of the industrialized countries in global GDP—particularly the United States and Europe—makes the role of the industrialized countries more modest but firm GDP growth rate an important contributor to growth of the global economy. A drop in the latter's growth rate by 1–2 percentage points would weaken the global economic engine's performance by roughly 0.5–1 percentage points, with serious ramifications for the development prospects, as presently structured, of many LICs.

A further uncertainty rests on the likely policy dynamics that will characterize some of the key industrialized countries. Can these countries muster the political will to address the principal sources of looming fiscal pressure? To introduce policies that will weaken or strengthen the prospects for a resurgent and sustainable growth? How strong will be the downward pull of demographics on labor force growth, employment levels, and, potentially, productivity growth looking ahead? Although there have been some encouraging developments in the United States, the United Kingdom, and Germany, whether in the area of climate change, health care cost containment, or fiscal consolidation, the potential for political paralysis still appears far more likely than that of dynamic political activism.

The important point is the fact of considerable uncertainty. Explicit consideration of uncertainty should underlie the approach taken by LICs in formulating their development strategies. Most LICs now rely on the consensus short-term forecasts provided semiannually by the principal international financial institutions (IFIs). This includes the International Monetary Fund's World Economic Outlook (2009 a, 2009b), the World Bank's Global Economic Prospects 2009 (World Bank 2008), and the Organisation for Economic Co-operation and Development's Economic Outlook (OECD 2009). Given that the industrialized countries dominate the governance of these institutions, there is probably an optimistic bias to these forecasts. They tend to assume the prospect of reasonable policy actions and do not assume any change in the structural dynamics of industrialized economies (e.g., the sources of their growth) or in the likely configuration of global imbalances or in relative real exchange rates.

For countries engaged in long-term economic decision making, sole reliance on such scenarios would appear problematic and risky. Specifically, such scenarios do not provide an alternative vision of how the global economy might evolve over the medium to long term. More pessimistic perspectives or ones that embody more complicated political and economic interactions tend to be relegated to negative voices in the academic community (e.g., Nouriel Roubini before the last crisis) and some outliers in the investment bank world. Are there other viable scenarios that LICs should be considering?

It is easy to envisage a set of circumstances flowing from today's economic situation that could lead the global economy toward one of the outcomes expressed in the three medium-term scenarios. One, "the legacy of past excesses continues to haunt," appears unambiguously negative. One, entailing "a modest resumption of growth," is hardly the most optimistic but certainly appears plausible. In these two scenarios, little progress would be made by industrialized countries in fundamentally addressing the underlying sources of the recent crisis. This is particularly worrisome, since these countries now have to deal not only with the consequences of the policy measures adopted during the crisis—namely, expanded government debt levels and enhanced liquidity in the financial sector—but also with the challenges associated with looming demographic trends. The third scenario—"be careful for what you wish for"—appears, on the surface, relatively optimistic in terms of future global economic growth. But it also has many features that could prove a source of difficulties for many LICs if it were to eventuate. Highlights of the three scenarios follow:

Scenario One: The Legacy of Past Excesses Continues to Haunt, or a Faltering Global Economy

- Global growth relatively limited if not stagnant over the next five years, as industrialized countries cannot sustain a fiscal stimulus to sustain demand, China's growth falters, and only India and Brazil are able to maintain buoyant growth
- China's growth slows sharply as a consequence of overextended financial sector, problematic infrastructural expenditure, and need to contain inflationary pressures
- Dollar strengthens substantially against the euro; China is forced to accept a significant real appreciation of the renminbi, principally due to inflation
- Primary commodity prices fall from 2009 levels, reflecting weak global demand
- Affected by weak economic growth, intensified political instability is observed in many African countries that had previously been well-governed
- Unemployment increases in industrialized countries, putting pressure on remittances and employment prospects for existing or new migrants
- European Union forced to impose stronger conditionality in its fiscal

surveillance, as euro remains substantially weakened by speculative capital market pressures on fiscally weak members

Scenario Two: A Modest Resumption of Growth, or the Plausible Option

- Modest resumption of growth in 2010 in industrialized countries, but at low levels. China and India remain the principal buttress for global growth
- Little change in renminbi-dollar exchange rates, with only limited change in dollar-euro-yen-pound relationships
- Strengthening of U.S. current account position, modest reduction in China's current account surplus, but with past global imbalances continuing
- Continuing high unemployment in industrialized countries
- Limited rebound of primary commodity prices from 2009 levels
- Continuing high probability of another financial crisis, with low interest rates in industrialized countries leading to risk-taking in emerging market countries
- Industrialized countries constrained by high public debt in their capacity to use fiscal policy for stimulative purposes

Scenario Three: Be Careful What You Wish For, or Resumed Economic Growth

- Global economic growth resumes from pre-2008 levels, reflecting buoyant China, India, and the US and a modest rebound of confidence in other industrialized countries
- Resumed trends for integration into the global economy by emerging market and some low income countries
- China unwilling to accept real appreciation of the renminbi; global current account imbalances persist
- Primary commodity prices surge, not only for raw materials but for foodstuffs; the latter proves a source of political instability for many low income countries
- Many low income countries are focus of intense FDI interest from emerging market countries, but with adverse effects on governance and corruption levels in many of the poorest countries
- Technology-driven improvements in energy efficiency prove insufficient to offset growing emissions with resumed growth, raising further alarms about climate change
- Higher growth creates enhanced pressure on water resources, leading

to outbreaks of regional conflict. Global economic growth resumes from pre-2008 levels, reflecting buoyant China, India, and the United States and a modest rebound of confidence in other industrialized countries

- Resumed trends for integration into the global economy by emerging market and some low income countries
- China unwilling to accept real appreciation of the renminbi; global current account imbalances persist
- Primary commodity prices surge, not only for raw materials but for foodstuffs; the latter proves a source of political instability for many low income countries
- Many low income countries are the focus of intense FDI interest from emerging market countries but with adverse effects on governance and corruption levels in many of the poorest countries
- Technology-driven improvements in energy efficiency prove insufficient to offset growing emissions with resumed growth, raising further alarms about climate change.
- Higher growth creates enhanced pressure on water resources, leading to outbreaks of regional conflict.

The major consequence of the first two scenarios for LICs would be a continued weak global growth environment not propitious for either manufactured or primary commodity exporters, a dampened terms of trade for primary producers, and continuing weakness in remittance incomes from emigrants in the industrialized world. Continuing high levels of private sector financial flows would continue to be available but limited only to LICs capable of providing a low-risk environment and with strong growth from domestic sources capable of providing potential investment opportunities for infrastructure and energy restructuring. In contrast, the more optimistic third scenario nevertheless poses certain risks, namely, the persistence of significant global imbalances threatening a renewed crisis in the future; the difficulties that food-importing LICs would face; and the risks of weak governance. Climate change concerns would also loom in the future for many equatorial African countries as well as many in South Asia.

Other Scenarios

But these are just three potential speculative scenarios! LICs should consider others. One potential approach would be for LICs to use the occasional long-term scenarios produced periodically by some of the key scenario building organizations, such as the National Intelligence Council's *Global Trends 2025* or Shell International's scenarios for 2025 (Shell International 2005).[2] Typically, such scenario exercises provide at least three and possibly four potential views of the state of the world looking ahead two to three decades. They are always characterized as plausible and realistic portrayals of alternative ways in which the global political and economic situation might evolve. Almost certainly, some of these scenarios would portray a picture widely at variance with the conventional wisdom underlying mainstream forecasts, highlighting the kinds of important structural shifts that can be plausibly imagined as the consequence of events and policy actions that could flow from the current situation.

Unfortunately, while the scenarios produced by these organizations do provide contrasting visions, they often lack the quantification necessary, particularly for the short and medium term, that would allow them to used for developing contrasting forecasts that could be considered in formulating policies. LICs might thus wish to independently, and more boldly—perhaps through the agency of their Inter-Governmental Group of 24 (also known as the G-24)—formulate their own set of scenarios. Alternatively, they might seek to key off the National Intelligence Council's scenarios and at least explore the short-term or medium-term implications of a significantly slower global growth scenario over the next decade, with industrialized countries the principal source of that slower growth and with some dampened linkage effects on Asia. Other potential scenarios could explore the impact of a structural break that might entail significant reconfiguration of key relative prices, including with respect to the structure of exchange rates among the principal currencies, real interest rate levels, and global inflation rates. They might also explore alternative assumptions on the likely growth in demand for primary commodities.

The important point about such scenarios is that they should be plausible and credible, with a clear perspective on how the economic situation might evolve toward them. One cannot easily attach probabilities as to their likelihood, anymore than one can attach such probabilities to the so-called consensus forecasts of the IFIs. But their plausibility would give them sufficient weight that an LIC policymaker could explore their potential implications when plotting out an LIC's medium and longer-term development policy strategy.

For an individual LIC, the objective of such an exercise would be twofold. First, it would be necessary to explore the consequences for its real economy and macro aggregates of alternative scenarios, clarifying what would be the principal effects on aggregate demand, the budget, the current account, and, particularly for commodity producers, the terms of trade. Second, the objective would be to assess what would be the policy configuration of the government in the event that a given scenario was seen as likely to durably prevail over the next decade.

To illustrate the role that such scenarios could play, assume there was a plausible chance that government tax and aid receipts will be substantially lower than has been projected or that the prospects for export receipts and remittances are substantially below past trends. How this would this affect budgetary policy or exchange rate policy or investment strategies? Similarly, if Asian economies continue to prove more dynamic than those of the West, what would be the implications for the structure of government investment or the focus of policies with respect to direct foreign investment? Most likely, many domestic policy priorities would be unchanged across alternative scenarios. But in some areas, strong prioritization efforts might be needed that would significantly shift budget allocations at the margin.

Another value of such an exercise would be to provide greater attention to the need for ensuring flexibility in policy regimes. Given that there is uncertainty as to which scenario is likely to prevail, providing for the possibility of being able to adapt policies readily would minimize the losses that would be associated with a scenario that diverges importantly from the baseline.

Paradigm Shift II: Do Potential Structural Trends Suggest Development Policies That Should Be More Actively Explored?

The phrasing of the above question clearly implies that the core of what development economists would prescribe as the traditional development paradigm remains valid: the emphasis on the development of human capital—improved health and provision of universal primary and even secondary education; investments in public infrastructure services—in particular, in telecommunications, energy, water and sanitation, transport, ports—that provide a platform for incentivizing private investment and facilitate productivity growth; adopting technologies at the frontier that are usable in an LIC context as much as possible; strengthening of policies, institutions, and governance in order to ensure that the public sector provides a secure and safe environment and a competent regulatory framework; and, finally, a market-oriented policy framework that is underpinned by sound macroeconomic policies. These were prerequisites for the rapid growth of countries in Southeast and East Asia, in the former centrally planned economies of Eastern Europe, and in the nascent growth observed in Brazil and India.

Underscoring the role of these core elements of the traditional development policy paradigm should not be seen as mere lip service. The number of LICs that will not realize the Millennium Development Goals set by the

United Nations by 2015 highlights the inadequacy of policies and governance frameworks in many countries and the insufficiency of the budgetary resources being provided for education and health. The same deficiencies apply when one examines both the financial requirements for a minimal infrastructure package and the likely availability of funding (Heller 2010; World Bank 2006, 2008). Such countries will have a far more difficult time in simply standing still, let alone competing in the more challenging policy environment of the twenty-first century. The absence of an educated population will also make them less resilient in the face of the threats posed by natural disasters and policy shocks.

But the effects of the recent financial crisis, the thrust of technological progress as well as incipient structural change in demographics and the environment suggest that at the margin, the thrust and focus of many development policies should be reexamined and probably modified. In a number of areas, one might even consider a more fundamental refocusing, with implications at the margin for budgetary policy. Six broad areas are the starting point for such reconsideration.

1. Demographic Change and Migration Patterns

Two looming demographic trends will affect global migration patterns in the coming years: (1) the incipient aging of the industrialized West and subsequently of many emerging market economies (particularly of Southeast Asia and China) and (2) the prospective growth of populations and a youth bulge in many LICs of Africa, the Middle East, and South Asia.

The aging of the West will create potentially challenging stress fractures in the labor markets of those countries that will witness a decline in the size of their active labor force and growing needs in support of their elderly populations. The latter trend of a burgeoning youth population in other countries will challenge the capacity of many LICs to provide employment opportunities for a rapidly growing labor force.[3]

Given the abundance of the working age populations of the low-income world and the likelihood of relatively high fertility rates continuing for at least a decade or so, investments in human capital as an exportable service would appear an obvious element of any development strategy. Those LICs that move expeditiously in this direction are likely to gain a head start that would put them ahead of competitors as a source of supply.

A possible nursing shortage in many countries with a large older demographic and the likelihood of an influx of nurses from the Philippines is a good example of an interrelationship between the two different demographics. There is little doubt that industrialized countries and eventually China will witness a substantial increase in demand for long-term nurses and care workers to service the needs of people over 65 and over 85, as these age groups are expected to increase dramatically. With the increase in these age groups will come an increase in people with various forms of dementia and in need of assistance in with the daily functions of life. The future will also witness further pressures in some industrialized countries for increased labor force participation by women, who typically serve as caretakers for family members.

There is one country in particular, the Philippines, that over the years has invested heavily in nurse-training programs, which have graduated far more nurses than were employable in the Philippines itself. These nurses have emigrated, primarily to industrialized countries, yielding the Philippines significant remittance income. This model of training workers for the prospect of emigration and the potential for remittances would seem even more relevant to many LICs looking forward, particularly as the needs of the aging countries extend beyond technical nursing to home care and other less skill-intensive caregiving roles.

The potential for increased migration to fill the prospective gaps in labor-short industrial and emerging market economies offers many potential gains for LICs. Commentators have long noted the role that remittances have played in the last decade or so in supporting both investments and consumption in the countries from which these migrants have come. More recently, there is awareness that the potential development gains from migration may be even more significant. Michael Clemens devotes an entire chapter to this idea in this volume. Successful migrants can not only be the source of remittance transfers but may also remain actively engaged in their original countries, investing in businesses, providing human capital expertise in the formation and management of such businesses, and fostering further migration, all in a relatively virtuous cycle.

Thus, one facet of a revised development paradigm would be for LICs to recognize that their "welfare" has a transnational character. Specifically, the success of their migrants in their destination countries is of substantial value to the welfare of the citizens who remain in their origin country.

This encompasses more than the provision of remittance transfers to family members who have not migrated (wives, children, and other relatives). Rather, fostering an active and successful program of migration, particularly if it facilitates what is now known as "circular migration" (defined below), can be a pivotal element of a successful development strategy for the twenty-first century LIC.[4]

Circular migration arises when one observes active engagement by migrants in their former home country, including movement *to and from* that country even while the migrant may be formally integrated into the legal environment of the destination country, including as a citizen. Migrants who can be productively employed and integrated in their destination countries not only can remit transfers for consumption but remain actively engaged in their original home countries in the form of direct investments, engagement in local businesses, encouragement of involvement in the global economy by family members, transfer of new knowledge and skills (including the fostering of the use of modern technologies), a source of financing for governments (i.e., as purchasers of diaspora bonds), and potentially resettlers at the time of retirement. Such circular migrants can be key instruments of development.[5]

Success for such a strategy necessarily has implications not only in narrow terms with respect to migration but also for the thrust and focus of education and training policies, since the potential negative consequences of migration in terms of brain drain also need to be considered. In effect, education and health policies need to explicitly take into account both an LIC's local needs for manpower and the potential sources of demand that may derive from recipient countries, both in the industrialized West and the emerging markets of Asia.

From the perspective of an LIC, there are a number of policies that need to be put in place to actively exploit these opportunities. Elements of such policies are already observable in several low- and middle-income countries (notably, the Philippines, Ghana, Mauritius), but with these few exceptions, a far more comprehensive and directed strategy toward exploiting these potentialities is needed, both domestically and diplomatically with potential recipient countries. Such policies would include

- *Active consideration of dimensions and characteristics of labor market needs in industrialized and emerging market countries as their demand for particular types of skilled migrants emerges.* These demands will emerge progressively, first, as the nature of the pressures from the retirements of the baby boom population develop in Europe, Japan, and the United States; then as demands develop for long-term care workers as older people themselves move into the over 80 age group; and finally, as one observes increased numbers of older people in a decade or so in emerging market countries. Even earlier, in the case of China and some of the higher income countries of South and Southeast Asia, the rapid aging of their working age populations might begin to create a scarcity of low-cost unskilled workers even before their populations become significantly aged.
- *Development of education programs that are responsive to the potential needs for labor by these sources of demand.* This may entail policies to educate and train more workers than are needed with given job skills

in the origin country and workers who are trained specifically to obtain jobs outside the origin country.

- *Efforts at facilitating migration to potential destination countries.* There are numerous dimensions that need to be more actively considered—twinning with destination country labor search organizations as well private sources of demand; helping migrants to understand the nature of the labor markets of potential destination countries; helping them deal with the formal visa and legal requirements of such countries; facilitating dual citizenship for such migrants (at least from the perspective of the sending country); facilitating ease of mobility back and forth between the country of destination and the origin country; negotiation of mechanisms to facilitate the transfer of earned social entitlements in the destination county for migrants who choose to retire to their original home country.[6]

- *Active efforts to exploit relative differences in demand among potential recipient countries.* LICs can seek to play off those countries that are willing to foster a more secure legal environment for residency of their migrants relative to those countries that offer fewer incentives. From a development perspective, those destination countries that are prepared to provide a more secure legal environment can better foster circular migration—for example, allowing people to move back and forth without difficult visa requirements and allowing dual citizenship more often—should be the focus of origin country efforts at job placement and incentives.

- *Promotion of links with diaspora communities by consular offices of origin countries in destination countries.* Much greater effort could be made by origin countries to facilitate remittances through low-cost channels, to encourage involvement with the home country in terms of potential investment opportunities, and to incentivize the purchase of diaspora bonds floated by the origin country government.

2. Building Ties with Asia

Even before the current crisis, China, to a significant extent, and India to a lesser, had begun to build economic ties with many LICs, particularly in Africa. The focus of these efforts has principally been to secure assured sources of natural resources. But given that these economies are likely to become the most dynamic sources of global growth, building more sophisticated relationships will become even more important. The possibilities are numerous, ranging from subcontracting relationships in manufacturing, agricultural supply, tourism opportunities, and as indicated above, migrant labor for construction or services. In many respects, this mirrors the relationship that has developed in the last several decades between the Gulf states and workers from South Asia.[7] Exploiting these opportunities may be easier in some ways in relation to India, because of the language commonality with many Anglophone countries, but harder in others as India itself has a large low-income population and its own low-income states represent an obvious competitor in many of these areas. Efforts at greater links with China would require a more conscious effort in terms of human capital investments, particularly in Chinese language studies in the universities. A similar initiative would be warranted in strengthening ties with Brazil, another emerging market powerhouse.

This argument is not meant to imply that economic relationships with the industrialized countries will diminish or become unimportant, but rather that the dynamics of growth will become more centered in the Asian region. In the same way as multinational corporations from the West moved to integrate Asian firms into their production processes, LICs in Africa and Latin America should intensify their efforts to promote similar efforts to attract the major corporations of emerging market countries.

3. Global Investment

Another possible avenue of development for LICs would be to intensify efforts to capitalize on the potential availability of global capital sources seeking investment opportunities and the need to mobilize domestic sources of capital. One further implication of the potential change in the global environment is the prospect that one might see more, rather than less, availability of global savings in search of opportunities for profitable investment. Equally, the increasingly difficult fiscal positions of the advanced industrialized countries threaten to limit the magnitude of overseas development assistance available to LICs. The implications are several:

- *Multiple factors influence foreign direct investment choices (i.e., availability of adequate infrastructure, depth and extent of local and neighboring markets), so efforts at strengthened governance will be an important prerequisite for providing confidence to foreign investors exploring the potential of alternative countries for direct foreign investment.* This is particularly important as more countries seek to mount large infrastructural investment programs with reliance on public-private partnerships (PPPs). Having a clear policy framework for PPPs in place, and a capacity to manage them will be essential if resources are to be obtained for infrastructural investments outside those sectors where they have been easily acquired (such as the telecommunications sector).

- *Multilateral development banks should be encouraged to develop new insurance products that can facilitate risk management among LICs in the context of heightened risks.* There are a number of likely adverse potential developments where the capacity to manage risk at low cost remains thin in the private sector. These include natural disasters and drought conditions associated with climate change, as well as the potential for continued future shocks in the financial sector similar to those that occurred in 2007–8. Some movement has occurred—one sees the development of catastrophe bonds and regional climate insurance funds. But efforts to broaden the range of insurable risks and the potential number of insured could broaden the size of the market. The importance of such an initiative would allow LICs to lessen the extent to which they are reliant on industrialized countries for emergency grants and loans in the context of natural disasters. This is particularly important, given that the industrialized countries might prove more constrained in their capacity to provide aid resources in the context of tight fiscal positions.
- *The necessity to exploit the domestic resource mobilization potential associated with the demographic transition—falling fertility and increasing life expectancy—will be particularly critical.* The lesson of the emerging market and high-income countries that have successfully developed since the mid-twentieth century is the importance of capitalizing on the period when the share of the working age population is high in the total population and the dependency burden is low. For countries where women are presently discriminated against in the labor force, the growth opportunities wasted by the underutilization of women will not easily be recaptured.
- *The pursuit of sound macroeconomic policies was an essential element of the development policy paradigm even before the current crisis.* The example of some emerging market economies that overcame past records of poor macroeconomic management and are now able to borrow internationally in domestic currencies suggests that access to international capital markets for sound investment opportunities is not beyond the scope of many LICs. The standard litany of sound fiscal and monetary policy remains a fundamental prerequisite for policy, particularly in light of the weakened public debt positions of many LICs forced to respond to the crisis with countercyclical measures. Countries that were cautious about getting too much exposure to exotic financial products, that were cautious about their pace of capital market liberalization, and that maintained a strong foreign exchange reserve position proved better able to weather the storm of the recent financial crisis. Accepting the need for greater flexibility in exchange rates is

particularly important considering the strong possibility of a significant realignment of major currencies in the years ahead.

4. Regional Integration

The difference in starting points among LICs poses particular challenges in the context of the likelihood of a significant slowing of demand emanating from the industrialized countries as a consequence of population aging. LICs in Asia, being already significantly integrated in trade and subcontracting relationships with the larger economies of Asia, particularly China, are likely to continue to benefit from these relationships as China and India emerge as important powerhouses of the global economy. Central American countries likewise are reasonably integrated with the United States, Canada, and Mexico. In contrast, regions that are less well integrated, notably sub-Saharan Africa, will be hard pressed to establish comparable trading relationships unless these countries are able to strengthen their governance and institutional frameworks and improve the quality of their relatively abundant human resource stock. The potential for enhanced diversification of sources of demand thus may be determined by whether African countries are able to mobilize sufficient resources and political will for regional integration projects. This would involve the construction and maintenance of transport networks that could facilitate low-cost commerce with many land-locked states. This would provide an enhanced incentive for foreign investments in industries that could exploit the larger domestic markets that would be associated with regional integration.

5. Challenges of Commodity Exporters

The recent decade has seen many primary commodity producers benefiting from the strong surge in growth from emerging market economies. In sub-Saharan Africa, a number have been able to mobilize resources for investment by enhanced direct foreign investment in the mining sector by EMEs, including by the future sale of mining income. The demand for raw materials extends beyond the minerals sector to include countries with forestry reserves, also a source of tension in the context of pressures to limit deforestation in relation to climate change mitigation. For many LICs, the issue is whether what might be seen as the traditional and appropriate "development policy paradigm" can be implemented, rather than ignored.

Many primary commodity-exporting LICs, rather than using such resources for investments and for a transition to the time when the resources are depleted, have used the income from the exploited assets for consumption (at best, or for corruption at worst). Given the continuing growth in the active labor force of these countries (given high fertility rates), the urgency of using the income earned from natural resources for investments in other sectors that can generate productive employment is particularly critical and in principle would require an active industrialized policy. This challenge is particularly great for those LICs whose reserves of such minerals is limited, such that misuse results in the waste of a real patrimony that could have been converted to other forms of physical or human capital conducive to further growth. For those LICs with oil reserves, the likelihood of continued strong demand and rising real prices can be assumed to be great, given the likelihood of difficulties in securing an adequate regime for climate change mitigation. But the principal challenge they face is to ensure that the exploitation of the resources optimize the income that might be realized, given the potential price effects that might derive from the imposition of a form of carbon tax regime.

6. Climate Change

Climate change will require policy actions to begin the process of adaptation and foster mitigation. For the former, this would encompass new efforts to ensure that the agricultural sector will be able to address changes in the pattern of precipitation and temperature levels. For countries with major urban centers near the coast, or with large low-lying areas, sea level rise over the next several decades will wreak havoc in the absence of efforts to adapt now and preemptively limit the impact of these future changes.

Some LICs may also be able to benefit from investments that can generate solar energy products or produce biofuels. The latter would work particularly well in areas of the Sahel that don't compete with agricultural land, and for which some crops might be viable, e.g., *Jatropha curcas,* which requires little water but which can be a source for biodiesel fuel. Developing countries also should be emphasizing, in the context of the continuing climate change negotiations, the desirability of industrialized countries pursuing intensified investments in solar battery technologies that could be exploited in a LIC context and for the transfer of technology regimes without patents and licensing requirements. Low-carbon development will need to be mainstreamed into development policies. LICs and EMEs will need to underscore that their willingness to pursue mitigation efforts as part of a global coalition will require adequate funding from the industrialized world. This would also include obtaining funds for forest preservation. LICs will need to give intense thought to how to ensure that the channeling of any such funds is allocated for development and mitigation purposes but without adverse effects on the competitiveness of their economies (Edenhofer and Brunner 2009).

Conclusion

There is still much preoccupation in the financial pages with whether the recovery from the crisis will be V-shaped, or W-shaped, or elongated U-shaped. All of these questions rest on the premise of a return to the underlying structure of growth that preceded the crisis. In this chapter, I suggest that the crisis was a wake-up call, highlighting both the many aspects of the previous structure of growth that were unsustainable and the many structural forces associated with demographic trends, climate change, and technological change that may shift the balance of economic relations in the global economy. This has important implications for LICs. The major forces influencing the global economy are exogenous to them, so their task is to devise strategies for maximizing growth in a highly uncertain world where the past is no longer necessarily a good source of guidance as to which policies to pursue. But the vulnerabilities exposed by the past, are very much in evidence, as is the cost of addressing them. And many of the forces that will influence the future economic policy environment have long been understood. The challenge for LICs is thus to adapt their policy strategies to the new realities that the crisis has revealed. The development paradigms of the last few years that presume a business as usual global policy environment must now be at least viewed under the optic of a significant degree of uncertainty if not skepticism. At a minimum, LICs need to be flexible in their policy structures, responsive to the changing center of gravity of the global economy, attuned to the changing demands that will arise from the aging of the advanced economies, and preemptive to the implications of a warming globe.

Notes

1. This would exclude middle income and emerging market economies such as China or India.
2. Some World Bank staff also constructed scenarios for 2020 (World Bank 2006), though this publication did not represent an official perspective of the Bank and it was a one-off exercise.
3. Michael Clemens's chapter "A Labor Mobility Agenda for Development" discusses in depth the development benefits of enhanced immigration flows from LICs to industrialized countries.
4. See Swedish Presidency of the European Union (2009), Newland (2009), Mazzucato (2009), and Solomon and Cholewinski (2009).
5. There are obvious limits to the advantages of circular migration. At some point, migrants may so successfully integrate within their destination countries that their links to their origin countries may weaken and diminish. But this may only prove significant over several generations.

6. Reference is often made to the "paradox of permanency," that is, that the more secure the resident rights of migrants in their country of destination, the more likely they are to circulate and to be economically engaged with their home country!

7. The recent recession also highlights the vulnerabilities of such a strategy, with the sharp downturn in demand in the Persian Gulf states for the emigrant workers from Bangladesh, Sri Lanka, and India.

References

Auerbach, Alan J. and William G. Gale. 2009. "The Economic Crisis and the Fiscal Crisis: 2009 and Beyond: An Update." Washington, DC: Brookings Institution.

Edenhofer, Ottmar, and Steffen Brunner. 2009. "Adapt, Mitigate, or Die? The Fallacy of a False Tradeoff." *CESifo Forum* 10(3): 14–17.

El-Erian, Mohamed. 2009. "Insight: Decoupling versus Recoupling," *Financial Times*, August 10, 2009.

European Commission, Economic and Financial Affairs Directorate-General. 2009. "The 2009 Ageing Report: Economic and Budgetary Projections for the EU-27 Member States (2008–2060), *European Economy* 2.

Ferguson, Niall. 2009. "A Runaway Deficit May Soon Test Obama's Luck," *Financial Times*, August 10, 2009.

Heller, Peter S. 2010. "People and Places: Can They Align to Bring Growth to Africa" Working Paper. Washington, DC: Center for Global Development.

Horton, Mark, Manmohan Kumar, and Paolo Mauro. 2009. "The State of Public Finances: A Cross-Country Fiscal Monitor." *IMF Staff Position Note* SPN/09/21.

IMF. 2009a. *World Economic Outlook* (October). Washington, DC: IMF.

———. 2009b. *World Economic Outlook UPDATE* (July). Washington, DC: IMF.

Jackson, Richard, and Charles Freeman. 2009. *China's Long March to Retirement Reform: The Graying of the Middle Kingdom Revisited* Washington, DC: CSIS.

Krugman, Paul. 2009. "World Out of Balance," *The New York Times*, November 15, 2009.

Mazzucato, Valentina. 2009. "Circular Migration and Development." Paper presented at the conference on Labour Migration and Its Development Potential in the Age of Mobility, October 15–16, Malmö, Sweden.

Newland, Kathleen. 2009. "Circular Migration: The Paradox of Permanency." Paper presented at the conference on Labour Migration and Its Development Potential in the Age of Mobility, October 15–16, Malmö, Sweden.

OECD. 2009. *Economic Outlook* 85. Paris: OECD.

Shell International. 2005. *The Shell Global Scenarios to 2025*. The Hague, the Netherlands: Shell International.

Solomon, Michele Klein, and Ryszard Cholewinski. 2009. *Facilitating Regular Labor Migration to the EU: Partnerships between EU Member States and Third Countries of Origin.* Paper presented at conference on Labour Migration and Its Development Potential in the Age of Mobility, October 15–16, Sweden.

Swedish Presidency of the European Union. 2009. *Chairperson's Conclusions.* Paper presented at the conference on Labour Migration and Its Development Potential in the Age of Mobility, October 15–16, Sweden.

U.S. National Intelligence Council. 2009. *Global Trends 2025.* Washington, DC: U.S. National Intelligence Council.

Wolf, Martin. 2009. "The Recession Tracks the Great Depression," *Financial Times,* June 16, 2009.

World Bank. 2006. *Are You Ready for the Future: Rehearsing for the Future, the World and Development in 2020.* Washington, DC: World Bank.

———. 2008. *Global Economic Prospects 2009.* Washington, DC: World Bank.

World Economic Forum. 2009. *Global Risks 2009.* Geneva: World Economic Forum.

What Crisis?

Francis Fukuyama

Precedents and Preconditions

This volume is a reflection on the impact of the Wall Street financial crisis of 2008–9 and the ways in which it may change how people around the world will think about strategies to promote development in the future. The crisis has already produced the largest and likely longest-lasting recession in the United States since the Great Depression and led to a downturn that affected virtually all parts of the world. For a few critical weeks in the aftermath of the bankruptcy of Lehman Brothers in September 2008, the global financial system began to lock up, with companies around the world finding they had lost access not just to long-term capital but also to short-term financing to pay workers and suppliers. The real possibility of a collapse of the banking system portended a descent into a repeat of the Great Depression of the 1930s.

The 2008–9 crisis was different from other recent financial crises because it began not in the developing world, as in the case of the Asian financial crisis, but in the heart of global capitalism, the United States. Moreover, it began for reasons intrinsic to the American model of capitalism. That is, the United States had been strongly promoting a market-friendly, lightly regulated model of development for the generation following Ronald Reagan's presidency, something that in the developing world came to be known as the "Washington consensus." But while the crisis had many complex causes, surely one of the most important was the failure of the United States to regulate the vast shadow financial sector that had emerged in the 2000s, where new financial instruments like collateralized debt obligations and credit default swaps allowed many financial institutions to evade existing regulatory limits on leverage and risk. To put things perspective, the credit default swap market—which operated free of regulation—increased from $180 billion to $39 trillion between 1997 and 2008. Many of these contracts were written by lightly regulated entities such as AIG. The enormity of the ensuing crisis was what prompted the *Financial Times* to run a series of articles at the end of 2008 portentously entitled, "The Future of Capitalism."

The last time that a global depression originated on Wall Street, the impact on development policies and also on world politics were devastating. The Great Depression brought on, in its mildest form, a shift away from strict monetarism to Keynesian demand management and far more active involvement in economic regulation on the parts of governments all over the world. But more important, it delegitimated capitalism as such and paved the way for the rise of Marxist and fascist movements around the world. (Recall here we are using "liberal" in its economic, rather than political, sense of laissez-faire and minimal government intervention.) The collapse of the world economy undermined belief in liberal democracy as well and set the stage for the rise of fascism and the Second World War. The shift away from free markets persisted for another 40 years, until the stagflation of the 1970s gave rise to the Reagan-Thatcher revolution in whose wake we are currently living.

One of the motives for putting this volume together, then, was to see what kinds of long-term impacts the financial crisis might have on the way that people thought about development going forward. There has already been a substantial shift toward much heavier government intervention in economic life, most particularly in the United States, where the state had propped up not just banks but the auto industry, and passed landmark legislation increasing regulation of the financial sector. But will the crisis lead to a much broader discrediting of capitalism and markets, as in the 1930s? Will the "Anglo-Saxon" model of capitalism be laid to rest and replaced by another alternative? Will the crisis further strengthen antidemocratic forces around the world, given the close association of market capitalism with democracy? Or will the crisis lead to a more positive reformist path, where appropriate corrections are made to failures of oversight and regulation? And what are the changes that are likely to take place with regard to international institutions tasked with preventing and mitigating such crises in the future? The answers to these questions do not lie simply in economic policies and theories but rather in the way that such policies interact with politics, both within individual countries, and in their cross-border relationships with one another.

Models of Development Going into and out of the Crisis

As the chapter by Mitchell Orenstein points out, there were at least three models of capitalism going into the crisis. The first was the free market model of the United States and Britain (also known as the Anglo-Saxon or neoliberal model), the second was the European social model, and the last was the authoritarian state capitalism model of Russia and China. The first of these involved a small government providing basic public goods, with a bias toward low levels of regulation, private ownership, low taxes, and free trade. In this model, a market economy is closely tied to a democratic political system, in which the state encourages pluralistic participation in both the economy and polity. The European social model accepted the primacy of capitalism and markets but leavened it with heavy doses of regulation, state direction, and intervention for social objectives. While the state is clearly more heavy-handed here in taxation and intervention than in the free market case, the economy is also tied to a democratic and open political system. Finally, the model of authoritarian capitalism links a market economy to an authoritarian (or in the Russian case, an electoral authoritarian) political system. The state owns productive assets on a much greater scale than in the first two models, regulates the market economy more rigidly, and is itself not subject to democratic accountability or a strong rule of law.

In addition to these three models, one might describe variant 3.5, which is an export-led growth model that would put China not in the same basket as Russia but rather with Japan, South Korea, Singapore, Taiwan, and other East Asian fast developing countries. In the export model, the state intervenes to guide economic development much more strongly than in the free market one, while respecting private property rights. But in contrast to the European social model, the state provides relatively limited social protections or welfare benefits, focusing its objectives instead on industrial policies that seek to maximize growth through the promotion of exports. Such countries can be democratic (Japan or South Korea and Taiwan after the 1980s) or authoritarian (China or South Korea and Taiwan up to the 1980s). The authoritarian variants have more leeway to make large, rapid decisions but may suffer in the long run from problems of accountability and legitimacy.

During the 1980s and 1990s, the free market model was strongly promoted by the United States under the guise of the "Washington consensus," a term coined by John Williamson to describe a group of policies devised largely in response to the Latin American debt crisis of the 1980s (Williamson 1989). As Williamson himself and other early proponents of the Washington consensus have argued, much of the original thrust of the policy was indeed consensual and revolved around sensible macroeconomic policies that sought to keep budgets in balance, money supplies stable, and currencies sound. They were devised, as Liliana Rojas-Suarez points out in her chapter, in response to the clear-cut policy mistakes made by many Latin American governments in the years leading up to the debt crisis. The broad acceptance of basic Washington consensus principles (with the exception of some countries like Venezuela) was one of the reasons why Latin America could ride out the 2008–9 storm without severe damage.

The free market model evolved over time, however, into what Arvind Subramanian labels the "foreign finance fetish" model, which was something not necessarily intended by the Washington consensus' original formulators. While the United States promoted free trade, deregulation, and privatization among emerging market, transitional, and developing countries, it often put what seemed to be particular emphasis on the opening of capital accounts and the liberalization of financial sectors.

While the welfare-maximizing benefits of free trade have been fairly well documented, the advantages of full capital mobility are much less clear (Bhagwati 1998). The reasons for this have to do with the fundamental differences between the financial sector and sectors in the "real" economy. Free capital markets can indeed allocate capital efficiently. But large interconnected financial institutions can also take risks that impose huge negative externalities on the rest of the economy in a way that large manufacturing firms cannot. Financial assets are more fungible and liquid than real ones and thus far more susceptible to herd behavior and what John Maynard Keynes labeled "animal spirits."

The substantial benefits of financial liberalization can be realized, then, only under relatively stringent governance conditions. Not only does there have to be regulatory oversight of the financial sector, but macroeconomic policy must be also subject to strict discipline since capital can so readily flee at the first sign of trouble. While promoters of the free market model paid lip service to the need for regulation, the emphasis during the 1980s and early 1990s was far more heavily on macroeconomic balance and liberalization. Countries like Mexico, Russia, South Korea, Argentina, and Thailand that followed American advice in opening up their capital accounts soon found themselves subject to massive inflows of liquidity, followed by highly destabilizing outflows when conditions deteriorated. The crises that followed induced many East Asian countries to control capital inflows much more strictly and to begin the accumulation of dollar reserves as buffers against future external shocks.

One of the paradoxical consequences of the 2008–9 financial crisis may thus be to finally teach Americans and Britons what the East Asians had figured out over a decade ago, namely, that unregulated financial sectors were disasters-in-waiting. At the conclusion of the Asian crisis, many U.S.-based policymakers and economists shifted their recommendations from rapid capital account liberalization to "sequencing," that is, liberalization only after a strong regulatory system had been put in place. There was little thought devoted, however, to whether certain developing countries were capable of putting regulation in place in a timely fashion or what an appropriate regulatory regime would look like. But it was also clear that they did not fully internalize the new message that they were preaching, because they did not apply it to their own case. What's sauce for the goose is sauce for the gander: if capital account liberalization without regulatory oversight is dangerous for Thailand or Mexico, the emergence of a huge, unregulated shadow finance sector trading collateralized debt obligations and credit default swaps should be equally dangerous for the United States.

So the first clear consequence of the 2008–9 crisis for development strategies should be an end to the foreign finance fetish, as the Mitchell Orenstein and Arvind Subramanian chapters suggest. Those countries that followed fetish the most closely, like those in Eastern Europe, Ireland, or Iceland, were the hardest hit by the crisis and face the toughest recoveries. Just as for Wall Street, the strong growth records these countries amassed during the 2002–7 period proved to be something of a mirage, reflecting the easy availability of credit and high leverage ratios rather than strong fundamentals. As Liliana Rojas-Suarez suggests, a strong domestic banking system remains a far more reliable shield against external shocks than one dominated by foreign capital.

Subramanian argues, however, that translating a theoretical lesson into actual policy may be more problematic than this analysis suggests, due to the concentrated interests of those seeking foreign finance and the dispersed nature of the victims of financial crisis. He notes that that repeated crises in the global financial system have not caused many borrowers to draw back (though many Asian countries did reverse course after the 1997–98 crisis). The future of the foreign finance fetish will ultimately be resolved politically. It will depend on the degree of pain that various polities (including the United States) experienced as a result of earlier lack of caution, as well as the degree to which populist anger can be channeled into sensible reforms. I will return to the question of whether the crisis was severe enough at the end of the chapter.

The foreign finance fetish is only the reverse side of the "export fetish," however, since every dollar of capital flowing across an international border has to be balanced by a dollar of exports moving in the opposite direction. There are various versions of the export fetish, ranging from the directed credits used heavily during Japan and Korea's high growth periods, to export licensing, to the subsidization of technology and R&D. China's version of industrial policy was different still: by managing its exchange rate against the dollar at a low level and engaging in massive financial repression to prevent the consequent influx of dollars from driving up domestic prices, the Chinese government has hugely privileged domestic exporters as a group, at the expense of both their foreign rivals and domestic consumers. As Yasheng Huang points out in his chapter, this outcome occurred not simply as a result of exchange rate policy but through the deliberate closing off of credit to rural producers after the 1980s.

Export fetishism continues to exist in its various forms throughout Asia, with Japan, Korea, Taiwan, and other countries continuing to run trade surpluses and accumulate reserves. As long as the countries doing this were relatively small in relation to the global market, export fetishism was a viable strategy. But China has now surpassed Japan as the world's second-largest economy and has a much higher export-to-GDP ratio than other large economies. Amassing export surpluses is not a viable policy at this scale.

Observers for many years have been warning that China and other Asian exporters needed to shift their economies to rely on greater domestic demand. As the chapters by Huang and Minxin Pei suggest, however, this adjustment is not happening in the wake of the crisis. The massive stimulus package put in place by the Chinese government to counter falling export demand does not boost consumer spending on the part of China's vast, underserved rural population but rather pushes funds toward exactly the same set of manufacturers and exporters that have powered growth up to now. The reasons for this are ultimately political: while China is not a democracy, the communist party needs to respond to the well-organized interests represented by developers and wealthy local governments more than the dispersed interests of the rural poor—at least until the time the latter rise up in a general rebellion.

This, then, possibly points to a fundamental weakness in the authoritarian version of export fetishism: the basic lack of accountability in the political system means that the government can make rapid decisions (like the stimulus package), but at the expense of important social actors whose lack of voice may ultimately prove destabilizing to the system as a whole.

Coming out of the crisis, the free market model would appear to be the most seriously damaged, particularly with respect to its emphasis on financial sector liberalization; the export fetishist model slightly less so, as a consequence of the unsustainability of a model dependent on high U.S. demand; and the European social model the least perturbed. In the last case, the social protections that looked like drags on growth during boom years proved to be effective automatic stabilizers in downturns. In terms of development strategies for low-income countries, however, the European social model is also the least relevant, given the high costs in fiscal outlays, state capacity, and good governance that are the preconditions for its success.

Authoritarian capitalism, it turns out, is really not a single model as the divergent fates of Russia and China indicate. In contrast to China, Russia's economic base is undiversified and heavily dependent on energy exports, its financial structure and capitalization far less sound, and its central government more corrupt and less capable.

Russia, China, and would-be authoritarian capitalist states like Venezuela or Iran sometimes work together diplomatically but are not typically seen as a single model to be emulated. This will have important consequences for the way that the financial crisis is interpreted in coming years. When the Great Depression unfolded, there was an alternative economic and political model, undergirded by a single systematic ideology, waiting in the wings in the form of communism. Today's authoritarian capitalists may be united in opposition to American foreign policy, but there is little else ideologically that binds them. It is hard for a developing country without energy resources to aspire to emulate Russia or Venezuela. China might constitute a more plausible general model but seems to have more interest in locking up access to resources than in promoting itself as a country to be emulated.

The absence of a single authoritarian *capitalist* model is important for the fate of democracy in the aftermath of the crisis. While democratic governance is widely regarded in the West as a good thing in itself, its popularity around the world has risen and fallen historically on the basis of perceptions about the ways in which it is linked to economic growth. Again, the precedent of the 1930s, when capitalism and democracy collapsed in tandem in many countries, should be sobering. As Larry Diamond points out in his chapter, however, it is not clear that the current crisis will have comparable effects. The world was already heading into a democratic recession before the crisis struck, with a clear reversal of what Samuel Huntington (1991) had labeled the "third wave" of democratization. Elections in developing countries since the crisis have been relatively reassuring, with no particular trend toward populist radicalism evident.

But if the "Beijing consensus" is not likely to replace the Washington consensus anytime soon, the crisis has accelerated the de facto shift in power away from the United States and toward emerging market countries

like China and Brazil. While there are signs of economic recovery in the
United States, it does not seem likely that the United States will return to
robust economic growth quickly, while China has moved ahead in 2009–10
at a breathtaking pace. We are thus closer to what Fareed Zakaria (2008) has
labeled the "post-American" world. China has not proven to be as adept an
exporter of ideas as of manufactured goods, so the shift in actual influence
will continue to lag the change raw economic performance.

Other New Ideas

At this writing, it would appear that new ideas in development after the
financial crisis are likely to be reformist and incremental rather than radical
or revolutionary. There will not be a massive retreat either from free markets
or democracy; but there will be greater regulation and government involvement in economic development. Beyond this, the authors in this volume
suggest new ideas—or at least, new looks at old ideas—in at least four major
areas: (1) industrial policy, (2) public sector reform, (3) international organization, and (4) social policy.

A new look at industrial policy. In his chapter, World Bank chief economist Justin Lin suggests that the time is right for a new look at more active
forms of government intervention, of the sort that was practiced by many
East Asian governments over the past two generations. Many American observers, who were always skeptical of traditional industrial policy, believed
that the Asian financial crisis put the last nail in the coffin of state promotion of development due to widespread abuses of "crony capitalism." There
was, on the U.S. side of the Pacific, an expectation that Asian countries
would move increasingly toward a free market model wherein capital was
allocated by markets alone and governments stayed out of the picture. Behind the American promotion of the foreign finance fetish were the ideas
that the most important "binding constraint" to growth was the supply of
capital and that demand for capital would take care of itself. But the financial crisis of 2007–9 should have raised many doubts concerning the value
of cheap foreign capital and also of capital per se as a sufficient engine of
growth. Abundant capital does not always flow into productive investment
but ends up powering asset bubbles of various sorts, in real estate, in commodities, and in other goods. In the meantime, opportunities for the productive uses of capital were unexploited due to bottlenecks, lack of comple-
mentarities, and missing public goods.

Lin does not suggest a return to the kinds of structural industrial policies of the 1950s, whereby governments planned and implemented large
transitions in national economies. Instead, he suggests a more nuanced approach in which governments promote the development of complementary

technologies, look to shared infrastructural needs, and generally promote industrialization in a more incremental fashion. This is in fact what China has been doing in recent years—not through the picking of "winners" but rather in macroeconomic policies designed to promote the export sector as a whole, through management of the currency and massive investments in infrastructure.

The extent to which other developing countries should reconsider industrial policy in the wake of the crisis is, in my view, more of a political than an economic question. The problem with historical industrial policy was never an economic one. The East Asian development experience proved that many kinds of industrial policy, if carried out by competent and disciplined governments, could promote extremely rapid economic growth. Import substitution and infant industry protection, though commonly derided by American policymakers, was commonly practiced in both Asia and Latin America to good effect during the 1950s and 1960s and led to very high rates of growth in both regions. Problems arose when the protected sectors and infant industries grew up and became capable of competing on global markets. In Asia, policymakers were able to gradually remove protections and force companies to stand on their own. In Latin America, governments never forced domestic producers to compete globally and tended to retain protections long after they were necessary. All of this was driven by political factors like the need to maintain employment in parastatal companies or to pay off key political interest groups.

Any developing country considering implementing an industrial policy needs, therefore, to look hard not just at the policy model being adopted but also at the political economy of going down this route. Does the bureaucracy have sufficient technical capacity to design and execute a proper policy? Are there sufficient fiscal resources to sustain it? And will it be possible to shut down the initiative once it has either achieved its goals or else proves to be ineffective? It should be sobering to note that a very high proportion of successful industrial policies have all clustered in East Asia, where historical traditions of technocratic governance and respect for authority have yielded reasonably competent outcomes. Whether a given government in Africa or Latin America can achieve the results of a South Korea, Taiwan, or China should be a key consideration.

Social safety nets and social policy. One of the legacies of the era preceding the financial crisis was a downplaying of social policy in favor of strategies emphasizing efficiency and growth. Ronald Reagan and Margaret Thatcher came to power attacking the modern welfare state, which they regarded as tremendously overgrowth and dysfunctional. The original Washington consensus did not place particular emphasis on social safety nets or the need for sharing the benefits of growth. Indeed, the Washington consensus as implemented in various structural adjustment packages imposed by international financial institutions in this period tended to focus on the need for fiscal austerity, and many budgets were balanced by cutting back social sector spending. Intellectually, a large literature developed surrounding the unintended consequences of social policy, the tendency of middle class or elite groups to capture programs intended for the poor, or the inability of the public sector overseeing social spending to ever perform efficiently.

Many of these criticisms were well taken; a lot of traditional social policy did produce moral hazard or was captured or developed into an entitlement mentality that undermined the prospects for fiscal balance. Nonetheless, repeated financial crisis and the ensuing recessions or depressions set off by them also underscored the fact that the instability of modern capitalism regularly creates victims who, through no fault of their own, are thrown out of work or otherwise see their livelihoods disappear. If for no other reason, governments have found that they have to offer social protections if they are to stay in power. The impact of financial crisis is, moreover, the most devastating for the poor, and so elementary considerations of justice demand action to protect them.

Apart from transitional safety nets to protect vulnerable people from periodic crisis, economic growth and development need to be shared more broadly. Highly unequal societies, like many of those in Latin America, are not productive in the long run of either stable democracy or sustained growth. The legitimacy of liberal democracy is often undermined by the ability of elite groups to dominate the electoral process or by the failure of democratic government to produce tangible benefits for the poor. Economic growth, for its part, can occur under conditions of extreme inequality and often actually contributes to the widening of existing inequalities. But, in such countries, growth tends to be interrupted periodically by political protest and conflict over the failure to share the benefits of growth.

If the world is moving away from the small-government, unregulated model of the Reagan-Thatcher years, it is clear that social policy will need a new look as well. A lot of experimentation with social safety nets has been going on *force majeure* as a result of the financial crisis. Many governments around the world have learned the lessons of the 1970s and don't want to return to out-of-control social sector spending and yet need to come up with fiscally sustainable approaches to social protection.

José Antonio Ocampo in his chapter points to the particular issue of universal social policies as a possible outcome of the present crisis. Latin America had developed many innovative new social programs during the 1990s and 2000s to deal with its persistently high level of inequality and poverty, like the conditional cash transfer programs pioneered in Mexico and Brazil. While some of these programs have had a measurable effect in reducing inequality, they are targeted at the poor and raise a number of difficult questions for the future. Targeted programs are more costly to administer, risk politicization as politicians begin to perceive them as sources of patronage, and potentially stigmatize their beneficiaries. In the political economy of redistribution, moreover, taxation of wealthier citizens to support the poor is often a much harder sell than a universal program that potentially benefits the middle class as well. But if a transition from targeted to universal programs is to be made, serious questions of fiscal sustainability arise. Developing countries have fewer fiscal resources to begin with and have much greater difficulties taxing their own populations to pay for broad-ranging social benefits.

New forms of international cooperation. Virtually all of the contributors to the present volume have underscored the fact that the financial crisis has made much more urgent the development of new mechanisms for coordinating international cooperation on a variety of fronts. One of the few concrete results of the events of 2008–9 was the emergence of the G-20 as a replacement for the G-7 as the primary locus for economic policy coordination. The expansion of the G-7 to include large developing countries like China, India, and Brazil was broadly seen as an overdue recognition of the importance of large emerging market countries. In addition, at the spring 2009 London conference of the G-20 the heads of state pledged to increase the capital available to the International Monetary Fund to $750 billion. After a brief period in 2006–7 when people speculated it may have lost its function, the IMF ended up supporting Hungary, Iceland, Ukraine, Pakistan, and Latvia whose solvency was severely threatened by the financial crisis. Another important longer-term motive for expanding the IMF was to reduce incentives for self-insurance that was in some ways responsible for the emergence of the global structural imbalances that in turn fed the crisis itself. It is obvious that on balance, most countries cannot protect themselves from international volatility by running trade surpluses and building up dollar reserves as a standard development model. It was precisely to insure against temporary balance of payments risks that the IMF was created in the first place.

As the chapter by Kemal Derviş and the introduction by Nancy Birdsall indicate, however, neither the revitalization of the G-20 or of the IMF will in themselves be enough to either forestall a future crisis or to successfully mitigate its effects. For countries to trust their fates to the IMF in the future requires not just a larger capital base, but a shift away from an old IMF that was widely seen as arrogant and all too willing to set gratuitous and unhelpful conditions as a condition for its lending. However, the IMF cannot abandon all conditionality, if for no other reason than its fiduciary responsibility to its shareholders. But what the exact conditions will be for future lending is not at present clear.

Furthermore, while the G-20 may appear more legitimate than the G-7, it has neither proved itself as an effective decision-making institution nor even consolidated its own institutional structure. Some of the global economy's most important and intractable issues, like the bilateral structural imbalances between the United States and China, are not likely to be settled in this forum.

Finally, there are a host of other new international coordination issues that, while not resulting from the crisis, will need to be addressed even as the international community deals with crisis-related matters. As Derviş point out, high on this list is carbon abatement and global warming, which will have very large downstream implications for developing countries. Also in their chapters, Michael Clemens and Peter Heller discuss broader issues of how demographic change across borders affects development issues, Clemens by suggesting a new look at how migrants shape the societies they leave as much as the ones they move to and Heller by exploring how cultural attitudes influence economic choices and how demographic problems—such as a lack of young people—in one country can be offset by a larger number of that age group in another country.

Public sector reform. Many of the contributors to this volume and the conference on which it was based have pointed to the need not just for larger but also for more capable public sectors. It stands to reason that if the crisis shows the need for greater prudential regulation of finance, the capacity to regulate must somehow be created. This is by no means a trivial question. In the United States, the manifest regulatory failures of the 2000s were underpinned by a series of factors, including underfunding of regulatory agencies, the inability of government to attract high-quality personnel in competition with the private sector, the difficulty of regulators to keep up with a rapidly developing industry, political constraints on regulation, and finally a broad ideological climate that was hostile to regulation. That climate is clearly changing now in the wake of the crisis, but the capacity problems still remain acute. Regulation typically aims at closing the barn door on horses that have already escaped; forward-looking regulation that anticipates or at least keeps up with a rapidly changing environment is extremely difficult to put in place.

It is not just in the area of financial sector regulation that greater public capacity is needed, however. Past efforts at industrial policy have been hobbled by the absence of a competent, politically shielded group of technocrats to carry it out. Any new look at social safety nets or universal social policies will require new implementing bureaucracies and new approaches to design and implementation to minimize moral hazard problems. And new international organizations will also have to build capacity on an international level, something that is politically easy to undertake, but extremely difficult to do well.

As Lant Pritchett's chapter indicates, public sector reform is far more difficult to accomplish than many other types of development initiatives. He points out that organizational capacity is nonlinear, something that emerges out of the capacities of the individuals who make up organizations, and yet different from their sum. Despite nearly 15 years during which development agencies like the World Bank or Britain's Department of International Development have been investing in anticorruption and good governance programs, the measurable results have been slender (World Bank 2008). One issue for the World Bank in particular is the fact that it has to work through governments, which are the source of the problem. It is constrained from working directly with civil society and other social actors that can better hold governments accountable for their actions.

There are at least three major constraints preventing the emergence of better public sectors. The first is the overtly political nature of government dysfunction. International donors typically have seen the problem as one of technical capacity, but bureaucracies often serve governments that are rent-seeking coalitions whose self-interest is different from the ideal of impersonal public service. Outside donors typically do not have the leverage to force change, with the partial exception of mechanisms like the European Union's accession process.

Second, the most effective institutions are often ones that have been modified to fit the particular social characteristics of the country in which they are applied. The development of institutions in the West was the product of a long and painful process, with factors exogenous to the economy (e.g., the need to mobilize for war) playing a large part in incentivizing institutional creation and reform. Institutions like rule of law will often not work unless there is a normative buy-in to their content, something that often doesn't happen when formal rules are simply copied from external sources.

And finally, state building depends for its success on a parallel process of nation building. That is, unless a society has a clear sense of national identity and public interest, individual actors will not show greater loyalty to it than to their ethnic group, tribe, or patronage network. Nation building is the deliberate creation of national identity based on common language, history, culture, and symbols; it is not something that outsiders to a society can typically promote, nor is it something that many national leaders are capable of undertaking.

What Crisis?

At the moment of this writing, we do not know when and how the United States, Europe, and other big economies will emerge from the 2008–9 financial crisis. While many countries around the world are experiencing a V-shaped setback, the V could turn into a W, and the U.S. economy could look more L-shaped over the next few years. If there is a second leg to the crisis the long-term implications will obviously go well beyond those suggested by the authors in this present volume.

That being said, what is remarkable about the crisis is how little impact it has had on long-term thinking and policies, despite characteristics that might have led one to expect otherwise. While democratic governments in places like Iceland have been brought down and replaced, there has so far been no broad shift in the political climate to the left or extreme right as occurred during the Great Depression. Indeed, the European parliamentary elections of June 2009, as well as the German election of September 2009 and the British parliamentary elections of 2010, improved the position of the center-right rather than the left. A growing global consensus hostile to market capitalism does not seem to be much in evidence anywhere.

Indeed, one might even argue that the heroic measures undertaken by central banks and finance ministries around the world to avoid a deepening of the crisis worked a little too well. By rapidly flooding finance sectors with liquidity and rescuing insolvent institutions, they converted private risk and debt into public liabilities. Stimulus packages like those undertaken by the United States and China may have countered the short-run downturn, but at the cost of a deteriorating fiscal position in the case of the United States, and potential overheating in the case of China. Large, too-big-to-fail financial institutions that were at the heart of the crisis are now solvent and making money again, but with even stronger implicit guarantees that governments will not let them collapse in the future. While everyone has talked about structural imbalances leading to the crisis, no one has acted to address their root causes (except to the extent that American consumers have to buy less as a result of recession and credit crunch).

In the political economy of reform, it is often the case that things have to get worse before they can get better. It took the Great Depression to persuade Americans to put the basic components of the U.S. welfare state in place and to create a more modern regulatory structure. Populist anger is always a dangerous thing, since it can turn against the wrong causes. (An example is Congressman Ron Paul's efforts to reduce the Federal Reserve's autonomy with regard to monetary policy.) But wise political leadership can make use of that anger to build consensus in favor of necessary but painful policy change.

The political opportunity presented by the crisis looks as if it is slipping away. Despite the passage of a Dodd-Frank financial regulation bill in 2010, it is not clear that the regulatory system at a national level will be able to control the systemic risks posed by large financial institutions. And at an international level, it is not clear that the relatively modest steps taken so far, like the shift from the G-7 to G-20, will be nearly adequate to ensure the level of policy coordination required. So in the end, it may turn out that the great crisis of 2008–9, while hugely destructive on a popular level, was actually not severe enough to bring about long-term, constructive policy change.

References

Bhagwati, Jagdish. 1998. "The Capital Myth: The Difference between Trade in Widgets and Dollars." *Foreign Affairs* 77(May–June): 7–12.

Huntington, Samuel. 1991. *The Third Wave: Democratization in the Late Twentieth Century.* Norman: University of Oklahoma Press.

Williamson, John. 1990. "What Washington Means by Policy Reform." In *Latin American Readjustment: How Much Has Happened?* edited by John Williamson. Washington, DC: Peter G. Peterson Institute for International Economics.

World Bank Independent Evaluation Group. 2008. "Public Sector Reform: What Works and Why?" Available at http://siteresources.worldbank.org/EXTPUB SECREF/Resources/psr_eval.pdf

Zakaria, Fareed. 2008. *The Post-American World.* New York: W. W. Norton.

Contributors

Nancy Birdsall is president of the Center for Global Development. Dr. Birdsall is the author of numerous publications on labor markets, human resources, economic inequality, the relationship between income distribution and growth, and other development issues. She serves on various boards, including the Population Council, and is special adviser to the administrator of the United Nations Development Program. Dr. Birdsall received her Ph.D. from Yale University.

Michael Clemens is a senior fellow at the Center for Global Development, where he leads the Migration and Development initiative. Dr. Clemens's current research focuses on the effects of international migration on people from and in developing countries. Dr. Clemens received his Ph.D. from Harvard University.

Kemal Derviş was the head of the United Nations Development Program, the UN's global development network, from August 2005 to February 2009. A book entitled *General Equilibrium Models for Development Policy*, which he co-authored, was published by Cambridge University Press in 1982 and became a widely used textbook in development economics in the 1980s. In cooperation with the Center for Global Development, Dr. Derviş has published a new book entitled *A Better Globalization* (Brookings Press, March

2005), which deals with global development issues and international institutional reform. Dr. Derviş received his Ph.D. from Princeton University.

Larry Diamond is a senior fellow at the Hoover Institution and at the Freeman Spogli Institute for International Studies, where he also directs the Center for Democracy, Development, and the Rule of Law. Dr. Diamond is the founding co-editor of the *Journal of Democracy* and also serves as senior consultant (and previously was co-director) at the International Forum for Democratic Studies of the National Endowment for Democracy. Diamond has edited or co-edited some thirty-six books on democracy, including the recent titles *How People View Democracy* and *Assessing the Quality of Democracy*, both published by the Johns Hopkins University Press. Dr. Diamond received his Ph.D. from Stanford University.

Francis Fukuyama is Olivier Nomellini Senior Fellow at the Freeman Spogli Institute for International Studies (FSI), resident in FSI's Center on Democracy, Development, and the Rule of Law at Stanford University. Dr. Fukuyama has written widely on issues relating to questions concerning democratization and international political economy. His most recent book is *America at the Crossroads: Democracy, Power, and the Neoconservative Legacy* (Yale University Press, 2006). His next book, *The Origins of Political Order*, will be published in the spring of 2011 by Farrar, Straus and Giroux. Dr. Fukuyama received his Ph.D. from Harvard University.

Peter S. Heller is a senior adjunct professor of international economics at the Johns Hopkins University Paul H. Nitze School of Advanced International Studies. The former deputy director of the Fiscal Affairs Department of the International Monetary Fund, he has advised both industrial and developing countries on broad macroeconomic policy strategies for over 30 years. Dr. Heller wrote *Who Will Pay? Coping with Aging Societies, Climate Change and Other Long-Term Fiscal Challenges* (International Monetary Fund, 2003). Dr. Heller received his Ph.D. from Harvard University.

Yasheng Huang is professor of political economy and international management at Massachusetts Institute of Technology's Sloan School of Management. In collaboration with other scholars, Dr. Huang is conducting research on a range of projects including higher education in China, production of scientific knowledge in China, on entrepreneurship, and on FDI. His most recent book is *Capitalism with Chinese Characteristics: Entrepreneurship and the State* (Cambridge University Press, 2008, Chinese edition, 2010). Dr. Huang received his Ph.D. from Harvard University.

Justin Yifu Lin is World Bank chief economist and senior vice president of development economics. Building on a distinguished career as one of China's leading economists. Dr. Lin has undertaken an ambitious research program that examines the industrialization of rapidly developing countries and sheds new light on the causes of lagging growth in poor regions. Dr. Lin received his Ph.D. from the University of Chicago.

José Antonio Ocampo is a professor of Professional Practice in International and Public Affairs and director, Economic and Political Development Concentration at the School of International and Public Affairs, Columbia University. Dr. Ocampo is the author of numerous books and articles on macroeconomics policy and theory, economic development, international trade and economic history. His recent publications include *Stability with Growth: Macroeconomics, Liberalization and Development*, with Joseph E. Stiglitz, Shari Spiegel, Ricardo French-Davis, and Deepak Nayyar (Oxford University Press, 2006). Dr. Ocampo received his Ph.D. from Yale University.

Mitchell A. Orenstein is the S. Richard Hirsch Associate Professor of European Studies at the Johns Hopkins University Paul H. Nitze School of Advanced International Studies. Dr. Orenstein's work focuses on the international political economy of policy reform, exploring the ways that democratic polities seek to adapt and adjust to economic pressures of globalization and liberal economic reforms. Dr. Orenstein received his Ph.D. from Yale University.

Minxin Pei is a professor of government at Claremont McKenna College and director of the Keck Center for International and Strategic Studies. Dr. Pei's research focuses on democratization in developing countries, economic reform and governance in China, and U.S.-China relations. Dr. Pei is the author of *From Reform to Revolution: The Demise of Communism in China and the Soviet Union* (Harvard University Press, 1994) and *China's Trapped Transition: The Limits of Developmental Autocracy* (Harvard University Press, 2006). Dr. Pei received his Ph.D. from Harvard University.

Lant Pritchett is currently professor of the Practice of International Development and Faculty Chair of the Masters in Public Policy in International Development (MPA/ID) program at Harvard's Kennedy School of Government. He worked for years for the World Bank, serving in a number of capacities and living in different regions of the world. He has published widely in economics journals and in specialized journals on demography, education, and health. Dr. Pritchett received his Ph.D. from Massachusetts Institute of Technology.

Liliana Rojas-Suarez is a senior fellow at the Center for Global Development with expertise on Latin America and on financial services and the development impact of global financial flows. Dr. Rojas-Suarez is also the chair of the Latin American Shadow Financial Regulatory Committee (CLAAF). Her most recent book is *Growing Pains in Latin America: An Economic Growth Framework as Applied to Brazil, Colombia, Costa Rica, Mexico, and Peru* (Center for Global Development, 2009). Dr. Rojas-Suarez received her Ph.D. from the University of Western Canada.

Arvind Subramanian is senior fellow jointly at the Peterson Institute for International Economics and the Center for Global Development and senior research professor at the Johns Hopkins University. Dr. Subramanian has written on growth, trade, development, institutions, aid, oil, India, Africa, the WTO, and intellectual property, and has published widely in academic and other journals. His book, *India's Turn: Understanding the Economic Transformation*, was published in 2008 by Oxford University Press. Dr. Subramanian received his Ph.D. from the University of Oxford.

Index

accession process, 45, 323

accountability: authoritarian state, 313, 316; institutional vs. organizational, 229-32, 234, 257; public sector, 14, 320, 323

accounting standards, 178

Africa: economy size, 260-61; global governance, 22, 195, 197; income gap, 56, 265, 279-80; migration, 21, 265, 272, 278-79; policies, 2, 7, 12, 14, 79, 295, 306; recession, 51, 54-55, 247-50, 252, 254, 257. *See also individual countries*

agriculture, 45, 93, 102-3, 144, 184n2

aid /aid systems: changing attitudes, 22, 74-75, 257, 261, 282; remittances vs., 272

appreciation, 136

Argentina: crisis, 162, 164-65, 184n4, 185n13, 249-52, 255; development, 133, 142-45, 147, 150-51

Asia: building ties, 303-4, 306; crisis, 5, 15-16, 19, 72, 170, 184n6, 315, 321; exports, 164-65, 316; foreign aid, 22; industrial policy, 6, 23, 289, 318-19; liberalization, 37-39; market policy, 7-9, 33, 313; prior financial crisis, x, 8, 70-72, 80n6, 114, 272, 311, 315, 318; recession, 249-50, 252-53;

257; recovery, viii, 5, 22, 50-51, 56, 314-15, 321; social policy, 10-12. *See also individual countries and currencies*

assets, real: capital investments, 54, 75, 178, 318-19; liquidity, 71-73, 119, 293, 314; recession, 52-54, 118. *See also* reserve currency

austerity programs, 41-42, 44-45

authoritarian state capitalism, 30, 37-38, 43-46; major economies, 33-35, 47n1, 117-18, 313, 316-18

autocratic policymaking, 6, 13-14, 128, 313, 319

automobile industry, 42, 44, 126, 292

balance sheets, 51, 59, 73, 119, 122, 138-39, 173, 177

bankruptcy, 72

banks/banking system: China, 88, 91, 102, 108n3, 117, 119, 124, 128, 131n29; crisis, viii, 41-42, 44, 311, 324; developing countries, 7-9, 20; domestic vs. foreign, 41, 70, 75, 125, 175-77, 315; Latin America, 138, 145, 167, 174-77, 185n20, 186n21; reform, 11-12, 17, 202, 305; state ownership, 34, 44-45, 80n3, 88, 102, 128